Thomas Aquinas

On Faith and Reason

Thomas Aquinas

On Faith and Reason

Edited, with Introductions, by
STEPHEN F. BROWN

Hackett Publishing Company
Indianapolis/Cambridge

Cover design by Listenberger Design & Associates
Interior design by Meera Dash

Printed in the United States of America

1 2 3 4 5 6 7   03 02 01 00 99

For further information, please address

Hackett Publishing Company, Inc.
P. O. Box 44937
Indianapolis, Indiana 46244–0937

Library of Congress Cataloging-in-Publication Data
Thomas, Aquinas, Saint, 1225?–1274.
    [Selections. English. 1999]
    On faith and reason / edited, with introductions, by
Stephen F. Brown.
       p. cm.
    Includes bibliographical references.
    ISBN 0-87220-457-X (alk. paper).
    ISBN 0-87220-456-1 (pbk.: alk. paper)
    1. Faith and reason—Christianity.   I. Brown, Stephen F.   II. Title.
BT50.T4813 1999
231'.042—dc21   98-50833
                                           CIP

CONTENTS

PREFACE

In 1997, Hackett Publishing Company reissued *Basic Writings of Saint Thomas Aquinas*, edited in 1945 by Anton C. Pegis. This massive two-volume collection of texts from the *Summa Theologica* and the *Summa contra Gentiles* of Saint Thomas Aquinas covers many areas of his philosophy and theology. In the hope of making these texts more serviceable to college and university students, the editorial board also has chosen to publish them in a number of separate volumes and under a different format. This volume, *On Faith and Reason*, includes Aquinas's texts from the *Summa Theologica* that deal with faith and reason and with the knowledge of God that might be gained from both sources. These sources present a God who is one and triune and a God who became man. This volume not only picks up the texts of the original edition but also adds others that complement and clarify the more terse presentation that at times is found in the *Summa Theologica*. This is the case, for example, with our addition of Question 2 of Aquinas's *Exposition of the "De Trinitate" of Boethius* (On the Trinity). The new format also permits us to add other types of Aquinas's works. The *Summa Theologica* and even the *Exposition* follow the technical schoolroom method of the Middle Ages. A more specialized set of volumes offers the opportunity to introduce other forms of Aquinas's teaching into the present book: his commentaries on Scripture and his sermons. Thus in the part dealing with the God who became man, we will employ texts from Aquinas's *Commentary on the Gospel of Saint John* and sections from his *Sermon on the Apostles' Creed*. These additions allow the readers to see Thomas Aquinas at work in the three forms of teaching required to become a Master of Sacred Scripture in the medieval universities: *reading* (explaining the Scripture texts), *disputing* (debating the difficulties raised by the Scripture texts), and *preaching* (proclaiming according to sound understanding of the Scripture message).

We are grateful to those who have given permission to use the texts added to Pegis's original *Summa Theologica* selections. First of all, we are indebted to the Pontifical Institute of Mediaeval Studies at the University of Toronto for allowing us to use Question 2 of Father Armand Maurer's translation of the *Exposition of the "De Trinitate" of Boethius*, published under the title *Faith, Reason and Theology*. Likewise, we are grateful to Dr. Thomas Gallagher of Magi Books for permission to use two lectures from Aquinas's *Commentary on the Gospel of Saint John*. Finally, we wish to thank the editors of Sophia Institute Press in Manchester, New Hampshire, for granting permission to quote three sections from Thomas's *Sermon on the Apostles' Creed*, published under the title *St. Thomas Aquinas: The Three Greatest Prayers*. Our gratitude also goes out to Shirley Gee, my administrative assistant, and to Philip Wodzinski, as assistant to my assistant, for their patient efforts and technical assistance. Finally, I would like to thank my wife, Marie, for freeing me from other obligations, which generously permitted me to finish this endeavor.

Stephen F. Brown
Boston College

GENERAL INTRODUCTION

The World of Saint Augustine

Over the centuries, Augustine of Hippo and Thomas of Aquino have been rightly considered the two wisest and most profound theologians of the Christian Church. With Augustine, we encounter a man born in a pagan world, who wrestled most humanly with life's temptations and deceits, discovered the hidden presence of God even in his mother Monica's nagging, and realized that his soul's hunger for fulfillment ultimately could be found only in the tranquillity of that order where all things outside the soul are properly related to it, where all things within the soul listen to its highest aspirations, and where the soul itself, even in its most noble moments, is not the center of reality. The fundamental yearning of its being, as the being of every creature, is for its creator. His *Confessions* begin with the cry of his too-late-discovered awareness that "Thou has made us for thyself, O Lord, and our hearts are restless until they rest in Thee."[1]

Augustine's *Confessions* records contingent events for their necessary implications and recounts temporal moments for their eternal dimensions. He uses his childhood account of joining friends to steal pears, a story that on the surface might seem laughable, to search the depths of his soul. He there finds, in a variation on the Genesis story of the forbidden fruit, that he and his friends—and all men—have an original flaw that tempts them to seek evil even if for no other reason than because they simply refuse to submit to anything above themselves. His account recalls his everyday passions resisting and resenting the higher, more eternal voices of his soul that themselves wanted only to enslave him. His soul finally realizes what the most lofty Stoic philosopher never realized: Even at its highest point, the soul itself is not supreme, but a creature of the loving God who must be confessed. Augustine's *Confessions*, in effect, cannot be reduced to an autobiography. It is a declaration of the essential Gospel message as it has been understood by the Christian Church; it is the proclamation of every secular soul who, like Augustine, discovers that the meaning of life can be found only in the scriptural message expounded by the Christian community.

On a theoretical level, Augustine's *On Christian Doctrine (De doctrina Christiana)* outlines his effort to unify all knowledge under the divine

---

[1] Augustine, *Confessions*, I, c. 1.

plan or Wisdom. In brief, his book is a search for the tranquillity derived from God's order. Divine Wisdom exists in the mind of God. It is revealed in the Scriptures in a special way to those with faith. It is also manifested to all in the rhythmic order of the natural world. Philosophers have perceived and described this natural order, yet with no awareness of its created character. They have only half seen it. The Scriptures thus bring a more penetrating and corrective light to humankind's understanding of the natural order of visible reality, manifesting another of its dimensions, its created nature. Yet the Scriptures rely on the natural world for gaining a better understanding of its message. An understanding of "The kingdom of heaven is like a mustard seed" starts with a knowledge of a mustard seed and its characteristics. The Scriptures therefore use human language and natural examples. In *On the Trinity (De Trinitate)*, Augustine tells us: "I will not be hesitant to inquire into the substance of God either by reading the Scriptures or studying creatures. For, both are offered to us for our consideration, so that He may Himself be sought, and Himself may also be loved—he who both inspired the Scriptures and created the creaturely world."[2] To know more deeply the true nature of the scriptural examples, we must realize that they are signs or symbols. By Christian definition, pagan philosophy on its own falls short of a full explanation. Yet philosophy is necessary, in the sense that it provides examples that point beyond themselves. Scripture and philosophy are thus intertwined as sources of our knowledge of the depths of the wisdom and knowledge of God. The philosophical sciences, dealing with *exempla*, have no independent and complete message. They achieve a greater meaning to the extent that they serve to illustrate a higher message: Creatures not only exist, but they also are created by the Goodness of God. Creatures belong to a larger plan or Wisdom than their own.

Hence all the philosophical sciences—the liberal and mechanical arts and Platonic philosophy—become enobled. By themselves, they were incomplete. As elevated examples of something more important, however, they became more. In the opening chapter of *On the Trinity*, Augustine warns against the rude understanding of examples:

> He who thinks that God is white or red, is in error; and yet these things are found in the body. Again, he who thinks of God as now forgetting and now remembering, or anything of the same kind, is nonetheless in error; and yet these things are found in the mind. But he who thinks that God is of such

---

[2]Augustine, *The Trinity*, II, preface.

powers as to have generated Himself, is so much the more in error, because not only does God not so exist, but neither does the spiritual nor the bodily creature; for there is nothing whatever that generates its own existence.[3]

Examples must be employed in a manner beyond their ordinary meaning if they are to illustrate higher truths. Faith thus needs reason and creation to help it attain a deeper understanding of divine Wisdom. Nevertheless, faith never must cede to a person's reason; that is, it never should be measured, reduced, and judged by reason in order to appear to be reasonable on a person's own terms.

Augustine's educational orientation was focused on the learning believer. He saw the need to adjust his teaching to the level of the student. In the first book of his *Soliloquies*, he summarizes his method of teaching:

Even though someone's eyes might rightly be called healthy, we endanger them if we set out to show them what they are still not capable of seeing. These eyes must first be trained, and their love for the light must be delayed and nursed along. First, certain things ought to be shown to them that are not luminous in themselves but may be seen in the light, such as a piece of clothing, or a wall, or some such object. Later, they should be shown something that, although still not luminous in itself, will shine more brilliantly in the light, such as a piece of silver or gold, or other similar things—but these still must not be illuminated so brightly as to injure the eyes. Then, perhaps, the ordinary fire we find on earth should be shown, then the stars, followed by the moon, then the creeping dawn and the brilliance of the sunrise. Sooner or later, either by going through the whole gamut or skipping certain steps, such a person will grow as accustomed as he can to the various bright objects and will finally, without hesitation and with great delight, come to behold the sun. This is how the best teachers deal with seekers of wisdom who only see it dimly but at least do see it to some extent. For it is the role of good training to lead a person to Wisdom by a progression, since we could hardly count on reaching it without such an orderly approach.[4]

Augustine's *Confessions* reveals that this is the method he learned from the Divine Teacher who led him to Himself. The stages of the journey to God are more explicitly presented in his treatise *On the Measure of the Soul (De quantitate animae)*, but they are no better manifested in their concreteness and subtlety than in Augustine's *Confessions*.

---

[3]Augustine, *The Trinity*, I, c. 11, n. 1. [4]Augustine, *Soliloquies*, I, c. 13, n. 23.

The World and Life of Saint Thomas

Thomas Aquinas lived in a different world than did Augustine—a Christian world, where Augustine's vision reigned. By the thirteenth century, nonetheless, the basic plan of Augustine's *On Christian Doctrine*, with the liberal and mechanical arts serving as handmaids to the understanding of Scripture, had become highly formalized. Universities had begun to supersede the monastic, palace, and cathedral schools. The new universities were split into the preparatory faculty of arts and the more advanced faculties of theology, medicine, and law. In the arts faculty of the universities, new challenges to Augustine's vision were appearing. Aristotle, Plato's disciple and critic, was arriving with all his intellectual luggage.

Backpacks of Aristotelian logic arrived long before Aristotle's heavier substantive baggage did; Boethius (died c. 524), his first porter, had translated some of his logical works in the Patristic era, whereas the rest of Aristotle's *Organon*, that is, his instrumental or logical works, arrived in Latin versions in the twelfth century. Bit by bit, Aristotle's whole philosophical corpus appeared, including his treatises on the natural world, the heavens, and the nature of the soul, and terminating with the *Politics* in the 1260s. The *Politics* is unique in having arrived with no ancient commentaries to help Thomas Aquinas and his contemporaries. The reception of Aristotle's other works, however, was significantly different. Christians, such as Aquinas, could find help (along with challenging complications) in understanding Aristotle's works by attending to the prior commentaries of Arab teachers, such as Avicenna and Averroës, or Jewish scholars, such as Avicebron and Maimonides, who also functioned within a world of divine revelation.

The era of Thomas Aquinas at Paris was a time of great assimilation in philosophy. By 1255 the arts faculty, a preparatory faculty that had focused on the seven liberal arts (grammar, logic, rhetoric, arithmetic, geometry, astronomy, and music), officially became a philosophy faculty—an Aristotelian philosophy faculty. New materials from Aristotle provided medieval Christians, for the first time, with a natural view of the world—a competing view based on reason alone. How should they deal with this challenge?

Thomas Aquinas did much of his preparatory work in the liberal arts at the *studium* established by Frederick II in Naples, a school that later became part of the University of Bologna. He then went to the University of Paris in 1245 and quite likely completed his study of the liberal arts there. It was a time when Aristotle's vision of reality was gaining appreciation. Aquinas took Aristotle's philosophy seriously. Throughout his career he wrote detailed commentaries on Aristotle's *On the Soul, Physics, Meteors, Perihermenias, Posterior Analytics, Ethics,* the first part of *Politics, Metaphysics, On Heaven and the World,* and *On Generation and Corruption.* In 1248 Aquinas went to Cologne, where the Dominicans were just opening a general *studium.* Although he followed the courses of Albert the Great on Pseudo-Dionysius's *On the Divine Names* and Aristotle's *Nicomachean Ethics,* he also began his study of the Bible, writing cursory commentaries on Isaiah, Jeremiah, and Lamentations. Later, as a Master of the Bible or Sacred Scripture he would move on to more detailed commentaries on Job, on the Gospels of Matthew and John, and on the Letters of Paul.

After his studies in Cologne, in 1252 Aquinas returned to Paris, where he was a Bachelor commenting on Peter Lombard's *Sentences.* He served as Regent Master in Paris from 1256 to 1259. These are the years of some of his detailed Scripture commentaries (such as *On the Book of Job*), as well as his *Disputed Questions on Truth* and his *Exposition of the "De Trinitate" of Boethius.* In 1259, Aquinas returned to his native Italy, where for nine years he taught at Naples, Orvieto, and Rome. During this sojourn he wrote some of his strongest theological treatises: the *Summa contra Gentiles* (On the Truths of the Catholic Faith) and the First Part of the *Summa Theologica.* A second period of teaching at Paris, 1268–1272, saw him deeply involved in the chief philosophical debates of that period. His treatises *On the Eternity of the World* and *On the Unity of the Intellect* owe their existence to these debates. In these years he also composed many of his commentaries on Aristotle's works and wrote Part Two of the *Summa Theologica.* In 1272, he returned as Regent Master to Naples. There he wrote the portion of Part Three of the *Summa Theologica* that remained incomplete. Some scholars also date Thomas's short, incomplete systematic work, *The Compendium of Theology,* during this last period of his life. Aquinas died on his way to the Council of Lyon on March 7, 1274.

The Medieval Methods of Teaching

In the *Inaugural Sermon* Aquinas delivered as he began his career as Master of Sacred Scripture in 1256, he indicated the three offices or functions of a Master at the University of Paris: "These three functions, preaching, lecturing and disputing are mentioned in *Titus 1:9,* 'So that he will be capable of exhorting people' (this refers to preaching) 'in sound teaching' (this refers to lecturing) 'and of defeating those who contradict' (this refers to disputing)."[5] These offices were already classic responsibilities, noted at least since Peter Cantor's *Verbum abbreviatum* (Abbreviated word) at the end of the twelfth century.[6]

Aquinas *preached* at least twenty university sermons, many of them in Paris. He also preached on the Ten Commandments, the Lord's Prayer, the Hail Mary, and the Apostles' Creed. This volume includes selected parts of Aquinas's *Sermon on the Apostles' Creed*. It shows that Aquinas paid close attention to Peter Cantor's ordering of the offices of the Master. For Cantor, the reading of Scripture and theological disputation were proper preparations for sound preaching.[7] Aquinas's *Sermon on the Apostles' Creed* well illustrates his close reading of sacred Scripture, his solid reflections on the Christian Church's teaching about the divinity and humanity of Christ, and his strong opposition to heretical misunderstandings of this teaching.

Aquinas *lectured* in the medieval sense of the term: a public reading and explanation of each line of the text. Of course, simple public readings were the task of those in training to become Masters. These simple lessons were called cursory lectures, where the Bachelor merely ran the students through the text to give them a sense of the work as a whole. Aquinas's beginning lectures on Isaiah and Jeremiah at Cologne were of this type. It is, however, Aquinas the Master who is extremely impressive. Whether he is explaining in detail the Gospel of Matthew, the Gospel of John, or Aristotle's *Nicomachean Ethics* or *Metaphysics*, it is hard to miss his organizational genius, his attention to detail, and his masterful insights. His scriptural lectures demonstrate his vast knowledge of the whole of the Scriptures and of the numerous commentaries of the Fathers of the Church on the scriptural passages he attempts to unfold.

Finally, Aquinas *disputed*. This occurred not only in the formal exercises titled disputations, such as the *Disputed Questions on Truth* or *Disputed Questions on the Power of God*, but also in his *Quodlibet Questions* (*Quaestiones de quolibet*) that could be about anything (*de quolibet*) and in

---

[5]*Albert and Thomas, Selected Writings* (The Classics of Western Spirituality), trans. S. Tugwell (New York: Paulist Press, 1988), 358.   [6]Peter Cantor, *Verbum abbreviatum*, c. 1 (PL 205, 25): "In tribus igitur consistit exercitium sacrae scripturae, circa lectionem, disputationem et predicationem." (The study of Sacred Scripture consists of three functions: lecturing, disputing and preaching.) [7]*Ibid.*: "Post lectionem igitur sacrae Scripturae et dubitabilium per disputationem inquisitionem, et non prius, praedicandum est. . . ." (Therefore, one should preach after the reading of sacred Scripture and attempting to solve doubtful things through disputation, and not before. . . .).

all the questions that make up his *Summae* and *Commentary on the Sentences of Lombard*. To gain a sense of the extent of the general exercise of a disputation or a question, it might help to consider the explanation of one of Aquinas's contemporaries, the Franciscan Richard Rufus. Explaining the various duties of a Master of Sacred Scripture, this is what he says about a "question" and its more developed form, a "disputation": " . . . We untie knots, we explain difficult passages, we determine ambiguous points, and, to the extent that it is possible, we bring light to obscure places."[8]

The medieval *quaestio*, from which the *disputatio* developed as its most mature form, is not your ordinary question. This is important to realize for understanding most of the texts in this volume. People do not ordinarily ask questions while someone is preaching. They do, however, ask questions when someone is reading publicly in a classroom. They might not understand the meaning of a word or a historical reference. The medieval reading or *lectio* thus had a certain questioning aspect to it. For instance, if a *lector* (lecturer) were reading St. Paul's Letter to the Galatians to students and read about Abraham and his sons, perhaps a student who had not read the Genesis texts that speak about Abraham and his sons might ask: "Who were Abraham's sons?" This is a factual question that can be answered quite simply. When you study the Scriptures more deeply, however, you might have more difficult questions. "Why," for instance, "did Christ have to be both God and man in order to redeem us from our sins?" An answer to this question requires more than knowing a fact, such as a name. It requires knowing *why* something is the way it is, that you *understand* the reason for something. Masters dealt with this latter type of question. The development of this kind of questioning has a long history, but a simplification is that the medievals developed a method for forming questions that would require students to understand a number of ideas in order to answer them. Such questions did not promote memorization or factual knowledge, though they would suppose it as background. Rather, they forced students to think, and they did it by starting them off with a puzzle they then had to try to solve.

The puzzles generally were formed in this way: You are given a question that requires you to think. Then you are given two sets of arguments that disagree with each other. One set tells you that the answer to the

---

[8]Richardus Rufus, *Commentarium in I librum Sententiarum*, prol. (Oxford: cod. Balliol 62, f. 6rb): " . . . . "Nodosa enodamus, difficilia explanmus, ambigua certificamus, obscura, prout possibile est, elucidamus."

question is yes, and its arguments give you reasons for the yes answer. Then, another set of arguments tells you that the answer is no and provides reasons for answering no. It is next up to the teacher and students to figure out the better answer and then to tell those defending the other opinion why their arguments are not convincing.

Such questions are central to the medieval university method of study. They are meant to strengthen and develop the student's understanding of the faith. The questions are at times only methodical, in the sense that they do not imply a real doubt. A question such as "Does God exist?" does not mean the teacher asking it doubts God's existence. It is posed to overcome arguments or objections against God's existence, and it forces students to seek more solid arguments supporting God's existence. In brief, the *quaestio* is a methodical exercise that, according to Richard Rufus, helps students to untie knots or solve conflicts, explain difficulties, settle ambiguities, and bring light to their understanding of the Scriptures.

The Texts Included in This Volume

One twelfth-century theologian, Peter Lombard (1095–1160), made an organized collection of these more theoretical or nonfactual questions relating to the Bible. Since it contained among the yes and no arguments for each question a large number of opinions or sentences from the Bible, the writings of the Fathers of the early Christian Church, the declarations of church councils, and church legal decisions, the book was called *The Sentences*. From the time of Alexander of Hales (c. 1235) until the period shortly after Martin Luther, all the Masters of Sacred Scripture made commentaries on Lombard's *Sentences* as part of their training. Thomas Aquinas thus made a *Commentary on Lombard's "Sentences."* Not only is it a work of his training years, but it is also a work done "according to the manner of Saint-Jacques." On many points it resembles closely the commentaries of his Dominican contemporaries at Saint-Jacques in Paris: Peter of Tarentaise, Humbert of Rome, and Bombolognus of Bologna. Already, however, Aquinas's differences are noticeable: more than two thousand citations from Aristotle's works and indications that Aquinas considered the principle of organization in Lombard's *Sentences* to be seriously lacking. As Jean-Pierre Torrell recently put it:

> [With the *Sentences* of Lombard] we are dealing with a compendium of materially juxtaposed questions rather than a treatise ordered around a central idea. The author in no way emphasizes the contours of his rather loose plan. Thomas, by contrast, gets the most out of what he does not hes-

itate to call the Master's *intentio*: he proposes to organize the theological material with God as the center and everything else around Him, according to the relationships that they maintain with Him, whether they come from Him as their first cause or return to Him as to their final end.[9]

When Aquinas went to rework the *Sentences* years later in Rome, he abandoned the project and decided to write his *Summa Theologica* (also called *Summa Theologiae*) as an alternatively organized gathering of the various questions concerning theology.[10] Aquinas's *Summa Theologica*, his greatest achievement, was composed during the later years of his life, beginning with Part One around 1265 in Rome. Part Two was composed in Paris in 1271–72. Part Three probably was begun in Paris and was continued in Naples in 1273 but never finished. Later disciples completed it, using the materials of Aquinas's *Commentary on Lombard's "Sentences."* A major portion of this volume will be based on Aquinas's well-respected *Summa Theologica*.

Also during his first teaching years in Paris, namely in 1257–58, Aquinas wrote what seems to be the sole thirteenth-century commentary on Boethius's theological tractate *On the Trinity*. Though a work he never completed, the *Exposition of the "De Trinitate" of Boethius* contains discussions on the role of reason in examinations of the truths of the Christian faith that complement his treatment of theology in the *Summa Theologica*. It also expands notably on the variety of roles reason plays in theological study beyond the claims made in the more terse *Summa Theologica*.

A third textual component of this volume is taken from Aquinas's *Commentary on the Gospel of Saint John*. It demonstrates the *lectio* or lecture method of Aquinas, but, more important, it examines the scriptural and Patristic bases for the claim that Christ is God (and man). As Aquinas puts it in the prologue to his commentary:

> For while the other Evangelists treat principally of the mysteries of the humanity of Christ, John, especially and above all, makes known the divinity of Christ in his Gospel. . . . Still, he does not ignore the mysteries of his humanity. He did this because, after the other Evangelists had written their

---

[9]Jean Pierre. Torrell, *Saint Thomas Aquinas*, trans. Robert Royal (Washington, DC: The Catholic University of America Press, 1996), I, 43.   [10]L. E. Boyle, "Alia Lectura fratris Thomae," in *Mediaeval Studies* 45 (1983): 418–429; and M. F. Johnson, "Alia lectura fratris thome: A List of the New Texts found in Lincoln College, Oxford, MS. Lat. 95," *Recherches de Théologie ancienne et médiévale* 57 (1990): 34–61.

Gospels, heresies had arisen concerning the divinity of Christ, to the effect that Christ was purely and simply a man, as Ebion and Cerinthus falsely thought. And so John the Evangelist, who had drawn the truth about the divinity of the Word from the very fountain-head of the divine breast, wrote this Gospel at the request of the faithful. And in it he gives us the doctrine of the divinity of Christ and refutes all heresies.[11]

The final set of texts in this volume are taken from Aquinas's *Sermon on the Apostles' Creed*. Some have called this sermon, delivered to the people of Naples at the Church of St. Dominic, "A *Summa* for the simple."[12] Yet, in this sermon Aquinas examines all the misunderstandings of the basic beliefs of the Christian faith, and in this work he especially proclaims the "sound doctrine" concerning Christ that is a hallmark of true faith. Indeed, it is more than "A *Summa* for the simple," since its simple message really is a summary of the teaching found in the *Summa Theologica*, the *Summa contra Gentiles*, and the *Compendium of Theology*.

---

[11]Thomas Aquinas, *Commentary on the Gospel of Saint John*, pro. (*ed. cit.*), 26.
[12]Cf. Ralph McInerny's introduction to *The Three Greatest Prayers* (*ed. cit.*), x.

I

FAITH, REASON, AND
THEOLOGICAL KNOWLEDGE

The treatise on faith in Saint Thomas Aquinas's *Compendium of Theology* begins with these words:

> Faith is a certain foretaste of that knowledge which is to make us happy in the life to come. The Apostle says, in *Hebrews* 11:1, that faith is "the substance of things to be hoped for," as though implying that faith is already, in some preliminary way, inaugurating in us the things that are to be hoped for, that is, future beatitude.[1]

In what way do believers in this life have a foretaste of the knowledge they hope to have in the future life? First of all, from listening to the revealed Scriptures, any believer can derive a knowledge that God created the world and that Christ was poor and humble and suffered and died on the cross. This kind of knowledge, of course, does not exhaust the message of the Scriptures, but it provides a sense of the kind of knowledge believers can obtain through faith. Through the liturgy of the Christian Church, they can learn much more as they recall and celebrate Christ's death and resurrection, listen to the Scriptural readings, and follow the instruction of the homilies. Furthermore, theologians, such as Peter Lombard, collected much more data concerning the truths of the Christian faith from the Scriptures and from the Fathers of the church who have commented on the Scriptures. From their writings Christian believers can gain even deeper insight into the truths revealed by God. Yet when we read the prologue of the *Summa Theologica*, Aquinas seems somewhat disappointed with the *Sentences* of Lombard and the other *Summae* that imitate it. Many of the questions contained in these books seem useless to him, or they derive from a questionable order that such books follow, or they arise by happenstance, such as from an impressive disputation where certain questions came up and thus were included in a later *summa*. It is as though Aquinas were saying that despite the superior message of the Scriptures and the books based on them, the manner

---

[1]Thomas Aquinas, *Compendium of Theology*, trans. Cyril Vollert. (St. Louis: B. Herder Book Company, 1947), 5.

in which this message is presented lacks the proper organization it deserves.

Peter Comestor presented a similar argument when he wrote his *Scholastic History (Historia Scholastica)*. The Scriptures are like an impenetrable forest; therefore, we need a summary of biblical history that provides a thread to their unified story so that we can find our way through the biblical forest. Aquinas is looking for more than the historical thread that unifies the long and complex biblical story. He is searching for the logical thread that can lead us through the scriptural trees. Lombard's *Sentences* still would keep a student helplessly wandering. It might be a useful work for those familiar with the woods, but beginners need a better map.

Certainly, the Scriptures provide a more lofty and true view of reality than any purely human invention has produced. No philosopher had dreamed of the goal of human life as it is presented in the Scriptures. Attaining that beatitude required the knowledge of certain truths that are beyond the attainment of human reason left to itself. Yet from the viewpoint of logical organization, the stories of the bible, the unified biblical history of Peter Comestor, and the *Sentences* of Peter Lombard and the *Summae* of his followers all fall short. The substance of Aristotle's philosophy is dwarfed before all these portrayals of reality. Nevertheless, the organization of the realities that "the Philosopher" treats is superior. Aquinas's *Summa Theologica* is his effort to bring to sacred teaching a logical order superior to that of his Christian predecessors. He wanted to discover the *ordo disciplinae*, the order that exists among the realities of the Christian faith—the divine or theological order.

In its fullness this order exists in the Divine Wisdom. It is the order we hope to see in the light of glory. What can we glimpse of that order in this life? We have been given two other lights to help us: the light of faith and the light of reason. Reason on its own can lead us to see some idea of the divine order, but experience teaches us that few true philosophers exist, and even they have spent a good part of their life encapsulated in inherited opinions that had to be unlearned or were misdirected by unbalanced emotions. Furthermore, even the "truths" they discover are tarnished with errors.[2] The light of faith is thus necessary if we are to approach closer to the divine order of reality. For faith assists us not only to know what is above reason, such as the Trinity and the Incarnation, but it also helps us to arrive more quickly at the aspects of the divine plan that can be known by reason. If people were left to reason alone, the search for the

---

[2] *Summa Theologica*, I, q. 1, a. 1.

knowledge of God is the last pursuit they would be prone to undertake. Indeed, very few of them would search, so faith makes the knowledge of divinity more widespread. Besides, human reason is deficient concerning God; thus faith is necessary for the sake of certitude. "And, consequently, in order that men might have knowledge of God, free of doubt and uncertainty, it was necessary for divine truths to be delivered to them by way of faith, being told to them, as it were, by God Himself Who cannot lie."[3] Nonetheless, faith not only assists and corrects reason; it also, as we have said, leads believers beyond reason. The articles of the Christian faith, enunciated in the Creed, lead us into a new world: into a world where God is a God in three Persons and a God who became incarnate and suffered and died to redeem fallen humankind. It does not take Christian faith to know that Jesus died; but it does take Christian faith to know that the Jesus who suffered and died was both God and man.

Faith and reason work in complex ways within Aquinas's intellectual world. In this first part, we will look at his conscious declarations about what he is doing. It also would be helpful to keep in mind Aquinas's other works, such as *On the Truths of the Catholic Faith (Summa contra Gentiles)* and *Commentary on Peter Lombard's "Sentences,"* to develop a richer picture of his views on the diverse roles of faith and reason. With these as a background, the present texts provide an adequate picture of Aquinas's view on the interplay of faith and reason.

We might begin with Aquinas's question on whether the teaching of the scriptural message can be a science.[4] Through it, we become aware that Aquinas is asking not only if the study of divine revelation can be better organized, but also if it can be organized the way Aristotle has organized his sciences. As a general portrait of sciences, Aristotle in the *Posterior Analytics* distinguished two types of sciences. A simple or pure science begins with its own self-evident principles. Geometry and mathematics might serve as examples. Other sciences are dependent or subalternated sciences. They accept the pure or simple sciences from the experts in these fields and apply them to another field. Optics borrows, or accepts on the authority of a geometrician, certain principles about lines. Because these principles help explain optics data, a student of optics uses them to deal with lines of vision. Optics thus is a science, but a dependent one. The same might be said of music composers. They are not mathemati-

---

[3]*Summa Theologica*, II-II, q. 2, a. 4. [Not in this volume]   [4]*Summa Theologica*, I, q. 1, a. 2.

cians. Yet they borrow the teachings of mathematicians; that is, they take them on faith and use them fruitfully to compose their music.

Aquinas uses these analogies or examples to illustrate how the scientific form of sacred teaching might work. Like optics and musical composition, the study of revealed truth—let's call it *Theology* with a capital *T* to distinguish it from Aristotle's *theology*—can be a subalternated or dependent science.[5] It depends on or is subalternated to the *evident knowledge* (science in the strict sense) God and the blessed have. What God has revealed, He has evident knowledge of; what God has revealed to people in this life, the blessed see, so they also have evident knowledge of the realities believers accept on faith. Thus, in a parallel way, believers in this life can have science of the same realities, not, of course, evident knowledge but knowledge passed down by God's revelation. Like the student of optics or music, they take their principles or starting points on faith given by God, who has evident knowledge of them. Yet just as optics and music are real, though dependent or subalternate, sciences, so the scientific study of Christian revelation, dependent as it is on the revelation received on the most reliable divine authority, is science. Believers in this world can have this knowledge, and they hope to have evident knowledge or science in the strict sense when they join the blessed who have preceded them.[6]

One of the chief characteristics of Aristotelian science is that it is deductive. From certain principles or premises accepted because of their self-evidence or, in the case of theology, because of their divinely guaranteed certainty, one can by following faithfully the laws of logic arrive at sure conclusions. These certain conclusions can be science in the strict sense if they are based on evidence. Or they can be science in the subalternated sense if they are based on principles or premises accepted from authority that itself has evidence.[7] Certainly, warrant exists for a claim that the deductively structured argumentations of theology are scientific if they have certain or sure principles or premises. Indeed, throughout the history of the Christian understanding of revelation, a certain kind of deduction, in the sense of making explicit what was already implicitly in

---

[5]In the Second Article of Question 2 of Aquinas's *Exposition of the "De Trinitate" of Boethius*, he speaks of two sciences concerning the divine. See Aquinas's Reply, especially the second part. [6]*Summa Theologica*, I, q. 1, a. 2. [7]In his *Commentary on the "Sentences" of Peter Lombard*, Aquinas uses the expressions *"quasi" principia* and *"quasi" conclusiones* to say that the theological premises or principles are, strictly speaking, not evident but that they act in a parallel way to the way philosophical principles or premises act in relation to philosophical conclusions.

the Scriptures, has been admitted as necessary. We find such "deductions" in declarations of the councils that oppose heretical interpretations of the Trinity or Christ and in the explicit articles of the various formulations of the Creeds. Aquinas, in his view of theology, sees such procedures as an important aspect of its study. Theological conclusions, drawn from revealed premises, follow as "explicitations" of basic theological principles or premises. Theology, then, is not just carrying out in a mechanical way the rules of logic. It is deepening, by its deductions, the understanding of the richer message of the scriptural revelation and of the divine mysteries contained therein.

Another side of this explicitation process also shows the scientific organization Aquinas desires. When he deals with the object of faith in the opening question of the Second Part of Part Two, he tells us in the Seventh Article that even some of the articles of the Creed, which serve as the principles or premises for deducing other truths, have a certain hierarchy among them:

> In like manner, all the articles are contained implicitly in certain primary truths of faith, such as God's existence, and His providence over the salvation of man, according to *Heb.* xi: "He that cometh to God, must believe that He is, and is a rewarder to them that seek Him." For the being of God includes all that we believe to exist in God eternally, and in these our happiness consists, while belief in His providence includes all those things which God dispenses in time for man's salvation, and which are the way to that happiness; and in this way, again, some of those articles which follow from these are contained in others. Thus faith in the Redemption of mankind includes implicitly the Incarnation of Christ, His Passion and so forth.

If the mark of a wise man is to order things properly, then Aquinas's efforts to discover the wise order of reality according to God's plan would qualify his well-ordered form of Christian teaching as a wisdom participating in the Divine Wisdom. Not only, then, is theology a science. It is the highest and noblest science, providing the divine order within which all the other sciences have their place.

But reason can bring even more to the principles of this wise form of Christian teaching than establishing their order. Here again Aquinas follows Aristotle's lead. When Aristotle analyzed the nature of science, he realized that not all ideas could be proved scientifically if we meant they could be proved by deduction. We always need premises to arrive at a conclusion, and not all premises can be established by a previous deduction. We otherwise would be caught in an infinite regress. We therefore must have some premises that are not conclusions of a previous argument but that are first principles. For Aristotle, a premise such as "The same thing cannot be and not be at the same time under the same aspect" is not established by a prior argument. It is just self-evident. If we were to deny it, we would see that our denial implies that we admit it, since we imply that to deny and not deny the same thing at the same time under the same aspect are not the same thing. We cannot prove first principles. The case is similar in the study of revealed truths. The articles of Christian faith are first principles.

Aquinas's identification of theology's first principles with the articles of the faith is a significant move on his part. Some twenty years before Aquinas, William of Auxerre also spoke of theology as deductive. However, the premises or principles he started from were those closer to the senses: that the Son of God was a man, that he was humble, meek, and patient.[8] For Aquinas, the premises were the articles of the faith expressed in the Creed. In his more scientific study of theology, he centered his attention more on the essential elements of the faith. He does not concentrate on premises that are first known by us but on principles or articles that are in themselves more essential to the faith.

It is important to note, furthermore, that the articles of the Christian faith cannot be demonstrated or proved by argument. They are accepted because believers accept that God has revealed them. They trust that God knows these first principles or articles of the faith and that He has revealed them according to the understanding and acceptance by the Christian Church. As first principles, they can be accepted only because the First Truth, God, who has both knowledge and veracity, guarantees them. Aquinas indicates, however, that reason does not shy away from the first principles of the Christian faith:

> They are also defended against those who attack them, as the Philosopher argues against those who deny principles. Moreover they are clarified by certain analogies, just as principles that are naturally known are made evident by induction but not proved by demonstrative reasoning.[9]

In the years following Aquinas, the double aspect of his thought—focusing on drawing out through deductive processes new truths that are already contained in the revealed articles of the Creed and attending to the primary principles or revealed articles of the faith themselves—split

---

[8]William of Auxerre, *Summa aurea*, pro. ed. J. Bibaillier (Paris: Grottaferrata, 1980), 17. [9]*Exposition of Boethius*, q. 2, a. 2, Reply to 4.

in two. In the middle of the fourteenth century, the Augustinian Hermit, Gregory of Rimini, stressed that the habit students developed in the theology faculty should be solely deductive. In other words, they did not need to bring reason to bear on the source or principles of the Christian faith. We accept them on faith, and reason in no way justifies Scripture or the Creeds. Theology accepts these divine sources on faith and draws out new explicit truths already contained there:

> But it is established that every such element of knowledge either is expressly contained in Sacred Scripture or is deducible from what is contained there. Otherwise, the Scriptures would not suffice for our salvation and for the defense of our faith, etc. Yet Augustine tells us that the Scriptures do suffice in the last chapter of Book II of *On Christian Doctrine*, when he says: "Whatever a man might learn outside of Scripture, if it is harmful, it is condemned in the Sacred Writings; if it is useful, then it is already found there."[10]

Gregory of Rimini chided anyone who claimed that Saint Augustine used reason to support the fundamental truths of the faith: "Where in the aforesaid books did Augustine prove these truths from probable propositions or from any other sources taken from worldly teachings? I think that he could not find any such sources, but will only find this: that he proved these truths from the authorities of the Scriptures."[11]

In taking this position, Gregory strongly opposed the early fourteenth-century Franciscan theologian, Peter Aureoli, who focused primarily, and almost exclusively, on what he called declarative theology. Declarative theology emphasized the principles or articles of the faith, defending them against heretics and explaining and confirming them to confused believers. It did this by bringing forth arguments from other sciences that give support for the articles of the faith, by explaining the meaning of the terms that express these articles, or by responding to

---

[10]Gregory of Rimini, *Lectura super Primum Sententiarum*, pro., a. 2 ed. D. Trapp et Venicius Marcolino (Berlin De Gruyter, 1981), p. 19: "Sed constat quod quodlibet tale vel expresse secundum se continetur in sacra scriptura vel ex contentis in ea deducitur, alioquin non ipsa sufficeret ad nostram salutem et nostrae fidei defensionem etc.; contra Augustinum, II *De doctrina Christiana*, capitulo ultimo dicentem quod 'quidquid homo extra didicerit, si noxium, ibi damnatur; si utile est, ibi invenitur.'" [11]Gregory of Rimini, *ibid.*: "Ubi in praedictis libris praedictas veritates probavit Augustinus ex propositionibus probabilibus aut aliis qualibuscumque ex mundanis sumptis doctrinis? Puto quod invenire non poterit, sed hoc solum inveniet quod ex auctoritabibus probavit scripturae."

doubts raised against them. By developing such skills of support, clarifi-cation, and defense, theologians do not *produce* conviction so that they can affirm these truths without the fear of error. They are already convinced through faith. Instead they develop a habit distinct from faith, allowing them to clarify what they already unhesitatingly believe and to defend these truths against doubts and challenges raised in their regard.[12]

Studied fully, Aquinas's works reveal that both aspects of theology are necessary, that is, that the intellectual habits theology students develop must be both deductive and declarative.[13] In so contending, Aquinas brings a fuller use of reason to the scientific form of Christian teaching he aims at in his comprehensive theological works.

---

[12]Peter Aureoli, *Scriptum in I Sententiarum, prooemium*, nn. 92–129. ed, E. M. Buy-taert. (St. Bonaventure, NY: The Franciscan Institute, 1953), 159–166.
[13]On deductive and declarative theology, see Stephen F. Brown, "Peter of Candia's Hundred-Year 'History' of the Theologian's Role," *Medieval Philosophy and The-ology* I (1991), 156–190; and "Declarative and Deductive Theology in the Early Fourteenth Century," *Miscellanea Mediaevalia* 26 (1998), 648–655.

THE SCIENTIFIC ASPECTS

Summa Theologica
Prologue

The doctor of Catholic truth ought not only to instruct the proficient, but also to teach beginners. As St. Paul says, *As unto little ones in Christ, I gave you milk to drink, no meat (1 Cor.* iii, 1–2). For this reason it is our purpose in the present work to treat of the things which belong to the Christian religion in such a way as befits the instruction of beginners.

For we have observed that beginners in this doctrine have been considered hampered by what various authors have written. They have been hampered partly because of the multiplication of useless questions, articles and arguments; partly, too, they have been hampered because those things that are needful for them to know are not taught according to the order of discipline, but rather according as the order of exposition in books demands, or according to the occasion for disputation arises; and partly they have been hampered because frequent repetition brought about weariness and confusion in the minds of the readers.

It will be our endeavor to avoid these and other like faults. With confidence in God's help, we shall try, following the needs of the subject matter, to set forth briefly and clearly the things which pertain to sacred doctrine.

Part One
Question 1
The Nature and Domain of Sacred Doctrine
(In Ten Articles)

To place our purpose within definite limits, we must first investigate the nature and domain of sacred doctrine. Concerning this there are ten points of inquiry:—

(1) Whether sacred doctrine is necessary? (2) Whether it is a science? (3) Whether it is one or many? (4) Whether it is speculative or practical?

Source: Basic Writings of Saint Thomas Aquinas, edited and annotated by Anton C. Pegis (Indianapolis: Hackett Pub. Co., 1997). Reprinted by permission of the publisher.

(5) How it is compared with other sciences? (6) Whether it is a wisdom? (7) Whether God is its subject-matter? (8) Whether it is argumentative? (9) Whether it rightly employs metaphors and similes? (10) Whether the Sacred Scripture of this doctrine may be expounded in different senses?

First Article
Whether, Besides the Philosophical Disciplines, Any Further Doctrine Is Required?

We proceed thus to the First Article:—

Objection 1. It seems that, besides the philosophical disciplines, we have no need of any further doctrine. For man should not seek to know what is above reason: *Seek not the things that are too high for thee* (*Ecclus.* iii. 22). But whatever is not above reason is sufficiently considered in the philosophical disciplines. Therefore any other doctrine besides the philosophical disciplines is superfluous.

Objection 2. Further, doctrine can be concerned only with being, for nothing can be known, save the true, which is convertible with being. But everything that is, is considered in the philosophical disciplines—even God Himself; so that there is a part of philosophy called theology, or the divine science, as is clear from Aristotle.[1] Therefore, besides the philosophical disciplines, there is no need of any further doctrine.

On the contrary, It is written (*2 Tim.* iii. 16): *All Scripture inspired of God is profitable to teach, to reprove, to correct, to instruct in justice.* Now Scripture, inspired of God, is not a part of the philosophical disciplines discovered by human reason. Therefore it is useful that besides the philosophical disciplines there should be another science—*i.e.,* inspired of God.

I answer that, It was necessary for man's salvation that there should be a doctrine revealed by God, besides the philosophical disciplines investigated by human reason. First, because man is directed to God as to an end that surpasses the grasp of his reason: *The eye hath not seen, O God, besides Thee, what things Thou hast prepared for them that wait for Thee* (*Isa.* lxiv. 4). But the end must first be known by men who are to direct their intentions and actions to the end. Hence it was necessary for the salvation of man that certain truths which exceed human reason should be made known to him by divine revelation. Even as regards those truths about God which human reason can investigate, it was necessary that man be taught by a divine revelation. For the truth about God, such as reason can know it, would only be known for a few, and that after a long

---

[1]*Metaph.*, V, 1 (1026a 19).

time, and with the admixture of many errors; whereas man's whole salvation, which is in God, depends upon the knowledge of this truth. Therefore, in order that the salvation of men might be brought about more fitly
and more surely, it was necessary that they be taught divine truths by
divine revelation. It was therefore necessary that, besides the philosophical disciplines investigated by reason, there should be a sacred doctrine
by way of revelation.

Reply Obj. 1. Although those things which are beyond man's knowledge may not be sought for by man through his reason, nevertheless, what
is revealed by God must be accepted through faith. Hence the sacred text
continues, *For many things are shown to thee above the understanding of man*
(*Ecclus.* iii. 25). And in such things sacred doctrine consists.

Reply Obj. 2. Sciences are diversified according to the diverse nature of
their knowable objects. For the astronomer and the physicist both prove
the same conclusion—that the earth, for instance, is round: the astronomer by means of mathematics (*i.e.*, abstracting from matter), but the
physicist by means of matter itself. Hence there is no reason why those
things which are treated by the philosophical disciplines, so far as they
can be known by the light of natural reason, may not also be treated by
another science so far as they are known by the light of the divine revelation. Hence the theology included in sacred doctrine differs in genus
from that theology which is part of philosophy.

Second Article
Whether Sacred Doctrine Is a Science?

We proceed thus to the Second Article:—

Objection 1. It seems that sacred doctrine is not a science. For every science proceeds from self-evident principles. But sacred doctrine proceeds
from articles of faith which are not self-evident, since their truth is not
admitted by all: *For all men have not faith* (2 *Thess.* iii. 2) Therefore sacred
doctrine is not a science.

Obj. 2. Further, science is not of individuals. But sacred doctrine treats
of individual facts, such as the deeds of Abraham, Isaac and Jacob, and the
like. Therefore sacred doctrine is not a science.

On the contrary, Augustine says that *to this science alone belongs that
whereby saving faith is begotten, nourished, protected and strengthened.*[2] But
this can be said of no science except sacred doctrine. Therefore sacred
doctrine is a science.

---

[2]*De Trin.*, XIV, 1 (PL 42, 1037).

I answer that, Sacred doctrine is a science. We must bear in mind that there are two kinds of sciences. There are some which proceed from principles known by the natural light of the intellect, such as arithmetic and geometry and the like. There are also some which proceed from principles known by the light of a higher science: thus the science of optics proceeds from principles established by geometry, and music from principles established by arithmetic. So it is that sacred doctrine is a science because it proceeds from principles made known by the light of a higher science, namely, the science of God and the blessed. Hence, just as music accepts on authority the principles taught by the arithmetician, so sacred doctrine accepts the principles revealed by God.

Reply Obj. 1. The principles of any science are either in themselves self-evident, or reducible to the knowledge of a higher science; and such, as we have said, are the principles of sacred doctrine.

Reply Obj. 2. Individual facts are not treated in sacred doctrine because it is concerned with them principally; they are rather introduced as examples to be followed in our lives (as in the moral sciences), as well as to establish the authority of those men through whom the divine revelation, on which this sacred scripture or doctrine is based, has come down to us.

Third Article
Whether Sacred Doctrine Is One Science?

We proceed thus to the Third Article:—

Objection 1. It seems that sacred doctrine is not one science, for according to the Philosopher *that science is one which treats only of one class of subjects.*[3] But the creator and the creature, both of whom are treated in sacred doctrine, cannot be grouped together under one class of subjects. Therefore sacred doctrine is not one science.

Obj. 2. Further, in sacred doctrine we treat of angels, corporeal creatures and human morality. But these belong to separate philosophical sciences. Therefore sacred doctrine cannot be one science.

On the contrary, Holy Scripture speaks of it as one science: *Wisdom gave him the knowledge [scientiam] of holy things (Wis.* x. 10).

I answer that, Sacred doctrine is one science. The unity of a power or habit is to be gauged by its object, not indeed, in its material aspect, but as regards the formality under which it is an object. For example, man, ass, stone, agree in the one formality of being colored; and color is the formal object of sight. Therefore, because Sacred Scripture (as we have said)

---

[3] *Post. Anal.,* I, 28 (87a 38).

considers some things under the formality of being divinely revealed, all things which have been divinely revealed have in common the formality of the object of this science. Hence, they are included under sacred doctrine as under one science.

Reply Obj. 1. Sacred doctrine does not treat of God and creatures equally, but of God primarily, and of creatures only so far as they are referable to God as their beginning or end. Hence the unity of this science is not impaired.

Reply Obj. 2. Nothing prevents inferior powers or habits from being diversified by objects which yet agree with one another in coming together under a higher power or habit; because the higher power or habit regards its own object under a more universal formality. Thus, the object of the *common sense* is the sensible, including, therefore, whatever is visible or audible. Hence the *common sense*, although one power, extends to all the objects of the five senses. Similarly, objects which are the subject-matter of different philosophical sciences can yet be treated by this one single sacred doctrine under one aspect, namely, in so far as they can be included in revelation. So that in this way sacred doctrine bears, as it were, the stamp of the divine science, which is one and simple, yet extends to everything.

Fourth Article
Whether Sacred Doctrine Is a Practical Science?

We proceed thus to the Fourth Article:—

Objection 1. It seems that sacred doctrine is a practical science, for a practical science is that which ends in action, according to the Philosopher.[4] But sacred doctrine is ordained to action: *Be ye doers of the word, and not hearers only* (*Jas.* I. 22). Therefore sacred doctrine is a practical science.

Obj. 2. Further, sacred doctrine is divided into the Old and the New Law. But law belongs to moral science, which is a practical science. Therefore sacred doctrine is a practical science.

On the contrary, Every practical science is concerned with the things man can do; as moral science is concerned with human acts, and architecture with buildings. But sacred doctrine is chiefly concerned with God, Who is rather the Maker of man. Therefore it is not a practical but a speculative science.

---

[4]*Metaph.*, Ia, 1 (993b 21).

I answer that, Sacred doctrine, being one, extends to things which belong to the different philosophical sciences, because it considers in each the same formal aspect, namely, so far as they can be known through the divine light. Hence, although among the philosophical sciences some are speculative and others practical, nevertheless sacred doctrine includes both; as God, by one and the same science, knows both Himself and His works.

Still, it is more speculative than practical, because it is more concerned with divine things than with human acts; though even of these acts it treats inasmuch as man is ordained by them to the perfect knowledge of God, in which consists eternal beatitude. This is a sufficient answer to the Objections.

Fifth Article
Whether Sacred Doctrine Is Nobler than Other Sciences?

We proceed thus to the Fifth Article:—

Objection 1. It seems that sacred doctrine is not nobler than other sciences, for the nobility of a science depends on its certitude. But other sciences, the principles of which cannot be doubted, seem to be more certain than sacred doctrine; for its principles—namely, articles of faith—can be doubted. Therefore other sciences seem to be nobler.

Obj. 2. Further, it is the part of a lower science to draw upon a higher; as music draws upon arithmetic. But sacred doctrine does draw upon the philosophical disciplines; for Jerome observes, in his Epistle to Magnus, that *the ancient doctors so enriched their books with the doctrines and thoughts of the philosophers, that thou knowest not what more to admire in them, their profane erudition or their scriptural learning.*[5] Therefore sacred doctrine is inferior to other sciences.

On the contrary, Other sciences are called the handmaidens of this one: *Wisdom sent her maids to invite to the tower* (*Prov.* ix. 3).

I answer that, Since this science is partly speculative and partly practical, it transcends all other sciences, speculative and practical. Now one speculative science is said to be nobler than another either by reason of its greater certitude, or by reason of the higher dignity of its subject-matter. In both these respects this science surpasses other speculative sciences: in point of greater certitude, because other sciences derive their certitude from the natural light of human reason, which can err, whereas this derives its certitude from the light of the divine science, which cannot err;

---

[5]*Epist.* LXX (PL 22, 668).

in point of the higher dignity of its subject-matter, because this science treats chiefly of those things which by their sublimity transcend human reason, while other sciences consider only those things which are within reason's grasp. Of the practical sciences, that one is nobler which is ordained to a more final end, as political science is nobler than military science; for the good of the army is directed to the good of the state. But the purpose of this science, in so far as it is practical, is eternal beatitude, to which as to an ultimate end the ends of all the practical sciences are directed. Hence it is clear that from every standpoint it is nobler than other sciences.

Reply Obj. 1. It may well happen that what is in itself the more certain may seem to us the less certain because of the weakness of our intellect, *which is dazzled by the clearest objects of nature; as the owl is dazzled by the light of the sun.*[6] Hence the fact that some happen to doubt about the articles of faith is not due to the uncertain nature of the truths, but to the weakness of the human intellect; yet the slenderest knowledge that may be obtained of the highest things is more desirable than the most certain knowledge obtained of the lowest things, as is said in *De Animalibus* xi.[7]

Reply Obj. 2. This science can draw upon the philosophical disciplines, not as though it stood in need of them, but only in order to make its teaching clearer. For it accepts its principles, not from the other sciences, but immediately from God, by revelation. Therefore it does not draw upon the other sciences as upon its superiors, but uses them as its inferiors and handmaidens: even so the master sciences make use of subordinate sciences, as political science or military science. That it thus uses them is not due to its own defect or insufficiency, but to the defect of our intellect, which is more easily led by what is known through natural reason (from which proceed the other sciences), to that which is above reason, such as are the teachings of this science.

Sixth Article
Whether This Doctrine Is a Wisdom?

We proceed thus to the Sixth Article:—

Objection 1. It seems that this doctrine is not a wisdom. For no doctrine which borrows its principles is worthy of the name of wisdom, seeing that the wise man directs, and is not directed.[8] But this doctrine borrows its principles. Therefore it is not a wisdom.

---

[6]Aristotle, *Metaph.*, Ia, 1 (993b 9).   [7]Aristotle, *De Part. Anim.*, I, 5 (644b 31).
[8]Aristotle, *Metaph.*, I, 2 (982a 18).

Obj. 2. Further, it is a part of wisdom to prove the principles of other sciences. Hence it is called the chief of sciences, as is clear in *Ethics* vi.[9] But this doctrine does not prove the principles of other sciences. Therefore it is not a wisdom.

Obj. 3. Further, this doctrine is acquired by study, whereas wisdom is acquired by God's inspiration, and is accordingly numbered among the gifts of the Holy Spirit (*Isa.* xi. 2). Therefore this doctrine is not a wisdom.

On the contrary, It is written (*Deut.* iv. 6): *This is your wisdom and understanding in the sight of nations.*

I answer that, This doctrine is wisdom above all human wisdoms not merely in any one order, but absolutely. For since it is the part of a wise man to order and to judge, and since lesser matters can be judged in the light of some higher cause, he is said to be wise in any genus who considers the highest cause in that genus. Thus in the realm of building, he who plans the form of the house is called wise and architect, in relation to the subordinate laborers who trim the wood and make ready the stones: thus it is said, *As a wise architect I have laid the foundation* (*1 Cor.* iii. 10). Again, in the order of all human life, the prudent man is called wise, inasmuch as he directs his acts to a fitting end: thus it is said, *Wisdom is prudence to a man* (*Prov.* x. 23). Therefore, he who considers absolutely the highest cause of the whole universe, namely God, is most of all called wise. Hence wisdom is said to be the knowledge of divine things, as Augustine says.[10] But sacred doctrine essentially treats of God viewed as the highest cause, for it treats of Him not only so far as He can be known through creatures just as philosophers knew Him—*That which is known of God is manifest in them* (*Rom.* I. 19)—but also so far as He is known to Himself alone and revealed to others. Hence sacred doctrine is especially called a wisdom.

Reply Obj. 1. Sacred doctrine derives its principles, not from any human science, but from the divine science, by which, as by the highest wisdom, all our knowledge is ordered.

Reply Obj. 2. The principles of the other sciences either are evident and cannot be proved, or they are proved by natural reason in some other science. But the knowledge proper to this science comes through revelation, and not through natural reason. Therefore it is not its business to prove the principles of the other sciences, but only to judge them. For whatsoever is found in the other sciences contrary to the truth of this science must be condemned as false. Hence, it is said: *Destroying counsels and every height that exalteth itself against the knowledge of God* (*2 Cor.* x. 4, 5).

---

[9]Aristotle, *Eth.*, VI, 7 (1141a 20). Cicero, *De Officiis*, II, 2 (p. 80).

[10]*De Trin.*, XII, 14 (PL 42, 1009).—Cf.

Reply Obj. 3. Since judgment pertains to wisdom, in accord with a twofold manner of judging there is a twofold wisdom. A man may judge in one way by inclination, as whoever has the habit of a virtue judges rightly of what is virtuous by his very inclination towards it. Hence it is the virtuous man, as we read,[11] who is the measure and rule of human acts. In another way, a man may judge by knowledge, just as a man learned in moral science might be able to judge rightly about virtuous acts, though he had not virtue. The first manner of judging divine things belongs to that wisdom which is numbered as a gift of the Holy Spirit: *The spiritual man judgeth all things (1 Cor.* ii. 15). And Dionysius says: *Hierotheus is taught not only as one learning, but also as experiencing divine things.*[12] The second manner of judging belongs to this doctrine, inasmuch as it is acquired by study, though its principles are obtained by revelation.

Seventh Article
Whether God Is the Subject-Matter of This Science?

We proceed thus to the Seventh Article:—

Objection 1. It seems that God is not the subject-matter of this science. For, according to the Philosopher,[13] in every science the essence of its subject is presupposed. But this science cannot presuppose the essence of God, for Damascene says: *It is impossible to express the essence of God.*[14] Therefore God is not the subject-matter of this science.

Obj. 2. Further, whatever conclusions are reached in any science must be comprehended under the subject-matter of that science. But in Holy Scripture we reach conclusions not only concerning God, but concerning many other things, such as creatures and human morality. Therefore God is not the subject-matter of this science.

On the contrary, The subject-matter of a science is that of which it principally treats. But in this science the treatment is mainly about God; for it is called theology, as treating of God. Therefore God is the subject-matter of this science.

I answer that, God is the subject-matter of this science. The relation between a science and its subject-matter is the same as that between a habit or a power and its object. Now properly speaking the object of a power or habit is that under whose formality all things are referred to that power or habit, as man and stone are referred to sight in that they are colored. Hence the colored is the proper object of sight. But in sacred

---

[11]Aristotle, *Eth.,* X, 5 (1176a 17).   [12]*De Div. Nom.,* II, 9 (PG 3, 648).
[13]*Post. Anal.,* I, 1 (71a 13).   [14]*De Fide Orth.,* I, 4 (PG 94, 797).

doctrine all things are treated under the aspect of God, either because they are God Himself, or because they refer to God as to their beginning and end. Hence it follows that God is in very truth the subject-matter of this science. This is made clear also from the principles of this science, namely, the articles of faith, for faith is about God. The subject-matter of the principles and of the whole science must be the same, since the whole science is contained virtually in its principles.

Some, however, looking to what is treated in this science, and not to the aspect under which it is treated, have asserted the subject-matter of this science to be something other than God—that is, either things and signs,[15] or the works of salvation,[16] or the whole Christ, that is, the head and members.[17] Of all these things, in truth, we treat in this science, but so far as they are ordered to God.

Reply Obj. 1. Although we cannot know in what consists the essence of God, nevertheless in this doctrine we make use of His effects, either of nature or of grace, in the place of a definition, in regard to whatever is treated in this doctrine concerning God; even as in some philosophical sciences we demonstrate something about a cause from its effect, by taking the effect in the place of a definition of the cause.

Reply Obj. 2. Whatever other conclusions are reached in this sacred doctrine are comprehended under God, not as parts or species or accidents, but as in some way ordained to Him.

Eighth Article
Whether Sacred Doctrine Is Argumentative?

We proceed thus to the Eighth Article:—

Objection 1. It seems this doctrine is not argumentative. For Ambrose says: *Put arguments aside where faith is sought.*[18] But in this doctrine faith especially is sought: *But these things are written that you may believe (Jo.* xx. 31). Therefore sacred doctrine is not argumentative.

Obj. 2. Further, if it is argumentative, the argument is either from authority or from reason. If it is from authority, it seems unbefitting its dignity, for the proof from authority is the weakest form of proof according to Boethius.[19] But if from reason, this is unbefitting its end, because,

---

[15]Peter Lombard, *Sent.*, I, i, 1 (I, 14); cf. St. Augustine, *De Doc. Christ.*, I, 2 (PL 34, 19).   [16]Hugh of St. Victor, *De Sacram.*, Prol., 2 (PL 176, 183). [17]Robert Grosseteste, *Hexaëm.* (p. 176); Robert Kilwardby, *De Nat. Theol.* (p. 17).   [18]*De Fide*, I, 13 (PL 16, 570).   [19]*In Top. Cicer.*, I (PL 64, 1166); *De Differ. Top.*, III (PL 64, 1199).

according to Gregory, *faith has no merit in those things of which human reason brings its own experience.*[20] Therefore sacred doctrine is not argumentative.

On the contrary, The Scripture says that a bishop should *embrace that faithful word which is according to doctrine, that he may be able to exhort in sound doctrine and to convince the gainsayers* (*Tit.* i. 9).

I answer that, As the other sciences do not argue in proof of their principles, but argue from their principles to demonstrate other truths in these sciences, so this doctrine does not argue in proof of its principles, which are the articles of faith, but from them it goes on to prove something else; as the Apostle argues from the resurrection of Christ in proof of the general resurrection (*1 Cor.* xv, 12). However, it is to be borne in mind, in regard to the philosophical sciences, that the inferior sciences neither prove their principles nor dispute with those who deny them, but leave this to a higher science; whereas the highest of them, viz., metaphysics, can dispute with one who denies its principles, if only the opponent will make some concession; but if he concedes nothing, it can have no dispute with him, though it can answer his arguments. Hence Sacred Scripture, since it has no science above itself, disputes argumentatively with one who denies its principles only if the opponent admits some at least of the truths obtained through divine revelation. Thus, we can argue with heretics from texts in Holy Scripture, and against those who deny one article of faith we can argue from another. If our opponent believes nothing of divine revelation, there is no longer any means of proving the articles of faith by argument, but only of answering his objections—if he has any—against faith. Since faith rests upon infallible truth, and since the contrary of a truth can never be demonstrated, it is clear that the proofs brought against faith are not demonstrations, but arguments that can be answered.

Reply Obj. 1. Although arguments from human reason cannot avail to prove what belongs to faith, nevertheless, this doctrine argues from articles of faith to other truths.

Reply Obj. 2. It is especially proper to this doctrine to argue from authority, inasmuch as its principles are obtained by revelation; and hence we must believe the authority of those to whom the revelation has been made. Nor does this take away from the dignity of this doctrine, for although the argument from authority based on human reason is the weakest, yet the argument from authority based on divine revelation is

---

[20]*In Evang.*, II, hom. 26 (PL 76, 1197).

the strongest. But sacred doctrine also makes use of human reason, not, indeed, to prove faith (for thereby the merit of faith would come to an end), but to make clear other things that are set forth in this doctrine. Since therefore grace does not destroy nature, but perfects it, natural reason should minister to faith as the natural inclination of the will ministers to charity. Hence the Apostle says: *Bringing into captivity every understanding unto the obedience of Christ (2 Cor.* x. 5). Hence it is that sacred doctrine makes use also of the authority of philosophers in those questions in which they were able to know the truth by natural reason, as Paul quotes a saying of Aratus: *As some also of your own poets said: For we are also His offspring (Acts* xvii. 28). Nevertheless, sacred doctrine makes use of these authorities as extrinsic and probable arguments, but properly uses the authority of the canonical Scriptures as a necessary demonstration, and the authority of the doctors of the Church as one that may properly be used, yet merely as probable. For our faith rests upon the revelation made to the apostles and prophets, who wrote the canonical books, and not on the revelations (if any such there are) made to other doctors. Hence Augustine says: *Only those books of Scripture which are called canonical have I learned to hold in such honor as to believe their authors have not erred in any way in writing them. But other authors I so read as not to deem anything in their works to be true, merely because of their having so thought and written, whatever may have been their holiness and learning.*[21]

Ninth Article
Whether Holy Scripture Should Use Metaphors?

We proceed thus to the Ninth Article:—

Objection 1. It seems that Holy Scripture should not use metaphors. For that which is proper to the lowest science seems not to befit this science, which holds the highest place of all. But to proceed by the aid of various similitudes and figures is proper to poetic, the least of all the sciences. Therefore it is not fitting that this science should make use of such similitudes.

Obj. 2. Further, this doctrine seems to be intended to manifest truth. Hence a reward is held out to those who manifest it: *They that explain me shall have life everlasting (Ecclus.* xxiv. 31). But by such similitudes truth is hidden. Therefore to put forward divine truths under the likeness of corporeal things does not befit this doctrine.

---

[21]*Epist.* LXXXII, 1 (PL 33, 277).

Obj. 3. Further, the higher creatures are, the nearer they approach to the divine likeness. If therefore any creature be taken to represent God, this representation ought chiefly to be taken from the higher creatures, and not from the lowly; yet this is often found in the Scriptures.

On the contrary, It is written (*Osee* xii. 10): *I have multiplied visions, and I have used similitudes by the ministry of the prophets.* But to put forward anything by means of similitudes is to use metaphors. Therefore sacred doctrine may use metaphors.

I answer that, It is befitting Holy Scripture to put forward divine and spiritual truths by means of comparisons with material things. For God provides for everything according to the capacity of its nature. Now it is natural to man to attain to intellectual truths through sensible things, because all our knowledge originates from sense. Hence in Holy Scripture spiritual truths are fittingly taught under the likeness of material things. This is what Dionysius says: *We cannot be enlightened by the divine rays except they be hidden within the covering of many sacred veils.*[22] It is also befitting Holy Scripture, which is proposed to all without distinction of persons—*To the wise and to the unwise I am a debtor* (*Rom.* i. 14)—that spiritual truths be expounded by means of figures taken from corporeal things, in order that thereby even the simple who are unable by themselves to grasp intellectual things may be able to understand it.

Reply Obj. 1. Poetry makes use of metaphors to produce a representation, for it is natural to man to be pleased with representations. But sacred doctrine makes use of metaphors as both necessary and useful.

Reply Obj. 2. The ray of divine revelation is not extinguished by the sensible imagery wherewith it is veiled, as Dionysius says;[23] and its truth so far remains that it does not allow the minds of those to whom the revelation has been made, to rest in the likenesses, but raises them to the knowledge of intelligible truths; and through those to whom the revelation has been made others also may receive instruction in these matters. Hence those things that are taught metaphorically in one part of Scripture, in other parts are taught more openly. The very hiding of truth in figures is useful for the exercise of thoughtful minds, and as a defense against the ridicule of the unbelievers, according to the words, *Give not that which is holy to dogs* (*Matt.* vii. 6).

Reply Obj. 3. As Dionysius says,[24] it is more fitting that divine truths should be expounded under the figure of less noble than of nobler bodies; and this for three reasons. First, because thereby men's minds are the better

---

[22]*De Cael. Hier.*, I, 2 (PG 3, 121).   [23]*Ibid.*   [24]*Op. cit.*, II, 2 (PG 3, 136).

freed from error. For then it is clear that these things are not literal descriptions of divine truths, which might have been open to doubt had they been expressed under the figure of nobler bodies, especially in the case of those who could think of nothing nobler than bodies. Second, because this is more befitting the knowledge of God that we have in this life. For what He is not is clearer to us than what He is. Therefore similitudes drawn from things farthest away from God form within us a truer estimate that God is above whatsoever we may say or think of Him. Third, because thereby divine truths are the better hidden from the unworthy.

Tenth Article
Whether in Holy Scripture a Word May Have Several Senses?

We proceed thus to the Tenth Article:—

Objection 1. It seems that in Holy Scripture a word cannot have several senses, historical or literal, allegorical, tropological or moral, and anagogical. For many different senses in one text produce confusion and deception and destroy all force of argument. Hence no argument, but only fallacies, can be deduced from a multiplicity of propositions. But Holy Scripture ought to be able to state the truth without any fallacy. Therefore in it there cannot be several senses to a word.

Obj. 2. Further, Augustine says that *the Old Testament has a fourfold division: according to history, etiology, analogy, and allegory.*[25] Now these four seem altogether different from the four divisions mentioned in the first objection. Therefore it does not seem fitting to explain the same word of Holy Scripture according to the four different senses mentioned above.

Obj. 3. Further, besides these senses, there is the parabolical, which is not one of these four.

On the contrary, Gregory says: *Holy Scripture by the manner of its speech transcends every science, because in one and the same sentence, while it describes a fact, it reveals a mystery.*[26]

I answer that, The author of Holy Scripture is God, in Whose power it is to signify His meaning, not by words only (as man also can do), but also by things themselves. So, whereas in every other science things are signified by words, this science has the property that the things signified by the words have themselves also a signification. Therefore that first signification whereby words signify things belongs to the first sense, the historical or literal. That signification whereby things signified by words have themselves also a signification is called the spiritual sense, which is based on

---

[25]*De Util. Cred.*, III (PL 42, 68).   [26]*Moral.*, XX, 1 (PL 76, 135).

the literal, and presupposes it. Now this spiritual sense has a threefold division. For as the Apostle says (*Heb.* x. 1) the Old Law is a figure of the New Law, and Dionysius says *the New Law itself is a figure of future glory.*[27] Again, in the New Law, whatever our Head has done is a type of what we ought to do. Therefore, so far as the things of the Old Law signify the things of the New Law, there is the allegorical sense; so far as the things done in Christ, or so far as the things which signify Christ, are signs of what we ought to do, there is the moral sense. But so far as they signify what relates to eternal glory, there is the anagogical sense. Since the literal sense is that which the author intends, and since the author of Holy Scripture is God, Who by one act comprehends all things by His intellect, it is not unfitting, as Augustine says,[28] if, even according to the literal sense, one word in Holy Scripture should have several senses.

Reply Obj. 1. The multiplicity of these senses does not produce equivocation or any other kind of multiplicity, seeing that these senses are not multiplied because one word signifies several things, but because the things signified by the words can be themselves signs of other things. Thus in Holy Scripture no confusion results, for all the senses are founded on one—the literal—from which alone can any argument be drawn, and not from those intended allegorically, as Augustine says.[29] Nevertheless, nothing of Holy Scripture perishes because of this, since nothing necessary to faith is contained under the spiritual sense which is not elsewhere put forward clearly by the Scripture in its literal sense.

Reply Obj. 2. These three—history, etiology, analogy—are grouped under the literal sense. For it is called history, as Augustine expounds,[30] whenever anything is simply related; it is called etiology when its cause is assigned, as when Our Lord gave the reason why Moses allowed the putting away of wives—namely, because of the hardness of men's hearts (*Matt.*, xix, 8); it is called analogy whenever the truth of one text of Scripture is shown not to contradict the truth of another. Of these four, allegory alone stands for the three spiritual senses. Thus Hugh of St. Victor includes the anagogical under the allegorical sense, laying down three senses only—the historical, the allegorical and the tropological.[31]

Reply Obj. 3. The parabolical sense is contained in the literal, for by words things are signified properly and figuratively. Nor is the figure

---

[27]*De Eccles. Hier.*, V, 2 (PG 3, 501).   [28]*Confess.*, XII, 31 (PL 32, 844).   [29]*Epist.* XCIII, 8 (PL 33, 334).   [30]*De Util. Cred.*, 3 (PL 42, 68). [31]Cf. *De Sacram.*, I, 4 (PL 176, 184).—Cf. also *De Scriptur. et Scriptor. Sacris*, 3 (PL 175, 11).

itself, but that which is figured, the literal sense. When Scripture speaks of God's arm, the literal sense is not that God has such a member, but only what is signified by this member, namely, operative power. Hence it is plain that nothing false can ever underlie the literal sense of Holy Scripture.

THE DECLARATIVE ASPECTS

Exposition of the "De Trinitate" of Boethius
Question 2
On Making the Divine Knowledge Known

There are four questions concerning this topic:

1. Is it permissible to make divine realities an object of investigation?

2. Can there be a science of divine realities?

3. Is it permissible to use philosophical arguments and authorities in the science of faith whose object is God?

4. Should divine realities be veiled by obscure and novel words?

Article One
Is It Permissible to Make Divine
Realities an Object of Investigation?

We proceed to the first article as follows:

It does not seem right to inquire by reasoning into things divine.

1. For it is said in Ecclesiasticus 3:22: "Seek not what is too high for you, and search not into what is above your ability." But divine things especially are too high for us, and more particularly those held on faith. Therefore it is not permissible to investigate these matters.

2. Punishment is only inflicted for some fault. But, as is said in Proverbs 25:27: "He who is a searcher of majesty shall be overwhelmed by glory." Therefore it is not permitted to investigate thoroughly what belongs to the majesty of God.

3. Ambrose says:[1] "Away with arguments if you are looking for faith." But faith is necessary in divine things, especially concerning the Trinity. Therefore in this subject it is not permitted to investigate the truth by reasoning.

Source: Reprinted from Thomas Aquinas, *Faith, Reason and Theology*, edited and translated by Armand A. Maurer, pp. 35–55, by permission of the publisher. © 1987 by the Pontifical Institute of Mediaeval Studies, Toronto.

[1]St. Ambrose, *De fide* 1.13.84, PL 16:570.

4. Speaking of generation in God, Ambrose says:[2] "It is not right to inquire into these high mysteries. One may know that the Son is begotten; it is not right to discuss how he is begotten." For the same reason, then, it is not permitted to inquire by means of arguments into anything connected with the Trinity.

5. As Gregory says,[3] "Faith has no merit where human reason supplies proof." But it is wrong to do away with the merit of faith. Therefore it is not right to investigate matters of faith by reason.

6. All honor ought to be given to God. But secrets are to be respected by keeping silence about them. Thus Dionysius[4] speaks of "honoring by silence the hidden truth which is above us." This agrees with the words of Psalm 64:2, according to Jerome's text:[5] "Praise is silent before you, O God"; that is, silence itself is your praise. Therefore we ought to refrain in silence from inquiring into divine realities.

7. As the Philosopher says,[6] no one can travel to infinity, because the purpose of every movement is to reach an end, which is not present in infinity. But God is infinitely remote from us. Now investigation is a kind of progression of reason toward the object under inquiry. So it seems that we ought not to inquire into divine realities.

On the contrary, we have the words of 1 Peter 3:15: "Always be prepared to make a defence to any one who calls you to account for the faith[7] that is in you." But this is impossible unless we inquire rationally into what we hold on faith. Therefore a rational investigation into matters of faith is necessary.

2. As Titus 1:9 says, it is the duty of a bishop "to give instruction in sound doctrine and also to confute those who contradict it." But only by arguments can we refute those contradicting the faith. Therefore it is necessary to use reasoning in matters of faith.

3. Augustine says[8] that "with the help of the Lord our God we shall endeavor to give a reason for that very thing which they demand, namely that the Trinity is one God." Therefore we can use reasoning in inquiring into the Trinity.

---

[2]Ibid., 1.10.65, PL 16: 566A.   [3]St. Gregory, *Hom.* 26.1, PL 76:1197C.
[4]Pseudo-Dionysius, *De caelesti hierarchia* 15.19, PG 3:340B.   [5]St. Jerome,
Liber psalmorum, ps. 65, PL 28:1236C.   [6]Aristotle, *De caelo* 1.7 (274b11–13).
[7]The Greek text of the Bible reads "hope." St. Thomas follows a variant reading
of the Vulgate. See L. Elders, *Faith and Science*, p. 42.   [8]St. Augustine, *De
Trinitate* 1.2.4, CCL 50:31.

4. Augustine says in his treatise against Felician:[9] "[Although in matters of faith it is easier to believe qualified testimony than to investigate by reasoning, nevertheless] because you not altogether unfittingly acknowledge both of these—since you do not omit to acknowledge testimony as well as the aforesaid reasoning—I am ready to proceed with you in this controversy on lines you have approved," that is, I shall use both reasoning and authority. Therefore the same conclusion follows.

Reply: Because our perfection consists in our union with God, we must have access to the divine to the fullest extent possible, using everything in our power, that our mind might be occupied with contemplation and our reason with the investigation of divine realities. As Psalm 72:28 says: "It is good for me to adhere to my God." So Aristotle[10] rejects the opinion of those who held that we should not meddle with what is divine, but only with what is human. "But we must not follow those," he says, "who advise us, being human, to think of human things, and, being mortal, of mortal things, but must, so far as we can, make ourselves immortal, and strain every nerve to live in accord with what is best in us."

In this regard, however, it is possible to go wrong in three ways. First, by presumption, delving into the divine in such a way that one tries to grasp it fully. This presumption is denounced in Job 11:7: "Can you search out the footprints of God and perfectly discover the Almighty?" Hilary also states:[11] "Do not plunge yourself into that mystery and secret of unimaginable birth. Do not immerse yourself in it, presuming to comprehend the heights of intelligence; rather, understand that they are incomprehensible."

Second, one may err because in matters of faith he makes reason precede faith, instead of faith precede reason, as when someone is willing to believe only what he can discover by reason. It should in fact be just the opposite. Thus Hilary says:[12] "Begin by believing, inquire, press forward, persevere."

Third, by pursuing his speculation into the divine beyond the measure of his ability. Romans 12:3 says: "I bid every one of you not to be more wise than is necessary to be wise, but to be wise with sobriety, each according to the measure of faith that God has assigned him." For everyone has not been endowed in equal measure, so that what is beyond the ability of one is not beyond the ability of another.

---

[9]The treatise is in fact by Vigilius Thapsensis, *De unitate Trinitatis* 2, PL 42:1158. [10]Aristotle, *Nic. Ethics* 10.7 (1177b31–34). [11]St. Hilary, *De Trinitate* 2.10 and 11, CCL 62:48.11–13 and 49.14–16. [12]Ibid., 2. 10, CCL 62:48.13.

Replies to Opposing Arguments

Reply to 1. Those matters are said to be too high for us that go beyond our capacity, not those that are by nature of greater worth. For the more a person occupies himself with what is of greater value, provided that he keeps within the limits of his ability, the greater perfection he will reach. But should he exceed the measure of his ability even in the slightest matters, he easily falls into error. Thus the Gloss on Romans 12:3 says:[13] "Heretics are made in two ways: they fall into error and depart from the truth because they go beyond their limits when they concern themselves with the creator or with creatures."

Reply to 2. To investigate thoroughly is, as it were, to conduct an inquiry to the very end. But it is unlawful and presumptuous for anyone to inquire into the divine as though he will reach the end of comprehending it.

Reply to 3. Where faith is at stake there is no room for arguments opposed to faith or for those that attempt to precede it, but there is a place for those that in a due manner follow upon it.

Reply to 4. It is not permitted to investigate the heavenly mysteries with the intention of fully comprehending them. This is clear from the words that follow: "One may know that the Son is begotten; it is not right to discuss how he is begotten." He who discusses the manner of that birth tries to know what that birth is, though we can know *that* divine realities are but not *what* they are.

Reply to 5. There are two kinds of human reasoning. One is demonstrative, compelling the mind's assent. There can be no place in matters of faith for this kind of reasoning, but there can be in disproving claims that faith is impossible. For although matters of faith cannot be demonstratively proved, neither can they be demonstratively disproved. If this sort of reasoning were brought forward to prove what is held on faith, the merit of faith would be destroyed, because the assent to it would not be voluntary but necessary. But persuasive reasoning, drawn from analogies to the truths of faith, does not take away the nature of faith because it does not render them evident, for there is no reduction to first principles intuited by the mind. Neither does it deprive faith of its merit, because it does not compel the mind's assent but leaves the assent voluntary.

Reply to 6. God is indeed respected by silence, but this does not mean that we may say nothing whatever about him, or inquire into him, but that we should understand that however much we may say or inquire about

---

[13]*Glossa ordinaria* 3. col. 1994D.

him, we realize that we fall short of fully understanding him. Thus it is said in Ecclesiasticus 43:32: "When you praise the Lord, exalt him as much as you can; for he will surpass even that."

Reply to 7. Since God is infinitely distant from creatures, no creature progresses toward God so as to equal him, either in what it receives from him or in knowing him. So the goal of the creature's progress is not something infinitely remote from the creature; but every creature is drawn to be more and more like God, as far as it is able.[14] So also the human mind should always be aroused to know more and more about God in the manner proper to it. Thus Hilary says:[15] "The person who with piety pursues the infinite may sometimes find it beyond his reach, but by advancing he makes progress."

Article Two
Can There Be a Science of Divine Realities?[16]

We proceed to the second article as follows:

It seems that there cannot be a science of the divine realities that are matters of faith.

1. For wisdom is different from science, and wisdom treats of the divine.[17] Therefore science does not.

2. As is said in the *Posterior Analytics*,[18] every science must presuppose knowledge of what its subject is. But, as Damascene says,[19] we can in no way know what God is. Therefore there can be no science of God.

3. It belongs to every science to study the parts and attributes of its subject.[20] But God, being a simple form, neither has parts into which he may be analyzed, nor can he be the subject of attributes.[21] Therefore there can be no science about God.

4. In every science reasoning comes before assent, for in the sciences demonstration is the cause of the assent to the objects of knowledge. But in objects of belief the opposite must be the case: as we have said,[22] the

---

[14]See St. Thomas, *Contra gentiles* 3.19.   [15]St. Hilary, *De Trinitate* 2.10, CCL 62: 48. 14–16.   [16]See St. Thomas, *Sent.* 1, prol, q. un, a. 3, q. 2; *Summa theol.* 1.1.2.   [17]See St. Augustine, *De Trinitate* 12.15.25, CCL 50:379.   [18]Aristotle, *Post. Anal.* 1.1 (71a11–13).   [19]St. John Damascene, *De fide ortho-doxa* 1.2 and 4, ed. Buytaert, pp. 15.40–45 and 19.3–5, 20.33.   [20]See Aristotle, *Post. Anal.* 1.1.7, 10 (71a12, 75a39–b2, 76b11–16); St. Thomas, *In Peri herm.* 1, lect. 1, n. 3, ed. Leonine 1:8; *In Post. Anal.* 1, lect. 2, n. 2, ed. Leonine 1:142.   [21]See Boethius, *De Trinitate* 2, p. 10.29–30, 42–43 and p. 12.48–49   [22]See above, a. 1, Reply, p. 27.

assent of faith precedes reasoning. Therefore there can be no science of divine realities, especially those accepted on faith.

5. Every science proceeds from self-evident principles which everyone accepts on hearing, or from principles that are trustworthy because of them. But the articles of faith, which are the first principles in matters of faith, are not of this sort. As has been said,[23] they are neither self-evident nor can they be resolved by demonstration to self-evident principles. Consequently there can be no science about the divine realities held on faith.

6. Faith is concerned with realities that are not evident,[24] whereas science is concerned with those that are evident, because science brings to light the objects with which it deals. Therefore there can be no science of the divine realities held on faith.

7. Every science begins with understanding, because it is from the intellectual perception of principles that we arrive at the scientific knowledge of conclusions. But in matters of faith understanding does not come at the beginning but at the end, as is said in Isaiah 7:9:[25] "Unless you shall have believed, you will not understand." Hence there can be no science of the divine realities held by faith.

On the contrary, we have the words of Augustine:[26] "To this science I attribute only that whereby the most wholesome faith, which leads to true blessedness, is begotten, protected and strengthened." Therefore there is a science concerning matters of faith.

2. The same point is clear from the words of Wisdom 10:10: "Wisdom . . . gave him the science of the saints." This can only be understood to refer to that which distinguishes holy people from the wicked, namely the science of faith.

3. The Apostle, speaking of the knowledge possessed by the faithful in 1 Corinthians 8:7, says: "However, not all possess this science." From this the same conclusion follows.

Reply: The nature of science consists in this, that from things already known conclusions about other matters follow of necessity. Seeing that

---

[23]See above, a. 1, Reply to 5, p. 28.   [24]See Hebrews 11:1.   [25]This is the reading of the Septuagint. The Vulgate reads: "If you will not believe, you shall not continue" *(Si non credideritis, non permanebitis).* See St. Jerome, *Commentaria in Esaiam prophetam* 3, PL 24:107A, CCL 73:99.84–88.   [26]St. Augustine, *De Trinitate* 14.1.3, CCL 50:424. The text of Aquinas mistakenly refers to book 12.

this is possible in the case of divine realities, clearly there can be a science about them. Now the knowledge of divine things can be interpreted in two ways. First, from our standpoint, and then they are knowable to us only through creatures, the knowledge of which we derive from the senses. Second, from the nature of divine realities themselves. In this way they are eminently knowable of themselves, and although we do not know them in their own way, this is how they are known by God and the blessed.

Accordingly there are two kinds of science concerning the divine. One follows our way of knowing, which uses the principles of sensible things in order to make the Godhead known. This is the way the philosophers handed down a science of the divine, calling the primary science "divine science." The other follows the mode of divine realities themselves, so that they are apprehended in themselves. We cannot perfectly possess this way of knowing in the present life, but there arises here and now in us a certain sharing in, and a likeness to, the divine knowledge, to the extent that through the faith implanted in us we firmly grasp the primary Truth itself for its own sake. And as God, by the very fact that he knows himself, knows all other things as well in his way, namely, by simple intuition without any reasoning process, so may we, from the things we accept by faith in our firm grasping of the primary Truth, come to know other things in our way, namely by drawing conclusions from principles.[27] Thus the truths we hold on faith are, as it were, our principles in this science, and the others become, as it were, conclusions.[28] From this it is evident that this science is nobler than the divine science taught by the philosophers, proceeding as it does from more sublime principles.

Replies to Opposing Arguments

Reply to 1. Wisdom is not contrasted with science as though they were opposed to each other, but because wisdom adds an additional note to science. Wisdom, as the Philosopher says,[29] is the chief of all the sciences, because, being concerned with the highest principles, it directs all the other sciences. That is also why it is called the goddess of sciences in the beginning of the *Metaphysics*.[30] And this is even truer of the science that not only treats of the highest causes, but comes from them.[31] Now, since it belongs to the wise to direct others, so this most lofty science, which

---

[27]See St. Thomas, *Contra gentiles* 2.1.5. [Not in this volume]   [28]See St. Thomas, *Summa Theol.* I, q. 1, a. 7.   [29]Aristotle, *Nic. Ethics* 6.7 (1141a18–20). [30]Aristotle, *Metaph.* 1.2 (983a6).   [31]See St. Thomas, *Summa Theol.* I, q. 1, a. 6.

directs and puts order in the other sciences, is called wisdom,[32] just as in the "mechanical" arts they are called wise who draw up the plans for others, for example, architects.[33] The name "science" is left for the other less noble disciplines. In line with this, science is contrasted with wisdom as a property with a definition.[34]

Reply to 2. As we said above, when causes are known through their effects knowledge of the effect takes the place of knowledge of the essence of the cause, and this is necessary in sciences that treat of realities knowable through themselves. Consequently, in order that we have a science of God, we need not first know what he is. Or we may reply that in divine science knowledge of what God is not takes the place of knowledge of what he is, for just as one thing is distinguished from others by what it is, so also by the knowledge of what it is not.

Reply to 3. By the parts of the subject in a science are to be understood not only subjective or integral parts,[35] but anything whatsoever, a knowledge of which is required for a knowledge of the subject, because a science is concerned with all matters of this sort only insofar as they are related to its subject. By attributes are meant whatever can be proved of anything, whether they are negative attributes or relations to other things. Many attributes of this sort can be proved of God, both from naturally known principles and from the principles of faith.

Reply to 4. In every science there are some items that function as principles and others that function as conclusions. The reasoning introduced in sciences precedes assent to the conclusions, but it follows assent to the principles because it flows from them. Now in divine science the articles of faith are like principles and not like conclusions. They are also defended against those who attack them, as the Philosopher[36] argues against those who deny principles.[37] Moreover they are clarified by certain analogies, just as principles that are naturally known are made evident by induction but not proved by demonstrative reasoning.

---

[32]See St. Thomas, *Contra gentiles* I, q. 1, a. 1. [Not in this volume]   [33]See Aristotle, *Metaph.* 1.1 (981a30–b3).   [34]The meaning of this enigmatic statement seems to be that wisdom is distinguished from science by something outside the definition of science, namely wisdom's office of directing the other sciences, as a property is distinguished from a definition as something outside the definition, for example, the capability of laughter is outside the definition "rational animal." See J. Owens, "A Note on Aquinas, *In Boeth. de Trin.*, 2, 2, ad 1ᵐ," *The New Scholasticism* 59 (1985), 102–108.   [35]For the meaning of these kinds of parts, see St. Thomas, *Summa Theol.* 2–2.48, a. un.   [36]Aristotle, *Metaph.* 4.4–6 (1005b35–1011b22).   [37]See St. Thomas, *Summa Theol.* I, q .1, a. 8.

Reply to 5. Even some of the sciences taught on the purely human level use principles that are not known to everyone, but they must be presupposed as established by higher sciences. Thus subalternate sciences employ principles that are presupposed and believed on the authority of higher sciences, and these principles are self-evident only to the higher sciences. It is in this way that the articles of faith, which are the principles of this science, are related to God's knowledge, because what is self-evident in the knowledge God has of himself is presupposed in our science,[38] and they are believed on the word of him who reveals them to us through his witnesses, in much the same way as a physician accepts the testimony of a scientist when he says that there are four elements.

Reply to 6. The evidence of a science is the result of the evidence of its principles, for a science does not make its principles evident, but because the principles are evident it renders its conclusions evident. In this way the science we are speaking about does not make matters of faith apparent, but by them it brings to light other things in the way we can be certain about the primary beings.[39]

Reply to 7. Understanding is always the primary source of every science, but it is not always its proximate source. Sometimes the proximate starting point of a science is belief, as is clear in the subalternated sciences. The proximate source of their conclusions is belief in truths presupposed as established by a higher science. Their primary source, however, is the knowledge of the higher scientist who, through his understanding, is certain about these matters of belief. Similarly the proximate starting point of this [divine] science is faith, but its primary source is the divine understanding, in which we put our faith. The purpose of our believing, however, is to arrive at an understanding of what we believe.[40] It is as if a scientist on a lower level acquired the science of a scientist on a higher level; he would then come to know and to understand what he formerly only believed.

Article Three
Is It Permissible to Use Philosophical Reasoning and Authorities in the Science of Faith, Whose Object Is God?

We proceed to the third article as follows:

It seems that in matters of faith it is not permissible to use philosophical reasoning.

---

[38]See ibid., 1.1.6, ad 1ᵐ. [39]See St. Thomas, *De veritate* q. 14, a. 9, ad 3ᵐ.
[40]See St. Thomas, *Sent.* 1, prol. q. un. a. 3, q. 3; *Quodlibet* 4, q. 9, a. 3.

1. According to 1 Corinthians 1:17, "Christ did not send me to baptize but to preach the gospel, and not with eloquent wisdom," that is, "in the teaching of the philosophers," as the Gloss says.[41] And on the verse 1:20: "Where is the debater of this age?" the Gloss comments: "The debater is he who unravels the secrets of nature: such as these God does not accept as preachers."[42] Again, commenting on 2:4: "And my speech and my preaching was not in the persuasive words of human wisdom," the Gloss says: "Although my words were persuasive, they were not so because of human wisdom, like the words of pseudo-apostles."[43] From all this it seems that it is not permissible to use philosophical reasoning in matters of faith.

2. Commenting on Isaiah 15:1: "Ar is laid waste in a night," the Gloss say,[44] "Ar means the adversary, namely worldly knowledge, which is an enemy of God." Therefore we ought not to use worldly knowledge in matters that concern God.

3. Ambrose states:[45] "The mystery of faith is free from philosophical reasoning." Therefore, where it is a question of faith, it is not lawful to use the arguments and sayings of the philosophers.

4. Jerome[46] tells how in a vision he was scourged by divine judgment because he had read books of Cicero, how the bystanders prayed that he might be pardoned because of his youth, and then how he would insist on being tortured if he ever again read books of the pagans. Calling to witness the name of God, he cried: "O Lord, if I ever possess and read secular books, I have denied you." Therefore if it is wrong to study and read them, much less is it permissible to use them in treatises about God.

5. Secular wisdom is often represented in Scripture by water, divine wisdom by wine. But in Isaiah 1:22, innkeepers are blamed for mixing water with wine. Consequently those teachers should be condemned who mingle philosophical doctrines with sacred teaching.

6. As Jerome says:[47] "We ought not to use the same language as heretics. But heretics use the teachings of philosophy in order to distort the

---

[41]*Glossa ordinaria* 5, col. 201A. See Peter Lombard, *Glossa*, PL 191:1541B.
[42]*Glossa ordinaria* 6, col. 202D. See Peter Lombard, ibid., PL 191:1542D.
[43]Peter Lombard, ibid., PL 191:1548B. See *Glossa interlinearis* 6, col. 209–210.
[44]*Glossa ordinaria* 4, fol. 35rA.   [45]This statement is not from St. Ambrose but from Peter Lombard, *Sent.* 3, d. 22, c. 1, ed. Grottaferrata 2:136.8–9. See St. Ambrose, *De fide* 1.13.84, PL 16:570D.   [46]See St. Jerome, *Ep.* 22.30, CSEL 54:190.7–191.7.   [47]This statement has not been found in Jerome's gloss on Hosea. See *Glossa ordinaria* on Hosea 2:16; 4, fol. 336rA.

faith, as is said in the Gloss on Proverbs 7:16 and Isaiah 15:5.[48] Therefore Catholics ought not to use them in their treatises.

7. Just as every science has its own principles,[49] so also does sacred doctrine, namely the articles of faith. But the other sciences proceed incorrectly if one science takes the principles of another; rather, each ought to proceed from its own principles, as the Philosopher teaches.[50] Therefore neither does sacred doctrine proceed correctly if anyone uses the teachings of philosophy.

8. If someone's teaching is rejected in a certain matter, his authority is weakened as a support for another. Thus Augustine says[51] that if we should grant any mistake in sacred Scripture, its authority as a support of faith will be destroyed. But sacred doctrine repudiates the teaching of the philosophers on many points because they are found to have made many mistakes. Therefore their authority is incapable of supporting anything.

On the contrary, the Apostle in Titus 1:12 uses a line of the poet Epimenides: "The Cretans are always liars, evil beasts, lazy gluttons"; in 1 Corinthians 15:33 he refers to the words of Menander: "Bad company ruins good morals"; and in Acts 17:28 to the Athenians he quotes the words of Aratus: "For we are indeed his (that is, God's) offspring."[52] Consequently it is also permissible for other teachers of sacred Scripture to make use of philosophical arguments.

2. Jerome,[53] after mentioning several teachers of sacred Scripture like Basil, Gregory and certain others, adds, "All these so filled their books with the teachings and opinions of the philosophers that one does not know what to admire more in them, their secular learning or their knowledge of the Scriptures." They would not have acted like this had it been unlawful or useless.

3. Jerome wrote:[54] "If you love a captive woman, that is, worldly wis-

---

[48]See *Glossa ordinaria* on Proverbs 7:16; 3, col. 1634DE; and on Isaiah, 15:5; 4, fol. 35C. [49]See Q. 6, a. 1, ed. Decker, p. 205.13–15, trans. Maurer, pp. 63–64; *In Post. Anal.* 1, lect. 41 and 43, ed. Leonine 1:306–307, n. 9–12 and 317, n. 13. [50]Aristotle, *Post. Anal.* 1.7 (75a38–b20). [51]St. Augustine, Ep. 28 *ad Hieronymum* (to Jerome) 3.5 and 3.3, CSEL 34 (pt. 1), 111.8–13 and 108.5–10. [52]Taken from St. Jerome, *Ep. 70 ad Magnum* (to Magnus), CSEL 54:701.9–11, 15–702.1. For Epimenides, see *The Pre-Socratic Philosophers*, ed. K. Freeman, p. 31. For Menander, see *Thais*, fragm. 197, ed. A. Koerte, *Menandri quae supersunt*, p. 2. For Aratus, see *Phaenomena*, v. 5, ed. E. Maass. [53]St. Jerome, ibid., CSEL 54:706.14–707.3 [54]St. Jerome, *Ep. 56 ad Pammachium* (to Pammachius), n. 8, CSEL 54:658.3–10. See also *Ep. 21 ad Damasum* (to Damasus), n. 13, CSEL 54:122.13–123.3 and 124.3–7; *Ep. 70 ad Magnum*, n. 2, CSEL 54:702.6–14.

dom, and you are enthralled by her beauty, make her bald; do away with her alluring hair and verbal graces, along with her hard nails.[55] Wash her with the lye of which the prophet speaks,[56] and then reclining with her say:[57] 'Her left hand is under my head, and her right hand will embrace me.' Then will the captive woman bear you many children, and from a Moabitess she will become an Israelite woman to you."[58] Therefore it is fruitful for one to use worldly wisdom.

4. Augustine states:[59] "I shall not be sluggish in seeking after the substance of God, whether through his Scripture or through his creature." Now the knowledge about creatures is set forth in philosophy. Therefore it is not unfitting for someone to use philosophical reasoning in sacred doctrine.

5. Augustine writes[60]: "If those who are called philosophers have said things by chance that are true and in agreement with our faith, we must not only have no fear of them but appropriate them for our own use from those who are their unlawful possessors." And so the same conclusion follows.

6. Commenting on Daniel 1:8: "But Daniel resolved that he would not defile himself with the king's rich food," the Gloss says:[61] "If anyone who is ignorant of mathematics should write against the mathematicians, or knowing nothing of philosophy should attack the philosophers, who, even though himself a laughingstock, would not laugh?" But seeing that a teacher of sacred Scripture must at times oppose the philosophers, it is necessary for him to make use of philosophy.

Reply:[62] The gifts of grace are added to nature in such a way that they do not destroy it, but rather perfect it. So too the light of faith, which is imparted to us as a gift, does not do away with the light of natural reason given to us by God. And even though the natural light of the human mind is inadequate to make known what is revealed by faith, nevertheless what is divinely taught to us by faith cannot be contrary to what we are endowed with by nature. One or the other would have to be false, and since we have both of them from God, he would be the cause of our error, which is impossible. Rather, since what is imperfect bears a resemblance

---

[55]See Jeremiah 2:22.   [56]See Deut. 21:13.   [57]Cant. of Canticles 2:6.
[58]See Ruth 4:5, 10.   [59]St. Augustine, *De Trinitate* 2. prooem, 1, CCL
50:80.15–16.   [60]St. Augustine, *De doctrina Christiana* 2.40.60, CCL
32:73.1–4.   [61]*Glossa ordinaria*, 4, fol. 295rA. See St. Jerome, PL
25:497A.   [62]See St. Thomas, *Summa theol.* 1.1.8 and 2–2.1.5, ad 2 and 3;
Contra gentiles 1.2 and 9; *Sent.*, 1, prol. a. 5; *Quodlibet* 4, q. 9, a. 3. *De rationibus fidei*, 2, ed. Leonine 40:B58.

to what is perfect, what we know by natural reason has some likeness to what is taught to us by faith.

Now just as sacred doctrine is based on the light of faith, so philosophy is based on the natural light of reason. So it is impossible that the contents of philosophy should be contrary to the contents of faith, but they fall short of them. The former, however, bear certain likenesses to the latter and also contain certain preambles to them, just as nature itself is a preamble to grace. If anything, however, is found in the sayings of the philosophers contrary to faith, this is not philosophy but rather an abuse of philosophy arising from faulty reasoning. Therefore it is possible to refute an error of this sort by philosophical principles, either by showing that it is entirely impossible or that it is not necessary. For, as matters of faith cannot be demonstratively proved, so some assertions contrary to them cannot be demonstratively shown to be false; it can, however, be shown that they lack necessity.

Accordingly we can use philosophy in sacred doctrine in three ways.

First, in order to demonstrate the preambles of faith, which we must necessarily know in [the act of] faith. Such are the truths about God that are proved by natural reason, for example, that God exists, that he is one, and other truths of this sort about God or creatures proved in philosophy and presupposed by faith.

Second, by throwing light on the contents of faith by analogies, as Augustine[63] uses many analogies drawn from philosophical doctrines in order to elucidate the Trinity.

Third, in order to refute assertions contrary to the faith, either by showing them to be false or lacking in necessity.

Those, however, who use philosophy in sacred doctrine can err in two ways. In one way by making use of teachings that are contrary to the faith, which consequently do not belong to philosophy but are a corruption and abuse of it. Origen was guilty of this. In another way by including the contents of faith within the bounds of philosophy, as would happen should somebody decide to believe nothing but what could be established by philosophy. On the contrary, philosophy should be brought within the bounds of faith, as the Apostle says in 2 Corinthians 10:5 "We . . . take every thought captive to obey Christ."

Replies to Opposing Arguments
Reply to 1. All these statements show that the teaching of the philoso-

---

[63]St. Augustine, *De Trinitate* 9–12 and 14–15, CCL 50:292–380 and 421–533.

phers is not to be used as though it held first place, in such a way that the truth of faith should be believed because of it. But this does not prevent teachers of sacred doctrine from being able to use it in a secondary role. Thus, commenting on the Apostle's words in the same letter (1:19): "I will destroy the wisdom of the wise," the Gloss states:[64] "He says this, not because God can condemn the understanding of truth, but because he rejects the wisdom of those who rely on their own erudition." In order that all that belongs to faith should not be attributed to human power or wisdom, but to God alone, it was the will of God that the primitive apostolic preaching should have been marked by weakness and simplicity.[65] Nevertheless the power and secular wisdom that have come afterward show, by the triumph of the faith, that both as to power and wisdom the world is subject to God.

Reply to 2. Secular wisdom is said to be opposed to God in regard to its abuse, as when heretics misuse it, but not in regard to its truth.

Reply to 3. The mystery of faith is said to be free from philosophical reasoning because, as has been said, it is not confined within the bounds of philosophy.

Reply to 4. Jerome was so attached to pagan literature that in a way he held sacred Scripture in contempt, as he himself says:[66] "If when I came to myself I began to read the prophets, I was disgusted by their unpolished style." Nobody doubts that this deserves criticism.

Reply to 5. As the Master [Peter Lombard] says,[67] reasoning should not be based on figurative language. Dionysius also states that symbolic theology does not offer proofs, especially when it is interpreted by a writer who lacks authority. It can, however, be said that a mixture is not thought to have occurred when one of two items comes into the possession of the other, but when both of them are changed in their nature.[68] So those who use the works of the philosophers in sacred doctrine, by bringing them into the service of faith, do not mix water with wine, but rather change water into wine.

Reply to 6. Jerome speaks of the language created by heretics in accord with their errors. The philosophical disciplines are different; only their misuse leads to error, and so they should not be avoided on this account.

---

[64]Peter Lombard, *Glossa*, PL 191:1543A.   [65]See St. Thomas, *De rationibus fidei* 7, ed. Leonine 40:B67.   [66]St. Jerome, *Ep. 22*, n. 30, CSEL 54:189.17. [67]Peter Lombard, *Sent.* 3, d. 11, c. 2, n. 4, ed. Grottaferrata 2:80.3–4. See St. Thomas, *Sent.*, prol. q. un. a. 5c.   [68]For St. Thomas' doctrine of mixed bodies, see *De mixtione elementorum*, ed. Perrier, pp. 19–22; *Summa theol.* 1.76.4, ad 4; *Contra gentiles* 2.56.

Reply to 7. Interrelated sciences are such that one can use the principles of another. Sciences that come later employ the principles of prior sciences, whether the later be higher or lower in dignity. Thus metaphysics, which is the highest of the sciences, makes use of the conclusions established in the lower sciences. Similarly theology, to which all the other sciences are so to speak ancillary and propaedeutic in its coming into being, though they are of lesser dignity, can use the principles of all the other sciences.[69]

Reply to 8. Insofar as sacred doctrine uses philosophical teachings in its own interest, it does not welcome them because of the authority of their authors but on account of the reasonableness of what they say. What is well said it takes; the rest it rejects. But when it uses them to refute other writers, it does so because they are accepted as authorities by those who are refuted, for the witness of opponents carries greater weight.

Article Four
Should Divine Realities Be Veiled by
Obscure and Novel Words?[70]

We proceed to the fourth article as follows:

It seems that in the science of faith divine realities should not be veiled with obscure words.

1. For, as Proverbs 14:6 says, "Knowledge is easy for a man of understanding." Therefore it ought not to be presented in cryptic language.

2. Ecclesiasticus 4:28 says, "Hide not your wisdom in her beauty," and Proverbs 11:26: "The people curse him who holds back grain." The Gloss understands by *grain* "preaching."[71] Therefore the words of sacred doctrine ought not to be hidden.

3. It is said in Matthew 10:27: "What I tell you in the dark, utter in the light." The Gloss interprets *in the dark* to mean "in mystery," and *utter in*

---

[69]See St. Thomas, *Sent.*, prol. q. un. a. lc, ed. Mandonnet 1:8; *Summa theol.* 1.1.5, sed contra and ad 2. The notion of philosophy as the handmaid of theology is found in Philo. See H. A. Wolfson, *Philo* 1:149–151.   [70]See St. Thomas, *Sent.* 1, d. 34, q. 3, a. 1, 2; *Summa theol.* 1.1.9, ad 2. The background of this question is the rule of secrecy practiced by the early Church, later called the "discipline of the secret" *(disciplina arcani)*. See *The Oxford Dictionary of the Christian Church*, ed. F. L. Cross; 2nd ed. rev. F. L. Cross and E. A. Livingstone, p. 409. St. Thomas takes the occasion of Boethius' appeal to the discipline to insist that a teacher should adapt his words to the capacity of his hearers.   [71]*Glossa ordinaria* 3, col. 1651–1652; *Glossa interlinearis*, lin. 10(a).

the light to mean "openly."[72] So the mysteries of faith ought rather to be disclosed than hidden by difficult language.

4. Teachers of the faith have obligations to the learned and to the unlearned, as is clear from Romans 1:14. Therefore they ought to talk in such a way that they can be understood by both the great and the simple, that is, without obscure language.

5. Wisdom 7:13 says: "I learned without guile and impart without grudging." But the one who hides wisdom does not impart it. Therefore he seems to be guilty of jealousy.

6. Augustine states:[73] "The interpreters of sacred Scripture should not speak as though they were proposing themselves for interpretation, but in all their words their first and greatest endeavor should be to make themselves understood as much as possible by such clearness of style that the person who does not understand is very stupid."

On the contrary, Matthew 7:6 says: "Do not give dogs what is holy; and do not throw your pearls before swine." The Gloss comments on this: "What is hidden is more eagerly sought after; what is concealed appears more worthy of reverence; what is searched for longer is more dearly prized."[74] Therefore, since the sacred teachings should be regarded with the utmost reverence, it seems that they ought not to be made accessible to the public, but taught in obscure language.

2. Dionysius says: "You should not commit to everyone all the holy doctrines of the sublime episcopal order, but only to the godlike teachers of sacred things of the same rank as yourself." In other words, teach the divine praises, which include all the sacred writings, only to your peers. But if they were written in clear language, they would be obvious to all. So the mysteries of faith should be concealed in obscure language.

3. Luke 8:10 is to the point. He says: "To you," that is, to the perfect, "it has been given to know the secrets of the kingdom of God," that is, an understanding of the Scriptures, as is clear from the Gloss, "but for others they are in parables."[75] So there are some things that should be hidden by obscure language.

Reply: A teacher should so measure his words that they help rather than hinder his hearer. Now there are some things which can harm nobody when they are heard, for example, the truths everyone is bound to

---

[72]*Glossa ordinaria* 5, fol. 37v, *Glossa interlinearis*, lin. o. [73]St. Augustine, *De doctrina Christiana* 4.8.22, CCL 32:131.11–132.15. [74]*Glossa ordinaria* 5, fol. 28rB. [75]Ibid., fol. 146v; *Glossa interlinearis*, lin. a.

know. These should not be concealed but taught openly to everyone. There are other matters, however, that would be harmful to those hearing them if they were openly presented. This can happen in two ways. First, if the secrets of faith were revealed to unbelievers who detest the faith, for they would receive them with ridicule. Hence the Lord says in Matthew 7:6: "Do not give dogs what is holy," and Dionysius states:[76] "Concealing the holy truths, guard them from the profane crowd as something unchanging." Second, when abstruse doctrines are taught to the uneducated they take an occasion of error from what they do not fully understand. Thus the Apostle says in 1 Corinthians 3:1–2: "But I, brethren, could not address you as spiritual men, but as babes in Christ. I fed you with milk, not solid food." Commenting on Exodus 21:33: "When someone leaves a pit open," etc., Gregory says:[77] "Anyone who now perceives the depths in the sacred words, should hide in silence their sublime meaning when in the presence of those who do not understand them, so that he will not hurt by interior scandal an immature believer or an unbeliever who might become a believer." These matters, therefore, ought to be concealed from those to whom they might do harm.

In speaking, however, it is possible to discriminate. Certain things can be explained to the wise in private which we should keep silent about in public. Thus Augustine says:[78] "There are some passages which are not understood in their proper force or are understood with difficulty, no matter how great, how comprehensive, or how clear the eloquence with which they are handled by the speaker. These should be spoken to a public audience only rarely, if there is some urgent reason, or never at all." In writing, however, this distinction does not hold because a written book can fall into the hands of anybody. Therefore these matters should be concealed with obscure language, so that they will benefit the wise who understand them and be hidden from the uneducated who are unable to grasp them. This puts a burden on no one, for those who understand will go on reading them and those who do not are not obliged to read them at all. So Augustine continues:[79] "In books that are written in such a style that, when understood, they themselves so to speak grip the reader's attention, but, when not understood, give no trouble to those who do not care to read them, we must not neglect the duty of bringing truths, though very hard to understand, to the knowledge of others."

---

[76]Pseudo-Dionysius, *De caelesti hierarchia* 2, 5, PG 3:145C.   [77]St. Gregory, *Moralia* 17.26.38, CCL 143A:872. See *Glossa ordinaria* 1, col. 697B.   [78]St. Augustine, *De doctrina Christiana* 9.23, CCL 32:132.1–5.   [79]Ibid.

Replies to Opposing Arguments

Reply to 1. This text is not to the point. It does not mean that the teaching of the wise is easy in the active sense, that is, that they teach easily, but rather in the passive sense, that they are easily taught. This is clear from the Gloss.[80]

Reply to 2. These texts refer to one who conceals what he ought to reveal. Thus Ecclesiasticus 4:28 says immediately before: "Do not refrain from speaking in the time of salvation." The fact is not denied that what should be hidden ought to be concealed in obscure language.

Reply to 3. The teaching of Christ should be publicly and openly preached, so that it is clear to everyone what is good for him to know, but not that what is not good for him to know be made public.

Reply to 4. The obligation of the teachers of sacred Scripture to the wise and the unwise does not extend to their proposing the same things to both, but to telling each what is appropriate to them.

Reply to 5. It is not from jealousy that difficult truths are hidden from the masses, but rather, as has been said,[81] from due discretion.

Reply to 6. Augustine is referring to interpreters who speak to the people, not to those who teach something in writing. This is clear from his next words.[82]

---

[80]*Glossa ordinaria* 3, col. 1662D.   [81]See above, Reply, pp. 40–41.   [82]The words that follow are: " . . . or the reason why what we say is not understood, or is understood rather slowly, lies not in our manner of speaking, but in the difficulty and subtlety of the matters which we are trying to explain and make clear."

DIMENSIONS OF FAITH

Summa Theologica
Second Part of Part Two
Question 1
On Faith
(In Ten Articles)

Having to treat now of the theological virtues, we shall begin with Faith, secondly we shall speak of Hope,[1] and thirdly, of Charity.[2]

The treatise on Faith will be fourfold: (1) of faith itself; (2) of the corresponding gifts, science and understanding;[3] (3) of the opposite vices;[4] (4) of the precepts pertaining to this virtue.[5]

About faith itself we shall consider: (1) its object; (2) its act;[6] (3) the habit of faith.[7]

Under the first head there are ten points of inquiry: (1) Whether the object of faith is the First Truth? (2) Whether the object of faith is something complex or incomplex, *i.e.*, whether it is a thing or a proposition? (3) Whether anything false can come under faith? (4) Whether the object of faith can be anything seen? (5) Whether it can be anything known? (6) Whether the things to be believed should be divided into a certain number of articles? (7) Whether the same articles are of faith for all times? (8) Of the number of articles. (9) Of the manner of embodying the articles in a symbol. (10) Who has the right to propose a symbol of faith?

First Article
Whether the Object of Faith Is the First Truth?

We proceed thus to the First Article:—

Objection 1. It would seem that the object of faith is not the First Truth. For it seems that the object of faith is that which is proposed to us to be believed. Now not only things pertaining to the Godhead, *i.e.*, the First

---

Source: Basic Writings of Saint Thomas Aquinas, edited and annotated by Anton C. Pegis (Indianapolis: Hackett Pub. Co., 1997). Reprinted by permission of the publisher.

[1] Q. 17. [Not in this volume]   [2] Q. 23. [Not in this volume]   [3] Q. 8. [Not in this volume]   [4] Q. 10. [Not in this volume]   [5] Q. 16. [Not in this volume]   [6] Q. 2.   [7] Q. 4.

Truth, are proposed to us to be believed, but also things concerning Christ's human nature, the sacraments of the Church, and the condition of creatures. Therefore the object of faith is not only the First Truth.

Obj. 2. Further, Faith and unbelief have the same object since they are opposed to one another. Now unbelief can be about all things contained in Holy Scripture, for whichever one of them a man denies, he is considered an unbeliever. Therefore faith also is about all things contained in Holy Scripture. But there are many things therein concerning man and other creatures. Therefore the object of faith is not only the First Truth, but also created truth.

Obj. 3. Further, Faith is co-divided against charity, as stated above.[8] Now by charity we love not only God, Who is the highest Good, but also our neighbor. Therefore the object of faith is not only the First Truth.

On the contrary, Dionysius says that *faith is about the simple and everlasting truth.*[9] Now this is the First Truth. Therefore the object of faith is the First Truth.

I answer that, The object of every cognitive habit includes two things: first, that which is known materially, and is the material object, so to speak, and, secondly, that whereby it is known, which is the formal aspect of the object, Thus, in the science of geometry, the conclusions are what is known materially, while the formal aspect of the science consists in the means of demonstration, through which the conclusions are known.

Accordingly, if in faith we consider the formal aspect of the object, it is nothing else than the First Truth. For the faith of which we are speaking does not assent to anything, except because it is revealed by God. Hence faith bases itself on the divine Truth as on its means. If, however, we consider materially the things to which faith assents, they include not only God, but also many other things, which, nevertheless, do not come under the assent of faith except as bearing some relation to God, inasmuch as, namely, through certain effects of the divine operation man is helped on his journey towards the enjoyment of God. Consequently, from this point of view also the object of faith is, in a way, the First Truth, inasmuch as nothing comes under faith except in relation to God; even as the object of the medical art is health, for it considers nothing save in relation to health.

Reply Obj. 1. Things concerning Christ's human nature, the sacraments of the Church, or any creatures whatever, come under faith in so far as by them we are directed to God, and inasmuch as we assent to them because of the divine Truth.

---

[8]*S. T.,* I–II, q. 62, a. 3. [Not in this volume]   [9]*De Div. Nom.,* VII, 4 (PG 3, 872).

The same answer applies to the Second Objection, as regards all things contained in Holy Scripture.

Reply Obj. 3. Charity also loves our neighbor because of God, so that its object, properly speaking, is God, as we shall show further on.[10]

Second Article
Whether the Object of Faith Is Something Complex, Such as a Proposition?

We proceed thus to the Second Article:—

Objection 1. It would seem that the object of faith is not something complex such as a proposition. For the object of faith is the First Truth, as was stated above. Now the First Truth is something simple. Therefore the object of faith is not something complex.

Obj. 2. Further, The exposition of faith is contained in the symbol. Now the symbol does not contain propositions, but things; for it is not stated therein that God is almighty, but: *I believe in God . . . almighty.* Therefore the object of faith is not a proposition but a thing.

Obj. 3. Further, Faith is succeeded by vision, according to *1 Cor.* xiii. 12: *We see now through a glass in a dark manner; but then face to face. Now I know in part, but then I shall know even as I am known.* But the object of the heavenly vision is something simple, for it is the divine essence. Therefore the faith of the wayfarer is also.

On the contrary, Faith is a mean between science and opinion. Now the mean is in the same genus as the extremes. Since, then, science and opinion are about propositions, it seems that faith is likewise about propositions; so that its object is something complex.

I answer that, The thing known is in the knower according to the mode of the knower. Now the mode proper to the human intellect is to know the truth by composition and division, as we stated in the First Part.[11] Hence things that are simple in themselves are known by the intellect with a certain complexity, just as on the other hand the divine intellect knows, without any complexity, things that are complex in themselves.

Accordingly, the object of faith may be considered in two ways. First, as regards the thing itself which is believed, and thus the object of faith is something simple, namely, the thing itself about which we have faith; secondly, on the part of the believer, and in this respect the object of faith is something complex, such as a proposition.

---

[10]Q. 25, a. 1. [Not in this volume]   [11]*S. T.*, I, q. 85, a. 5. [Not in this volume]

Hence in the past both opinions have been held with a certain amount of truth.[12]

Reply Obj. 1. This argument considers the object of faith on the part of the thing believed.

Reply Obj. 2. The symbol mentions the things about which faith is, in so far as the act of the believer is terminated in them, as is evident from the manner of speaking about them. Now the act of the believer does not terminate in a proposition, but in a thing. For we do not form propositions, except in order to have knowledge about things through their means; and this is true of faith as well as of science.

Reply Obj. 3. The object of the heavenly vision will be the First Truth seen in itself, according to *1 John* iii. 2: *We know that when He shall appear, we shall be like to Him: because we shall see Him as He is.* Hence that vision will not be by way of a proposition, but by way of simple understanding. On the other hand, by faith, we do not apprehend the First Truth as it is in itself. Hence the comparison fails.

Third Article
Whether Anything False Can Come under Faith?

We proceed thus to the Third Article:—

Objection 1. It would seem that something false can come under faith. For faith is co-divided against hope and charity. Now something false can come under hope, since many hope to have eternal life, who will not obtain it. The same may be said of charity, for many are loved as being good, who, nevertheless, are not good. Therefore something false can be the object of faith.

Obj. 2. Further, Abraham believed that Christ would be born, according to *John* viii. 56: *Abraham your father rejoiced that he might see My day; he saw it, and was glad.* But after the time of Abraham, God might not have taken flesh, for it was merely because He willed that He did; so that what Abraham believed about Christ would have been false. Therefore the object of faith can be something false.

Obj. 3. Further, The ancients believed in the future birth of Christ, and many continued so to believe, until they heard the preaching of the Gospel. Now, when once Christ was born, even before He began to preach, it was false that Christ was yet to be born. Therefore something false can come under faith.

---

[12]Cf. Philip the Chancellor and William of Auxerre in M.-D. Chenu, "Contribution à l'histoire du traité de la foi. Commentaire historique de la IIa IIae, q. 1, a. 2" in *Mélanges thomistes* (*Bibliothèque Thomiste*, III; Le Saulchoir, Kain, 1923) p. 132.

Obj. 4. Further, It is a matter of faith that one should believe that the true Body of Christ is contained in the Sacrament of the altar. But it might happen that the bread was not rightly consecrated, and that there was not Christ's true Body there, but only bread. Therefore something false can come under faith.

On the contrary, No virtue that perfects the intellect is related to what is false, considered as the evil of the intellect, as the Philosopher declares.[13] Now faith is a virtue that perfects the intellect, as we shall show further on.[14] Therefore nothing false can come under it.

I answer that, Nothing comes under any power, habit or act, except by means of the formal aspect of the object. Thus color cannot be seen except by means of light, and a conclusion cannot be known save through the means of demonstration. Now it has been stated that the formal aspect of the object of faith is the First Truth. Hence nothing can come under faith, save in so far as it stands under the First Truth, under which nothing false can stand; just as neither can non-being stand under being, nor evil under goodness. It follows therefore that nothing false can come under faith.

Reply Obj. 1. Since the true is the good of the intellect, but not of the appetitive power, it follows that all the virtues which perfect the intellect exclude the false altogether, because it belongs to the nature of a virtue to be related to the good alone. On the other hand, those virtues which perfect the appetitive part do not entirely exclude the false, for it is possible to act in accordance with justice or temperance, while having a false opinion about what one is doing. Therefore, since faith perfects the intellect, whereas hope and charity perfect the appetitive part, the comparison between them fails.

Nevertheless, neither can anything false come under hope, for a man hopes to obtain eternal life, not by his own power (since this would be an act of presumption), but with the help of grace; and if he perseveres therein, he will obtain eternal life surely and infallibly.

In like manner, it belongs to charity to love God, wherever He may be; so that it matters not to charity whether God be in the individual whom we love for God's sake.

Reply Obj. 2. That *God would not take flesh,* considered in itself, was possible even after Abraham's time; but in so far as it stands in God's foreknowledge, it has a certain necessity of infallibility, as was explained in the First Part,[15] and in this way it comes under faith. Hence, in so far as it comes under faith, it cannot be false.

---

[13]*Eth.,* VI, 2 (1139b 13; a. 27).   [14]Q. 4, a. 2 and 5.   [15]*S. T.,* I, q. 14, a. 13. [Not in this volume]

Reply Obj. 3. After Christ's birth, to believe in Him was to believe in Christ's birth at some time or other. The fixing of the time, however, wherein some were deceived, was not due to their faith, but to a human conjecture. For it is possible for a believer to have a false opinion through a human conjecture, but it is quite impossible for a false opinion to be the outcome of faith.

Reply Obj. 4. The faith of the believer is not directed to such and such species of bread, but to the fact that the true Body of Christ is under the species of sensible bread when it is rightly consecrated. Hence, if it be not rightly consecrated, it does not follow that anything false comes under faith.

Fourth Article
Whether the Object of Faith Can Be Something Seen?

We proceed thus to the Fourth Article:—

Objection 1. It would seem that the object of faith is something seen. For our Lord said to Thomas (*Jo.* xx. 29): *Because thou hast seen Me, Thomas, thou hast believed.* Therefore vision and faith regard the same object.

Obj. 2. Further, The Apostle, while speaking of the knowledge of faith, says (*1 Cor.* xiii. 12): *We see now through a glass in a dark manner.* Therefore what is believed is seen.

Obj. 3. Further, Faith is a spiritual light. Now something is seen under every light. Therefore faith is about things seen.

Obj. 4. Further, *Every sense is a kind of sight*, as Augustine states.[16] But faith is of things heard, according to *Rom.* x. 17: *Faith . . . cometh by hearing.* Therefore faith is about things seen.

On the contrary, The Apostle says (*Heb.* xi. 1) that *faith is the evidence of things that appear not.*

I answer that, Faith signifies the assent of the intellect to that which is believed. Now the intellect assents to a thing in two ways. First, through being moved to assent by its very object, which is known either by itself (as in the case of first principles, which are held by the habit of understanding), or through something else already known (as in the case of conclusions which are held by the habit of science). Secondly, the intellect assents to something, not through being sufficiently moved to this assent by its proper object, but through an act of choice, whereby it turns voluntarily to one side rather than to the other. Now if this be accompanied by doubt and fear of the opposite side, there will be opinion; while, if there be certainty and no fear of the other side, there will be faith.

---

[16] *Serm.* CXII, 6 (PL 38, 646).

Now those things are said to be seen which, of themselves, move the intellect or the senses to knowledge of them. Therefore it is evident that neither faith nor opinion can be of things seen either by the senses or by the intellect.

Reply Obj. 1. Thomas *saw one thing, and believed another.* He saw the Man and, believing Him to be God, he made profession of his faith, saying: *My Lord and my God.*[17]

Reply Obj. 2. Those things which come under faith can be considered in two ways. First, in particular, and in this way they cannot be seen and believed at the same time, as was shown above. Secondly, in general, that is, under the common aspect of credibility; and in this way they are seen by the believer. For he would not believe unless, on the evidence of signs, or of something similar, he saw that they ought to be believed.

Reply Obj. 3. The light of faith makes us see what we believe. For just as, by the habits of the other virtues, man sees what is becoming to him in respect of that habit, so, by the habit of faith, the human mind is inclined to assent to such things as are becoming to a right faith, and not to assent to others.

Reply Obj. 4. Hearing is of words signifying what is of faith, but not of the things themselves that are believed. Hence it does not follow that these things are seen.

Fifth Article
Whether Those Things That Are of Faith
Can Be an Object of Science?

We proceed thus to the Fifth Article:—

Objection 1. It would seem that those things that are of faith can be an object of science. For where science is lacking there is ignorance, since ignorance is the opposite of science. Now we are not in ignorance of those things we have to believe, since ignorance of such things belongs to unbelief, according to *1 Tim.* i. 13: *I did it ignorantly in unbelief.* Therefore things that are of faith can be an object of science.

Obj. 2. Further, Science is acquired by arguments. Now sacred writers employ arguments to inculate things that are of faith. Therefore such things can be an object of science.

Obj. 3. Further, Things which are demonstrated are an object of science, since a *demonstration is a syllogism that produces science.* Now certain matters of faith have been demonstrated by the philosophers, such as the

---

[17]St. Gregory, *In Evang.*, II, hom. 26 (PL 76, 1202).

existence and unity of God, and so forth. Therefore things that are of faith can be an object of science.

Obj. 4. Further, Opinion is further from science than faith is, since faith is said to stand between opinion and science. Now opinion and science can, in a way, be about the same object, as is stated in *Posterior Analytics i.*[18] Therefore faith and science can be about the same object also.

On the contrary, Gregory says that *when a thing is manifest, it is the object, not of faith, but of perception.*[19] Therefore things that are of faith are not the object of perception, whereas what is an object of science is the object of perception. Therefore there can be no faith about things which are an object of science.

I answer that, All science is derived from self-evident and therefore *seen* principles; and so all objects of science must needs be, in a fashion, seen.

Now, as was stated above, it is impossible that one and the same thing should be believed and seen by the same person. Hence it is equally impossible for one and the same thing to be an object of science and of belief for the same person. It may happen, however, that a thing which is an object of vision or science for one, is believed by another; for we hope to see some day what we now believe about the Trinity, according to *1 Cor.* xiii. 12: *We see now through a glass in a dark manner; but then face to face.* And this vision the angels possess already, so that what we believe, they see. In like manner, it may also happen that what is an object of vision or scientific knowledge for one man, even in the state of a wayfarer, is, for another man, an object of faith, because he does not know it by demonstration.

Nevertheless, that which is proposed to be believed equally by all is equally unknown by all as an object of science. Such are the things which are of faith absolutely. Consequently, faith and science are not about the same things.

Reply Obj. 1. Unbelievers are in ignorance of things that are of faith, for neither do they see or know them in themselves, nor do they know them to be credible. The faithful, on the other hand, know them, not as by demonstration, but by the light of faith which makes them see that they ought to believe them, as was stated above.

Reply Obj. 2. The arguments employed by holy men to prove things that are of faith are not demonstrations; they are either persuasive argu-

---

[18]Aristotle, *Post. Anal.*, I, 33 (89a 25).   [19]*In Evang.*, II, hom. 26 (PL 76, 1202).

ments showing that what is proposed to our faith is not impossible, or else they are proofs drawn from the principles of faith, *i.e.*, from the authority of Holy Scripture, as Dionysius declares.[20] Whatever is based on these principles is as well proved in the eyes of the faithful as a conclusion drawn from self-evident principles is in the eyes of all. Hence, again, theology is a science, as we stated at the outset of this work.[21]

Reply Obj. 3. Things which can be proved by demonstration are reckoned among what is of faith, not because they are believed absolutely by all, but because they are a necessary presupposition to matters of faith; so that those who do not know them by demonstration must possess them at least by faith.

Reply Obj. 4. As the Philosopher says, *science and opinion about the same object can certainly be in different men,*[22] as we have stated above about science and faith; yet it is possible for one and the same man to have science and faith about the same thing relatively, *i.e.*, in relation to the object, but not in the same respect. For it is possible for the same person, about one and the same object, to know one thing and to have an opinion about another; and, in like manner, one may know by demonstration the unity of God, and believe that there are three Persons in God. On the other hand, in one and the same man, about the same object, and in the same respect, science is incompatible with either opinion or faith, but for different reasons. For science is incompatible with opinion about the same object absolutely, for the reason that science demands that its object should be deemed impossible to be otherwise, whereas it is essential to opinion that its object should be deemed possible to be otherwise. But that which is the object of faith, because of the certainty of faith, is also deemed impossible to be otherwise; and the reason why science and faith cannot be about the same object, and in the same respect, is because the object of science is something seen, whereas the object of faith is the unseen, as was stated above.

Sixth Article
Whether Those Things That Are of Faith
Should Be Divided into Certain Articles?

We proceed to the Sixth Article:—

Objection 1. It would seem that those things that are of faith should not be divided into certain articles. For all things contained in Holy Scripture

---

[20]*De Div. Nom.*, II, 2 (PG 3, 640).   [21]*S. T.*, I, q. 1, a. 2.   [22]*Post. Anal.*, I, 33 (89b 2).

are matters of faith. But these, by reason of their multitude, cannot be reduced to a certain number. Therefore it seems superfluous to distinguish certain articles of faith.

Obj. 2. Further, Material differences can be multiplied indefinitely, and therefore art should take no notice of them. Now the formal aspect of the object of faith is one and indivisible, as was stated above, viz. the First Truth; so that matters of faith cannot be distinguished in respect of their formal object. Therefore no notice should be taken of a material division of matters of faith into articles.

Obj. 3. Further, It has been said by some that *an article is an indivisible truth concerning God, exacting our belief.*[23] Now belief is a voluntary act, since, as Augustine says, *no man believes against his will.*[24] Therefore it seems that matters of faith should not be divided into articles.

On the contrary, Isidore says: *An article is a glimpse of divine truth, tending thereto.*[25] Now we can get a glimpse of divine truth only by way of some distinction, since things which in God are one, are manifold in our intellect. Therefore matters of faith should be divided into articles.

I answer that, The term *article* is apparently derived from the Greek, for the Greek ἄρθρον, which the Latin renders *articulus*, signifies a fitting together of distinct parts; and so the small parts of the body which fit together are called the articulations of the member. Likewise, in the Greek grammar, articles are parts of speech which are affixed to words to show their gender, number or case. Again, in rhetoric, articles are parts that fit together in a sentence, for Tully says that an article is composed of words each pronounced singly and separately, *e.g., Your passion, your voice, your look, have struck terror into your foes.*[26]

Hence matters of Christian faith are said to contain distinct articles in so far as they are divided into parts which fit together. Now the object of faith is something unseen concerning God, as was stated above. Consequently, any matter that, for a special reason, is unseen, is a special article; whereas when there are several matters unknown under the same aspect,

---

[23]Cf. J.-M. Parent, "La notion du dogme au XIIIe siècle" (*Études d'histoire littéraire et doctrinale du XIIIe siècle*, 1932) p. 149.   [24]*Tract.* XXVI, super *Ioann.*, VI, 44) PL 35, 1607).   [25]St. Albert, *In III Sent.*, d. xxiv, a. 4 (XXVIII, 449), and St. Bonaventure, *In III Sent.*, d. xxiv, a. 3, q. 2 (III, 527), mentioning St. Isidore. But Philip the Chancellor refers to the same definition without mentioning the author of it.—Cf. J.-M. Parent, "La notion du dogme . . . ," p. 149.   [26]Pseudo-Cicero, *Rhetor. ad Herenn.*, IV, 19 (p. 135).

we are not to distinguish various articles. Thus one encounters one difficulty in seeing that God suffered, and another in seeing that He rose again from the dead, and so the article of the Resurrection is distinguished from the article of the Passion. But that He suffered, died and was buried, present the same difficulty, so that if one be accepted, it is not difficult to accept the others; and hence all these belong to one article.

Reply Obj. 1. Some things proposed to our belief are in themselves of faith, while others are of faith, not in themselves, but only in relation to others; even as in the sciences certain propositions are put forward on their own account, while others are put forward in order to manifest others. Now, since the chief object of faith consists in those things which we hope to see in heaven, according to *Heb.* xi. 1: *Faith is the substance of things to be hoped for*, it follows that those things are in themselves of faith, which order us directly to eternal life. Such are the Trinity of Persons in Almighty God, the mystery of Christ's Incarnation, and the like; and these are distinct articles of faith. On the other hand, certain things in Holy Scripture are proposed to our belief, not chiefly on their own account, but for the manifestation of those mentioned above: *e.g.*, that Abraham had two sons, that a dead man rose again at the touch of Eliseus' bones, and the like, which are related in Holy Scripture for the purpose of manifesting the divine majesty or the Incarnation of Christ; and such things should not form distinct articles.

Reply Obj. 2. The formal aspect of the object of faith can be taken in two ways: first, on the part of the thing believed, and thus there is one formal aspect of all matters of faith, viz., the First Truth; and from this point of view there is no distinction of articles. Secondly, the formal aspect of matters of faith can be considered from our point of view, and thus the formal aspect of a matter of faith is that it is something unseen; and from this point of view there are various distinct articles of faith, as we saw above.

Reply Obj. 3. This definition of an article is taken from an etymology of the word as derived from the Latin, rather than in accordance with its real meaning, as derived from the Greek. Hence it does not carry much weight. Yet even then it could be said that, although faith is exacted of no man by a necessity of coercion, since belief is a voluntary act, yet it is exacted of him by a necessity of the end, since *he that cometh to God must believe that He is, and without faith it is impossible to please God*, as the Apostle declares (*Heb.* xi. 6).

Seventh Article
Whether the Articles of Faith Have
Increased in the Course of Time?

We proceed thus to the Seventh Article:—

Objection 1. It would seem that the articles of faith have not increased in the course of time. For, as the Apostle says (*Heb.* xi. 1), *faith is the substance of things to be hoped for.* Now the same things are to be hoped for at all times. Therefore, at all times, the same things are to be believed.

Obj. 2. Further, Development has taken place in the sciences devised by man, because of defects in the knowledge of those who discovered them, as the Philosopher observes.[27] Now the doctrine of faith was not devised by man, but was delivered to us by God, as is stated in *Ephes.* ii. 8: *It is the gift of God.* Since, then, there can be no lack of knowledge in God, it seems that knowledge of matters of faith was perfect from the beginning, and did not increase as time went on.

Obj. 3. Further, The operation of grace proceeds in an orderly fashion no less than the operation of nature. Now nature always makes a beginning with perfect things, as Boethius states.[28] Therefore it seems that the operation of grace also began with perfect things, so that those who were the first to deliver the faith knew it most perfectly.

Obj. 4. Further, Just as the faith of Christ has reached us through the Apostles, so too, in the Old Testament, the knowledge of faith was delivered by the early patriarchs to those who came later, according to *Deut.* xxxii. 7: *Ask thy father, and he will declare to thee.* Now the Apostles were most fully instructed about the mysteries, for *they received them more fully than others, even as they received them earlier,* as the *Gloss* says on *Rom.* viii. 23: *Ourselves also who have the first-fruits of the Spirit.*[29] Therefore it seems that knowledge of matters of faith has not increased as time went on.

On the contrary, Gregory says that *the knowledge of the holy fathers increased as time went on . . . ; and the nearer they were to Our Savior's coming, the more fully did they receive the mysteries of salvation.*[30]

I answer that, The articles of faith stand in the same relation to the doctrine of faith, as self-evident principles to teaching based on natural reason. Among these principles there is a certain order, so that some are contained implicitly in others; and thus all principles are reduced, as to their first principle, to this one: *The same thing cannot be affirmed and*

---

[27]*Metaph.*, I *a*, I (993a 30; b ii).   [28]*De Consol.*, III, prose 10 (PL 63, 764).
[29]*Glossa interl.* (VI, 19r); Peter Lombard, *In Rom.*, super VIII, 23 (PL 191, 1444).
[30]*In Ezech.*, II, hom. 16 (PL 76, 980).

denied at the same time, as the Philosopher states.[31] In like manner, all the articles are contained implicitly in certain primary truths of faith, such as God's existence, and His providence over the salvation of man, according to *Heb.* xi.: *He that cometh to God, must believe that He is, and is a rewarder to them that seek Him.* For the being of God includes all that we believe to exist in God eternally, and in these our happiness consists, while belief in His providence includes all those things which God dispenses in time for man's salvation, and which are the way to that happiness; and in this way, again, some of those articles which follow from these are contained in others. Thus faith in the Redemption of mankind includes implicitly the Incarnation of Christ, His Passion and so forth.

Accordingly, we must conclude that, as regards the substance of the articles of faith, they have not received any increase as time went on; since whatever those who lived later have believed, was contained, albeit implicitly, in the faith of those Fathers who preceded them. But there was an increase in the number of articles believed explicitly, since to those who lived in later times some were known explicitly which were not known explicitly by those who lived before them. Hence the Lord said to Moses (*Exod.* vi. 2, 3): *I am the God of Abraham, the God of Isaac, the God of Jacob . . . and My name Adonai I did not show them.* David also said (*Ps.* cxviii. 100): *I have had understanding above ancients;* and the Apostle says (*Ephes.* iii. 5) that the mystery of Christ, *in other generations was not known, as it is now revealed to His holy apostles and prophets.*

Reply Obj. 1. Among all men the same things were always to be hoped for. But as they did not acquire this hope save through Christ, the further they were removed from Christ in point of time, the further they were from obtaining what they hoped for. Hence the Apostle says (*Heb.* xi. 13): *All these died according to faith, not having received the promises, but beholding them afar off.* Now the further off a thing is, the less distinctly is it seen; and so those who were near Christ's advent had a more distinct knowledge of the good things to be hoped for.

Reply Obj. 2. Progress in knowledge occurs in two ways. First, on the part of the teacher, be he one or many, who makes progress in knowledge as time goes on; and this is the kind of progress that takes place in the sciences devised by man. Secondly, on the part of the learner. Thus the master, who has perfect knowledge of an art, does not deliver it all at once to his disciple from the very outset, for he would not be able to take it all in, but he suits his teaching to the disciple's capacity and instructs him little

---

[31]*Metaph.*, III, 6 (1011b 20).

by little. It is in this way that men made progress in the knowledge of faith as time went on. Hence the Apostle (*Gal.* iii. 24) compares the state of the Old Testament to childhood.

Reply Obj. 3. Two causes are requisite before actual generation can take place, namely, an agent and matter. In the order of the active cause, the more perfect is naturally first; and in this way nature makes a beginning with perfect things, since the imperfect is not brought to perfection, except by something perfect already in existence. On the other hand, in the order of the material cause, the imperfect comes first, and in this way nature proceeds from the imperfect to the perfect. Now in the manifestation of faith, God is as the active cause, having perfect knowledge from all eternity; while man is likened to matter in receiving the influx of God's action. Hence, among men, the knowledge of faith had to proceed from imperfection to perfection; and, although some men have functioned as active causes, through being teachers of the faith, nevertheless, *the manifestation of the Spirit is given* to such men for the common good, according to *1 Cor.* xii. 7. Hence the knowledge of faith was imparted to the Fathers, who were instructors in the faith, so far as was necessary at the time for the instruction of the people, either openly or in figures.

Reply Obj. 4. The ultimate consummation of grace was effected by Christ, and so the time of His coming is called the *time of fullness* (*Gal.* iv. 4). Hence those who were nearest to Christ, whether before, like John the Baptist, or after, like the Apostles, had a fuller knowledge of the mysteries of faith; for even with regard to man's state we find that the perfection of manhood comes in youth, and that a man's state is all the more perfect, whether before or after, the nearer it is to the time of his youth.

Eighth Article
Whether the Articles of Faith Are Suitably Formulated?

We proceed thus to the Eighth Article:—

Objection 1. It would seem that the articles of faith are unsuitably formulated. For those things which can be known by demonstration do not belong to faith in such a way as to be objects of belief among men, as was stated above. Now it can be known by demonstration that there is one God; and hence the Philosopher proves this,[32] and many other philosophers demonstrated the same truth. Therefore that *there is one God* should not be set down as an article of faith.

Obj. 2. Further, Just as it is necessary to faith that we should believe

---

[32] *Metaph.*, XI, 10 (1076a 4).

God to be almighty, so is it too that we should believe Him to be *all-knowing* and *provident for all*, about both of which points some have erred.[33] Therefore, among the articles of faith, mention should have been made of God's wisdom and providence, even as of His omnipotence.

Obj. 3. Further, To know the Father is the same thing as to know the Son, according to *John* xiv. 9: *He that seeth Me, seeth the Father also.* Therefore there ought to be but one article about the Father and Son, and, for the same reason, about the Holy Ghost.

Obj. 4. Further, The Person of the Father is not lesser than the Person of the Son, and of the Holy Ghost. Now there are several articles about the Person of the Holy Ghost, and likewise about the Person of the Son. Therefore there should be several articles about the Person of the Father.

Obj. 5. Further, Just as certain things are said, by appropriation, of the Person of the Father and of the Person of the Holy Ghost, so too is something appropriated to the Person of the Son, in respect of His Godhead. Now, among the articles of faith, a place is given to a work appropriated to the Father, viz., the creation, and likewise, a work appropriated to the Holy Ghost, viz., that *He spoke by the prophets.* Therefore the articles of faith should contain some work appropriated to the Son in respect of His Godhead.

Obj. 6. Further, The sacrament of the Eucharist presents a special difficulty over and above the other articles. Therefore, it should have been mentioned in a special article; and consequently it seems that there is not a sufficient number of articles.

On the contrary stands the authority of the Church which formulates the articles thus.[34]

I answer that, As was stated above, to faith those things belong essentially, the sight of which we shall enjoy in eternal life, and by which we are brought to eternal life. Now two things are proposed to us to be seen in eternal life, viz., the secret of the Godhead, to see which is to possess happiness, and the mystery of Christ's Incarnation, *by Whom we have access* to the glory of the sons of God, according to *Rom.* v. 2. Hence it is written (*Jo.* xvii. 3): *This is eternal life, that they may know Thee, the . . . true God, and Jesus Christ Whom Thou hast sent.* Therefore the first distinction in matters of faith is that some concern the majesty of the Godhead, while others pertain to the mystery of Christ's human nature, which is the *mystery of godliness* (*1 Tim.* iii. 16).

---

[33]Cf. *S. T.*, I, q. 14, a. 6 [Not in this volume]; q. 22, a. 2.   [34]*Symb. Nicaeno-Constantinopolitanum* (Denzinger, no. 86).

Now with regard to the majesty of the Godhead, three things are proposed to our belief: first, the unity of the Godhead, to which the first article refers; secondly, the trinity of the Persons, to which three articles refer, corresponding to the three Persons; and thirdly, the works proper to the Godhead. The first of these refers to the order of nature, in relation to which the article about the creation is proposed to us; the second refers to the order of grace, in relation to which all matters concerning the sanctification of man are included in one article; while the third refers to the order of glory, and in relation to this another article is proposed to us concerning the resurrection of the body and life everlasting. Thus there are seven articles referring to the Godhead.

In like manner, with regard to Christ's human nature, there are seven articles, the first of which refers to Christ's incarnation or conception; the second, to His virginal birth; the third, to His Passion, death and burial; the fourth, to His descent into hell; the fifth, to His resurrection; the sixth, to His ascension; the seventh, to His coming for the judgment. And thus there are fourteen articles in all.

Some, however, distinguish twelve articles, six pertaining to the Godhead, and six to the humanity.[35] For they include in one article the three articles about the three Persons, because we have one knowledge of the three Persons; while they divide the article referring to the work of glorification into two, viz., the resurrection of the body, and the glory of the soul. Likewise they unite the conception and nativity into one article.

Reply Obj. 1. By faith we hold many truths about God which the philosophers were unable to discover by natural reason, *e.g.*, about His providence and omnipotence, and that He alone is to be worshipped, all of which are contained in the one article of the unity of God.

Reply Obj. 2. The very name of the Godhead implies a kind of watching over things, as was stated in the First Part.[36] Now in beings having an intellect, power does not work save by the will and knowledge. Hence God's omnipotence includes, in a way, universal knowledge and providence. For He would not be able to do all He wills in things here below, unless He knew them, and exercised His providence over them.

Reply Obj. 3. We have but one knowledge of the Father, Son and Holy Ghost, as to the unity of the essence, to which the first article refers. But as to the distinction of the Persons, which is by the relations of origin, knowledge of the Father does indeed, in a way, include knowledge of the

---

[35]Cf. St. Bonaventure, *In Hexaëm.*, coll. VIII (V, 371).   [36]*S. T.*, I, q. 13, a. 8.
[Not in this volume]

Son, for He would not be Father, had he not a Son; and between them the bond is the Holy Ghost. From this point of view, there was a sufficient motive for those who referred one article to the three Persons. Since, however, with regard to each Person, certain points have to be observed, about which some happen to fall into error, looking at it in this way, we may distinguish three articles about the three Persons. For Arius believed in the omnipotence and eternity of the Father, but he did not believe the Son to be co-equal and consubstantial with the Father; hence the need for an article about the Person of the Son in order to settle this point. In like manner, it was necessary to appoint a third article about the Person of the Holy Ghost, against Macedonius. In the same way, Christ's conception and birth, like the resurrection and life everlasting, can from one point of view be united together in one article, in so far as they are ordained to one end; while, from another point of view, they can be distinct articles, inasmuch as each one separately presents a special difficulty.

Reply Obj. 4. It belongs to the Son and Holy Ghost to be sent to sanctify the creature; and about this several things have to be believed. Hence it is that there are more articles about the Persons of the Son and Holy Ghost than about the Person of the Father, Who is never sent, as we stated in the First Part.[37]

Reply Obj. 5. The sanctification of a creature by grace, and its consummation by glory, is also effected by the gift of charity, which is appropriated to the Holy Ghost, and by the gift of wisdom, which is appropriated to the Son; so that each work belongs by appropriation, but under different aspects, but to the Son and to the Holy Ghost.

Reply Obj. 6. Two things may be considered in the sacrament of the Eucharist. One is the fact that it is a sacrament, and in this respect it is like the other effects of sanctifying grace. The other is that Christ's body is miraculously contained therein, and thus it is included under God's omnipotence, like all other miracles which are ascribed to God's almighty power.

Ninth Article
Whether It Is Suitable for the Articles of Faith to Be Embodied in a Symbol?

We proceed thus to the Ninth Article:—

Objection 1. It would seem that it is unsuitable for the articles of faith to be embodied in a symbol. For Holy Scripture is the rule of faith, to

---

[37] *S. T.*, I, q. 43, a. 4. [Not in this volume]

which no addition or subtraction can lawfully be made, since it is written (*Deut.* iv. 2): *You shall not add to the word that I speak to you, neither shall you take away from it.* Therefore it was unlawful to make a symbol as a rule of faith, after Holy Scripture had once been published.

Obj. 2. Further, According the Apostle (*Ephes.* iv. 5) there is but *one faith.* Now the symbol is a profession of faith. Therefore it is not fitting that there should be many symbols.

Obj. 3. Further, The confession of faith, which is contained in the symbol, concerns all the faithful. But the faithful are not all competent to believe in God, but only those who have formed faith. Therefore it is unfitting for the symbol of faith to be expressed in the words: *I believe in one God.*

Obj. 4. Further, The descent into hell is one of the articles of faith, as was stated above. But the descent into hell is not mentioned in the symbol of the ancient Fathers. Therefore the latter is formulated inadequately.

Obj. 5. Further, Augustine, expounding the passage, *You believe in God, believe also in Me* (*Jo.* xiv. 1), says: *We believe Peter or Paul, but we speak only of believing "in" God.*[38] Since then the Catholic Church is merely a created being, it seems unfitting to say: *In the One, Holy, Catholic and Apostolic Church.*

Obj. 6. Further, A symbol is drawn up that it may be a rule of faith. Now a rule of faith ought to be proposed to all, and that publicly. Therefore every symbol, besides the symbol of the Fathers, should be sung at Mass. Therefore it seems unfitting to publish the articles of faith in a symbol.

On the contrary, The universal Church cannot err, since she is governed by the Holy Ghost Who is the Spirit of truth; for such was Our Lord's promise to His disciples (*Jo.* xvi. 13): *When He, the Spirit of truth, is come, He will teach you all truth.* Now the symbol is published by the authority of the universal Church. Therefore it contains nothing defective.

I answer that, As the Apostle said (*Heb.* xi. 6), *he that cometh to God, must believe that He is.* Now a man cannot believe, unless the truth be proposed to him that he may believe it. Hence the need for the truth of faith to be collected together, so that it might the more easily be proposed to all, lest through ignorance anyone might stray from the truth of faith. It is from being such a collection of the truths of faith that the symbol takes its name.

Reply Obj. 1. The truth of faith is contained in Holy Scripture diffusely, under various modes of expression, and sometimes obscurely, so

---

[38]*Tract.* XXIX, super *Ioann.*, VII, 17 (PL 35, 1631).

that, in order to gather the truth of faith from Holy Scripture, one needs long study and practice; and these are unattainable by all those who require to know the truth of faith, many of whom have no time for study, being busy with other affairs. And so it was necessary to gather together a clear summary from the sayings of Holy Scripture, to be proposed to the belief of all. This indeed was no addition to Holy Scripture, but something derived from it.

Reply Obj. 2. The same doctrine of faith is taught in all the symbols. Nevertheless, the people need more careful instruction about the truth of faith when errors arise, lest the faith of simple believers be corrupted by heretics. It was this that gave rise to the necessity of formulating several symbols, which in no way differ from one another, save that, because of the obstinacy of heretics, one contains more explicitly what another contains implicitly.

Reply Obj. 3. The confession of faith is drawn up in a symbol, in the person, as it were, of the whole Church, which is united together by faith. Now the faith of the Church is formed faith; since such is the faith to be found in all those who are of the Church not only outwardly but also by merit. Hence the confession of faith is expressed in a symbol, in a manner that is in keeping with formed faith, so that even if some of the faithful lack formed faith, they should endeavor to acquire it.

Reply Obj. 4. No error about the descent into hell had arisen among the heretics, so that there was no need to be more explicit on that point. For this reason it is not repeated in the symbol of the Fathers, but is supposed as already settled in the symbol of the Apostles. For a subsequent symbol does not cancel a preceding one; rather does it expound it, as was stated above.

Reply Obj. 5. If we say: *"In" the holy Catholic Church*, this must be taken verified in so far as our faith is directed to the Holy Ghost, Who sanctifies the Church; so that the sense is: *I believe in the Holy Ghost sanctifying the Church*. But it is better and more in keeping with the common use to omit the *in*, and say simply, *the holy Catholic Church*, as the Pope Leo observes.[39]

Reply Obj. 6. Since the symbol of the Fathers is an explanation of the symbol of the Apostles, and was drawn up after the faith was already spread abroad, and when the Church was already at peace, it is sung publicly in the Mass. On the other hand, the symbol of the Apostles, which was drawn up at the time of persecution, before the faith was made pub-

---

[39]Cf. Rufinus, *In Symb. Apost.* (PL 21, 373).

lic, is said secretly at Prime and Compline, as though it were against the darkness of past and future errors.

Tenth Article
Whether It Belongs to the Sovereign Pontiff
to Draw Up a Symbol of Faith?

We proceed thus to the Tenth Article:—

Objection 1. It would seem that it does not belong to the Sovereign Pontiff to draw up a symbol of faith. For a new edition of the symbol becomes necessary in order to explain the articles of faith, as was stated above. Now, in the Old Testament, the articles of faith were more and more explained as time went on, because the truth of faith became clearer through greater nearness to Christ, as was stated above. Since, then, this reason ceased with the advent of the New Law, there is no need for the articles of faith to be more and more explicit. Therefore it does not seem to belong to the authority of the Sovereign Pontiff to draw up a new edition of the symbol.

Obj. 2. Further, No man has the power to do what is forbidden under pain of anathema by the universal Church. Now it was forbidden under pain of anathema by the universal Church to make a new edition of the symbol. For it is stated in the acts of the first council of Ephesus that after the symbol of the Nicene council had been read through, *the holy synod decreed that it was unlawful to utter, write or draw up any other creed than that which was defined by the Fathers assembled at Nicaea together with the Holy Ghost,*[40] and this under pain of anathema. The same was repeated in the acts of the council of Chalcedon.[41] Therefore it seems that the Sovereign Pontiff has no authority to publish a new edition of the symbol.

Obj. 3. Further, Athanasius was not a Sovereign Pontiff, but patriarch of Alexandria, and yet he published a symbol which is sung in the Church. Therefore it does not seem to belong to the Sovereign Pontiff, any more than to other bishops, to publish a new edition of the symbol.

On the contrary, The symbol was drawn up by a general council. Now such a council cannot be convoked otherwise than by the authority of the Sovereign Pontiff, as is stated in the *Decretals.*[42] Therefore it belongs to the authority of the Sovereign Pontiff to draw up a symbol.

---

[40]*Conc. Ephes.*, actio VI (Denzinger, no. 125).   [41]*Conc. Chalced.*, actio V (Mansi, VII, 109).   [42]Gratian, *Decretum*, I, xvii, 4 (I, 51).

I answer that, As was stated above, a new edition of the symbol becomes necessary in order to set aside the errors that may arise. Consequently to publish a new edition of the symbol belongs to that authority which is empowered to decide matters of faith definitely, so that all may hold them with unshaken faith. Now this belongs to the authority of the Sovereign Pontiff, *to whom the more important and more difficult questions that arise in the Church are referred,* as is stated in the *Decretals.*[43] Hence Our Lord said to Peter whom he made Sovereign Pontiff (*Luke* xxii. 32): *I have prayed for thee,* Peter, *that thy faith fail not, and thou, being once converted, confirm thy brethren.* The reason for this is that there should be but one faith in the whole Church, according to *1 Cor.* i. 10: *That you all speak the same thing, and that there be no schisms among you;* and this could not be secured unless any question of faith that may arise be decided by him who presides over the whole Church, so that the whole Church may hold firmly to his decision. Consequently it belongs to the sole authority of the Sovereign Pontiff to publish a new edition of the symbol, as do all other matters which concern the whole Church, such as to convoke a general council, and so forth.

Reply Obj. 1. The truth of faith is sufficiently explicit in the teaching of Christ and the Apostles. But since, according to *2 Pet.* iii. 16, some men are so evil-minded as to pervert the apostolic teaching and other doctrines and Scriptures to their own destruction, it was necessary as time went on to express the faith more explicitly against the errors which arose.

Reply Obj. 2. This prohibition and sentence of the council was intended for private individuals, who have no business to decide matters of faith; for this decision of the general council did not take away from a subsequent council the power of drawing up a new edition of the symbol, containing, not indeed a new faith, but the same faith with greater explicitness. For every council has taken into account that a subsequent council would expound matters more fully than the preceding council, if this became necessary through the rise of some heresy. Consequently, this belongs to the Sovereign Pontiff, by whose authority the council is convoked, and its decision confirmed.

Reply Obj. 3. Athanasius drew up a declaration of faith, not under the form of a symbol, but rather by way of an exposition of doctrine, as appears from his way of speaking. But since it contained briefly the whole truth of faith, it was accepted by the authority of the Sovereign Pontiff, so as to be considered as a rule of faith.

---

[43]*Ibid.,* 5 (I, 52).

Question 2
On the Interior Act of Faith
(*In Ten Articles*)

We must now consider the act of faith, and (1) the interior act; (2) the exterior act.[1]

Under the first head there are ten points of inquiry: (1) What is *to believe*, which is the interior act of faith? (2) In how many ways is it expressed? (3) Whether it is necessary for salvation to believe in anything above natural reason? (4) Whether it is necessary to believe those things that are attainable by natural reason? (5) Whether it is necessary for salvation to believe certain things explicitly? (6) Whether all are equally bound to explicit faith? (7) Whether explicit faith in Christ is always necessary for salvation? (8) Whether it is necessary for salvation to believe in the Trinity explicitly? (9) Whether the act of faith is meritorious? (10) Whether human reason diminishes the merit of faith?

First Article
Whether to Believe Is to Think with Assent?

We proceed thus to the First Article:—

Objection 1. It would seem that to believe is not to think with assent. Because the Latin word *cogitatio* [*thought*] implies an inquiry, for *cogitare* [*to think*] seems to be equivalent to *coagitare*, i.e., *to discuss together.* Now Damascene says that faith is *an assent without inquiry.*[2] Therefore thinking has no place in the act of faith.

Obj. 2. Further, Faith resides in the reason, as we shall show further on.[3] Now to think is an act of the cogitative power, which belongs to the sensitive part, as was stated in the First Part.[4] Therefore thought has nothing to do with faith.

Obj. 3. Further, To believe is an act of the intellect, since its object is truth. But assent seems to be an act, not of the intellect, but of the will, even as consent is, as was stated above.[5] Therefore to believe is not to think with assent.

On the contrary, This is how *to believe is* defined by Augustine.[6]

I answer that, To think can be taken in three ways. First, in a general

---

[1]Q. 3. [2]*De Fide Orth.*, IV, 11 (PG 94, 1128). [3]Q. 4, a. 2. [4]*S. T.*, I, q. 78, a. 4. [Not in this volume] [5]Q. 1, q. 4; I–II, q. 15, a. 1. [Not in this volume] [6]*De Praedest. Sanct.*, II (PL 44, 963).

way for any kind of actual consideration of the intellect, as Augustine observes: *By understanding I mean now the power whereby we understand when thinking.*[7] Secondly, *to think* is more strictly taken for that consideration of the intellect which is accompanied by some kind of inquiry, and which precedes the intellect's arrival at the stage of perfection that comes with the certitude of vision. In this sense Augustine says that *the Son of God is not called the Thought, but the Word of God. When our thought realizes what we know and takes form therefrom, it becomes our word. Hence the Word of God must be understood without any thinking on the part of God, for there is nothing there that can take form, or be unformed.*[8] In this way thought is, properly speaking, the movement of the soul while yet deliberating, and not yet perfected by the clear vision of truth. Since, however, such a movement of the soul may be one of deliberation either about universal intentions, which belongs to the intellectual part, or about particular intentions, which belongs to the sensitive part, hence it is that *to think* is taken secondly for an act of the deliberating intellect, and thirdly for an act of the cogitative power.

Accordingly, if *to think* be understood broadly according to the first sense, then *to think with assent* does not express completely what is meant by *to believe;* for, in this way, a man thinks with assent even when he considers what he knows by science or what he understands. If, on the other hand, *to think* be understood in the second way, then this expresses completely the nature of the act of believing. For among the acts belonging to the intellect, some have a firm assent without any such kind of thinking, as when a man considers the things that he knows by science or what he understands, for this consideration is already formed. But some acts of the intellect have unformed thought devoid of a firm assent, whether they incline to neither side, as in one who *doubts;* or incline to one side rather than the other, but because of some slight motive, as in one who *suspects;* or incline to one side, yet with fear of the other, as in one who *opines.* But this act, *to believe*, cleaves firmly to one side, in which respect belief has something in common with science and understanding; yet its knowledge does not attain the perfection of clear vision, wherein it agrees with doubt, suspicion and opinion. Hence it is proper to the believer to think with assent; so that the act of believing is distinguished from all the other acts of the intellect which are about the true or the false.

Reply Obj. 1. Faith has not that inquiry of natural reason which demonstrates what is believed, but an inquiry into those things whereby a man

---

[7]*De Trin.*, XIV, 7 (PL 42, 1044).   [8]*Op. cit.*, XV, 16 (PL 42, 1079).

is induced to believe, for instance, that such things have been uttered by God and confirmed by miracles.

Reply Obj. 2. To think is not taken here for the act of the cogitative power, but for an act of the intellect, as was explained above.

Reply Obj. 3. The intellect of the believer is determined to one object, not by the reason, but by the will, and so assent is taken here for an act of the intellect as determined to one object by the will.

Second Article
Whether the Act of Faith Is Suitably Distinguished as Believing God, Believing in a God, and Believing in God?

We proceed thus to the Second Article:—

Objection 1. It would seem that the act of faith is unsuitably distinguished as believing God, believing in a God, and believing in God. For one habit has but one act. Now faith is one habit since it is one virtue. Therefore it is unreasonable to say that there are several acts of faith.

Obj. 2. Further, That which is common to all acts of faith should not be reckoned as a particular kind of act of faith. Now *to believe God* is common to all acts of faith, since faith is founded on the First Truth. Therefore it seems unreasonable to distinguish it from certain other acts of faith.

Obj. 3. Further, That which can be said of unbelievers cannot be called an act of faith. Now unbelievers can be said to believe that there is a God. Therefore it should not be reckoned an act of faith.

Obj. 4. Further, Movement towards the end belongs to the will, whose object is the good and the end. Now to believe is an act, not of the will, but of the intellect. Therefore *to believe in God*, which implies movement towards an end, should not be reckoned as a species of that act.

On the contrary is the authority of Augustine who makes this distinction.[9]

I answer that, The act of any power or habit depends on the relation of that power or habit to its object. Now the object of faith can be considered in three ways. For, since *to believe* is an act of the intellect, in so far as the will moves it to assent, as was stated above, the object of faith can be considered either on the part of the intellect, or on the part of the will that moves the intellect.

If it be considered on the part of the intellect, then two things can be observed in the object of faith, as was stated above.[10] One of these is the

---

[9] *Serm.* CXLIV, 2 (PL 38, 788); *Tract.* XXIX, super *Ioann.*, VII, 17 (PL 35, 1631).
[10] Q. 1, a. 1.

material object of faith, and in this way an act of faith is *to believe in a God*, because, as was stated above, nothing is proposed to our belief except inasmuch as it is referred to God.[11] The other is the formal aspect of the object, for it is the medium because of which we assent to such and such a point of faith; and thus an act of faith is *to believe God*, since, as was stated above, the formal object of faith is the First Truth,[12] to Which man gives his adhesion, so as to assent for Its sake to whatever he believes.

Thirdly, if the object of faith be considered in so far as the intellect is moved by the will, an act of faith is *to believe in God*. For the First Truth is referred to the will, through having the nature of an end.

Reply Obj. 1. These three do not denote different acts of faith, but one and the same act having different relations to the object of faith.

This suffices also for the *Reply* to the *Second Objection*.

Reply Obj. 3. Unbelievers cannot be said *to believe in a God* as we understand it in relation to the act of faith. For they do not believe that God exists under the conditions that faith determines; and hence they do not truly believe in a God, since, as the Philosopher observes, *to know simple things defectively is not to know them at all.*[13]

Reply Obj. 4. As was stated above, the will moves the intellect and the other powers of the soul to the end;[14] and in this respect an act of faith is *to believe in God*.

Third Article
Whether It Is Necessary for Salvation to
Believe Anything above the Natural Reason?

We proceed thus to the Third Article:—

Objection 1. It would seem unnecessary for salvation to believe anything above the natural reason. For the salvation and perfection of a thing seem to be sufficiently insured by its natural endowments. Now matters of faith surpass man's natural reason, since they are things unseen, as was stated above.[15] Therefore to believe seems unnecessary for salvation.

Obj. 2. Further, it is dangerous for man to assent to matters wherein he cannot judge whether that which is proposed to him be true or false, according to *Job* xii. 11: *Doth not the ear discern words?* Now a man cannot form a judgment of this kind in matters of faith, since he cannot reduce them back to first principles, by which all our judgments are guided.

---

[11]*Ibid.*   [12]*Ibid.*   [13]*Metaph.*, VIII, 10 (1051b 25).   [14]*S. T.*, I, q. 82, a. 4 [Not in this volume]; I-II, q. 9, a. 1.   [15]Q. 1, a. 4. [Not in this volume]

Therefore it is dangerous to believe in such matters. Therefore to believe is not necessary for salvation.

Obj. 3. Further, Man's salvation rests on God, according to *Ps.* xxxvi. 39: *But the salvation of the just is from the Lord. Now the invisible things of God are clearly seen, being understood by the things that are made; His eternal power also and divinity,* according to *Rom.* i. 20. But those things which are clearly seen by the understanding are not an object of belief. Therefore it is not necessary for man's salvation that he should believe certain things.

On the contrary, It is written (*Heb.* xi. 6): *Without faith it is impossible to please God.*

I answer that, Wherever one nature is subordinate to another, we find that two things concur towards the perfection of the lower nature, one of which is in terms of that nature's proper movement, while the other is in terms of the movement of the higher nature. Thus water by its proper movement moves towards the center, while according to the movement of the moon, it moves round the center by ebb and flow. In like manner, the spheres of the planets have their proper movements from west to east, while in accordance with the movement of the first heaven, they have a movement from east to west. Now the created rational nature alone is immediately ordered to God, since other creatures do not attain to the universal, but only to something particular, for they partake of the divine goodness either in *being* only, as inanimate things, or also in *living*, and in *knowing singulars*, as plants and animals; whereas the rational nature, inasmuch as it apprehends the universal notion of good and being, is immediately related to the universal principle of being.

Consequently the perfection of the rational creature consists not only in what belongs to it according to its nature, but also in that which it acquires through a supernatural participation of the divine goodness. Hence it was said above that man's ultimate happiness consists in a supernatural vision of God.[16] To this vision man cannot attain unless he be taught by God, according to *John* vi. 45: *Every one that hath heard of the Father and hath learned cometh to Me.* Now man acquires a share of this learning, not all at once, but a little at a time, according to the mode of his nature; and every one who learns thus must needs believe, in order that he may acquire science in a perfect degree. And so the Philosopher likewise remarks that *it behooves a learner to believe.*[17]

---

[16]*S. T.*, I, q. 12, a. 1 [Not in this volume]; I-II, q. 3, a. 8. [Not in this volume]   [17]*Soph. Elench.*, II (161b 3).

Hence, in order that a man arrive at the perfect vision of heavenly happiness, he must first of all believe God, as a disciple believes the master who is teaching him.

Reply Obj. 1. Since man's nature is dependent on a higher nature, natural knowledge does not suffice for its perfection, and some supernatural knowledge is necessary, as was stated above.

Reply Obj. 2. Just as man assents to first principles by the natural light of his intellect, so does a virtuous man, by the habit of virtue, judge rightly of things concerning that virtue; and in this way, by the light of faith which God bestows on him, a man assents to matters of faith and not to those which are against faith. Consequently, *there is no* danger or *condemnation to them that are in Christ Jesus,* and whom He has enlightened by faith.

Reply Obj. 3. In many respects, faith perceives the invisible things of God in a higher way than natural reason does in proceeding to God from His creatures. Hence it is written (*Ecclus.* iii. 25): *Many things are shown to thee above the understanding of man.*

Fourth Article
Whether It Is Necessary to Believe Those Things Which Can Be Proved by Natural Reason?

We proceed thus to the Fourth Article:—

Objection 1. It would seem unnecessary to believe those things which can be proved by natural reason. For nothing is superfluous in God's works, much less even than in the works of nature. Now it is superfluous to employ other means, where one already suffices. Therefore it would be superfluous to receive by faith things that can be known by natural reason.

Obj. 2. Further, Those things must be believed which are the object of faith. Now science and faith are not about the same object, as was stated above.[18] Since, therefore, all things that can be known by natural reason are an object of science, it seems that there is no need to believe what can be proved by natural reason.

Obj. 3. Further, All things knowable by science would seem to have one nature; so that if some of them are proposed to man as objects of faith, in like manner the others should also be believed. But this is not true. Therefore it is not necessary to believe those things which can be proved by natural reason.

On the contrary, It is necessary to believe that God is one and incorporeal; which things philosophers prove by natural reason.

---

[18]Q. 1, a. 5.

I answer that, It is necessary for man to receive by faith not only things which are above reason, but also those which can be known by reason; and this for three motives. First, in order that man may arrive more quickly at the knowledge of divine truth. For the science to whose province it belongs to prove the existence of God and many other such truths is the last of all to offer itself to human inquiry, since it presupposes many other sciences; so that it would be far along in life that man would arrive at the knowledge of God. The second reason is, in order that the knowledge of God may be more widespread. For many are unable to make progress in the study of science, either through dullness of ability, or through having a number of occupations and temporal needs, or even through laziness in learning; and all these persons would be altogether deprived of the knowledge of God, unless divine things were brought to their knowledge by way of faith. The third reason is for the sake of certitude. For human reason is very deficient in things concerning God. A sign of this is that philosophers, in their inquiry into human affairs by natural investigation, have fallen into many errors, and have disagreed among themselves. And consequently, in order that men might have knowledge of God, free of doubt and uncertainty, it was necessary for divine truths to be delivered to them by way of faith, being told to them, as it were, by God Himself Who cannot lie.

Reply Obj. 1. The inquiry of natural reason does not suffice mankind for the knowledge of divine truths, even of those that can be proved by reason; and so it is not superfluous if these be believed.

Reply Obj. 2. Science and faith cannot be in the same subject and about the same object; but what is an object of science for one can be an object of faith for another, as was stated above.[19]

Reply Obj. 3. Although all things that can be known by science have the notion of science in common, they do not all alike lead man to beatitude; and hence they are not all equally proposed to our belief.

Fifth Article
Whether Man Is Bound to Believe Anything Explicitly?

We proceed thus to the Fifth Article:—

Objection 1. It would seem that man is not bound to believe anything explicitly. For no man is bound to do what is not in his power. Now it is not in man's power to believe a thing explicitly, for it is written (*Rom.* x. 14, 15): *How shall they believe Him, of whom they have not heard? And how*

---

[19] *Ibid.*

shall they hear without a preacher? And how shall they preach unless they be sent? Therefore man is not bound to believe anything explicitly.

Obj. 2. Further, Just as we are directed to God by faith, so also are we by charity. Now man is not bound to keep the precepts of charity, but it is enough if he be ready to fulfill them. This is evidenced by the precept of Our Lord (*Matt.* v. 39): *If one strike thee on one cheek, turn to him also the other;* and by others of the same kind, according to Augustine's exposition.[20] Therefore neither is man bound to believe anything explicitly, but it is enough if he be ready to believe whatever God proposes to be believed.

Obj. 3. Further, The good of faith consists in a certain obedience, according to *Rom.* i. 5: *For obedience to the faith in all nations.* Now the virtue of obedience does not require man to keep certain fixed precepts, but it is enough that his mind be ready to obey, according to *Ps.* cxviii. 60: *I am ready and am not troubled, that I may keep Thy commandments.* Therefore it seems enough for faith, too, that man should be ready to believe whatever God may propose, without believing anything explicitly.

On the contrary, It is written (*Heb.* xi. 6): *He that cometh to God must believe that He is, and is a rewarder to them that seek Him.*

I answer that, The precepts of the Law, which man is bound to fulfill, concern acts of virtue which are the means of attaining salvation. Now an act of virtue, as was stated above, depends on the relation of the habit to its object.[21] But two things may be considered in the object of any virtue, namely, that which is the proper and direct object of that virtue, which is necessarily in every act of virtue, and that which is accidental and consequent to the object properly so called. Thus, it belongs properly and directly to the object of fortitude to face the dangers of death, and to charge at the foe with danger to oneself, for the sake of the common good; and yet that, in a just war, a man be armed, or strike another with his sword, and so forth, is reduced to the object of fortitude, but indirectly.

Accordingly, just as a virtuous act is required for the fulfillment of a precept, so is it necessary that the virtuous act should terminate in its proper and direct object; but, on the other hand, the fulfillment of the precept does not require that a virtuous act should terminate in those things which have an accidental or secondary relation to the proper and direct object of that virtue, except in certain places and at certain times.

We must, therefore, say that the direct object of faith is that whereby man is made one of the Blessed, as was stated above;[22] while the indirect

---

[20]*De Serm. Dom.*, I, 19 (PL 34, 1260).   [21]Q. 2, a. 2.   [22]Q. 1, a. 6, ad 1.

and secondary object comprises all things delivered by God to us in Holy Scripture, for instance, that Abraham had two sons, that David was the son of Jesse, and so forth. Therefore, as regards the primary points or articles of faith, man must believe them explicitly, just as he must have faith; but as to other points of faith, man is not bound to believe them explicitly, but only implicitly, or to be ready to believe them, in so far as he is prepared to believe whatever is contained in the divine Scriptures. Then alone is he bound to believe such things explicitly, when it is clear to him that they are contained in the doctrine of faith.

Reply Obj. 1. If we understand those things alone to be in a man's power, which we can do without the help of grace, then we are bound to do many things which we cannot do without the aid of healing grace, such as to love God and our neighbor, and likewise to believe the articles of faith. But with the help of grace we can do this, for this help *to whomsoever it is given from above it is mercifully given; and from whom it is withheld it is justly withheld, as a punishment of a previous, or at least of original, sin,* as Augustine states.[23]

Reply Obj. 2. Man is bound to love definitely those lovable things which are properly and directly the objects of charity, namely, God and neighbor. The objection refers to those precepts of charity which belong, as by a consequence, to the object of charity.

Reply Obj. 3. The virtue of obedience is seated, properly speaking, in the will; and hence the promptness of the will, which is subject to authority, suffices for the act of obedience, because it is the proper and direct object of obedience. But this or that precept is accidental or consequent to that proper and direct object.

Sixth Article
Whether All Are Equally Bound to Have Explicit Faith?

We proceed thus to the Sixth Article:—

Objection 1. It would seem that all are equally bound to have explicit faith. For all are bound to those things which are necessary for salvation, as is evident concerning the precepts of charity. Now it is necessary for salvation that certain things should be believed explicitly, as we have said. Therefore all are equally bound to have explicit faith.

Obj. 2. Further, No one should be put to a test in matters that he is not bound to believe explicitly. But simple persons are sometimes tested in

---

[23]Cf. *Epist.* CXC, 3 (PL 33, 860); *De Praedest. Sanct.*, VIII (PL 44, 971).

reference to the slightest articles of faith. Therefore all are bound to believe everything explicitly.

Obj. 3. Further, If the simple are bound to have, not explicit, but only implicit faith, their faith must needs be implied in the faith of the learned. But this seems unsafe, since it is possible for the learned to err. Therefore it seems that the simple should also have explicit faith; so that all are, therefore, equally bound to have explicit faith.

On the contrary, It is written (*Job* i. 14): *The oxen were ploughing, and the asses feeding beside them,* because, as Gregory expounds this passage, the simple, who are signified by the asses, ought, in matters of faith, to stay by the learned, who are denoted by the oxen.[24]

I answer that, The unfolding of matters of faith is the result of divine revelation, for matters of faith surpass natural reason. Now divine revelation reaches those of lower degree through those who are over them, in a certain order; to men, for instance, through the angels, and to the lower angels through the higher, as Dionysius explains.[25] In like manner, therefore, the unfolding of faith must needs reach men of lower degree through those of higher degree. Consequently, just as the higher angels, who illumine those who are below them, have a fuller knowledge of divine things than the lower angels, as Dionysius states,[26] so too, men of higher degree, whose business it is to teach others, are under obligation to have fuller knowledge of matters of faith, and to believe them more explicitly.

Reply Obj. 1. The unfolding of the articles of faith is not equally necessary for the salvation of all, since those of higher degree, whose duty it is to teach others, are bound to believe explicitly more things than others are,

Reply Obj. 2. Simple persons should not be put to the test about subtle questions of faith, unless they be suspected of having been corrupted by heretics, who are wont to corrupt the faith of simple people in such questions. If, however, it is found that they are free from obstinacy in their heterodox sentiments, and that it is due to their simplicity, it is no fault of theirs.

Reply Obj. 3. The simple have no faith implied in that of the learned, except in so far as the latter adhere to the divine teaching. Hence the Apostle says (1 *Cor.* iv. 16): *Be ye followers of me, as I also am of Christ.* Hence it is not human knowledge, but the divine truth, that is the rule of faith; and if any of the learned stray from this rule, he does not harm the faith of the simple ones, who think that the learned believe rightly— unless the simple hold obstinately to their individual errors, against the

---

[24]*Moral.*, II, 30 (PL 75, 578).   [25]*De Cael. Hier.*, IV, 3; VII, 3; VII, 2 (PG 3, 180; 209; 240).   [26]*Op. cit.*, XII, 2 (PG 3, 292).

faith of the universal Church, which cannot err, since Our Lord said: (*Luke* xxii. 32): *I have prayed for thee,* Peter, *that thy faith fail not.*

Seventh Article
Whether It Is Necessary for the Salvation of All That They Should Believe Explicitly in the Mystery of Christ?

We proceed thus to the Seventh Article:—

Objection 1. It would seem that it is not necessary for the salvation of all that they should believe explicitly in the mystery of Christ. For man is not bound to believe explicitly what the angels do not know; for the unfolding of faith is the result of divine revelation, which reaches man by means of the angels, as was stated above.[27] Now even the angels were in ignorance of the mystery of the Incarnation; and so, according to the commentary of Dionysius,[28] it is they who ask (*Ps.* xxiii. 8): *Who is this king of glory?* and (*Isa.* lxiii. I): *Who is this that cometh from Edom?* Therefore men were not bound to believe explicitly in the mystery of Christ's Incarnation.

Obj. 2. Further, It is evident that John the Baptist was one of the learned, and most nigh to Christ, Who said of him (*Matt.* xi. 11) that *there hath not risen among them that are born of women, a greater than* he. Now John the Baptist does not appear to have known the mystery of the Incarnation of Christ explicitly, since he asked Christ (*Matt.* xi. 3): *Art Thou He that art to come, or look we for another?* Therefore even the learned were not bound to explicit faith in Christ.

Obj. 3. Further, Many gentiles obtained salvation through the ministry of the angels, as Dionysius states.[29] Now it would seem that the gentiles had neither explicit nor implicit faith in Christ, since they received no revelation. Therefore it seems that it was not necessary for the salvation of all to believe explicitly in the mystery of Christ.

On the contrary, Augustine says: *Our faith is sound if we believe that no man, old or young, is delivered from the contagion of death and the bonds of sin, except by the one Mediator of God and men, Jesus Christ.*[30]

I answer that, As was stated above, the object of faith includes, properly and directly, that thing through which man obtains beatitude.[31] Now the mystery of Christ's Incarnation and Passion is the way by which men obtain beatitude; for it is written (*Acts* iv. 12): *There is no other name under heaven given to men, whereby we must be saved.* Therefore belief of some

---

[27]*S. T.*, I, q. 111, a. 1. [Not in this volume] 209). [29]*Op. cit.*, IX, 4 (PG 3, 261). [31]A. 5; q. 1, a. 6, ad 1.

[28]*De Cael. Hier.*, VII, 3 (PG 3, 209). [30]Cf. *Epist.* CXC, 2 (PL 33, 858).

kind in the mystery of Christ's Incarnation was necessary at all times and for all persons, but this belief differed according to differences of times and persons. The reason for this is that before the state of sin, man believed explicitly in Christ's Incarnation, in so far as it was intended for the consummation of glory, but not as it was intended to deliver man from sin by the Passion and Resurrection, since man had no foreknowledge of his future sin. He does, however, seem to have had foreknowledge of the Incarnation of Christ, from the fact that he said (*Gen.* ii. 24): *Wherefore a man shall leave father and mother, and shall cleave to his wife*, of which the Apostle says (*Ephes.* v. 32) that *this is a great sacrament . . . in Christ and the Church;* and it is incredible that the first man was ignorant about this sacrament.

But after sin, men believed explicitly in Christ, not only as to the Incarnation, but also as to the Passion and Resurrection, by which the human race is delivered from sin and death: for otherwise they would not have foreshadowed Christ's Passion by certain sacrifices both before and after the Law. The meaning of these sacrifices was known by the learned explicitly, while the simple folk knew it under the veil of the sacrifices, believing them to be directed by God to Christ's coming, and thus their knowledge was covered with a veil, so to speak. And, as was stated above, the farther they were from Christ, the more difficult they found it to know Christ's mysteries; and the nearer they were to Christ, the more distinct was their knowledge of Christ's mysteries.[32]

After grace had been revealed, both learned and simple folk are bound to explicit faith in the mysteries of Christ, chiefly as regards those which are observed throughout the Church, and publicly proclaimed, such as the articles that refer to the Incarnation, of which we have spoken above.[33] As to other minute points in reference to the articles of the Incarnation, men have been bound to believe them more or less explicitly according to each one's state and office.

Reply Obj. 1. The mystery of the Kingdom of God was not entirely hidden from the angels, as Augustine observes,[34] yet certain aspects thereof were better known to them when Christ revealed them to them.

Reply Obj. 2. It was not through ignorance that John the Baptist inquired of Christ's advent in the flesh, since he had clearly professed his belief therein, saying: *I saw, and I gave testimony, that this is the Son of God* (*Jo.* i. 34). Hence he did not say: *Art Thou He that hast come?* but *Art Thou He that art to come?* thus asking about the future, not about the past. Likewise it is not to be believed that he was ignorant of Christ's future Passion,

---

[32]Q. 1, a. 7.   [33]Q. 1, a. 8.   [34]*De Genesi ad Litt.*, V, 19 (PL 34, 334).

for he had already said (*ibid.* 29): *Behold the Lamb of God, behold Him who taketh away the sins of the world,* thus foretelling His future immolation; and since other prophets had foretold it, as may be seen especially in *Isaias* liii. We may therefore say with Gregory that he asked this question, being in ignorance as to whether Christ would descend into hell in His own Person.[35] But he was not ignorant of the fact that the power of Christ's Passion would be extended to those who were detained in Limbo, according to *Zach.* ix. 11: *Thou also, by the blood of Thy testament, hast sent forth Thy prisoners out of the pit, wherein is no water;* nor was he bound to believe explicitly, before its fulfillment, that Christ was to descend thither Himself.

It may also be replied that, as Ambrose observes in his commentary on *Luke* vii. 19, he made this inquiry, not from doubt or ignorance, but from devotion,[36] or again, with Chrysostom, that he inquired, not as though ignorant himself, but because he wished his disciples to be satisfied, on that point, by Christ;[37] and so the latter framed His answer so as to instruct the disciples, by pointing to the signs of His works.

Reply Obj. 3. Many of the gentiles received revelations of Christ, as is clear from their predictions. Thus we read (*Job* xix. 25): *I know that my Redeemer liveth.* The Sibyl too foretold certain things about Christ, as Augustine relates.[38] Moreover we read in the history of the Romans, that at the time of Constantine Augustus and his mother Helen a tomb was discovered, wherein lay a man on whose breast was a golden plate with the inscription: *Christ shall be born of a virgin, and in Him I believe. O sun, during the lifetime of Helen and Constantine, thou shalt see me again.*[39] If, however, some were saved without receiving any revelation, they were not saved without faith in a Mediator, for, though they did not believe in Him explicitly, they did, nevertheless, have implicit faith through believing in divine providence, since they believed that God would deliver mankind in whatever way was pleasing to Him, and according to the revelation of the Spirit to those who knew the truth, as is stated in *Job* xxxv. 11: *Who teacheth us more than the beasts of the earth.*

Eighth Article
Whether It Is Necessary for Salvation to
Believe Explicitly in the Trinity?

We proceed thus to the Eighth Article:—

Objection 1. It would seem that it was not necessary for salvation to

---

[35] *In Evang.*, I, hom. 6 (PL 76, 1095).   [36] *In Luc.*, V, super VII, 19 (PL 15, 1748).   [37] *In Matt.*, hom. XXXVI (PG 57, 418).   [38] *Contra Faust.*, XIII, 15 (PL 42, 290).   [39] Cf. Theophanes, *Chronographia*, A.C. 773 (PG 108, 917).

believe explicitly in the Trinity. For the Apostle says (*Heb.* xi. 6): *He that cometh to God must believe that He is, and is a rewarder to them that seek Him.* Now one can believe this without believing in the Trinity. Therefore it was not necessary to believe explicitly in the Trinity.

Obj. 2. Further, Our Lord said (*Jo.* xvii. 5, 6): *Father, . . . I have manifested Thy name to men,* which words Augustine expounds as follows: *Not the name by which Thou art called God, but the name whereby Thou art called My Father;*[40] and further on he adds: *In that He made this world, God is known to all nations; in that He is not to be worshipped together with false gods, "God is known in Judea"; but, in that He is the Father of this Christ, through Whom He takes away the sin of the world, He now makes known to men this name of His, which hitherto they knew not.* Therefore before the coming of Christ it was not known that Paternity and Filiation were in the Godhead; and so the Trinity was not believed explicitly.

Obj. 3. Further, That which we are bound to believe explicitly of God is the object of heavenly happiness. Now the object of heavenly happiness is the highest good, which can be understood to be in God, without any distinction of Persons. Therefore it was not necessary to believe explicitly in the Trinity.

On the contrary, In the Old Testament the Trinity of Persons is expressed in many ways. Thus at the very outset of *Genesis* it is written in manifestation of the Trinity: *Let us make man to Our image and likeness* (*Gen.* i. 26). Therefore from the very beginning it was necessary for salvation to believe in the Trinity.

I answer that, It is impossible to believe explicitly in the mystery of Christ, without faith in the Trinity, since the mystery of Christ includes that the Son of God took flesh; that He renewed the world through the grace of the Holy Ghost; and, again, that He was conceived by the Holy Ghost. Therefore just as, before Christ, the mystery of Christ was believed explicitly by the learned, but implicitly and under a veil, so to speak, by the simple, so too was it with the mystery of the Trinity. And consequently, when once grace had been revealed, all were bound to explicit faith in the mystery of the Trinity; and all who are born again in Christ have this bestowed on them by the invocation of the Trinity, according to *Matt.* xxviii. 19: *Going therefore teach ye all nations, baptizing them in the name of the Father, and of the Son and of the Holy Ghost.*

Reply Obj. 1. Explicit faith in those two things was necessary at all times and for all people; but it was not sufficient at all times and for all people.

---

[40] *Tract.* CVI, super *Ioann.* XVII, 6 (PL 35, 1909).

Reply Obj. 2. Before Christ's coming, faith in the Trinity lay hidden in the faith of the learned, but through Christ and the Apostles it was shown to the world.

Reply Obj. 3. God's highest goodness, as we understand it now through its effects, can be understood without the Trinity of Persons; but as understood in itself, and as seen by the Blessed, it cannot be understood without the Trinity of Persons. Moreover, the mission of the divine Persons brings us to heavenly happiness.

Ninth Article
Whether to Believe Is Meritorious?

We proceed thus to the Ninth Article:—

Objection 1. It would seem that to believe is not meritorious. For the principle of all merit is charity, as was stated above.[41] Now faith, like nature, is a preamble to charity. Therefore, just as an act of nature is not meritorious, since we do not merit by our natural gifts, so neither is an act of faith.

Obj. 2. Further, Belief is intermediate between opinion and scientific knowledge or the consideration of things known by science. Now the considerations of science are not meritorious, nor on the other hand is opinion. Therefore belief is not meritorious.

Obj. 3. Further, He who assents to a point of faith either has a sufficient motive for believing, or he has not. If he has a sufficient motive for his belief, this does not seem to imply any merit on his part, since he is no longer free to believe or not to believe; whereas if he has not a sufficient motive for believing, this is a mark of levity, according to *Ecclus.* xix. 4: *He that is hasty to give credit, is light of heart,* so that, seemingly, he gains no merit thereby. Therefore to believe is by no means meritorious.

On the contrary, It is written (*Heb.* xi. 33) that the saints *by faith . . . obtained promises,* which would not be the case if they did not merit by believing. Therefore to believe is meritorious.

I answer that, As was stated above, our actions are meritorious in so far as they proceed from free choice moved with grace by God.[42] Therefore every human act proceeding from free choice, if it be referred to God, can be meritorious. Now the act of believing is an act of the intellect assenting to divine truth at the command of the will moved by the grace of God, so that it is subject to free choice in relation to God; and consequently the act of faith can be meritorious.

---

[41]*S. T.*, I–II, q. 114, a. 4. [Not in this volume]

[42]*S. T.*, I–II, q. 114, a. 3 and 4. [Not in this volume]

Reply Obj. 1. Nature is compared to charity, which is the principle of merit, as matter to form; whereas faith is compared to charity as the disposition which precedes the ultimate form. Now it is evident that the subject or the matter cannot act by virtue of the form, nor can a preceding disposition, before the advent of the form; but after the advent of the form, both the subject and the preceding disposition act by virtue of the form, which is the chief principle of action, even as the heat of fire acts by virtue of the substantial form of fire. Accordingly, neither nature nor faith can, without charity, produce a meritorious act; but, when accompanied by charity, the act of faith is made meritorious thereby, even as an act of nature, and a natural act of free choice.

Reply Obj. 2. Two things may be considered in science, namely, the assent of the one who has science to the thing that he knows, and his consideration of that thing. Now the assent of science is not subject to free choice, because the knower is obliged to assent by the force of the demonstration; and so scientific assent is not meritorious. But the actual consideration of what a man knows by science is subject to his free choice, for it is in his power to consider or not to consider. Hence consideration of science may be meritorious if it be referred to the end of charity, *i.e.*, to the honor of God or the good of our neighbor. On the other hand, in the case of faith, both these things are subject to free choice, so that in both respects the act of faith can be meritorious. But in the case of opinion, there is no firm assent, since it is weak and infirm, as the Philosopher observes,[43] so that it does not seem to proceed from a perfect act of the will; and for this reason, as regards the assent, it does not appear to be very meritorious, though it can be as regards the actual consideration.

Reply Obj. 3. The believer has sufficient motive for believing, for he is moved by the authority of divine teaching confirmed by miracles, and, what is more, by the inward instigation of the divine invitation; and so he does not believe lightly. He has not, however, sufficient reason for scientific knowledge, and hence he does not lose the merit.

Tenth Article
Whether Reasons in Support of What We
Believe Lessen the Merit of Faith?

We proceed thus to the Tenth Article:—

Objection 1. It would seem that reasons in support of what we believe lessen the merit of faith. For Gregory says that *there is no merit in believing what is shown by reason.*[44] If, therefore, human reason provides sufficient

---

[43]*Post. Anal.*, I, 33 (80a 5).   [44]*In Evang.*, II, hom. 26 (PL 76, 1197).

proof, the merit of faith is altogether taken away. Therefore it seems that any kind of human reasoning in support of matters of faith diminishes the merit of believing.

Obj. 2. Further, Whatever lessens the measure of virtue, lessens the amount of merit, since *happiness is the reward of virtue,* as the Philosopher states.[45] Now human reasoning seems to diminish the measure of the virtue of faith, since it is essential to faith to be about the unseen, as was stated above.[46] Now the more a thing is supported by reasons, the less it is unseen. Therefore human reasons in support of matters of faith diminish the merit of faith.

Obj. 3. Further, Contrary things have contrary causes. Now an inducement in opposition to faith increases the merit of faith, whether it consist in persecution inflicted by one who endeavors to force a man to renounce his faith, or in an argument persuading him to do so. Therefore reasons in support of faith diminish the merit of faith.

On the contrary, It is written (*1 Pet.* iii. 15): *Being ready always to satisfy every one that asketh you a reason of that faith and hope which is in you.* Now the Apostle would not give this advice, if it would imply a diminution in the merit of faith. Therefore reason does not diminish the merit of faith.

I answer that, As we have stated above, the act of faith can be meritorious in so far as it is subject to the will, not only as to the use, but also as to the assent. Now human reasoning in support of what we believe may stand in a twofold relation to the will of the believer.—First, as preceding the act of the will, as, for instance, when a man either has not the will, or not a prompt will, to believe, unless he be moved by human reasons; and in this way human reasoning diminishes the merit of faith. In this sense it has been said above that, in moral virtues, a passion which precedes choice makes the virtuous act less praiseworthy.[47] For just as a man ought to perform acts of moral virtue because of the judgment of his reason, and not because of a passion, so he ought to believe matters of faith, not because of human reasoning, but because of the divine authority.—Secondly, human reasons may be consequent to the will of the believer. For when a man has a will ready to believe, he loves the truth he believes, he thinks out and takes to heart whatever reasons he can find in support thereof; and in this way, human reasoning does not exclude the merit of faith, but is a sign of greater merit. Thus, again, in moral virtues, a consequent passion is the sign of a more prompt will, as was stated above.[48] We have an indication of

---

[45]*Eth.,* I, 9 (1099b 16).   [46]Q. 1, a. 4 and 5.   [47]*S. T.,* I-II, q. 24, a. 3, ad 1 [Not in this volume]; q. 77, a. 6, ad 2. [Not in this volume]   [48]*S. T.,* I-II, q. 24, a. 3, ad 1. [Not in this volume]

this in the words of the Samaritans to the woman, who is a type of human reason: *We now believe, not for thy saying* (*Jo.* iv. 42).

Reply Obj. 1. Gregory is referring to the case of a man who has no will to believe what is of faith, unless he be induced by reasons. But when a man has the will to believe what is of faith, on the authority of God alone, although he may have reasons in demonstration of some of them, *e.g.*, of the existence of God, the merit of his faith is not, for that reason, lost or diminished.

Reply Obj. 2. The reasons which are brought forward in support of the authority of faith are not demonstrations which can bring intellectual vision to the human intellect; and so the unseen is not removed. But they remove obstacles to faith, by showing that what faith proposes is not impossible; and hence such reasons do not diminish the merit or the measure of faith. On the other hand, though demonstrative reasons in support of the preambles of faith, but not of the articles of faith, diminish the measure of faith, since they make the thing believed to be seen; yet they do not diminish the measure of charity, which makes the will ready to believe them, even if they were unseen. And so the measure of merit is not diminished.

Reply Obj. 3. Whatever is in opposition to faith, whether it consist in a man's thoughts, or in outward persecution, increases the merit of faith in so far as the will is shown to be more prompt and firm in believing. Hence the martyrs had more merit of faith, through not renouncing faith because of persecution; and even the wise have greater merit of faith, through not renouncing their faith because of the reasons brought forward by philosophers or heretics in opposition to faith. On the other hand, things that are favorable to faith do not always diminish the promptness of the will to believe, and therefore they do not always diminish the merit of faith.

Question 3
On the Exterior Act of Faith
(*In Two Articles*)

We must now consider the exterior act, viz., the confession of faith, under which head there are two points of inquiry: (1) Whether confession is an act of faith? (2) Whether confession of faith is necessary for salvation?

First Article
Whether Confession Is an Act of Faith?

We proceed thus to the First Article:—

Objection 1. It would seem that confession is not an act of faith. For the same act does not belong to different virtues. Now confession belongs to penance, of which it is a part. Therefore it is not an act of faith.

Obj. 2. Further, Man is sometimes deterred by fear, or some kind of confusion, from confessing his faith; and so the Apostle (*Ephes.* vi. 19) asks for prayers that it may be granted him *with confidence, to make known the mystery of the gospel.* Now it belongs to fortitude, which moderates daring and fear, not to be deterred from doing good because of confusion or fear. Therefore it seems that confession is not an act of faith, but rather of fortitude or constancy.

Obj. 3. Further, Just as the ardor of faith makes one confess one's faith outwardly, so does it make one do other external good works; for it is written (*Gal.* v. 6) that *faith . . . worketh by charity.* But other external works are not reckoned as acts of faith. Therefore neither is confession an act of faith.

On the contrary, The *Gloss* explains the words of *2 Thess.* i. 11 (*and the work of faith in power*) as referring to *confession, which is a work proper to faith.*[1]

I answer that, Exterior acts belong properly to that virtue to whose end they are specifically referred; and thus fasting is referred specifically to the end of abstinence, which is to curb the flesh, and consequently it is an act of abstinence.

Now confession of those things that are of faith is referred specifically, as to its end, to that which concerns faith, according to *2 Cor.* iv. 13: *Having the same spirit of faith, . . . we believe, and therefore we speak also.* For the exterior utterance is intended to signify the interior thought. Therefore, just as the interior thought of matters of faith is properly an act of faith, so too is the exterior confession of them.

Reply Obj. 1. A threefold confession is commended by the Scriptures. One is the confession of what belongs to faith, and this is a proper act of faith, since it is referred to the end of faith, as was stated above. Another is the confession of thanksgiving or praise, and this is an act of adoration [*latria*], for its purpose is to give outward honor to God, which is the end of adoration. The third is the confession of sins, which is ordained to the blotting out of sins, which is the end of penance, to which virtue it therefore belongs.

---

[1] *Glossa ordin.* (VI, 114B).

Reply Obj. 2. That which removes an obstacle is not an essential cause, but an accidental one, as the Philosopher proves.[2] Hence fortitude, which removes an obstacle to the confession of faith, viz., fear or shame, is not the proper and essential cause of confession, but an accidental one, so to speak.

Reply Obj. 3. Interior faith, with the aid of charity, causes all exterior acts of virtue by means of the other virtues, by commanding, but not eliciting them; whereas it produces the act of confession as its proper act, without the help of any other virtue.

Second Article
Whether Confession of Faith Is Necessary for Salvation?

We proceed thus to the Second Article:—

Objection 1. It would seem that confession of faith is not necessary for salvation. For a thing seems to be sufficient for salvation, if it is a means of attaining the end of virtue. Now the proper end of faith is the union of the human mind with divine truth, and this can be realized without any exterior confession. Therefore confession of faith is not necessary for salvation.

Obj. 2. Further, By outward confession of faith, a man reveals his faith to another man. But this is unnecessary save for those who have to instruct others in the faith. Therefore it seems that the simple folk are not bound to confession of faith.

Obj. 3. Further, Whatever may tend to scandalize and disturb others, is not necessary for salvation; for the Apostle says (*1 Cor.* x. 32): *Be without offence to the Jews and to the gentiles, and to the Church of God.* Now confession of the faith sometimes causes a disturbance among unbelievers. Therefore it is not necessary for salvation.

On the contrary, The Apostle says (*Rom.* x. 10): *With the heart we believe unto justice; but with the mouth, confession is made unto salvation.*

I answer that, Things that are necessary for salvation come under the precepts of the divine law. Now since confession of faith is something affirmative, it can only fall under an affirmative precept. Hence its necessity for salvation depends on how it falls under an affirmative precept of the divine law. Now affirmative precepts, as was stated above, do not bind for always, although they are always binding;[3] but they bind as to place and time and according to other due circumstances, in respect of which human acts have to be regulated in order to be acts of virtue.

---

[2]*Phys.*, VIII, 4 (255b 24).   [3]*S. T.*, I-II, q. 71, a. 5, ad 3 [Not in this volume]; q. 100, a. 10. [Not in this volume]

Thus, then, it is not necessary for salvation to confess one's faith at all times and in all places, but in certain places and at certain times, when, namely, by omitting to do so, we would deprive God of due honor, or our neighbor of a service that we ought to render him. Such would be the case of a man who, on being asked about his faith, were to remain silent, so as to make people believe either that he is without faith, or that the faith is false, or so as to turn others away from the faith; for in such cases as these, confession of faith is necessary for salvation.

Reply Obj. 1. The end of faith, even as of the other virtues, must be referred to the end of charity, which is the love of God and neighbor. Consequently, when God's honor and our neighbor's good demand, man should not be contented with being united by faith to God's truth, but ought to confess his faith outwardly.

Reply Obj. 2. In cases of necessity, where faith is in danger, every one is bound to proclaim his faith to others, either to give good example and encouragement to the rest of the faithful, or to check the attacks of unbelievers; but at other times it is not the duty of all the faithful to instruct others in the faith.

Reply Obj. 3. There is nothing commendable in making a public confession of one's faith, if it cause a disturbance among unbelievers, without any profit either to the faith or to the faithful. Hence Our Lord said (*Matt.* vii. 6): *Give not that which is holy to dogs, neither cast ye your pearls before swine . . . lest turning upon you, they tear you.* Yet, if there is hope of profit to the faith, or if there be urgency, a man should disregard the disturbance of unbelievers, and confess his faith in public. Hence it is written (*Matt.* xv. 12, 14) that when the disciples had said to Our Lord that *the Pharisees, when they heard this word, were scandalized,* He answered: *Let them alone, they are blind, and leaders of the blind.*

Question 4
On the Virtue Itself of Faith
(*In Eight Articles*)

We must now consider the virtue itself of faith, and, in the first place, faith itself; secondly, those who have faith;[1] thirdly, the cause of faith;[2] fourthly, its effects.[3]

---

[1] Q. 5.   [2] Q. 6.   [3] Q. 7.

Under the first head there are eight points of inquiry: (1) What is faith? (2) In what power of the soul does it reside? (3) Whether its form is charity? (4) Whether formed [*formata*] faith and formless [*informis*] faith are one identically? (5) Whether faith is a virtue? (6) Whether it is one virtue? (7) Of its relation to the other virtues. (8) Of its certitude as compared with the certitude of the intellectual virtues.

First Article
Whether This Is a Fitting Definition of Faith:
Faith Is the Substance of Things to Be Hoped for,
the Evidence of Things That Appear Not?

We proceed thus to the First Article:—

Objection 1. It would seem that the Apostle gives an unfitting definition of faith when he says (*Heb.* xi. 1): *Faith is the substance of things to be hoped for, the evidence of things that appear not.* For no quality is a substance, whereas faith is a quality, since it is a theological virtue, as was stated above.[4] Therefore it is not a substance.

Obj. 2. Further, Different virtues have different objects. Now things to be hoped for are the object of hope. Therefore they should not be included in a definition of faith, as though they were its object.

Obj. 3. Further, Faith is perfected by charity rather than by hope, since charity is the form of faith, as we shall state further on. Therefore the definition of faith should have included the thing to be loved rather than the thing to be hoped for.

Obj. 4. Further, The same thing should not be placed in different genera. Now *substance* and *evidence* are different genera, and neither is subalternate to the other. Therefore it is unfitting to state that faith is both *substance* and *evidence*. Therefore faith is unfittingly defined.

Obj. 5. Further, Evidence manifests the truth of the matter for which it is adduced. Now a thing is said to be apparent when its truth is made manifest. Therefore it seems to imply a contradiction to speak of the *evidence of things that appear not*, for an argument makes a previously obscure thing to be apparent. And so faith is unfittingly defined.

On the contrary, The authority of the Apostle suffices.

I answer that, Though some say that the above words of the Apostle are not a definition of faith,[5] because the definition reveals the quiddity and

---

[4] *S. T.*, I–II, q. 62, a. 3. [Not in this volume]   [5] Cf. Hugh of St. Victor, *De Sacram.*, I, x, 2 (PL 176, 330).

essence of a thing, as it is said in *Metaph*. vii.,[6] yet if we consider the matter rightly, this definition overlooks none of the points in reference to which faith can be defined, although the words themselves are not arranged in the form of a definition, just as the philosophers touch on the principles of the syllogism without employing the syllogistic form.

In order to make this clear, we must observe that since habits are known by their acts, and acts by their objects, faith, being a habit, should be defined by its proper act in relation to its proper object. Now the act of faith is to believe, as was stated above,[7] which is an act of the intellect determined to one object by the will's command. Hence an act of faith is related both to the object of the will, *i.e.*, to the good and the end, and to the object of the intellect, *i.e.*, to the true. And since faith, through being a theological virtue, as was stated above,[8] has one and the same thing for object and end, its object and end must, of necessity, be in proportion to one another. Now it has been already stated that the object of faith is the First Truth, as unseen, and whatever we hold because of it;[9] so that it must needs be under the aspect of something unseen that the First Truth is the end of the act of faith, which aspect is that of a thing hoped for, according to the Apostle (*Rom*. viii. 25): *We hope for that which we see not.* For to see the truth is to possess it, and no one hopes for what one has already, but for what one has not, as was stated above.[10]

Accordingly, the relation of the act of faith to its end, which is the object of the will, is indicated by the words: *Faith is the substance of things to be hoped for.* For we are wont to call by the name of substance the first beginning of a thing, especially when the whole subsequent thing is virtually contained in the first beginning. For instance, we might say that the first self-evident principles are the substance of science, because, namely, these principles are in us the first beginnings of science, the whole of which is itself contained in them virtually. In this way, then, faith is said to be the *substance of things to be hoped for*, for the reason that in us the first beginning of things to be hoped for is brought about by the assent of faith, which contains virtually all things to be hoped for. For we hope to be made happy through seeing the unveiled truth to which our faith cleaves, as was made evident when we were speaking of happiness.[11]

The relationship of the act of faith to the object of the intellect, considered as the object of faith, is indicated by the words, *evidence of things*

---

[6]Aristotle, *Metaph.*, VI, 4 (1030a 6); 5 (1031a 12); 12 (1037b 25).   [7]Q. 2, a. 1, ad 3; a. 2 and 9.   [8]*S. T.*, I-II, q. 62, a. 3. [Not in this volume]   [9]Q. 1, a. 1 and 4.   [10]*S. T.*, I-II, q. 67, a. 4. [Not in this volume]   [11]*S. T.*, I-II, q. 3, a. 8; q. 4, a. 3.

that appear not, where *evidence* is taken for the result of evidence. For evidence induces the intellect to adhere to a truth, and so the firm adhesion of the intellect to the non-apparent truth of faith is called *evidence* here. Hence another reading has *conviction*, because, namely, the intellect of the believer is convinced by divine authority, so as to assent to what it sees not.

Accordingly, if anyone would reduce the foregoing words to the form of a definition, he may say that *faith is a habit of the mind, whereby eternal life is begun in us, making the intellect assent to what is non-apparent.* In this way faith is distinguished from all other things pertaining to the intellect. For when we describe it as *evidence*, we distinguish it from opinion, suspicion and doubt, which do not make the intellect adhere to anything firmly; when we go on to say, *of things that appear not*, we distinguish it from science and understanding, the object of which is something apparent; and when we say that it is *the substance of things to be hoped for*, we distinguish the virtue of faith from faith commonly so called, which has no reference to the beatitude we hope for.

Whatever other definitions are given of faith are explanations of this one given by the Apostle. For when Augustine says that *faith is a virtue whereby we believe what we do not see*,[12] and when Damascene says that *faith is an assent without inquiry*,[13] and when others say that *faith is that certainty of the mind about absent things which surpasses opinion but falls short of science*,[14] these all amount to the same as the Apostle's words: *Evidence of things that appear not;* and when Dionysius says that *faith is the solid foundation of the believer, establishing him in the truth, and showing forth the truth in him*,[15] this comes to the same as *substance of things to be hoped for.*

Reply Obj. 1. *Substance*, here, does not stand for the supreme genus co-divided against the other genera, but for that likeness to substance which is found in each genus, namely, inasmuch as the first thing in a genus contains the others virtually and is said to be the substance thereof.

Reply Obj. 2. Since faith pertains to the intellect as commanded by the will, it must needs be directed, as to its end, to the objects of those virtues which perfect the will, among which is hope, as we shall prove further on.[16] For this reason the definition of faith includes the object of hope.

Reply Obj. 3. Love may be of the seen and of the unseen, of the present and of the absent. Consequently a thing to be loved is not so adapted to

---

[12]*Tract.* XL, super *Ioann.*, VIII, 32 (PL 35, 1690); *Quaest. Evang.*, II, 39, super *Luc.* XVII, 5 (PL 35, 1352). [13]*De Fide Orth.*, IV, 11 (PG 94, 1128). [14]Cf. Hugh of St. Victor, *De Sacram.*, I, x, 1 (PL 176, 330). [15]*De Div. Nom.*, VII, 4 (PG 3, 872). [16]Q. 18, a. 1. [Not in this volume]

faith, as a thing to be hoped for, since hope is always of the absent and the unseen.

Reply Obj. 4. *Substance* and *evidence*, as included in the definition of faith, do not denote various genera of faith, nor different acts, but different relationships of one act to different objects, as is clear from what has been said.

Reply Obj. 5. Evidence taken from the proper principles of a thing makes it apparent, whereas evidence taken from divine authority does not make a thing apparent in itself; and such is the evidence referred to in the definition of faith.

Second Article
Whether Faith Resides in the Intellect?

We proceed thus to the Second Article:—

Objection 1. It would seem that faith does not reside in the intellect as in its subject. For Augustine says that *faith resides in the believer's will.*[17] Now the will is a power distinct from the intellect. Therefore faith does not reside in the intellect.

Obj. 2. Further, The assent of faith to believe anything proceeds from the will obeying God. Therefore it seems that faith owes all its praise to obedience. But obedience is in the will. Therefore faith is in the will, and not in the intellect.

Obj. 3. Further, The intellect is either speculative or practical. Now faith is not in the speculative intellect, since this is not concerned with things to be sought or avoided, as is stated in *De Anima* iii.,[18] so that it is not a principle of operation, whereas *faith . . . worketh by charity (Gal.* v. 6). Likewise, neither is it in the practical intellect, the object of which is some true, contingent thing that can be made or done. For the object of faith is the eternal truth, as was shown above.[19] Therefore faith does not reside in the intellect.

On the contrary, Faith is succeeded by the heavenly vision, according to *1 Cor.* xiii. 12: *We see now through a glass in a dark manner; but then face to face.* Now vision is in the intellect. Therefore faith is likewise.

I answer that, Since faith is a virtue, its act must needs be perfect. Now for the perfection of an act proceeding from two active principles each of these principles must be perfect; for it is not possible for a thing to be sawn well, unless the sawyer possess the art, and the saw be well fitted for

---

[17]*De Praedest. Sanct.*, V (PL 44, 968).   [18]Aristotle, *De An.*, III, 9 (432b 28).
[19]Q. 1, a. 1.

sawing. Now, in a power of the soul, which is related to opposite objects, a disposition to act well is a habit, as was stated above.[20] Therefore an act that proceeds from two such powers must be perfected by a habit residing in each of them. But it has been stated above that to believe is an act of the intellect, inasmuch as the will moves it to assent.[21] And this act proceeds from the will and the intellect, both of which have a natural aptitude to be perfected by a habit, as we said above.[22] Consequently, if the act of faith is to be perfect, there needs to be a habit in the will as well as in the intellect: even as there needs to be the habit of prudence in the reason, besides the habit of temperance in the concupiscible part, in order that the act of that part be perfect. Now, to believe is immediately an act of the intellect, because the object of that act is *the true*, which pertains properly to the intellect. Consequently faith, which is the proper principle of that act, must needs reside in the intellect.

Reply Obj. 1. Augustine takes faith for the act of faith, which is said to depend on the believer's will in so far as his intellect assents to matters of faith at the command of the will.

Reply Obj. 2. Not only does the will need to be ready to obey, but also the intellect needs to be well disposed to follow the command of the will, even as the concupiscible part needs to be well disposed in order to follow the command of reason; and hence there needs to be a habit of virtue not only in the will commanding, but also in the intellect assenting.

Reply Obj. 3. Faith resides in the speculative intellect, as is clear from its object. But since this object, which is the First Truth, is the end of all our desires and actions, as Augustine proves,[23] it follows that faith worketh by charity just as *the speculative intellect becomes practical by extension.*[24]

Third Article
Whether Charity Is the Form of Faith?

We proceed thus to the Third Article:—

Objection 1. It would seem that charity is not the form of faith. For each thing derives its species from its form. When, therefore, two things are opposite members of a division, one cannot be the form of the other. Now faith and charity are stated to be opposite members of a division, as different species of virtue (*1 Cor.* xiii. 13). Therefore charity is not the form of faith.

---

[20]*S. T.*, I-II, q. 49, a. 4, ad 1; a. 2 and 3. [Not in this volume]   [21]A. 1; q. 2, a. 1, ad 3; a. 2 and 9.   [22]*S. T.*, I-II, q. 50, a. 4 and 5. [Not in this volume] [23]*De Trin.*, I, 8; 10 (PL 42, 831; 834).   [24]Aristotle, *De An.*, III, 10 (433a 15).

Obj. 2. Further, A form and the thing of which it is the form are in one subject, since out of them is produced what is one absolutely. Now faith is in the intellect, while charity is in the will. Therefore charity is not the form of faith.

Obj. 3. Further, The form of a thing is a principle thereof. Now obedience, rather than charity, seems to be the principle of believing on the part of the will, according to *Rom.* i. 5: *For obedience to the faith in all nations.* Therefore obedience, rather than charity, is the form of faith.

On the contrary, Each thing works through its form. Now faith works through charity. Therefore the love of charity is the form of faith.

I answer that, As appears from what has been said above, voluntary acts take their species from their end, which is the will's object.[25] Now that which gives a thing its species functions as a form in natural things. Therefore the form of any voluntary act is, in a manner, the end to which that act is directed, both because it takes its species from it, and because the mode of an action should correspond proportionately to the end. Now it is evident from what has been said that the act of faith is directed to the object of the will, *i.e.*, the good, as to its end; and this good which is the end of faith, viz., the divine Good, is the proper object of charity. Therefore charity is called the form of faith, in so far as the act of faith is perfected and formed by charity.

Reply Obj. 1. Charity is called the form of faith because it quickens the act of faith. Now nothing hinders one act from being quickened by different habits, and thus to be reduced to various species in a certain order, as was stated above when we were treating of human acts in general.[26]

Reply Obj. 2. This objection is true of an intrinsic form. But it is not thus that charity is the form of faith, but in the sense that it quickens the act of faith, as was explained above.

Reply Obj. 3. Even obedience, and hope likewise, and whatever other virtue might precede the act of faith, is quickened by charity, as we shall show further on.[27] Consequently, charity is spoken of as the form of faith.

Fourth Article
Whether Formless Faith Can Become Formed, or Formed Faith, Formless?

We proceed thus to the Fourth Article:—

Objection 1. It would seem that formless faith does not become

---

[25]*S. T.*, I-II, q. 1, a. 3; q. 18, a. 6. [Not in this volume]   [26]*S. T.*, I-II, q. 18, a. 7, ad 1. [Not in this volume]   [27]Q. 23, a. 8. [Not in this volume]

formed, or formed faith formless. For, according to *1 Cor.* xiii. 10, *when that which is perfect is come, that which is in part shall be done away.* Now formless faith is imperfect in comparison with formed faith. Therefore when formed faith comes, formless faith is done away, so that they are not one identical habit.

Obj. 2. Further, A dead thing does not become a living thing. Now formless faith is dead, according to *James* ii. 20: *Faith without works is dead.* Therefore formless faith cannot become formed.

Obj. 3. Further, God's grace, by its advent, has no less effect in a believer than in an unbeliever. Now by coming to an unbeliever it causes the habit of faith. Therefore when it comes to a believer, who hitherto had the habit of formless faith, it causes another habit of faith in him.

Obj. 4. Further, As Boethius says, *accidents cannot be altered.*[28] Now faith is an accident. Therefore the same faith cannot be at one time formed, and at another formless.

On the contrary, On the words, *Faith without works is dead* (*Jas.* ii. 20), the Gloss adds, *by which it lives once more.*[29] Therefore faith which was dead and formless becomes formed and living.

I answer that, There have been various opinions on this question. For some have said that formed and formless faith are distinct habits, but that when formed faith comes, formless faith is done away, and that, in like manner, when a man sins mortally, after having formed faith, a new habit of formless faith is infused into him by God.[30] But it seems unfitting that grace should deprive man of a gift of God by coming to him, and that a gift of God should be infused into man because of a mortal sin.

Consequently others have said that formed and formless faith are indeed distinct habits, but that, all the same, when formed faith comes, the habit of formless faith is not taken away, and that it remains together with the habit of formed faith in the same subject.[31] Yet again it seems unreasonable that the habit of formless faith should remain inactive in a person having formed faith.

We must therefore hold a different view, and say that formed and formless faith are one and the same habit. The reason is that a habit is diversified by that which pertains essentially to that habit. Now since faith is a perfection of the intellect, that pertains essentially to faith which pertains to the intellect. Now what pertains to the will does not pertain

---

[28]*In Cat. Arist.*, I (PL 64, 198).   [29]*Glossa interl.* (VI, 212v).   [30]William of Auxerre, *Summa Aurea*, III, tr. 15, q. 2 (208vb); q. 3 (209ra).   [31]Cf., St. Bonaventure, *In III Sent.*, d. xxiii, a. 2, q. 4 (III, 496).

directly to faith, so as to be able to diversify the habit of faith. But the distinction of formed from formless faith is in respect of something pertaining to the will, *i.e.*, charity, and not in respect of something pertaining to the intellect. Therefore formed and formless faith are not distinct habits.

Reply Obj. 1. The saying of the Apostle refers to those imperfect things from which imperfection is inseparable, for then, when the perfect comes, the imperfect must needs be done away. Thus with the advent of clear vision, faith is done away, because it is essentially of *the things that appear not*. When, however, imperfection is not inseparable from the imperfect thing, the same identical thing which was imperfect becomes perfect. Thus, childhood is not essential to man, and consequently the same identical subject, who was a child, becomes a man. Now formlessness is not essential to faith, but is accidental thereto, as was stated above. Therefore formless faith itself becomes formed.

Reply Obj. 2. That which makes an animal live is inseparable from an animal, because it is a form essential to it, viz., the soul; and consequently a dead thing cannot become a living thing, and a living and a dead thing differ specifically. On the other hand, that which gives faith its form, or makes it live, is not of the essence of faith. Hence there is no comparison.

Reply Obj. 3. Grace causes faith not only when faith begins anew to be in a man, but also as long as faith lasts. For it has been said above that God is always working man's justification, even as the sun is always lighting up the air.[32] Hence grace is not less effective when it comes to a believer than when it comes to an unbeliever; since it causes faith in both, in the former by confirming and perfecting it, in the latter by creating it anew.

We might also reply that it is accidental, namely, because of the disposition of the subject, that grace does not cause faith in one who has it already; just as, on the other hand, a second mortal sin does not take away grace from one who has already lost it through a previous mortal sin.

Reply Obj. 4. When formed faith becomes formless, faith is not changed, but its subject, the soul, which at one time has faith without charity, and at another time, with charity, is changed.

Fifth Article
Whether Faith Is a Virtue?

We proceed thus to the Fifth Article:—

Objection 1. It would seem that faith is not a virtue. For virtue is directed to the good, since *it is virtue that makes its subject good*, as the Phi-

---

[32]*S. T.*, I, q. 104, a. 1 [Not in this volume]; I-II, q. 109, a. 9. [Not in this volume]

losopher states.[33] But faith is directed to the true. Therefore faith is not a virtue.

Obj. 2. Further, Infused virtue is more perfect than acquired virtue. Now faith, because of its imperfection, is not placed among the acquired intellectual virtues, as the Philosopher states.[34] Much less, therefore, can it be considered an infused virtue.

Obj. 3. Further, formed and formless faith are of the same species, as was stated above. Now formless faith is not a virtue, since it is not connected with the other virtues. Therefore neither is formed faith a virtue.

Obj. 4. Further, The gratuitous graces and the fruits are distinct from the virtues. But faith is numbered among the gratuitous graces (1 *Cor.* xii. 9) and likewise among the fruits (*Gal.* v. 23). Therefore faith is not a virtue.

On the contrary, Man is justified by the virtues, since *justice is the whole of virtue* as the Philosopher states.[35] Now man is justified by faith, according to *Rom.* v. 1: *Being justified therefore by faith let us have peace,* etc. Therefore faith is a virtue.

I answer that, As was shown above, human virtue is the virtue by which human acts are rendered good.[36] Hence, any habit that is always the principle of a good act may be called a human virtue. Such a habit is formed faith. For since to believe is an act of the intellect assenting to the truth at the command of the will, two things are required that this act may be perfect. One is that the intellect should infallibly tend to its object, which is the true, while the other is that the act should be infallibly directed to the last end, because of which the will assents to the true; and both of these are to be found in the act of formed faith. For it belongs to the very nature of faith that the intellect should ever tend to the true, since nothing false can be the object of faith, as was proved above,[37] while the effect of charity, which is the form of faith, is that the soul always has its will directed to a good end. Therefore formed faith is a virtue.

On the other hand, formless faith is not a virtue, because, though the act of formless faith is duly perfect on the part of the intellect, it has not its due perfection on the part of the will. So, too, if temperance be in the concupiscible part without prudence being in the rational part, temperance is not a virtue, as was stated above,[38] because the act of temperance requires both an act of reason, and an act of the concupiscible part; even as the act of faith requires an act of the will, and an act of the intellect.

---

[33]*Eth.*, II, 6 (1106a 15; a 22).   [34]*Op. cit.*, VI, 3 (1139b 15).   [35]*Op. cit.*, V, 1 (1130a 9).   [36]*S. T.*, I-II, q. 56, a. 3. [Not in this volume]   [37]Q. 1, a. 3. [38]*S. T.*, I-II, q. 65, a. 1. [Not in this volume]

Reply Obj. 1. The true is itself the good of the intellect, since it is its perfection, and consequently faith has a relation to some good in so far as it directs the intellect to the true. Furthermore, it has a relation to the good considered as the object of the will, inasmuch as it is formed by charity.

Reply Obj. 2. The faith of which the Philosopher speaks is based on human reasoning in a conclusion which does not follow of necessity from its premises, and which is subject to be false. Hence such a faith is not a virtue. On the other hand, the faith of which we are speaking is based on the divine truth, which is infallible, and consequently its object cannot be anything false; so that faith of this kind can be a virtue.

Reply Obj. 3. Formed and formless faith do not differ specifically, as though they belonged to different species. But they differ as perfect and imperfect within the same species. Hence formless faith, being imperfect, does not satisfy the conditions of a perfect virtue, for *virtue is a kind of perfection.*[39]

Reply Obj. 4. Some say that the faith which is numbered among the gratuitous graces is formless faith.[40] But this is said without reason, since the gratuitous graces, which are mentioned in that passage, are not common to all the members of the Church. Hence the Apostle there says: *There are diversities of graces;* and again: *To one is given* this grace and *to another* that. Now formless faith is common to all the members of the Church, because its formlessness is not part of its substance, if we consider it as a gratuitous gift. We must therefore say that, in that passage, faith denotes a certain excellency of faith, for instance, *constancy in faith,* according to the Gloss, or the *word of faith.*[41]

Faith is numbered among the fruits in so far as it gives a certain pleasure in its act by reason of its certainty; and so the *Gloss* on the fifth chapter to the *Galatians,* where the fruits are enumerated, explains faith as being *certainty about the unseen.*[42]

Sixth Article
Whether Faith Is One Virtue?

We proceed thus to the Sixth Article:—

---

[39]Aristotle, *Phys.,* VII, 3 (246a 13; 247a 2).   [40]St. Bonaventure, *In III Sent.,* d. xxiii, a. 2, q. 4 (III, 494); St. Albert, *In III Sent.,* d. xxiii, a. 5, ad 5; a. 9 (XXVIII, 414; 421).   [41]*Glossa interl.,* super *I Cor.,* XII, 9 (VI, 52v).   [42]*Glossa interl.,* super *Gal.,* V, 22 (VI, 87v); Peter Lombard, *In Gal.,* super V, 22 (PL 192, 160).

Objection 1. It would seem that faith is not one. For just as faith is a gift of God, according to *Ephes.* ii. 8, so also wisdom and science are numbered among God's gifts, according to *Isa.* xi. 2. Now wisdom and science differ in this, that wisdom is about eternal things, and science about temporal things, as Augustine states.[43] Since, then, faith is about eternal things, and also about some temporal things, it seems that faith is not one virtue, but divided into several parts.

Obj. 2. Further, Confession is an act of faith, as was stated above.[44] Now confession of faith is not one and the same for all, since what we confess as past the fathers of old confessed as yet to come, as appears from *Isa.* vii. 14: *Behold a virgin shall conceive.* Therefore faith is not one.

Obj. 3. Further, Faith is common to all believers in Christ. But one accident cannot be in many subjects. Therefore all cannot have one faith.

On the contrary, The Apostle says (*Ephes.* iv. 5): *One Lord, one faith.*

I answer that, If we take faith as a habit, we can consider it in two ways. First, on the part of the object, and thus there is one faith. For the formal object of faith is the First Truth, by adhering to which we believe whatever is contained in faith. Secondly, on the part of the subject, and thus faith is diversified according as it is in various subjects. Now it is evident that faith, like any other habit, takes its species from the formal aspect of its object, but is individuated by its subject. Hence if we take faith for the habit by which we believe, it is one specifically, but differs numerically according to its various subjects. If, on the other hand, we take faith for that which is believed, then, again, there is one faith, since what is believed by all is one and the same thing; for though the things believed, which all agree in believing, be diverse from one another, yet they are all reduced to one.

Reply Obj. 1. Temporal matters, which are proposed to be believed, do not belong to the object of faith, except in relation to something eternal, viz., the First Truth, as was stated above.[45] Hence there is one faith of things both temporal and eternal. It is different with wisdom and science, which consider temporal and eternal matters under their proper natures.

Reply Obj. 2. This difference of past and future arises, not from any difference in the thing believed, but from the different relationships of believers to the one thing believed, as we have likewise mentioned above.[46]

Reply Obj. 3. This objection considers the numerical diversity of faith.

---

[43]*De Trin.*, XII, 14; 15 (PL 42, 1009; 1012).   [44]Q. 3, a. 1.   [45]Q. 1, a. 1.
[46]*S. T.*, I–II, q. 103, a. 4. [Not in this volume]

Seventh Article
Whether Faith Is the First of the Virtues?

We proceed thus to the Seventh Article:—

Objection 1. It would seem that faith is not the first of the virtues. For the *Gloss* on *Luke* xii. 4 (*I say to you My friends*) says that *fortitude is the foundation of faith.*[47] Now the foundation precedes that which is founded thereon. Therefore faith is not the first of the virtues.

Obj. 2. Further, The *Gloss* on *Psalm* xxxvi. 3 (*Be not emulous*) says that hope *leads on to faith.*[48] Now hope is a virtue, as we shall state further on.[49] Therefore faith is not the first of the virtues.

Obj. 3. Further, It was stated above that the intellect of the believer is moved, out of obedience to God, to assent to what belongs to faith. Now obedience also is a virtue. Therefore faith is not the first virtue.

Obj. 4. Further, Not formless but formed faith is the foundation, as the *Gloss* remarks on *1 Cor.* iii. 11.[50] Now faith is formed by charity, as was stated above. Therefore it is owing to charity that faith is the foundation; so that charity is the foundation even more than faith is (for the foundation is the first part of a building), and consequently it seems to precede faith.

Obj. 5. Further, The order of habits is taken from the order of acts. Now in the act of faith, the act of the will, which is perfected by charity, precedes the act of the intellect, which is perfected by faith, as the cause which precedes its effect. Therefore charity precedes faith. Therefore faith is not the first of the virtues.

On the contrary, The Apostle says (*Heb.* xi. 1) that *faith is the substance of things to be hoped for.* Now the substance of a thing has the nature of that which is first. Therefore faith is first among the virtues.

I answer that, One thing can precede another in two ways: first, essentially; secondly, by accident. Essentially faith precedes all other virtues. For since the end is the principle in matters of action, as was stated above,[51] the theological virtues, the object of which is the last end, must needs precede all the others. Now the last end must of necessity be present in the intellect before it is present in the will, since the will has no inclination for anything except in so far as it is apprehended by the intel-

---

[47]*Glossa ordin.* (V. 157A).—St. Ambrose, *In Luc.*, super XII, 4 (PL 15, 1817). [48]*Glossa interl.* (III, 136v).   [49]Q. 17, a. 1. [Not in this volume]   [50]*Glossa ordin.* (VI, 37E).—Cf. St. Augustine, *De Fide et Oper.*, XVI (PL 40, 215). [51]*S. T.*, I-II, q. 13, a. 3 [Not in this volume]; q. 34, a. 4, ad 1 [Not in this volume]; q. 57, a. 4. [Not in this volume]

lect. Hence, since the last end is present in the will by hope and charity, and in the intellect, by faith, the first of all the virtues must, of necessity, be faith, because natural knowledge cannot reach God as the object of heavenly beatitude, which is the aspect under which hope and charity tend towards Him.

On the other hand, some virtues can precede faith accidentally. For an accidental cause precedes its effect accidentally. Now that which removes an obstacle is a kind of accidental cause, according to the Philosopher;[52] and in this sense certain virtues may be said to precede faith accidentally, in so far as they remove obstacles to belief. Thus fortitude removes the inordinate fear that hinders faith; humility removes pride, whereby a man refuses to submit himself to the truth of faith. The same may be said of some other virtues, although there are no real virtues, unless faith be presupposed, as Augustine states.[53]

This suffices for the *Reply* to the *First Objection.*

Reply Obj. 2. Hope cannot lead to faith absolutely. For one cannot hope to obtain eternal happiness, unless one believes this possible, since hope does not tend to the impossible, as was stated above.[54] It is, however, possible for one to be led by hope to persevere in faith, or to hold firmly to faith; and it is in this sense that hope is said to lead to faith.

Reply Obj. 3. Obedience is twofold. For sometimes it denotes the inclination of the will to fulfill God's commandments. In this way, it is not a special virtue, but a general condition of every virtue, since all acts of virtue come under the precepts of the divine law, as was stated above.[55] In this sense, obedience is requisite for faith. In another way, obedience denotes an inclination to fulfill the commandments considered as a duty. In this way, it is a special virtue, and a part of justice; for a man does his duty towards his superior when he obeys him. In this sense, obedience follows faith, whereby man knows that God is his superior, Whom he must obey.

Reply Obj. 4. To be a foundation, a thing requires not only to come first, but also to be connected with the other parts of the building; since the building would not be founded on it unless the other parts adhered to it. Now the connecting bond of the spiritual edifice is charity, according to *Coloss.* iii. 14: *Above all . . . things have charity which is the bond of perfection.* Consequently, faith without charity cannot be the foundation; and yet it does not follow that charity precedes faith.

---

[52]*Phys.* VIII, 4 (255b 24).   [53]*Contra Julian.*, IV, 3 (PL 44, 750).   [54]*S. T.*, I-II, q. 40, a. 1. [Not in this volume]   [55]*S. T.*, I-II, q. 100, a. 2. [Not in this volume]

Reply Obj. 5. Some act of the will is required before faith, but not an act of the will quickened by charity. This latter act presupposes faith, because the will cannot tend to God with perfect love unless the intellect possesses a right faith about Him.

Eighth Article
Whether Faith Is More Certain than Science and the Other Intellectual Virtues?

We proceed thus to the Eighth Article:—

Objection 1. It would seem that faith is not more certain than science and the other intellectual virtues. For doubt is opposed to certitude, and so a thing would seem to be the more certain, through being less doubtful, just as a thing is the whiter, the less it has of an admixture of black. Now understanding, science and also wisdom are free of any doubt about their objects; whereas the believer may sometimes suffer a movement of doubt, and doubt about matters of faith. Therefore faith is no more certain than the intellectual virtues.

Obj. 2. Further, Sight is more certain than hearing. But *faith is through hearing* according to *Rom.* x. 17; whereas understanding, science and wisdom include some kind of intellectual vision. Therefore science and understanding are more certain than faith.

Obj. 3. Further, In matters concerning the intellect, the more perfect is the more certain. Now understanding is more perfect than faith, since faith is the way to understanding, according to another version of *Isa.* vii. 9: *If you will not believe, you shall not understand;*[56] and Augustine says that *faith is strengthened by science.*[57] Therefore it seems that science or understanding is more certain than faith.

On the contrary, The Apostle says (*1 Thess.* ii. 15): *When you had received of us the word of the hearing, i.e.,* by faith . . . *you received it not as the word of men, but, as it is indeed, the word of God.* Now nothing is more certain than the word of God. Therefore science is not more certain than faith, nor is anything else.

I answer that, As was stated above, two of the intellectual virtues are about contingent matter, viz., prudence and art;[58] and to these faith is preferable in point of certitude by reason of its matter, since it is about eternal things, which never change. But the other three intellectual virtues, viz., wisdom, science and understanding, are about necessary things,

---

[56]The Septuagint.   [57]*De Trin.*, XIV, 1 (PL 42, 1037).   [58]*S. T.*, I-II, q. 57, a. 4, ad 2; a. 5, ad 3. [Not in this volume]

as was stated above.[59] But it must be observed that wisdom, science and understanding may be taken in two ways: first, as intellectual virtues, according to the Philosopher;[60] secondly, for gifts of the Holy Ghost. If we consider them in the first way, we must note that certitude can be looked at in two ways. First, on the part of its cause, and thus a thing which has a more certain cause is itself more certain. In this way, faith is more certain than these three virtues because it is founded on the divine truth, whereas the aforesaid three virtues are based on human reason. Secondly, certitude may be considered on the part of the subject, and thus the more a man's intellect lays hold of a thing, the more certain it is. In this way, faith is less certain, because matters of faith are above the human intellect, whereas the objects of the aforesaid three virtues are not. Since, however, a thing is judged absolutely according to its cause, but relatively, according to a disposition on the part of the subject, it follows that faith is more certain absolutely, while the others are more certain relatively, *i.e.*, for us. Likewise, if these three be taken as gifts received in this present life, they are related to faith as to their principle, which they presuppose; so that in this way also faith is more certain.

Reply Obj. 1. This doubt is not on the side of the cause of faith, but on our side, in so far as we do not fully grasp with our intellect what belongs to faith.

Reply Obj. 2. Other things being equal, sight is more certain than hearing; but if the person from whom we hear surpasses greatly the seer's sight, hearing is more certain than sight. Thus a man of little science is more certain about what he hears on the authority of an expert in science, than about what is apparent to him according to his own reason; and much more is a man certain about what he hears from God, Who cannot be mistaken, than about what he sees with his own reason, which can be mistaken.

Reply Obj. 3. The gifts of understanding and science are more perfect than the knowledge of faith in the point of their greater clearness, but not in regard to more certain adhesion. For the whole certitude of the gifts of understanding and science arises from the certitude of faith, even as the certitude of the knowledge of conclusions arises from the certitude of the principles. But in so far as science, wisdom and understanding are intellectual virtues, they are based upon the natural light of reason, which falls short of the certitude of God's word, on which faith is founded.

---

[59]*S. T.*, I–II, q. 57, a. 5, ad 3. [Not in this volume]   [60]*Eth.*, VI, 3 (1139b 15).

Question 5
Concerning Those Who Have Faith
(*In Four Articles*)

We must now consider those who have faith, under which head there are four points of inquiry: (1) Whether there was faith in the angels, or in man, in their original state? (2) Whether the demons have faith? (3) Whether those heretics who err in one article have faith in the others? (4) Whether, among those who have faith, one has it more than another?

First Article
Whether There Was Faith in the Angels,
or in Man, in Their Original State?

We proceed thus to the First Article:—

Objection 1. It would seem that there was no faith, either in the angels or in man, in their original state. For Hugh of S. Victor says in his *Sentences* that *man cannot see God or things that are in God, because the eye of contemplation is closed in him.*[1] Now the angels, in their original state, before they were either confirmed in grace, or had fallen from it, had their eye opened to contemplation, since *they saw things in the Word*, according to Augustine.[2] Likewise, the first man, while in the state of innocence, appears to have had his eye open to contemplation; for Hugh of S. Victor says that *in his original state man knew his Creator, not by the mere outward perception of hearing, but by inward inspiration, not as believers now seek an absent God by faith, but by seeing Him clearly present to his contemplation.*[3] Therefore there was no faith in the angels and man in their original state.

Obj. 2. Further, The knowledge of faith is dark and obscure, according to *1 Cor.* xiii. 12: *We see now through a glass in a dark manner.* Now in their original state there was no obscurity either in the angels or in man, because obscurity is a punishment of sin. Therefore there could be no faith in the angels or in man, in their original state.

Obj. 3. Further, The Apostle says (*Rom.* x. 17) *that faith . . . cometh by hearing, and hearing by the word of God.* Now this could not apply to the angels and man in their original state, for then there was no hearing from another. Therefore, in that state, there was no faith either in man or in the angels.

---

[1]*De Sacram.*, I, x, 2 (PL 176, 330).   [2]*De Genesi ad Littl*, II, 8 (PL 34, 270).
[3]*De Sacram.*, I, vi, 14 (PL 176, 271).

On the contrary, It is written (*Heb.* xi. 6): *He that cometh to God must believe that He is, and is a rewarder to them that seek Him.* Now the original state of the angels and of man was one of approach to God. Therefore they had need of faith.

I answer that, Some say that there was no faith in the angels before they were confirmed in grace or fell from it, and in man before he sinned, by reason of the manifest contemplation that they had of divine things.[4] Since, however, *faith is the evidence of things that appear not,* according to the Apostle (*Heb.* xi. 1), and since *by faith we believe what we see not,* according to Augustine,[5] that manifestation alone excludes faith which renders apparent or seen the principal object of faith. Now the principal object of faith is the First Truth, the vision of which gives the happiness of heaven and takes the place of faith. Consequently, since the angels before their confirmation in grace, and man before sin, did not possess the happiness whereby God is seen in His essence, it is evident that the knowledge they possessed was not such as to exclude faith.

It follows, then, that the absence of faith in them could be explained only by their being altogether ignorant of the object of faith. And if man and the angels were created in a purely natural state, as some hold,[6] perhaps one might hold that there was no faith in the angels before their confirmation in grace, or in man before sin, because the knowledge of faith surpasses not only a man's, but even an angel's natural knowledge about God. Since, however, we have stated in the First Part that man and the angels were created with the gift of grace,[7] we must needs say that there was in them a certain beginning of hoped-for happiness, by reason of grace received but not yet consummated, which happiness was begun in their will by hope and charity, and in the intellect by faith, as stated above.[8] Consequently we must hold that the angels had faith before they were confirmed, and man, before he sinned.

Nevertheless we must observe that, in the object of faith, there is something formal, as it were, namely, the First Truth, surpassing all the natural knowledge of a creature, and something material, namely, the thing to which we assent while adhering to the First Truth. With regard to the former, before obtaining the happiness to come, faith is common to

---

[4]*Ibid.*—Cf. Peter Lombard, *Sent.*, IV, i, 5 (II, 747).   [5]*Tract.* XL, super *Ioann.* VIII, 32 (PL 35, 1690); *Quaest. Evang.*, II, 39, super *Luc.* XVII, 5 (PL 35, 1352).   [6]William of Auxerre, *Summa Aurea*, II, tr. 1, ch. 1 (fol. 35rb); St. Bonaventure, *In II Sent.*, d. xxix, a. 2, q. 2 (II, 703).—Cf. *S. T.*, I, q. 95, a. 1. [Not in this volume]   [7]*S. T.*, I, q. 62, a. 3 [Not in this volume]; q. 95, a. 1. [Not in this volume]   [8]Q. 4, a. 7.

all who have knowledge of God, by adhering to the First Truth; whereas with regard to the things which are proposed as the material object of faith, some are believed by one, and known manifestly by another, even in the present state, as we have shown above.[9] In this respect, too, it may be said that the angels before being confirmed, and man, before sin, possessed manifest knowledge about certain points in the divine mysteries, which now we cannot know except by believing them.

Reply Obj. 1. Although the words of Hugh of S. Victor are those of a master, and have the force of an authority, yet it may be said that the contemplation which removes the need of faith is heavenly contemplation, whereby the supernatural truth is seen in its essence. Now the angels did not possess this contemplation before they were confirmed, nor did man before he sinned; and yet their contemplation was of a higher order than ours, for by its means they approached nearer to God, and had manifest knowledge of more of the divine effects and mysteries than we can have knowledge of. Hence faith was not in them so that they sought an absent God as we seek Him, since by the light of wisdom He was more present to them than He is to us; although He was not so present to them as He is to the Blessed by the light of glory.

Reply Obj. 2. There was no obscurity of sin or punishment in the original state of man and the angels, but there was a certain natural obscurity in the human and angelic intellect in so far as every creature is darkness in comparison with the immensity of the divine light; and this obscurity suffices for the notion of faith.

Reply Obj. 3. In the original state there was no hearing anything from man speaking outwardly, but there was from God inspiring inwardly; and thus the prophets heard, according to the *Psalm* (lxxxiv. 9): *I will hear what the Lord God will speak in me.*

Second Article
Whether in the Demons There Is Faith?

We proceed thus to the Second Article:—

Objection 1. It would seem that the demons have no faith. For Augustine says that *faith depends on the believer's will;*[10] and this is a good will, since by it man wishes to believe in God. Since then no deliberate will of the demons is good, as was stated above,[11] it seems that in the demons there is no faith.

---

[9]Q. 1, a. 5.   [10]*De Praedest. Sanct.*, V (PL 44, 968).   [11]*S. T.*, I, q. 64, a. 2, ad 5. [Not in this volume]

Obj. 2. Further, Faith is a gift of divine grace, according to *Ephes.* ii. 8: *By grace you are saved through faith, . . . for it is the gift of God.* Now according to the *Gloss* on *Osee* iii. 1 (*They look to strange gods, and love the husks of the grapes*), the demons lost their gifts of grace by sinning.[12] Therefore faith did not remain in the demons after they sinned.

Obj. 3. Further, Unbelief would seem to be graver than other sins, as Augustine observes on *John* xv. 22 (*If I had not come and spoken to them, they would not have sin; but now they have no excuse for their sin*).[13] Now the sin of unbelief is in some men. Consequently, if the demons have faith, some men would be guilty of a sin graver than that of the demons, which seems unreasonable. Therefore in the demons there is no faith.

On the contrary, It is written (*Jas.* ii. 19): *The devils . . . believe and tremble.*

In answer that, As we have stated above, the believer's intellect assents to that which he believes, not because he sees it either in itself, or by resolving it to first self-evident principles, but because his will commands his intellect to assent.[14] Now, that the will moves the intellect to assent may be due to two causes. First, by the fact that the will is ordered towards the good; and in this way, to believe is a praiseworthy action. Secondly, because the intellect is convinced that it ought to believe what is said, though that conviction is not based on the evidence in the thing said. Thus, if a prophet, while preaching the word of God, were to foretell something, and were to give a sign, by raising a dead person to life, the intellect of a witness would be convinced so as to recognize clearly that God, Who lieth not, was speaking, although the thing itself foretold would not be evident in itself and consequently the notion of faith would not be removed.

Accordingly, we must say that faith is commended in the first sense in the faithful of Christ. And in this way faith is not in the demons, but only in the second way, for they see many evident signs, whereby they recognize that the teaching of the Church is from God, although they do not see the things themselves that the Church teaches, for instance, that there are three Persons in God, and so forth.

Reply Obj. 1. The demons are, in a way, compelled to believe by the evidence of signs, and so their will deserves no praise for their belief.

Reply Obj. 2. Faith, which is a gift of grace, inclines man to believe by giving him a certain affection for the good, even when that faith is form-

---

[12]*Glossa ordin.* (IV, 336E).—St. Jerome, *In Osee*, super III, 1 (PL 25, 883).
[13]*Tract.* LXXXIX, super *Ioann.* XV, 22 (PL 35, 1856).   [14]Q. 1, a. 4; q. 2, a. 1, ad 3; q. 4, a. 1 and 2.

less. Consequently, the faith which the demons have is not a gift of grace. Rather are they compelled to believe through their natural intellectual acumen.

Reply Obj. 3. The very fact that the signs of faith are so evident, that the demons are compelled to believe, is displeasing to them, so that their malice is by no means diminished by their belief.

Third Article
Whether a Man Who Disbelieves One Article of Faith Can Have Formless Faith in the Other Articles?

We proceed thus to the Third Article:—

Objection 1. It would seem that a heretic who disbelieves one article of faith can have formless faith in the other articles. For the natural intellect of a heretic is not more able than that of a Catholic. Now a Catholic's intellect needs the aid of the gift of faith in order to believe any article whatever of faith. Therefore it seems that heretics cannot believe any articles of faith without the gift of formless faith.

Obj. 2. Further, Just as faith contains many articles, so does one science, viz., geometry, contain many conclusions. Now a man may possess the science of geometry as to some geometrical conclusions, and yet be ignorant of other conclusions. Therefore a man can believe some articles of faith, without believing the others.

Obj. 3. Further, Just as man obeys God in believing the articles of faith, so does he also in keeping the commandments of the Law. Now a man can obey some commandments, and disobey others. Therefore he can believe some articles, and disbelieve others.

On the contrary, Just as mortal sin is contrary to charity, so is disbelief in one article of faith contrary to faith. Now charity does not remain in a man after one mortal sin. Therefore neither does faith, after a man disbelieves one article.

I answer that, Neither formed nor formless faith remains in a heretic who disbelieves one article of faith. The reason for this is that the species of every habit depends on the formal nature of the object, without which the species of the habit cannot remain. Now the formal object of faith is the First Truth, as manifested in Holy Scripture and the teaching of the Church, which proceeds from the First Truth. Consequently, whoever does not adhere, as to an infallible and divine rule, to the teaching of the Church, which proceeds from the First Truth manifested in Holy Scripture, has not the habit of faith, but holds that which is of faith otherwise than by faith. So, too, it is evident that a man whose mind holds a conclusion, without knowing how it is proved, has not scientific knowledge, but merely an opinion about it. Now it is manifest that he who adheres to the teaching of the Church, as to an infallible rule, assents to whatever the Church teaches. Otherwise, if, of the things taught by the Church, he holds what he chooses to hold, and rejects what he chooses to reject, he no longer adheres to the teaching of the Church as to an infallible rule, but to his own will. Hence it is evident that a heretic, who obstinately disbelieves one article of faith, is not prepared to follow the teaching of the Church in all things; but if he is not obstinate, he is no longer in heresy but only in error. Therefore it is clear that such a heretic with regard to one article has no faith in the other articles, but only a kind of opinion in accordance with his own will.

Reply Obj. 1. A heretic does not hold the other articles of faith, about which he does not err, in the same way as one of the faithful does, namely, by adhering absolutely to the divine truth, because in order to do so a man needs the help of the habit of faith; but he holds the things that are of faith by his own will and judgment.

Reply Obj. 2. The various conclusions of a science have their respective means of demonstration, one of which may be known without another, so that we may know some conclusions of a science without knowing the others. On the other hand, faith adheres to all the articles of faith by reason of one means, viz., because of the First Truth proposed to us in the Scriptures understood correctly according to the teaching of the Church. Hence whoever abandons this means is altogether lacking in faith.

Reply Obj. 3. The various precepts of the Law may be referred either to their respective proximate motives, and thus one can be kept without another; or to their primary motive, which is perfect obedience to God, in which a man fails whenever he breaks one commandment, according to *James* ii. 10: *Whosoever shall . . . offend in one point is become guilty of all.*

Fourth Article
Whether Faith Can Be Greater in One Man than in Another?

We proceed thus to the Fourth Article:—

Objection 1. It would seem that faith cannot be greater in one man than in another. For the quantity of a habit is taken from its object. Now whoever has faith believes everything that is of faith, since by failing in one point a man loses his faith altogether, as was stated above. Therefore it seems that faith cannot be greater in one than in another.

Obj. 2. Further, Those things which consist in a maximum cannot be *more* or *less*. Now the notion of faith consists in a maximum because it requires that man should adhere to the First Truth above all things. Therefore faith cannot be *more* or *less*.

Obj. 3. Further, Faith is to knowledge by grace as the understanding of principles is to natural knowledge, since the articles of faith are the first principles of knowledge by grace, as was shown above.[15] Now the understanding of principles is possessed in equal degree by all men. Therefore faith is possessed in equal degree by all the faithful.

On the contrary, Wherever we find great and little, there we find more and less. Now in faith we find great and little, for Our Lord said to Peter (*Matt.* xiv. 31): *O thou of little faith, why didst thou doubt?* And to the woman he said (*Matt.* xv. 28): *O woman, great is thy faith!* Therefore faith can be greater in one than in another.

I answer that, As was stated above, the quantity of a habit may be considered from two points of view:[16] first, on the part of the object; secondly, on the part of its participation by the subject. The object of faith may be considered in two ways: first, according to its formal aspect; secondly, according to the material object which is proposed to be believed. Now the formal object of faith is one and simple, namely the First Truth, as was stated above.[17] Hence in this respect there is no diversity of faith among believers, but it is specifically one in all, as was stated above.[18] But the things which are proposed as the matter of our belief are many and can be received more or less explicitly; and in this respect one man can believe explicitly more things than another, so that faith can be greater in one man because of the greater explicitness of faith.

If, on the other hand, we consider faith from the point of view of its participation by the subject, this happens in two ways, since the act of faith proceeds both from the intellect and from the will, as was stated above.[19] Consequently a man's faith may be described as being greater, in one way, on the part of his intellect, because of its greater certitude and firmness, and, in another way, on the part of his will, because of his greater promptitude, devotion or confidence.

Reply Obj. 1. A man who obstinately disbelieves a thing that is of faith has not the habit of faith, and yet he who does not explicitly believe all, while he is prepared to believe all, has that habit. In this respect, one man has greater faith than another, on the part of the object, in so far as he believes more things, as was stated above.

---

[15]Q. 1, a. 7.   [16]*S. T.*, I-II, q. 52, a. 1 and 2 [Not in this volume]; q. 112, a. 4. [Not in this volume]   [17]Q. 1, a. 1.   [18]Q. 4, a. 6.   [19]A. 2; q. 1, a. 4; q. 2, a. 1, ad 3; a. 9; q. 4, a. 1 and 2.

Reply Obj. 2. It is of the nature of faith that one should give the first place to the First Truth. But among those who do this, some submit to it with greater certitude and devotion than others; and in this way faith is greater in one than in another.

Reply Obj. 3. The understanding of principles follows from man's very nature, which is equally shared by all; whereas faith follows from the gift of grace, which is not equally in all, as was explained above.[20] Hence the comparison fails.

Nevertheless, the virtual power of principles is more known to one than to another, according to the greater capacity of intellect.

Question 6
On the Cause of Faith
(*In Two Articles*)

We must now consider the cause of faith, under which head there are two points of inquiry: (1) Whether faith is infused into man by God? (2) Whether formless faith is a gift of God?

First Article
Whether Faith Is Infused into Man by God?

We proceed thus to the First Article:—

Objection 1. It would seem that faith is not infused into man by God. For Augustine says that *science begets faith in us, and nourishes, defends and strengthens it.*[1] Now those things which science begets in us seem to be acquired rather than infused. Therefore faith does not seem to be in us by divine infusion.

Obj. 2. Further, That to which man attains by hearing and seeing seems to be acquired by him. Now man attains to belief both by seeing miracles and by hearing the teachings of faith; for it is written (*Jo.* iv. 53): *The father . . . knew that it was at the same hour, that Jesus said to him, Thy son liveth; and himself believed, and his whole house;* and (*Rom.* x. 17) it is said that *faith is through hearing.* Therefore man attains to faith by acquiring it.

---

[20]*S. T.*, I-II, q. 112, a. 4. [Not in this volume]

[1]*De Trin.*, XIV, 1 (PL 42, 1037).

Obj. 3. Further, That which depends on a man's will can be acquired by him. *But faith depends on the believer's will,* according to Augustine.[2] Therefore faith can be acquired by man.

On the contrary, It is written (*Ephes.* ii. 8, 9): *By grace you are saved through faith, and that not of yourselves . . . that no man may glory . . . for it is the gift of God.*

I answer that, Two things are requisite for faith. First, that the things which are of faith should be proposed to man; and this is necessary in order that man believe something explicitly. The second thing requisite for faith is the assent of the believer to the things which are proposed to him. Accordingly, as regards the first of these, faith must needs be from God. For the things which are of faith surpass human reason, and hence they do not come to man's knowledge, unless God reveals them. To some, indeed, they are revealed by God immediately, as those things which were revealed to the Apostles and prophets, while to some they are proposed by God in sending preachers of the faith, according to *Rom.* x. 15: *How shall they preach, unless they be sent?*

As regards the second, viz., man's assent to the things which are of faith, we may observe a twofold cause, one of external inducement, such as seeing a miracle, or being persuaded by someone to embrace the faith; neither of which is a sufficient cause, since of those who see the same miracle, or who hear the same sermon, some believe, and some do not. Hence we must assert another and internal cause, which moves man inwardly to assent to what belongs to faith.

The Pelagians held that this cause was nothing else than man's free choice,[3] and consequently they said that the beginning of faith is from ourselves, inasmuch as, namely, it is in our power to be ready to assent to the things which are of faith, but that the consummation of faith is from God, Who proposes to us the things we have to believe. But this is false, for since, by assenting to what belongs to faith, man is raised above his nature, this must needs come to him from some supernatural principle moving him inwardly; and this is God. Therefore faith, as regards the assent which is the chief act of faith, is from God moving man inwardly by grace.

Reply Obj. 1. Science begets and nourishes faith by way of external persuasion afforded by some science; but the chief and proper cause of faith is that which moves man inwardly to assent.

---

[2]*De Praedest. Sanct.,* V (PL 44, 968). (Denzinger, no. 178).

[3]Cf. *Conc. Arausic.,* II (529), can. 5

Reply Obj. 2. This argument likewise refers to the cause that proposes outwardly the things that are of faith, or persuades man to believe by words or deeds.

Reply Obj. 3. To believe does indeed depend on the will of the believer; but man's will needs to be prepared by God with grace, in order that he may be raised to things which are above his nature, as was stated above.

Second Article
Whether Formless Faith Is a Gift of God?

We proceed thus to the Second Article:—

Objection 1. It would seem that formless faith is not a gift of God. For it is written (*Deut.* xxxii. 4) that *the works of God are perfect.* Now formless faith is something imperfect. Therefore it is not the work of God.

Obj. 2. Further, Just as an act is said to be deformed through lacking its due form, so too faith is called formless when it lacks the form due to it. Now the deformed act of sin is not from God, as was stated above.[4] Therefore neither is formless faith from God.

Obj. 3. Further, Whomsoever God heals, He heals wholly; for it is written (*Jo.* vii. 23): *If a man receives circumcision on the Sabbath-day, that the law of Moses may not be broken, are you angry at Me because I have healed the whole man on the Sabbath-day?* Now faith heals man from unbelief. Therefore whoever receives from God the gift of faith is at the same time healed from all his sins. But this is not done except by formed faith. Therefore formed faith alone is a gift of God, and consequently formless faith is not from God.

On the contrary, A *Gloss* on 1 *Cor.* xiii. 2 says that *the faith which lacks charity is a gift of God.*[5] Now this is formless faith. Therefore formless faith is a gift of God.

I answer that, Formlessness is a privation. Now it must be noted that privation sometimes belongs to the notion of a species, whereas sometimes it does not, but supervenes in a thing already possessed of its proper species. Thus privation of the due equilibrium of the humors belongs to the nature of the species of sickness, while darkness does not belong to the nature of the species of a diaphanous body, but supervenes in it. Since, therefore, when we assign the cause of a thing, we intend to assign the cause of that thing as existing in its proper species, it follows that what is not the cause of a privation cannot be assigned as the cause of the thing to

---

[4]*S. T.*, I-II, q. 79, a. 2. [Not in this volume]   [5]Peter Lombard, *Sent.*, III, xxiii, 4 (II, 657); *In I Cor.*, super XIII, 2 (PL 191, 1659).—Cf. *Glossa ordin.* (VI, 54A).

which that privation belongs as belonging to the nature of its species. For we cannot assign, as the cause of a sickness, something which is not the cause of a disturbance in the humors; though we can assign, as cause of a diaphanous body, something which is not the cause of the darkness, which does not belong to the nature of the diaphanous body. Now the formlessness of faith does not belong to the nature of the species of faith, since faith is said to be formless through lack of an extrinsic form, as was stated above.[6] Consequently, the cause of formless faith is that which is the cause of faith absolutely so called; and this is God, as was stated above. It follows, therefore, that formless faith is a gift of God.

Reply Obj. 1. Formless faith, though it is not absolutely perfect with the perfection of a virtue, is, nevertheless, perfect with a perfection that suffices for the nature of faith.

Reply Obj. 2. The deformity of an act belongs to the nature of the species of an act, considered as a moral act, as was stated above;[7] for an act is said to be deformed through being deprived of an intrinsic form, viz., the due commensuration of the act's circumstances. Hence we cannot say that God is the cause of a deformed act, for He is not the cause of its deformity, though He is the cause of the act as an act.

We may also reply that deformity denotes not only the privation of a due form, but also a contrary disposition; and so deformity is compared to the act as falsehood is to faith. Hence, just as the deformed act is not from God, so neither is a false faith; and as formless faith is from God, so, too, acts that are good of their very nature, though not quickened by charity, as is frequently the case in sinners, are from God.

Reply Obj. 3. He who receives faith from God, without charity, is healed from unbelief, not entirely (because the sin of his previous unbelief is not removed) but in part, namely, in that he ceases from committing such and such a sin. Thus it happens frequently that a man desists from one act of sin, through God causing him thus to desist, without desisting from another act of sin, through the instigation of his own malice. And in this way sometimes it is granted by God to a man to believe, and yet he is not granted the gift of charity; so, too, the gift of prophecy, or the like, is given to some without charity.

---

[6] Q. 4, a. 4.   [7]*S. T.*, I, q. 48, a. 1, ad 2 [Not in this volume]; I-II, q. 18, a. 5. [Not in this volume]

Question 7
On the Effects of Faith
(*In Two Articles*)

We must now consider the effects of faith, under which head there are two points of inquiry: (1) Whether fear is an effect of faith? (2) Whether the heart is purified by faith?

First Article
Whether Fear Is an Effect of Faith?

We proceed thus to the First Article:—

Objection 1. It would seem that fear is not an effect of faith. For an effect does not precede its cause. Now fear precedes faith, for it is written (*Ecclus.* ii. 8): *Ye that fear the Lord, believe in Him.* Therefore fear is not an effect of faith.

Obj. 2. Further, The same thing is not the cause of contraries. Now fear and hope are contraries, as was stated above,[1] and faith begets hope, as the *Gloss* observes on *Matt.* 1.[2] Therefore fear is not an effect of faith.

Obj. 3. Further, One contrary does not cause another. Now the object of faith is a good, which is the First Truth, while the object of fear is an evil, as was stated above.[3] But acts take their species from the object, according to what was stated above.[4] Therefore faith is not a cause of fear.

On the contrary, It is written (*Jas.* ii. 19): *The devils . . . believe and tremble.*

I answer that, Fear is a movement of the appetitive power, as was stated above.[5] Now the principle of all appetitive movements is apprehended good or evil, and consequently the principle of fear and of every appetitive movement must be an apprehension. But through faith there arises in us an apprehension of certain penal evils, which are inflicted in accordance with the divine judgment. In this way, then, faith is a cause of the fear whereby one dreads to be punished by God; and this is servile fear.

It is also a cause of filial fear, whereby one dreads to be separated from God, or whereby one shrinks from equalling oneself to Him, and holds Him in reverence, inasmuch as faith makes us appreciate God as an

---

[1]*S. T.*, I-II, q. 23, a. 2 [Not in this volume]; q. 40, a. 4, ad 1. [Not in this volume]
[2]Glossa interl. (V, 5r).   [3]*S. T.*, I-II, q. 42, a. 1. [Not in this volume]
[4]*S. T.*, I-II, q. 18, a. 2. [Not in this volume]   [5]*S. T.*, I-II, q. 41, a. 1 [Not in this volume]; q. 42, a. 1. [Not in this volume]

unfathomable and supreme good, separation from which is the greatest evil, and to which it is wicked to wish to be equaled. Of the first fear, viz., servile fear, formless faith is the cause, while formed faith is the cause of the second, viz., filial fear, because through charity it makes man to adhere to God and to be subject to Him.

Reply Obj. 1. Fear of God cannot altogether precede faith, because if we knew nothing at all about Him, with regard to rewards and punishments, concerning which faith teaches us, we should in no way fear Him. If, however, faith be presupposed in reference to certain articles of faith, for example the divine excellence, then reverential fear follows, the result of which is that man submits his intellect to God, so as to believe in all the divine promises. Hence the text quoted continues: *And your reward shall not be made void.*

Reply Obj. 2. The same thing in respect of contraries can be the cause of contraries, but not under the same aspect. Now faith begets hope in so far as it enables us to appreciate the prize which God awards to the just, while it is the cause of fear in so far as it makes us appreciate the punishments which He intends to inflict on sinners.

Reply Obj. 3. The primary and formal object of faith is the good which is the First Truth; but the material object of faith includes also certain evils, for instance, that it is an evil either not to submit to God, or to be separated from Him, and that sinners will suffer penal evils from God; and in this way faith can be the cause of fear.

Second Article
Whether Faith Has the Effect of Purifying the Heart?

We proceed thus to the Second Article:—

Objection 1. It would seem that faith does not purify the heart. For purity of the heart pertains chiefly to the affections, whereas faith is in the intellect. Therefore faith has not the effect of purifying the heart.

Obj. 2. Further, That which purifies the heart is incompatible with impurity. But faith is compatible with the impurity of sin, as may be seen in those who have formless faith. Therefore faith does not purify the heart.

Obj. 3. Further, If faith were to purify the human heart in any way, it would chiefly purify the intellect of man. Now it does not purify the intellect from obscurity, since it is a veiled knowledge. Therefore faith in no way purifies the heart.

On the contrary, Peter said (*Acts* xv. 9): *Purifying their hearts by faith.*

I answer that, A thing is impure through being mixed with baser things. For silver is not called impure when mixed with gold, which betters it, but when mixed with lead or tin. Now it is evident that the rational creature is more excellent than all temporal and corporeal creatures; so that it becomes impure through subjecting itself to temporal things by loving them. From this impurity the rational creature is purified by means of a contrary movement, namely, by tending to that which is above it, viz., God. The first beginning of this movement is faith, since *he that cometh to God must believe that He is,* according to *Heb.* xi. 6. Hence the first principle of the purification of the heart is faith; and if this be perfected through being quickened by charity, the heart will be perfectly purified thereby.

Reply Obj. 1. Things that are in the intellect are the principles of those which are in the appetite, in so far as it is the apprehended good that moves the appetite.

Reply Obj. 2. Even formless faith excludes a certain impurity which is contrary to it, viz., that of error, and which consists in this, that the human intellect adheres inordinately to things below itself, through wishing to measure divine things by the rule of sensible things. But when it is quickened by charity, then it is incompatible with any kind of impurity, because *charity covereth all sins (Prov.* x. 12).

Reply Obj. 3. The obscurity of faith does not pertain to the impurity of sin, but rather to the natural defect of the human intellect, according to the present state of life.

II

REASON AND THE NATURAL
KNOWLEDGE OF GOD

As we have seen, Thomas Aquinas's approach to the study of Theology involves two general focuses. One centers its attention on how premises lead to legitimate conclusions and thus to new or more explicit knowledge and, working in the opposite direction, on how conclusions are shown to be dependent on more fundamental premises or principles. The other approach concentrates on just the premises and principles and attempts to explain the meaning of the terms involved in these propositions so that they might be better understood. It also tries to defend them against attacks that bring difficulties or confusion and strives to support their truth by fitting analogies and confirming arguments. We might ask, as we begin Part II of this volume, if the fundamental truth of God's existence is a conclusion or a principle. Can it be proved, or is it a starting point that is either an article of the faith or a self-evident principle? Aquinas's answer is that the existence of God is not an article of Christian faith, nor is the proposition "God exists" self-evident. Rather, it is a conclusion gained by solid arguments. In Article Two of Question 2 (*Summa Theologica*, Part One), Aquinas tells us:

> The existence of God and other like truths about God, which can be known by natural reason, are not articles of faith, but are *preambles* to the articles; for faith *presupposes* natural knowledge, even as grace presupposes nature and perfection the perfectible. Nevertheless, there is nothing to prevent a man, who cannot grasp a proof, from accepting, as a matter of faith, something which *in itself* is capable of being scientifically known and demonstrated.[1]

A *preamble*, literally speaking, is something that walks ahead of something more important. The Greek Patristic writer, Clement of Alexandria (died c. 219), captured the same general idea when he spoke of the relationship of Greek philosophy to Christianity. He set up a parallel between how the Old Testament walked ahead of those of Jewish background and prepared them for the New Testament and how Greek philosophy walked

---

[1]*Summa Theologica*, I, q. 2, a. 2, Reply Obj. 1. Emphasis added.

ahead or disposed the non-Jewish world for the arrival of the Gospel. Aquinas, when he speaks of a *preamble* to faith, is not thinking primarily, as did Clement, of a divinely providential, historical preparation of the Greeks for accepting the truths of the Christian faith. He is thinking more fundamentally. Reason, *at any time*, if used well, among all its other aids, also disposes certain people to accept the Christian faith and leads reasonable people to see that some fundamental revealed truths about God and the world are in accord with nature and are naturally discoverable. Furthermore, when Aquinas speaks of faith as presupposing natural knowledge, he certainly does not mean that legitimate faith cannot exist without reason approving it. Rather, he indicates that "faith presupposes natural knowledge even as . . . perfection the perfectible." Faith perfects reason's potential. It completes it. It is not alien to reason, but instead brings it to the fulfillment it was created for. Of course, many Athenian roads do not lead to Jerusalem. Yet, Aquinas teaches that, despite its challenges, the Jerusalem road is the best route to Athens. "Grace perfects nature and perfection the perfectible." Faith helps reason to achieve its natural goal and even more.

Aquinas, because of Christian revelation and his own intellectual acumen, brought to the basic principles of Aristotle a fulfillment that went beyond the Philosopher's expectations. He provided a depth that Aristotle's principles never produced on their own. He used the Philosopher's principles most consistently, but he also extended them into a world given its existence by God. For Aristotle, the fundamental principles are act and potency. They are, for him, principles that attempt to explain the changes that occur to what in kind has existed forever. Individuals are not eternal, but, for Aristotle, species or kinds of things are. Socrates is not eternal, but humans, through Socrates, Plato, and their temporal predecessors and successors, are. Aquinas views reality differently, since he knows that people, even if we might for reason of debate admit the possibility that they always have existed, are still dependent on a Creator God. The basic elements for humans, and for every creature, need an extended explanation of act and potency. Within a Christian vision, we must not only explain the changes that occur to existing beings; but we also must explain their very existence.

For Aristotle, act and potency are principles that explain change in things that already exist. They explain different kinds of motion, such as change of color. If Socrates stays out in the sun, he changes from white to tan. More fundamentally, these principles also explain change from one kind of thing to another. An egg becomes a chicken. It was potentially a chicken; now it actually is a chicken. We thus see that accidental changes occur, such as a change of color, and substantial changes occur, such as a potential chicken (an egg) becoming an actual chicken (that rules the roost). However, for a Christian philosopher, such as Aquinas, a more fundamental category of change exists, and a more fundamental kind of act and potency. Even if for argument's sake we might admit that humans could well have lived from all eternity, and all the other species that make up the world we encounter, still, in every case, a more fundamental category is *existence*. No matter how things might change in their substantial or accidental forms of existence, their more basic change is from not existing to existing. Nothing in the world would exist without the divine Creator, even if their ways of existing, as people, as horses, and so on, manifest a continuity within creation. The most fundamental category of act and potency, therefore, is what explains act as existence and potency as the capacity to exist. It is true that created realities that already exist are capable of different forms of change, both accidental and substantial. But the explanation of change or motion or becoming is secondary to the type of change that causes a potential being or thing to exist, a change from what is nonexistent to what is existent. Aristotle's theory of act and potency thus needs an extended meaning within a Christian vision of God's creative goodness.

The whole composite of any created being, whether spiritual or material, allows it to have accidents. Such subjects are the matter or potency that receive different accidental forms or acts. So, once again, Aristotle's general theory of act and potency took on a similar yet different specification when Aquinas centered it on created being. When the theory focused on the subject and the different accidents that might inhere in or be linked to the subject, it followed Aristotle's teaching; yet when Aquinas applied it within the larger framework of essence and existence, he went beyond the Philosopher's vision of reality. He extended Aristotle's principles.

The application of Aristotle's theory of act and potency to particular types of created beings also occurs on the level of the composition of material realities. It specifies the principles of material beings in such a way that matter plays the role of potency, and form the role of act. Every material reality is composed of matter and form. The higher the level of the form, the higher the type of reality that exists. The form of an inanimate being is less than the form of an animate being. The form of a plant is less than the form of an animal. And the form of a human being is greater than the form of a brute. The higher the form, the higher the reality of the being so informed. For Aristotle, the heavenly substances who were separated from all matter were pure "forms" with no matter, and thus they were divine. The highest of these separated substances was the First Mover, who was the highest being, but not a qualitatively different kind of being. The First Mover was the first among equally pure separated substances. Some Christian authors attempted to define the separated substances, or angels, as different from God by saying all the angels were composed of matter and form. In this case, however, their matter was a spiritual matter. Aquinas saw no need to follow this path. The composition of essence and existence in angels was enough to make them composed and thus not divine. He saw no reason to add a further composition in angels to distinguish them from divine beings.

Besides the intrinsic principles of created things, Aquinas saw the need to admit extrinsic principles or causes. Aristotle had spoken of efficient causes, those that make things in the world change from one kind to another or from one intensity of a particular kind to another intensity of the same kind. Yet Aristotle never thought of his First or Unmoved Mover as the cause of existence. For him, the world always existed, and the only changes that needed to be explained were those from being this to being that or the changes that made a being achieve more of its fulfillment. He never had to explain the every existence of the concrete being. Aristotle's efficient cause explained the movement of beings presupposed as already existing. His is a philosophy of movement, not of existence. Aristotle also spoke of final causes or the goals that efficient causes pursue when they aim at a certain purpose in performing their actions. Final causes can be the chosen goals of those who exercise choice, or they can be the goals that things pursue due to the necessary drives built into their natures.

Keeping these Aristotelian principles in mind and realizing that Aquinas has extended their meaning, let us now turn to the five arguments that Aquinas gives for the existence of God in Article Three of Question 2 (*Summa Theologica*, Part One). Many of these five ways of proving God's existence derive from Aristotle.

The first way is based on the experience of motion or change in the world. Whatever changes occur do so because of the influence of an efficient cause that moves them. Now if this efficient cause is itself moved, then it must have a prior mover and so on. We must, then, finally arrive at a First Mover, or else there would be no movement at all. This Prime Mover everyone understands to be God.

Aquinas's second argument is founded on the hierarchy of causes and effects visible in the world. Such a series cannot be one that contains only caused causes, since these all would be effects. So, we must finally arrive at an efficient cause that is not caused, or else there would be no reasonable explanation for the effects we perceive. This Uncaused Cause we call God.

The third way of proving God's existence is based on our awareness that some beings come into existence and then go out of existence. They are technically what we might call possible: They can exist or they can *not* exist. But possibles cannot give themselves existence, so if any possible being attains actual existence, there must ultimately be a necessary being that gives it actuality. This Necessary Being we understand to be God.

Aquinas's fourth argument begins with the observation that things have various degrees of perfection, that some are more or less good, true, and noble. Now, things are considered "more or less" because to different degrees they approach a maximum. Such a maximum, then, must have the fullness of goodness, truth, and nobility, and also of being, since as Aristotle argues in II *Metaphysics*: that which is greatest in truth is also greatest in being. Furthermore, since the maximum in any class or genus of beings is the cause of all the realities in that genus—for example, fire is the cause of all levels of hot things—then there must be a maximum that transcends every genus and is the cause of the being, goodness, truth, and nobility of all "more or less" things. Such a perfect being we call God.

The fifth way of proving God's existence is grounded on the order found in the world. The example Aquinas employs of an arrow heading toward a target because it has been directed toward that goal by the archer hints at his intent. Many things in this world act consistently in the same way as they achieve the same purposes. The order by which they function with such consistency cannot be explained by chance. In relation to such consistent natures, there must be an intelligence that guides them toward their end. This Providential Guide we understand to be God.

We should consider a number of noteworthy points about these proofs. First, it is important to note that the major accent is on empirical grounds. This shows Aquinas's close link to Aristotle in his use of reason to establish God's existence. His approach is not that of St. Augustine's followers, who stress the interior to-be-discovered presence of God already existing in the human soul, which is examined in Article One of Question 2 (*Summa Theologica*, Part One). It is not just that Aquinas uses reason based on sense experience to establish the existence of God as a preamble to the faith, and that he does not consider God's existence as a self-evident truth or a truth accepted solely on faith. The very order of his subsequent questions draws out the implications of Aquinas's stress on the empirical in his five ways of proving the existence of God.

Despite the strength of these proofs for establishing the existence of God, they nevertheless manifest people's weakness, if left to themselves, in understanding the nature of God. Aquinas never makes the claim that humans by reason alone can come to a positive distinct knowledge of God's nature. We see that Aquinas's proofs describe God as Unmoved Mover, Uncaused Cause, and Infinite Perfection. Thus, what makes God distinct from other movers, causes, and perfections are negative attributes—unmoved, uncaused, and infinite. This negative approach is evident in regard to the first attribute Aquinas considers: God's simplicity. Fundamentally, it signifies that God is not composed in the way every creature is: He is not composed of essence and existence; he is not composed of substance and accidents; and he is not composed of matter and form.

When Aquinas turns to the positive attributes of God, such as goodness, perfection, and being, we discover that such positive attributes are common to both God and finite beings. We never grasp goodness, perfection, or being as it is proper to God. We begin with the level of goodness, perfection, or being we gain from created effects and argue to the existence of the divine cause. Still, because of the lack of proportion between goodness, perfection, or being as it is found in creatures and as it is found in God, we gain only an imperfect knowledge of God's nature. Nonetheless, we do grasp God to some extent by combining the knowledge we have of positive and negative attributes. If we begin only with certain positive concepts gained from creatures that do not necessarily have limits built into them—for example, being and the transcendental attributes of goodness and truth, we can rightly say that "God is good," and we mean by this that he is good, but not in the way we experience the finite expressions of goodness in creatures. Rather, he is good in a nonfinite and in an eminent or excellent way. As Aquinas says: "In this life we cannot see the essence of God; but we know God from creatures as their cause, and also by way of excellence and remotion."[2]

This traditional manner of dealing with the highest perfections, that is, perfections that do not necessarily contain limits, came to medieval authors from Pseudo-Dionysius, or Dionysius the Areopagite.[3] It is easy to accept the claim that pure perfections, such as being, goodness, and truth, do not have to include within them limitations. But what about life? Aquinas, following Dionysius, also explains how life can be predicated of God. It is necessary, of course, that he exclude the forms of life

---

[2]*Summa Theologica*, I, q. 13, a. 1. [Not in this volume]   [3]*Divine Names*, 13, 1.

that necessarily include limits from the forms of life we predicate of God. Life, nonetheless, does not imply limits in all its forms. Eating implies limits, walking implies limits, but understanding, despite its limits in creatures, does not by its very nature entail limits. Aquinas makes similar adjustments when he examines how will, love, justice, and mercy exist in God. They are present in the sense that they are positive perfections that by their very nature do not entail limits. Such mixed positive perfections are always affirmed of God after Aquinas has excluded the limits that might be in certain forms of these perfections. The negative and positive attributes thus continually work together to attain a better understanding of the supereminent way these perfections are affirmed of God.

Since God is the First Cause of all created beings, then it follows that God is the total cause of all the being of all finite beings. That is why we use the word "creation" to express divine causality, since God, in contrast to finite causes, does not simply transform existing things. He gives them their very existence. It should be added that God did not create or give existence to the universe necessarily, but freely. For, as extensive as the universe is, it is still as a whole a finite good, as all its parts are also finite goods. The only object that God necessarily must love is infinite goodness: God thus necessarily loves Himself. In regard to finite goods, however, God could choose to create, or he could choose not to create. Neither is he forced to create any particular kind of a universe. He could choose to create any universe that does not violate his attribute of wisdom. We can gather further implications for the understanding of creation if we attend to the interplay of the divine attributes of freedom and wisdom. We realize that divine freedom, as a wise freedom, is thus not tyrannical or arbitrary. Furthermore, since God's causality is total, he wisely rules over all creation. We give the name "providence" to this wise guidance of creation toward the realization of the goal he has built into it.

GOD'S EXISTENCE

Summa Theologica
Part One
Question 2
The Existence of God
(In Three Articles)

Because the chief aim of sacred doctrine is to teach the knowledge of God not only as He is in Himself, but also as He is the beginning of things and their last end, and especially of rational creatures, as is clear from what has been already said,[1] therefore, in our endeavor to expound this science, we shall treat: (1) of God; (2) of the rational creature's movement towards God;[2] (3) of Christ Who as man is our way to God.[3]

In treating of God there will be a threefold division:—

For we shall consider (1) whatever concerns the divine essence. (2) Whatever concerns the distinctions of Persons.[4] (3) Whatever concerns the procession of creatures from Him.[5]

Concerning the divine essence, we must consider:—

(1) Whether God exists? (2) The manner of His existence, or rather, what is *not* the manner of His existence.[6] (3) Whatever concerns His operations—namely, His knowledge,[7] will,[8] power.[9]

Concerning the first, there are three points of inquiry:—

(1) Whether the proposition *God exists* is self-evident? (2) Whether it is demonstrable? (3) Whether God exists?

First Article
Whether the Existence of God Is Self-Evident?

We proceed thus to the First Article:—

Source: *Basic Writing of Saint Thomas Aquinas*, edited and annotated by Anton C. Pegis (Indianapolis: Hackett Pub. Co., 1997). Reprinted by permission of the publisher.

[1]Q. I, a. 7.   [2]*S.T.*, II. [Not in this volume]   [3]*S.T.*, III. [Not in this volume]   [4]Q. 27. [Not in this volume]   [5]Q. 44. [Not in this volume]   [6]Q. 3.   [7]Q. 14. [Not in this volume]   [8]Q. 19.   [9]Q. 25. [Not in this volume]

Objection 1. It seems that the existence of God is self-evident. For those things are said to be self-evident to us the knowledge of which exists naturally in us, as we can see in regard to first principles. But as Damascene says, *the knowledge of God is naturally implanted in all.*[10] Therefore the existence of God is self-evident.

Obj. 2. Further, those things are said to be self-evident which are known as soon as the terms are known, which the Philosopher says is true of the first principles of demonstration.[11] Thus, when the nature of a whole and of a part is known, it is at once recognized that every whole is greater than its part. But as soon as the signification of the name *God* is understood, it is at once seen that God exists. For by this name is signified that thing than which nothing greater can be conceived. But that which exists actually and mentally is greater than that which exists only mentally. Therefore, since as soon as the name *God* is understood it exists mentally, it also follows that it exists actually. Therefore the proposition *God exists* is self-evident.

Obj. 3. Further, the existence of truth is self-evident. For whoever denies the existence of truth grants that truth does not exist: and, if truth does not exist, then the proposition *Truth does not exist* is true: and if there is anything true, there must be truth. But God is truth itself: *I am the way, the truth and the life* (*Jo.* xiv. 6). Therefore *God exists* is self-evident.

On the contrary, No one can mentally admit the opposite of what is self-evident, as the Philosopher states concerning the first principles of demonstration.[12] But the opposite of the proposition *God is* can be mentally admitted: *The fool said in his heart, There is no God* (*Ps.* lii. 1). Therefore, that God exists is not self-evident.

I answer that, A thing can be self-evident in either of two ways: on the one hand, self-evident in itself, though not to us; on the other, self-evident and to us. A proposition is self-evident because the predicate is included in the essence of the subject: *e.g., Man is an animal,* for animal is contained in the essence of man. If therefore, the essence of the predicate and subject be known to all, the proposition will be self-evident to all; as is clear with regard to the first principles of demonstration, the terms of which are certain common notions that no one is ignorant of, such as being and non-being, whole and part, and the like. If, however, there are some to whom the essence of the predicate and subject is unknown, the proposition will be self-evident in itself, but not to those who do not know the meaning of

---

[10]*De Fide Orth.*, I, 1; 3 (PG 94, 789; 793).   [11]*Post. Anal.*, I, 3 (72b 18).
[12]*Metaph.*, III, 3 (1005b 11) ; *Post. Anal.*, I, 10 (76b 23).

the predicate and subject of the proposition. Therefore, it happens, as Boethius says, that there are some notions of the mind which are common and self-evident only to the learned, as that incorporeal substances are not in space.[13] Therefore I say that this proposition, *God exists*, of itself is self-evident, for the predicate is the same as the subject, because God is His own existence as will be hereafter shown.[14] Now because we do not know the essence of God, the proposition is not self-evident to us, but needs to be demonstrated by things that are more known to us, though less known in their nature—namely, by His effects.

Reply Obj. 1. To know that God exists in a general and confused way is implanted in us by nature, inasmuch as God is man's beatitude. For man naturally desires happiness, and what is naturally desired by man is naturally known by him. This, however, is not to know absolutely that God exists; just as to know that someone is approaching is not the same as to know that Peter is approaching, even though it is Peter who is approaching; for there are many who imagine that man's perfect good, which is happiness, consists in riches, and others in pleasures, and other in something else.

Reply Obj. 2. Perhaps not everyone who hears this name *God* understands it to signify something than which nothing greater can be thought, seeing that some have believed God to be a body.[15] Yet, granted that everyone understands that by this name *God* is signified something than which nothing greater can be thought, nevertheless, it does not therefore follow that he understands that what the name signifies exists actually, but only that it exists mentally. Nor can it be argued that it actually exists, unless it be admitted that there actually exists something than which nothing greater can be thought; and this precisely is not admitted by those who hold that God does not exist.

Reply Obj. 3. The existence of truth in general is self-evident, but the existence of a Primal Truth is not self-evident to us.

Second Article
Whether It Can Be Demonstrated That God Exists?

We proceed thus to the Second Article:—

Objection 1. It seems that the existence of God cannot be demonstrated. For it is an article of faith that God exists. But what is of faith

---

[13]*De Hebdom.* (PL 64,1311).   [14]Q. 3, a. 4.   [15]Cf. *C. G.*, I, 20—Cf. also Aristotle, *Phys.*, I, 4 (187a 12) ; St. Augustine, *De Civit. Dei*, VIII, 2 : 5 (PL 41, 226; 239); *De Haeres.*, 46, 50, 86 (PL 42, 35; 39; 46); *De Genesi ad Litt.*, X, 25 (PL 34, 427); Maimonides, *Guide*, I, 53 (p. 72).

cannot be demonstrated, because a demonstration produces scientific knowledge, whereas faith is of the unseen, as is clear from the Apostle (*Heb.* xi. 1). Therefore it cannot be demonstrated that God exists.

Obj. 2. Further, essence is the middle term of demonstration. But we cannot know in what God's essence consists, but solely in what it does not consist, as Damascene says.[16] Therefore we cannot demonstrate that God exists.

Obj. 3. Further, if the existence of God were demonstrated, this could only be from His effects. But His effects are not proportioned to Him, since He is infinite and His effects are finite, and between the finite and infinite there is no proportion. Therefore, since a cause cannot be demonstrated by an effect not proportioned to it, it seems that the existence of God cannot be demonstrated.

On the contrary, The Apostle says: *The invisible things of Him are clearly seen, being understood by the things that are made* (*Rom.* i. 20). But this would not be unless the existence of God could be demonstrated through the things that are made; for the first thing we must know of anything is, whether it exists.

I answer that, Demonstration can be made in two ways: One is through the cause, and is called *propter quid,* and this is to argue from what is prior absolutely. The other is through the effect, and is called a demonstration *quia;* this is to argue from what is prior relatively only to us. When an effect is better known to us than its cause, from the effect we proceed to the knowledge of the cause. And from every effect the existence of its proper cause can be demonstrated, so long as its effects are better known to us; because, since every effect depends upon its cause, if the effect exists, the cause must pre-exist. Hence the existence of God, in so far as it is not self-evident to us, can be demonstrated from those of His effects which are known to us.

Reply Obj. 1. The existence of God and other like truths about God, which can be known by natural reason, are not articles of faith, but are preambles to the articles; for faith presupposes natural knowledge, even as grace presupposes nature and perfection the perfectible. Nevertheless, there is nothing to prevent a man, who cannot grasp a proof, from accepting, as a matter faith, something which in itself is capable of being scientifically known and demonstrated.

Reply Obj. 2. When the existence of a cause is demonstrated from an effect, this effect takes the place of the definition of the cause in proving

---

[16]*De Fide Orth.*, I, 4 (PG 94, 800).

the cause's existence. This is especially the case in regard to God, because, in order to prove the existence of anything, it is necessary to accept as a middle term the meaning of the name, and not its essence, for the question of its essence follows on the question of its existence. Now the names given to God are derived from His effects, as will be later shown.[17] Consequently, in demonstrating the existence of God from His effects, we may take for the middle term the meaning of the name *God*.

Reply Obj. 3. From effects not proportioned to the cause no perfect knowledge of that cause can be obtained. Yet from every effect the existence of the cause can be clearly demonstrated, and so we can demonstrate the existence of God from His effects; though from them we cannot know God perfectly as He is in His essence.

Third Article
Whether God Exists?

We proceed thus to the Third Article:—

Objection 1. It seems that God does not exist: because if one of two contraries be infinite, the other would be altogether destroyed. But the name *God* means that He is infinite goodness. If therefore, God existed, there would be no evil discoverable; but there is evil in the world. Therefore God does not exist.

Obj. 2. Further, it is superfluous to suppose that what can be accounted for by a few principles has been produced by many. But it seems that everything we see in the world can be accounted for by other principles, supposing God did exist. For all natural things can be reduced to one principle, which is nature; and all voluntary things can be reduced to one principle, which is human reason, or will. Therefore there is no need to suppose God's existence.

On the contrary, It is said in the person of God: *I am Who am* (*Exod.* iii 14).

I answer that, The existence of God can be proved in five ways.

The first and more manifest way is the argument from motion. It is certain, and evident to our senses, that in the world some things are in motion. Now whatever is moved is moved by another, for nothing can be moved except it is in potentiality to that towards which it is moved; whereas a thing moves inasmuch as it is in act. For motion is nothing else than the reduction of something from potentiality to actuality. But nothing can be reduced from potentiality to actuality, except by something in a

---

[17]Q. 13, a. 1. [Not in this volume]

state of actuality. Thus that which is actually hot, as fire, makes wood, which is potentially hot, to be actually hot, and thereby moves and changes it. Now it is not possible that the same thing should be at once in actuality and potentiality in the same respect, but only in different respects. For what is actually hot cannot simultaneously be potentially hot; but it is simultaneously potentially cold. It is therefore impossible that in the same respect and in the same way a thing should be both mover and moved, *i.e.*, that it should move itself. Therefore, whatever is moved must be moved by another. If that by which it is moved be itself moved, then this also must needs be moved by another, and that by another again. But this cannot go on to infinity, because then there would be no first mover, and consequently, no other mover, seeing that subsequent movers move only inasmuch as they are moved by the first mover; as the staff moves only because it is moved by the hand. Therefore it is necessary to arrive at a first mover, moved by no other; and this everyone understands to be God.

The second way is from the nature of efficient cause. In the world of sensible things we find there is an order of efficient causes. There is no case known (neither is it, indeed, possible) in which a thing is found to be the efficient cause of itself; for so it would be prior to itself, which is impossible. Now in efficient causes it is not possible to go on to infinity, because in all efficient causes following in order, the first is the cause of the intermediate cause, and the intermediate is the cause of the ultimate cause, whether the intermediate cause be several, or one only. Now to take away the cause is to take away the effect. Therefore, if there be no first cause among efficient causes, there will be no ultimate, nor any intermediate, cause. But if in efficient causes it is possible to go on to infinity, there will be no first efficient cause, neither will there be an ultimate effect, nor any intermediate efficient causes; all of which is plainly false. Therefore it is necessary to admit a first efficient cause, to which everyone gives the name of God.

The third way is taken from possibility and necessity, and runs thus. We find in nature things that are possible to be and not to be, since they are found to be generated, and to be corrupted, and consequently, it is possible for them to be and not to be. But it is impossible for these always to exist, for that which can not-be at some time is not. Therefore, if everything can not-be, then at one time there was nothing in existence. Now if this were true, even now there would be nothing in existence, because that which does not exist begins to exist only through something already existing. Therefore, if at one time nothing was in existence, it would have been impossible for anything to have begun to exist; and thus even now nothing would be in existence—which is absurd. Therefore, not all beings are merely possible, but there must exist something the existence of which is necessary. But every necessary thing either has its necessity caused by another, or not. Now it is impossible to go on to infinity in necessary things which have their necessity caused by another, as has been already proved in regard to efficient causes. Therefore we cannot but admit the existence of some being having of itself its own necessity, and not receiving it from another, but rather causing in others their necessity. This all men speak of as God.

The fourth way is taken from the gradation to be found in things. Among beings there are some more and some less good, true, noble, and the like. But *more* and *less* are predicated of different things according as they resemble in their different ways something which is maximum, as a thing is said to be hotter according as it more nearly resembles that which is hottest; so that there is something which is truest, something best, something noblest, and consequently, something which is most being for those things that are greatest in truth are greatest in being, as it is written in *Metaph*. ii[18] Now the maximum in any genus is the cause of all in that genus, as fire, which is the maximum of heat, is the cause of all hot things, as is said in the same book.[19] Therefore there must also be something which is to all beings the cause of their being, goodness, and every other perfection; and this we call God.

The fifth way is taken from the governance of the world. We see that things which lack knowledge, such as natural bodies, act for an end and this is evident from their acting always, or nearly always, in the same way, so as to obtain the best result. Hence it is plain that they achieve their end, not fortuitously, but designedly. Now whatever lacks knowledge cannot move towards an end, unless it be directed by some being endowed with knowledge and intelligent; as the arrow is directed by the archer. Therefore some intelligence; being exists by whom all natural things are directed to their end; and this being we call God.

Reply Obj. 1. As Augustine says: *Since God is the highest good, He would not allow any evil to exist in His works, unless His omnipotence and goodness were such as to bring good even out of evil.*[20] This is part of the infinite goodness of God, that He should allow evil to exist, and out of it produce good.

Reply Obj. 2. Since nature works for a determinate end under the direction of a higher agent, whatever is done by nature must be traced

---

[18]*Metaph*. 1a, 1 (993b 30).   [19]*Ibid*. (993b 25).   [20]*Enchir*., XI (PL 40, 236).

back to God as to its first cause. So likewise whatever is done voluntarily must be traced back to some higher cause other than human reason and will, since these can change and fail; for all things that are changeable and capable of defect must be traced back to an immovable and self-necessary first principle, as has been shown.

MANNER OF GOD'S EXISTENCE

Summa Theologica
Part One
Question 3
On the Simplicity of God
(*In Eight Articles*)

When the existence of a thing has been ascertained, there remains the further question of the manner of its existence, in order that we may know its essence. Now because we cannot know what God is, but rather what He is not, we have no means for considering how God is, but rather how He is not.

Therefore, we must consider (1) how He is not; (2) how He is known by us;[1] (3) how He is named.[2]

Now it can be shown how God is not, by removing from Him whatever does not befit Him—viz., composition, motion, and the like. Therefore (1) we must discuss His simplicity, whereby we remove composition from Him. And because whatever is simple in material things is imperfect and part of something else, we shall discuss (2) His perfection;[3] (3) His infinity;[4] (4) His immutability;[5] (5) His unity.[6]

Concerning His simplicity, there are eight points of inquiry: (1) Whether God is a body? (2) Whether He is composed of matter and form? (3) Whether in Him there is composition of quiddity or essence (or nature) and subject? (4) Whether there is in Him a composition of essence and being? (5) Whether He is composed of genus and difference? (6) Whether He is composed of subject and accident? (7) Whether He is in any way composite, or wholly simple? (8) Whether He enters into composition with other things?

First Article
Whether God Is a Body?

We proceed thus to the First Article:—

---

[1] Q. 12. [Not in this volume]   [2] Q. 13. [Not in this volume]   [3] Q. 4.
[4] Q. 7. [Not in this volume]   [5] Q. 9. [Not in this volume]   [6] Q. 11. [Not in this volume]

Objection 1. It seems that God is a body. For a body is that which has three dimensions. But Holy Scripture attributes three dimensions to God, for it is written: *He is higher than Heaven, and what wilt thou do? He is deeper than Hell, and how wilt thou know? The measure of Him is longer than the earth and broader than the sea* (*Job* xi. 8, 9). Therefore God is a body.

Obj. 2. Further, everything that has figure is a body, since figure is a quality of quantity. But God seems to have figure, for it is written: *Let us make man to our image and likeness* (*Gen.* i. 26). Now a figure is called an image, according to the text: *Who being the brightness of His glory and the figure, i.e.,* the image *of His substance* (*Heb.* i. 3). Therefore God is a body.

Obj. 3 Further, whatever has corporeal parts is a body. Now Scripture attributes corporeal parts to God. *Hast thou an arm like God?* (*Job* xl. 4); and *The eyes of the Lord are upon the just* (*Ps.* xxxiii. 16); and *The right hand of the Lord hath wrought strength* (*Ps.* cxvii, 16). Therefore God is a body.

Obj. 4. Further, posture belongs only to bodies. But something which supposes posture is said of God in the Scriptures: *I saw the Lord sitting* (*Isa.* vi. 1), and *He standeth up to judge* (*Isa.* iii 13). Therefore God is a body.

Obj. 5. Further, only bodies or things corporeal can be a local terminus *wherefrom* or *whereto*. But in the Scriptures God is spoken of as a local terminus *whereto*, according to the words, *Come ye to Him and be enlightened* (*Ps.* xxxiii. 6), and as a term *wherefrom: All they that depart from Thee shall be written in the earth* (*Jer.* xvii. 13). Therefore God is a body.

On the contrary, It is written in the Gospel of St. John (iv. 24): *God is a spirit.*

I answer that, It is absolutely true that God is not a body, and this can be shown in three ways. First, because no body moves unless it be moved, as is evident from induction. Now it has been already proved that God is the First Mover, Himself unmoved.[7] Therefore it is clear that God is not a body. Second, because the first being must of necessity be in act, and in no way in potentiality. For although in any single thing that passes from potentiality to actuality, the potentiality is prior in time to actuality, nevertheless, absolutely speaking, actuality is prior to potentiality; for whatever is the potentiality is reduced to actuality only by some being in actuality. Now it has been already proved that God in the First Being.[8] It is therefore impossible that in God there should be any potentiality. But every body is in potentiality, because the continuous, as such, is divisible to infinity. It is therefore impossible that God should be a body. Third, because God is the most noble of beings, as is clear from what has been said.[9] Now it is impossible for a body to be the most noble of beings. For a body is either animate

---

[7]Q. 2, a. 3.   [8]*Ibid.*   [9]*Ibid.*

or inanimate; and an animate body is manifestly nobler than any inanimate body. But an animate body is not animate precisely as body, or otherwise all bodies would be animate. Therefore its animation depends upon some other thing, as our body depends for its animation on the soul. Hence that by which a body is animate is nobler than the body. Therefore it is impossible that God should be a body.

Reply Obj. 1. As we have said above, Holy Scripture puts before us spiritual and divine things under the likenesses of corporeal things.[10] Hence, when it attributes three dimensions to God, under the comparison of corporeal quantity it designates His virtual quantity: thus, by depth, it signifies His power of knowing hidden things; by height, the transcendence of His excelling power; by length, the duration of His existence; by breadth, His act of love for all. Or as says Dionysius,[11] by the depth of God is meant the incomprehensibility of His essence, by length, the procession of His all-pervading power, by breadth, His overspreading all things, inasmuch as all things lie under His protection.

Reply Obj. 2. Man is said to be in the image of God, not as regards his body, but as regards that whereby he excels other animals. Hence, when it is said, *Let us make man to our image and likeness,* it is added, *And let him have dominion over the fishes of the sea* (*Gen.* I. 26). Now man excels all animals by his reason and intellect; hence it is according to his intellect and reason, which are incorporeal, that man is said to be in the image of God.

Reply Obj. 3. Corporeal parts are attributed to God in Scripture because of His actions, and this is owing to a certain likeness. For instance, the act of the eye is to see, and hence the eye attributed to God signifies His power of seeing intellectually, not sensibly; and so on with the other parts.

Reply Obj. 4. Whatever pertains to posture, likewise, is attributed to God only by a sort of likeness. He is spoken of as sitting, because of His unchangeableness and dominion; and as standing, because of His power of overcoming whatever withstands Him.

Reply Obj. 5. We draw near to God by no corporeal steps, since He is everywhere, but by the affections of the soul, and by the actions of that same soul do we withdraw from Him. Hence, to draw near or to withdraw signifies merely spiritual affection under the likeness of local motion.

Second Article
Whether God Is Composed of Matter and Form?

We proceed thus to the Second Article:—

---

[10]Q. 1. a. 9.   [11]*De Div. Nom.*, IX, 5 (PG 3, 913).

Objection 1. It seem that God is composed of matter and form. For whatever has a soul is composed of matter and form; since the soul is the form of the body. But Scripture attributes a soul to God; for it is mentioned in *Hebrews* (x. 38), where God says: *But My just man liveth by faith; but if he withdraw himself, he shall not please My soul.* Therefore God is composed of matter and form.

Obj. 2. Further, anger, joy, and the like are passions of the composite, as is said in *De Anima*, i.[12] But these are attributed to God in Scripture: *The Lord was exceeding angry with His people* (*Ps.* cv. 40). Therefore God is composed of matter and form.

Obj. 3. Further, matter is the principle of individuation. But God seems to be individual, for He cannot be predicated of many. Therefore He is composed of matter and form.

On the contrary, Whatever is composed of matter and form is a body, for dimensive quantity is the first property of matter. But God is not a body, as has been proved. Therefore, He is not composed of matter and form.

I answer that, It is impossible that matter be in God. First, because matter is that which exists in potentiality. But we have shown that God is pure act, without any potentiality. Hence it is impossible that God be composed of matter and form. Second, because everything composed of matter and form owes its perfection and goodness to its form, and therefore its goodness is participated, inasmuch as matter participates the form. Now the first good and the best—viz., God—is not a participated good, because the essential good is prior to the participated good. Hence it is impossible that God should be composed of matter and form. Third, because every agent acts by its form, and so the manner in which it has its form is the manner in which it is an agent. Therefore whatever is primarily and essentially an agent must be primarily and essentially form. Now God is the first agent, since He is the first efficient cause, as has been shown.[13] He is therefore of His essence a form, and not composed of matter and form.

Reply Obj. 1. A soul is attributed to God because of a similitude in acts; for, that we will anything, is due to our soul. Hence what is pleasing to His will is said to be pleasing to His soul.

Reply Obj. 2. Anger and the like are attributed to God because of a similitude in effects. Thus, because to punish is properly the act of an angry man, God's punishment is metaphorically spoken of as His anger.

Reply Obj. 3. Forms which can be received in matter are individuated by matter, which cannot be in another as in a subject since it is the first

---

[12]Aristotle, *De An.*, I, 1 (403a 3). [13]Q. 2, a. 3.

underlying subject; although form of itself, unless something else prevents it, can be received by many. But that form which cannot be received in matter, but is self-subsisting, is individuated precisely because it cannot be received in a subject; and such a form is God. Hence it does not follow that matter exists in God.

Third Article
Whether God Is the Same as His Essence or Nature?

We proceed thus to the Third Article:—

Objection 1. It seems that God is not the same as His essence or nature. For nothing is in itself. But the essence or nature of God—*i.e.*, The Godhead—is said to be in God. Therefore it seems that God is not the same as His essence or nature.

Obj. 2. Further, the effect is assimilated to its cause; for every agent produces its like. But in created things the *suppositum* is not identical with its nature; for a man is not the same as his humanity. Therefore God is not the same as His Godhead.

On the contrary, It is said of God that He is life itself, and not only that He is a living thing: *I am the way, the truth, and the life* (*Jo.* xiv. 6). Now the relation between Godhead and God is the same as the relation between life and a living thing. Therefore God is His very Godhead.

I answer that, God is the same as His essence or nature. To understand this, it must be noted that in things composed of matter and form, the nature or essence must differ from the *suppositum*, for the essence or nature includes only what falls within the definition of the species; as humanity includes all that falls within the definition of man, for it is by this that man is man, and it is this that humanity signifies that, namely, whereby man is man. Now individual matter, with all the individuating accidents, does not fall within the definition of the species. For this particular flesh, these bones, this blackness or whiteness, etc., do not fall within the definition of a man. Therefore this flesh, these bones, and the accidental qualities designating this particular matter, are not included in humanity; and yet they are included in the reality which is a man. Hence, the reality which is a man has something in it that humanity does not have. Consequently, humanity and a man are not wholly identical, but humanity is taken to mean the formal part of a man, because the principles whereby a thing is defined function as the formal constituent in relation to individuating matter. The situation is different in things not composed of matter and form, in which individuation is not due to individual matter—that is to say, to *this* matter—but the forms themselves are individuated of themselves. Here it is necessary that the forms themselves should be subsisting *supposita*. Therefore *suppositum* and nature in them are identified. Since, then, God is not composed of matter and form, He must be His own Godhead, His own Life, and whatever else is so predicated of Him.

Reply Obj. 1. We can speak of simple things only as though they were like the composite things from which we derive our knowledge. Therefore, in speaking of God, we use concrete nouns to signify His subsistence, because with us only those things subsist which are composite, and we use abstract nouns to signify His simplicity. In speaking therefore of Godhead, or life, or the like as being in God, we indicate the composite way in which our intellect understands, but not that there is any composition in God.

Reply Obj. 2. The effects of God do not imitate Him perfectly, but only as far as they are able. It pertains to defect in imitation that what is simple and one can be represented only by a multiplicity. This is the source of composition in God's effects, and therefore in them *suppositum* is not the same as nature.

Fourth Article
Whether Essence and Being Are the Same in God?

We proceed thus to the Fourth Article:—

Objection 1. It seems that essence and being [*esse*] are not the same in God. For if it be so, then the diving being has nothing added to it. Now being to which no addition is made is the being-in-general which is predicated of all things. Therefore it follows that God is being-in-general which can be predicated of everything. But this is false: *For men gave the incommunicable name to stones and wood (Wisd.* xiv. 21). Therefore God's being is not His essence.

Obj. 2. Further, we can know *whether* God exists, as was said above,[14] but we cannot know *what* He is. Therefore God's being is not the same as His essence—that is, as His quiddity or nature.

On the contrary, Hilary says: *In God being is not an accidental quality, but subsisting truth.*[15] Therefore what subsists in God is His being.

I answer that, God is not only His own essence, as has been shown, but also His own being. This may be shown in several ways. First, whatever a thing has besides its essence must be caused either by the constituent principles of that essence (like a proper accident that necessarily accompanies the species—as the faculty of laughing is proper to a man—and is

---

[14]Q. 2, a. 2.   [15]*De Trin.*, VII (PL 10, 208).

caused by the constituent principles of the species), or by some exterior agent,—as heat is caused in water by fire. Therefore, if the being of a thing differs from its essence, this being must be caused either by some exterior agent or by the essential principles of the thing itself. Now it is impossible for a thing's being to be caused only by its essential constituent principles, for nothing can be the sufficient cause of its own being, if its being is caused. Therefore that thing, whose being differs from its essence, must have its being caused by another. But this cannot be said of God, because we call God the first efficient cause. Therefore it is impossible that in God His being should differ from His essence.

Second, being is the actuality of every form or nature: for goodness and humanity are spoken of as actual, only because they are spoken of as being. Therefore, being must be compared to essence, if the latter is distinct from it, as actuality to potentiality. Therefor, since in God there is no potentiality, as shown above, it follows that in Him essence does not differ from being. Therefore His essence is His being. Third, just as that which has fire, but is not itself fire, is on fire by participation, so that which has being, but is not being, is a being by participation. But God is His own essence, as was shown above. If therefore, He is not His own being, He will be not essential, but participated, being. He will not therefore be the first being—which is absurd. Therefore, God is His own being, and not merely His own essence.

Reply Obj. 1. A thing-that-has-nothing-added-to-it can be understood in two ways. Either its essence precludes any addition (thus, for example, it is of the essence of an irrational animal to be without reason), or we may understand a thing to have nothing added to it, inasmuch as its essence does not require that anything should be added to it (thus the genus animal is without reason, because it is not of the essence of animal in general to have reason; but neither is it of the essence of animal to lack reason). And so the divine being has nothing added to it in the first sense; whereas being-in-general has nothing added to it in the second sense.

Reply Obj. 2. *To be* can mean either of two things. It may mean the act of being, or it may mean the composition of a proposition effected by the mind in joining a predicate to a subject. Taking *to be* in the first sense we cannot understand God's being (or His essence) ; but only in the second sense. We know that this proposition which we form about God when we say *God is*, is true; and this we know from His effects, as was said above.[16]

---

[16] Q. 2, a. 2.

Fifth Article
Whether God Is Contained in a Genus?

We proceed thus to the Fifth Article:—

Objection 1. It seems that God is contained in a genus. For a substance is a being that subsists of itself. But to be such a being is especially true of God. Therefore God is in the genus of substance.

Obj. 2. Further, each thing is measured by something of its own genus; as length is measured by length and numbers by number. But God is the measure of all substances, as the Commentator shows.[17] Therefore God is in the genus of substance.

On the contrary, Genus is prior in meaning to what it contains. But nothing is prior to God either really or in meaning. Therefore God is not in any genus.

I answer that, A thing can be in a genus in two ways: either absolutely and properly, as a species contained under a genus; or as being reducible to it, as principles and privations. For example, *point* and *unity* are reduced to the genus of quantity as its principles, while blindness and all other privations are reduced to the genus of habit. But in neither of these ways is God in a genus. That He cannot be a species of any genus may be shown in three ways. First, because a species is constituted of genus and difference. Now that from which the difference constituting the species is derived is always related to that from which the genus is derived as actuality is related to potentiality. For *animal* is derived from sensitive nature by concretion, for that is animal which has a sensitive nature. *Rational*, on the other hand, is derived from intellectual nature, because that is rational which has an intellectual nature. Now the intellectual is compared to the sensitive as actuality is to potentiality. The same argument holds good in other things. Hence, since in God potentiality is not added to actuality, it is impossible that He should be in any genus as a species. Second, since the being of God is His essence, if God were in any genus, He would have to be in the genus *being*, because, since genus is predicated essentially, it refers to the essence of a thing. But the Philosopher has shown that being cannot be a genus, for every genus has differences outside the generic essence.[18] Now no difference can exist distinct from being, for non-being cannot be a difference. It follows then that God is not in a genus. Third, because all members of one genus share in the quiddity or essence of the genus which is predicated of them essentially, but they differ in their

---

[17]*In Metaph.*, X, comm. 7 (VIII, 120 v). [18]*Metaph.*, II, 3 (998b 22).

being. For the being of man and of horse is not the same; nor is the being of this man and that man. Thus, in every member of a genus, being and quiddity—*i.e.*, essence—must differ. But in God they do not differ, as was shown in the preceding article. Therefore it is plain that God is not in a genus as if He were a species. From this it is also plain that He has no genus or difference, nor can there be any definition of Him; nor save through His effects, a demonstration of Him; for a definition is from genus and difference, and the means of a demonstration is a definition.

That God is not in a genus, as reducible to it as its principle, is clear from this, that a principle reducible to any genus does not extend beyond that genus: *e.g.*, a point is the principle of continuous quantity alone, and unity, of discontinuous quantity. But God is the principle of all being, as will later be shown.[19] Therefore He is not contained in any genus as its principle.

Reply Obj. 1. The name *substance* signifies not only what is being of itself—for being cannot of itself be a genus, as has been shown; but it also signifies an essence to which it belongs to be in this way—namely, of itself, which being, however, is not its essence. Thus it is clear that God is not in the genus of substance.

Reply Obj. 2. This objection turns upon proportionate measure, which must be homogeneous with what is measured. Now, God is not a measure proportionate to anything. Still, He is called the measure of all things, in the sense that everything has being only according as it resembles Him.

Sixth Article
Whether in God There Are Any Accidents?

We proceed thus to the Sixth Article:—

Objection 1. It seems that there are accidents in God. For substance cannot be an accident, as Aristotle says.[20] Therefore that which is accident in one, cannot, in another, be a substance. Thus it is proved that heat cannot be the substantial form of fire, because it is an accident in other things. But wisdom, power, and the like, which are accidents in us, are attributes of God. Therefore in God there are accidents.

Obj. 2. Further, in every genus there is a first principle. But there are many *genera* of accidents. If, therefore, the primal members of these genera are not in God, there will be many primal beings other than God—which is absurd.

---

[19]Q. 44, a. 1. [Not in this volume]   [20]*Phys.* 1, 3 (186b 4).

On the contrary, Every accident is in a subject. But God cannot be a subject, for *no simple form can be a subject*, as Boethius says.[21] Therefore in God there cannot be any accident.

I answer that, From all we have said, it is clear there can be no accident in God. First, because a subject is compared to its accidents as potentiality to actuality; for a subject is in some sense made actual by its accidents. But there can be no potentiality in God, as was shown. Second, because God is His own being, and as Boethius says, although that which is may have something superadded to it, this cannot happen to being itself.[22] Thus, a heated substance can have something extraneous to heat added to it, as whiteness, but heat itself can have nothing else than heat. Third, because what is essential is prior to what is accidental. Whence, as God is absolute primal being, there can be in Him nothing accidental. Neither can He have any essential accidents (as the capability of laughing is an essential accident of man), because such accidents are caused by the constituent principles of the subject. Now there can be nothing caused in God, since He is the first cause. Hence it follows that there is no accident in God.

Reply Obj. 1. Power and wisdom are not predicated of God and of us univocally, as will later be clear.[23] Hence it does not follow that there are accidents in God as there are in us.

Reply Obj. 2. Since substance is prior to its accidents, the principles of accidents are reducible to the principles of the substance as to that which is prior. Now God is not first as contained in the genus of substance; He is first in respect to all being, outside every genus.

Seventh Article
Whether God Is Altogether Simple?

We proceed thus to the Seventh Article:—

Objection 1. It seems that God is not altogether simple. For whatever is from God imitates Him. Thus from the first being are all beings, and from the first good are all goods. But in the things which God has made, nothing is altogether simple. Therefore neither is God altogether simple.

Obj. 2. Further, whatever is better must be attributed to God. But with us that which is composite is better than that which is simple: thus, chemical compounds are better than elements, and elements than the parts that compose them Therefore it cannot be said that God is altogether simple.

---

[21]*De Trin.*, II (PL 64,1250).   [22]*De Hebdom.* (PL 64, 1311).   [23]Q. 13, a. 6. [Not in this volume]

On the contrary, Augustine says, *God is truly and absolutely simple.*[24]

I answer that, The absolute simplicity of God may be shown in many ways. First, from the previous articles of this question. For there is neither composition of quantitative parts in God, since He is not a body; nor composition of form and matter; nor does His nature differ from His *suppositum*; nor His essence from His being; neither is there in Him composition of genus and difference, nor of subject and accident. Therefore, it is clear that God is in no way composite, but is altogether simple. Secondly, because every composite is posterior to its component parts, and is dependent on them; but God is the first being, as has been shown above.[25] Thirdly, because every composite has a cause, for things in themselves diverse cannot unite unless something caused them to unite. But God is uncaused, as has been shown above,[26] since He is the first efficient cause. Fourthly, because in every composite there must be potentiality and actuality (this does not apply to God) for either one of the parts actualizes another, or at least all the parts are as it were in potency with respect to the whole. Fifthly, because nothing composite can be predicated of any one of its parts. And this is evident in a whole made up of dissimilar parts; for no part of a man is a man, nor any of the parts of the foot, a foot. But in wholes made up of similar parts, although something which is predicated of the whole may be predicated of a part (as a part of the air is air, and a part of water, water), nevertheless certain things are predicable of the whole which cannot be predicated of any of the parts; for instance, if the whole volume of water is two cubits, no part of it can be two cubits. Thus in every composite there is something which is not itself. But, even if this could be said of whatever has a form, viz., that it has something which is not it itself, as in a white object there is something which does not belong to the essence of white, nevertheless, in the form itself there is nothing besides itself. And so, since God is absolute form, or rather absolute being, He can be in no way composite. Hilary touches upon this argument when he says: *God, Who is strength, is not made up of things that are weak; nor is He, Who is light, composed of thing that are dark.*[27]

Reply Obj. 1. Whatever is from God imitates Him, as caused things imitate the first cause. But it is of the essence of a thing caused to be in some way composite; because at least its being differs from its essence, as will be shown hereafter.[28]

Reply Obj. 2. With us composite things are better than simple things, because the perfection of created goodness is not found in one simple

---

[24]*De Trin.*, VI, 6 (PL 42, 928).   [25]Q. 2, a. 3.   [26]*Ibid.*   [27]*De Trin.*, VII (PL 10, 223).   [28]Q. 50, a. 2. [Not in this volume]

thing, but in many things. But the perfection of divine goodness is found in one simple thing, as will be shown hereafter.[29]

Eighth Article
Whether God Enters into the Composition of Other Things?

We proceed thus to the Eighth Article:—

Objection 1. It seems that God enters into the composition of other things, for Dionysius says: *The being of all things is that which is above being—the Godhead.*[30] But the being of all things enters into the composition of everything. Therefore God enters into the composition of other things.

Obj. 2. Further, God is a form; for Augustine says that, *the word of God which is God, is an uncreated form.*[31] But a form is part of a composite. Therefore God is part of some composite.

Obj. 3. Further, whatever things exist, in no way differing from each other, are the same. But God and primary matter exist, and in no way differ from each other. Therefore they are absolutely the same. But primary matter enters into the composition of things. Therefore so does God. Proof of the minor: whatever things differ, they differ by some differences, and therefore must be composite. But God and primary matter are altogether simple. Therefore they nowise differ from each other.

On the contrary, Dionysius says: *There can be no touching Him, i.e., God, nor any other union with Him by mingling part with part.*[32]

Further, the first cause rules all things without commingling with them, as it is said in the *Book of Causes.*[33]

I answer that, On this point there have been three errors. Some have affirmed that God is world-soul, as is clear from Augustine.[34] This is also the opinion of those who assert that God is the soul of the first heavens. Again, others[35] have said that God is the formal principle of all things; and this is said to have been the theory of the Almaricians.[36] The third error is that of David of Dinant,[37] who most stupidly taught that God was primary matter. Now all these contain manifest untruth, since it is not possible for God to enter into the composition of anything, either as a formal or a material principle. First, because we pointed out above that God

---

[29]Q. 4, a. 1; Q. 6, a. 3. [Not in this volume] [30]*De Cael. Hier.,* IV, 1 (PG 3, 177). [31]*Serm.* CXVII, 2 (PL 38, 662). [32]*De Div. Nom.,* II, 5 (PG 3, 643). [33]*De Causis,* XX (p. 177). [34]*De Civit. Dei,* VII, 6 (PL 41, 199). [35]Cf. *C. G.,* I, 27. [36]Cf. G. C. Capelle, *Amaury de Bène* (Paris: J. Vrin, 1932), pp. 42–50. [37]Cf. G. Théry, *David de Dinant* (Paris: J. Vrin, 1925), pp. 34–45.

is the first efficient cause.[38] Now the efficient cause is not identical numerically with the form of the thing caused, but only specifically: for man begets man. But primary matter can be neither numerically nor specifically identical with an efficient cause; for primary matter exists potentially, while the efficient cause exists actually. Secondly, because, since God is the first efficient cause, to act belongs to Him primarily and essentially. But that which enters into composition with anything does not act primarily and essentially, but rather the composite so acts; for the hand does not act, but the man by his hand and fire warms by its heat. Hence God cannot be part of a composite. Thirdly, because no part of a composite can be absolutely first among beings—not even matter, nor form, though they are the first parts of composites. For matter is merely potential, and potentiality is posterior absolutely to actuality, as is clear from the foregoing, while a form which is part of a composite is a participated form; and as that which participates is posterior to that which is essential, so likewise is that which is participated, as fire in ignited things is posterior to fire that is essentially such. Now it has been proved that God is absolutely the first being.[39]

Reply Obj. 1. The Godhead is called the being of all things as their efficient and exemplar cause, but not as being their essence.

Reply Obj. 2. The Word is an exemplar form, but not a form that is part of a composite.

Reply Obj. 3. Simple things do not differ by added differences,—for this belongs to composites. Thus man and horse differ by their differences, rational and irrational; which differences, however, do not differ from each other by other differences. Hence, to be quite accurate, it is better to say that they are, not different, but diverse. Hence, according to the Philosopher, *things are said to be diverse absolutely, but things which are different differ by something.*[40] Therefore, strictly speaking, primary matter and God do not differ, but are by their very being diverse. Hence it does not follow that they are the same.

Question 4

The Perfection of God

(*In Three Articles*)

Having considered the divine simplicity, we treat next of God's perfection. Now because it is in so far as it is perfect that everything is called

---

[38]Q. 2, a. 3.   [39]*Ibid.*   [40]*Metaph.*, IX, 3 (1054b 24).

good, we shall speak first of the divine perfection; secondly of the divine goodness.[1]

Concerning the first there are three points of inquiry:—

(1) Whether God is perfect? (2) Whether God is perfect universally, as having in Himself the perfections of all things? (3) Whether creatures can be said to be like God?

First Article
Whether God Is Perfect?

We proceed thus to the First Article:—

Objection 1. It seems that to be perfect does not belong to God. For we say that a thing is perfect if it is completely made. But it does not befit God to be made. Therefore, neither does it befit Him to be perfect.

Obj. 2. Further, God is the first beginning of things. But the beginnings of things seem to be imperfect, for a seed is the beginning of animals and plants. Therefore God is imperfect.

Obj. 3. Further, as has been shown above, God's essence is being itself.[2] But being itself seems most imperfect, since it is most universal and receptive of all modification. Therefore God is imperfect.

On the contrary, It is written: *Be you perfect as also your heavenly Father is perfect (Matt.* v. 48).

I answer that, As the Philosopher relates,[3] some ancient philosophers, namely, the Pythagoreans and Speusippus, did not predicate *best* and *most perfect* of the first principle. The reason was that the ancient philosophers considered only a material principle; and a material principle is most imperfect. For since matter as such is merely potential, the first material principle must be absolutely potential, and thus most imperfect. Now God is the first principle, not material, but in the order of efficient cause, which must be most perfect. For just as matter, as such, is merely potential, so an agent, as such, is in a state of actuality. Hence, the first active principle must needs be most actual, and therefore most perfect; for a thing is said to be perfect in proportion to its actuality, because we call that perfect which lacks nothing of the mode of its perfection.

Reply Obj. 1. As Gregory says: *Though our lips can only stammer, we yet chant the high things of God.*[4] For that which has not been made is improperly called perfect. Nevertheless, because things which come to be are then called perfect when from potentiality they are brought into actuality,

---

[1]Q. 5. [Not in this volume]   [2]Q. 3, a. 4.   [3]*Metaph.,* XI, 7 (1072b 30).
[4]*Moral.,* V, 36 (PL 75, 715).

this term *perfect* signifies by extension whatever is not wanting in actual being, whether this be by way of having been produced or not.

Reply Obj. 2. The material principle which with us is found to be imperfect, cannot be absolutely first, but is preceded by something perfect. For the seed, though it be the principle of the animal generated through it, has previous to it the animal or plant from which it came. Because, previous to that which is potential, must be that which is actual, since a potential being can be reduced to act only by some being already actual.

Reply Obj. 3. Being itself is the most perfect of all things, for it is compared to all things as that which is act; for nothing has actuality except so far as it is. Hence being is the actuality of all things, even of forms themselves. Therefore it is not compared to other things as the receiver is to the received, but rather as the received to the receiver. When therefore I speak of the being of man, or of a horse, or of anything else, being is considered as a formal principle, and as something received, and not as that to which being belongs.

Second Article
Whether the Perfections of All Things Are in God?

We proceed thus to the Second Article:—

Objection 1. It seems that the perfections of all things are not in God. For God is simple, as has been shown above,[5] whereas the perfections of things are many and diverse. Therefore the perfections of all things are not in God.

Obj. 2. Further, opposites cannot coexist. Now the perfections of things are opposed to each other, for each species is perfected by its own specific difference. But the differences by which a *genus* is divided, and *species* constituted, are opposed to each other. Therefore, because opposites cannot co-exist in the same subject, it seems that the perfections of all things are not in God.

Obj. 3. Further, a living thing is more perfect than what merely exists, and an intelligent thing than what merely lives. Therefore, to live is more perfect than to be, and to know than to live. But the essence of God is being itself. Therefore He has not the perfections of life, and knowledge, and other similar perfections.

On the contrary, Dionysius says that *God in His one existence prepossesses all things.*[6]

---

[5]Q. 3, a. 7.   [6]*De Div. Nom.*, V, 9 (PG 3, 825).

I answer that, All the perfections of all things are in God. Hence He is spoken of as universally perfect, because He lacks not (says the Commentator[7]) any excellence which may be found in any genus. This may be seen from two considerations.

First, because whatever perfection exists in an effect must be found in the producing cause: either in the same formality, if it is a univocal agent—as when man reproduces man; or in a more eminent degree, if it is an equivocal agent—thus in the sun is the likeness of whatever is generated by the sun's power. Now it is plain that the effect pre-exists virtually in the efficient cause; and although to pre-exist in the potentiality of a material cause is to pre-exist in a more imperfect way, since matter as such is imperfect, and an agent as such is perfect, still to pre-exist virtually in the efficient cause is to pre-exist not in a more imperfect, but in a more perfect, way. Since therefore God is the first producing cause of things, the perfections of all things must pre-exist in God in a more eminent way. Dionysius touches upon this argument by saying of God: *It is not that He is this and not that, but that He is all, as the cause of all.*[8]

Secondly, from what has been already proved,[9] God is being itself, of itself subsistent. Consequently, He must contain within Himself the whole perfection of being. For it is clear that if some hot thing has not the whole perfection of heat, this is because heat is not participated in its full perfection; but if this heat were self-subsisting, nothing of the virtue of heat would be wanting to it. Since therefore God is subsisting being itself, nothing of the perfection of being can be wanting to Him. Now all the perfections of all things pertain to the perfection of being; for things are perfect precisely so far as they have being after some fashion. It follows therefore that the perfection of no thing is wanting to God. This line of argument, too, is touched upon by Dionysius when he says that *God exists not in any single mode, but embraces all being within Himself, absolutely, without limitation, uniformly;*[10] and afterwards he adds that *He is very being to subsisting things.*[11]

Reply Obj. 1. Even as the sun, as Dionysius remarks, *while remaining one and shining uniformly, contains within itself first and uniformly the substances of sensible things, and many and diverse qualities; a fortiori should all things in a kind of natural unity pre-exist in the cause of all things;*[12] and thus

---

[7]*Metaph.,* V, comm. 21 (VIII, 62 r).   [8]*De Div. Nom.,* V, 8 (PG 3, 824).
[9]Q. 3, a. 4.   [10]*De Div. Nom.,* V, 4 (PG 3, 817).   [11]*Ibid.*   [12]*Op. cit.,*
V, 8 (PG 3, 824).

things diverse and in themselves opposed to each other pre-exist in God as one, without injury to His simplicity.

This suffices for the *Reply to the Second Objection.*

Reply Obj. 3. The same Dionysius says that, although being itself is more perfect than life, and life than wisdom, if they are considered as distinguished in idea, nevertheless, a living thing is more perfect than what merely is, because a living thing is also a being, and an intelligent thing is both a being and alive.[13] Although therefore being does not include life and wisdom, because that which participates being need not participate in every mode of being, nevertheless God's being includes in itself life and wisdom, because nothing of the perfection of being can be wanting to Him Who is subsisting being itself.

Third Article
Whether Any Creature Can Be Like God?

We proceed thus to the Third Article:—

Objection 1. It seems that no creature can be like God. For it is written (*Ps.* lxxxv. 8): *There is none among the gods like unto Thee, O Lord.* But of all creatures the most excellent are those which are called by participation gods. Therefore still less can other creatures be said to be like to God.

Obj. 2. Further, a likeness is a certain comparison. But there can be no comparison between things in diverse genera. Therefore neither can there be any likeness. Thus we do not say that sweetness is like whiteness. But no creature is in the same genus as God, since God is in no genus, as has been shown above.[14] Therefore no creature is like God.

Obj. 3. Further, we speak of those things as like which agree in form. But nothing can agree with God in form; for only in God is the essence being itself. Therefore no creature can be like to God.

Obj. 4. Further, among like things there is mutual likeness; for like is like to like. If therefore any creature is like God, God will be like some creature, which is against what is said by Isaias: *To whom have you likened God?* (xl. 18).

On the contrary, It is written: *Let us make man to our image and likeness* (*Gen.* i. 26), and: *When He shall appear, we shall be like to Him* (*1 John* iii. 2).

I answer that, Since likeness is based upon agreement or communication in form, it varies according to the many modes of communication in form. Some things are said to be like, which communicate in the same

---

[13]*Op. cit.,* V, 3 (PG 3, 817).   [14]Q. 3, a. 5.

form according to the same formality, and according to the same measure; and these are said to be not merely like, but equal in their likeness, as two things equally white are said to be alike in whiteness; and this is the most perfect likeness. In another way, we speak of things as alike which communicate in form according to the same formality, though not according to the same measure, but according to more or less, as something less white is said to be like another thing more white; and this is imperfect likeness. In a third way some things are said to be alike which communicate in the same form, but not according to the same formality; as we see in non-univocal agents. For since every agent reproduces itself so far as it is an agent, and everything acts in accord with its form, the effect must in some way resemble the form of the agent. If therefore the agent is contained in the same species as its effect, there will be a likeness in form between that which makes and that which is made, according to the same formality of the species; as man reproduces man. If however the agent and its effect are not contained in the same species, there will be a likeness, but not according to the formality of the same species; as things generated by the sun's power may reach some likeness of the sun, not indeed so as to receive the form of the sun in its specific likeness, but only in its generic likeness. Therefore, if there is an agent not contained in any genus, its effects will still more distantly reproduce the form of the agent, not, that is, so as to participate in the likeness of the agent's form according to the same specific or generic formality, but only according to some sort of analogy; as being itself is common to all. In this way all created things, so far as they are beings, are like God as the first and universal principle of all being.

Reply Obj. 1. As Dionysius says, when Holy Scripture declares that nothing is like God, it does not mean to deny all likeness to Him. *For, the same things can be like and unlike to God: like, according as they imitate Him, as far as He, Who is not imitable perfectly, can be imitated; unlike, according as they fall short of their cause,*[15] not merely in intensity and remission, as that which is less white falls short of that which is more white, but because they are not in agreement, specifically or generically.

Reply Obj. 2. God is not related to creatures as though belonging to a different genus, but as transcending every genus, and as the principle of all genera.

Reply Obj. 3. Likeness of creatures to God is not affirmed because of agreement in form according to the same formality of genus or species,

---

[15]*De Div. Nom.*, X, 7 (PG 3, 916).

but solely according to analogy, viz., inasmuch as God is essential being, whereas other things are beings by participation.

Reply Obj. 4. Although it may be admitted that creatures are in some way like God, it can in no way be admitted that God is like creatures; because, as Dionysius says: *A mutual likeness may be found between things of the same order, but not between a cause and that which is caused.*[16] For we say that a statue is like a man, but not conversely; so also a creature can be spoken of as in some way like God, but not that God is like a creature.

---

[16]*Op. cit.*, IX, 6 (PG 3, 913).

THE DIVINE OPERATIONS

Summa Theologica
Part One
Question 18
The Life of God
(*In Four Articles*)

Since to understand belongs to living beings, after considering the divine knowledge and intellect, we must consider the divine life. About this, four points of inquiry arise: (1) To whom does it belong to live? (2) What is life? (3) Whether life is properly attributed to God? (4) Whether all things in God are life?

First Article
Whether to Live Belongs to All Natural Things?

We proceed thus to the First Article:—

Objection 1. It seems that to live belongs to all natural things. For the Philosopher says that *movement is like a kind of life possessed by all things existing in nature.*[1] But all natural things participate in movement. Therefore all natural things partake in life.

Obj. 2. Further, plants are said to live, inasmuch as they have in themselves a principle of movement, of growth and decay. But local movement is naturally more perfect than, and prior to, movement of growth and decay, as the Philosopher shows.[2] Since, then, all natural bodies have in themselves some principle of local movement, it seems that all natural bodies live.

Obj. 3. Further, among natural bodies the elements are the less perfect. Yet life is attributed to them, for we speak of "living waters." Much more, therefore, have other natural bodies life.

On the contrary, Dionysius says that *The last echo of life is heard in the plants;*[3] whereby it is inferred that their life is life in its lowest degree. But inanimate bodies are inferior to plants. Therefore they have not life.

I answer that, We can gather to what things life belongs, and to what it does not, from such things as manifestly possess life. Now life manifestly

---

[1]*Phys.*, VIII, 1 (250b 14).   [2]*Op. cit.*, VIII, 7 (260a 28).   [3]*De Div. Nom.*, VI, 1 (PG 3, 856).

belongs to animals, for it is said in *De Vegetab.* i. that in animals life is manifest.[4] We must, therefore, distinguish living from lifeless things by comparing them to that by reason of which animals are said to live: and this it is in which life is manifested first and remains last. We say then that an animal begins to live when it begins to move of itself: and as long as such movement appears in it, so long is it considered to be alive. When it no longer has any movement of itself, but is moved only by another power, then its life is said to fail, and the animal to be dead. Whereby it is clear that those beings are properly called living that move themselves by some kind of movement, whether it be movement properly so called, as *the act of the imperfect* (*i.e.*, of a thing which exists in potentiality) is called movement; or movement in a more general sense, as when said of *the act of the perfect*, as *understanding* and *sensing* are called movements, as is said in *De Anima*, iii.[5] Accordingly, all things are said to be alive that determine themselves to movement or to operation of any kind: whereas those things that cannot by their nature do so cannot be called living, unless by some likeness.

Reply Obj. 1. These words of the Philosopher may be understood either of the first movement, namely, that of the celestial bodies, or of movement in its general sense. In either way movement is called the life, as it were, of natural bodies only metaphorically and not properly. The movement of the heavens is in the universe of corporeal natures as the movement of the heart, whereby life is preserved, is in animals. Similarly also every natural movement in respect to natural things has a certain likeness to the operations of life. Hence, if the whole corporeal universe were one animal, so that its movement came from an interior moving principle, as some in fact have held, in that case movement would really be the life of all natural bodies.

Reply Obj. 2. To bodies, whether heavy or light, movement does not belong, except in so far as they are displaced from their natural conditions, and are out of their proper place; for when they are in the place that is proper and natural to them, then they are at rest. Plants and other living things move with vital movement, in accordance with the disposition of their nature, but not by approaching thereto, or by receding from it, for in so far as they recede from such movement, so far do they recede from their natural disposition. Furthermore, *heavy and light bodies are moved by an extrinsic mover, either generating them and giving them form, or removing*

---

[4]Aristotle, *De Plantis*, I, 1 (815a 10).   [5]Aristotle, *De An.*, III, 7 (431a 6); I, 4 (408b 6).

obstacles from their way, as is said in *Physics* viii.[6] They do not therefore move themselves, as do living bodies.

Reply Obj. 3. Waters are called living that have a continuous current: for standing waters, that are not connected with a continually flowing source, are called dead, as in cisterns and ponds. This is merely a similitude, inasmuch as the movement they are seen to possess makes them look as if they were alive. Yet they do not have life in its real nature, since this movement of theirs is not from themselves but from the cause that generates them; as is the case with the movement of other heavy and light bodies.

Second Article
Whether Life Is an Operation?

We proceed thus to the Second Article:—

Objection 1. It seems that life is an operation. For nothing is divided except into parts of the same genus. But life is divided by certain operations, as is clear from the Philosopher[7] who distinguishes four kinds of life, namely, nourishment, sensation, local movement and understanding. Therefore life is an operation.

Obj. 2. Further, the active life is said to be different from the contemplative. But the contemplative is only distinguished from the active by certain operations. Therefore life is an operation.

Obj. 3. Further, to know God is an operation. But this is life, as is clear from the words of *John* xvii. 3, *Now this is eternal life, that they may know Thee, the only true God.* Therefore life is an operation.

On the contrary, The Philosopher says: *In living things to live is to be.*[8]

I answer that, As is clear from what has been said, our intellect, which knows the essence of a thing as its proper object, derives knowledge from sense, of which the proper objects are external accidents.[9] Hence it is that from external appearances we come to the knowledge of the essence of things. And because we name a thing in accordance with our knowledge of it, as is clear from what has already been said,[10] so from external properties names are often imposed to signify essences. Hence such names are sometimes taken strictly to denote the essence itself, the signification of which is their principal object; but sometimes, and less strictly, to denote the properties by reason of which they are imposed. And so we see that

---

[6]Aristotle, *Phys.*, VIII, 4 (255b 35).   [7]*De An.*, II, 2 (413a 22).   [8]*Op. cit.*, II, 4 (415b 13).   [9]Q. 17, a. 1 and 3. [Not in this volume]   [10]Q. 13, a. 1. [Not in this volume]

the word *body is* used to denote a particular genus of substances from the fact of their possessing three dimensions; and so it is sometimes taken to denote the dimensions themselves, in which sense body is said to be a species of quantity.

The same must be said of life. The name is given from a certain external appearance, namely, self-movement, yet not precisely to signify this, but rather a substance to which self-movement, or the application of itself to any kind of operation, belongs naturally. *To live*, accordingly, is nothing else than for a substance with such a nature *to be;* and *life* signifies this very fact, but abstractly, as *running* abstractly signifies *to run.* Hence *living* is not an accidental, but a substantial, predicate. Sometimes, however, life is used less properly for the operations from which its name is taken; and thus the Philosopher says that *to live is principally to sense or to understand.*[11]

Reply Obj. 1. The Philosopher here takes *to live* to mean an operation of life. Or it would be better to say that sensation and intelligence, and the like, are sometimes taken for the operations, sometimes for the being itself of those who are operating in this way. For he says that to be is to sense or to understand[12]—in other words, to have a nature capable of sensation or understanding. It is in this way that he distinguishes life by the four operations mentioned. For in this lower world there are four kinds of living things. It is the nature of some to be capable of nothing more than taking nourishment, and, as a consequence, of growing and generating. Others are able, in addition, to sense, as we see in the case of shellfish and other animals without movement. Others have the further power of moving from place to place, as perfect animals, such as quadrupeds, and birds, and so on. Others, as man, have the still higher perfection of understanding.

Reply Obj. 2. By vital operations are meant those whose principles are within the operator, and in virtue of which the operator produces such operations of itself. It happens, however, that there exist in men not merely such natural principles of certain operations as are their natural powers, but something over and above these, namely, habits inclining them in the manner of a nature to particular kinds of operations and rendering those operations pleasurable. Thus, as by a similitude, any kind of work in which a man takes delight, so that his bent is towards it, his time spent in it, and his whole life ordered with a view to it, is said to be the life of that man. Hence some are said to lead a life of self-indulgence, others a life of virtue. It is in this way that the contemplative life is distinguished

---

[11]*Eth.,* IX, 9 (1170a 18).   [12]*Ibid* (1170a 33).

from the active; and in this manner likewise to know God is said to be life eternal.

Wherefore the Reply to the third objection is clear.

Third Article
Whether Life Is Properly Attributed to God?

We proceed thus to the Third Article:—

Objection 1. It seems that life is not properly attributed to God. For things are said to live inasmuch as they move themselves, as was previously stated. But movement does not belong to God. Neither therefore does life.

Obj. 2. Further, in all living things we must needs suppose some principle of life. Hence it is said by the Philosopher that *the soul is the cause and principle of the living body.*[13] But God has no principle. Therefore life cannot be attributed to Him.

Obj. 3. Further, the principle of life in the living things around us is the vegetative soul. But this exists only in corporeal things. Therefore life cannot be attributed to incorporeal things.

On the contrary, It is said (*Ps.* lxxxiii. 3): *My heart and my flesh have rejoiced in the living God.*

I answer that, Life is most properly in God. In proof of which it must be considered that since a thing is said to live in so far as it operates of itself and not as moved by another, the more perfectly this power is found in anything, the more perfect is the life of that thing. In things that move and are moved three things are distinguished in order. In the first place, the end moves the agent: and the principal agent is that which acts through its own form (sometimes it does so through some instrument that acts by virtue, not of its own form, but of the principal agent, and does no more than execute the action). Accordingly, there are things that move themselves, not in relation to any form or end, which is naturally inherent in them, but only in relation to the execution of the movement: the form by which they act, and the end of the action are determined for them by their nature. Of this kind are plants, which move themselves according to their inherent nature, with regard only to executing the movements of growth and decay.

Other things have self-movement in a higher degree, that is, not only with relation to the execution of the movement, but even with relation to the form which is the principle of movement, which they acquire by

---

[13]*De An.*, II, 4 (415b 8).

themselves. Of this kind are animals, in which the principle of movement is not a naturally implanted form, but one received through sense. Hence the more perfect their sense, the more perfect is their power of self-movement. Such as have only the sense of touch, as shellfish, move only with the motion of expansion and contraction; and thus their movement hardly exceeds that of plants. Whereas such as have the power of sense in perfection, so as to recognize not only what is joined to them or touches them, but also objects apart from themselves, can move themselves to a distance by progressive movement.

Yet although animals of the latter kind receive through sense the form that is the principle of their movement, nevertheless they cannot of themselves propose to themselves the end of their operation or their movement, for this has been implanted in them by nature; and by natural instinct they are moved to any action through the form apprehended by sense. Hence such animals as move themselves in relation to an end that they themselves propose are superior to these. This can be done only by reason and intellect, whose province it is to know the proportion between the end and the means to that end, and duly co-ordinate them. Hence a more perfect degree of life is that of intelligent beings, for their power of self-movement is more perfect. This is shown by the fact that in one and the same man the intellectual power moves the sensitive powers; and these by their command move the organs of movement. Just as also in the arts we see that the art of using a ship, *i.e.*, the art of navigation, rules the art of ship-designing; and this in its turn rules the art that is only concerned with preparing the material for the ship.

But although our intellect moves itself to some things, yet others are set for it by nature, as are first principles, which it must accept, and the last end, which it cannot but will. Hence, although with respect to some things it moves itself, yet with regard to other things it must be moved by another. Hence, that being whose act of understanding is its very nature, and which, in what it naturally possesses, is not determined by another, must have life in the most perfect degree. Such is God; and hence in Him principally is life. From this the Philosopher concludes, after showing God to be intelligent, that God has life most perfect and eternal, since His intellect is most perfect and always in act.[14]

Reply Obj. 1. As is stated in *Metaph.* ix.,[15] action is twofold. Actions of one kind pass out to external matter, as to heat or to cut, while actions of the other kind remain in the agent, as to understand, to sense, and to will.

---

[14]*Metaph.*, XI, 7 (1072b 27).   [15]*Op. cit.*, VIII, 8 (1050a 22).

The difference between them is this, that the former action is the perfection, not of the agent that moves, but of the thing moved; whereas the latter action is the perfection of the agent. Hence, because movement is an act of the thing in movement, the latter action, in so far as it is the act of the operator, is called its movement, on the basis of the similitude that as movement is an act of the thing moved, so an action of this kind is the act of the agent. And although movement is an act of the imperfect, that is, of what is in potentiality, this kind of action is an act of the perfect, that is to say, of what is in act, as is stated in *De anima* iii.[16] In the sense, therefore, in which understanding is movement, that which understands itself is said to move itself. It is in this sense that Plato also taught that God moves Himself,[17] and not in the sense in which movement is an act of the imperfect.

Reply Obj. 2. As God is His own being and understanding, so He is His own life; and therefore He so lives that He has no principle of life.

Reply Obj. 3. Life in this lower world is bestowed on a corruptible nature, that needs generation to preserve the species, and nourishment to preserve the individual. For this reason life is not found here below apart from a vegetative soul: but this does not hold good among incorruptible beings.

Fourth Article
Whether All Things Are Life in God?

We proceed thus to the Fourth Article:—

Objection 1. It seems that not all things are life in God. For it is said (*Acts* xvii, 28), *In Him we live, and move, and are.* But not all things in God are movement. Therefore not all things are life in Him.

Obj. 2. Further, all things are in God as in their first exemplar. But all likenesses of an exemplar should be modeled after it. Since, then, not all things have life in themselves, it seems that not all things are life in God.

Obj. 3. Further, as Augustine says,[18] a living substance is better than a substance that does not live. If, therefore, things which in themselves have not life are life in God, it seems that things exist more truly in God than in themselves. But this appears to be false, since in themselves they exist actually, but in God potentially.

Obj. 4. Further, just as good things and things made in time are known by God, so are evils and things that God can make, but that never will be

---

[16]Aristotle, *De An.*, III, 7 (413a 6).   [17]Cf. above, q. 9, a. 1, ad 1.   [18]*De Vera Relig.*, XXIX (PL 34, 145).

made. If, therefore, all things are life in God, inasmuch as known by Him, it seems that even evils and things that will never be made are life in God, as known by Him, and this appears inadmissible.

On the contrary, It is said (*Jo.* i. 3, 4), *What was made, in Him was life.* But all things were made, except God. Therefore all things are life in God.

I answer that, In God to live is to understand, as was before stated. But in God intellect, the thing understood, and the act of understanding are one and the same. Hence whatever is in God as understood is the very living or life of God. Now, therefore, since all things that have been made by God are in Him as things understood, it follows that all things in Him are the divine life itself.

Reply Obj. 1. Creatures are said to be in God in a twofold sense. In one way, so far as they are contained and preserved by the divine power; even as we say that things that are in our power are in us. And thus creatures are said to be in God, even according to their existence in their own natures. In this sense we must understand the words of the Apostle when he says, *In Him we live, and move, and are;* since our living, being and moving are themselves caused by God. In another sense, things are said to be in God as in Him who knows them; in which sense they are in God through their proper likenesses, which are nothing other in God than the divine essence. Hence things as they are in this way in God are the divine essence. And since the divine essence is life but not movement, it follows that things existing in God in this manner are not movement, but life.

Reply Obj. 2. The thing modeled must be like the exemplar according to the form, not the mode of being. For sometimes the form has being of another kind in the exemplar from that which it has in the thing modeled. Thus the form of a house has immaterial and intelligible being in the mind of the architect; but in the house that exists outside his mind, material and sensible being. Hence the likenesses of these things, which do not have life in themselves, are life in the divine mind, as having a divine being in that mind.

Reply Obj. 3. If form only, and not matter, belonged to natural things, then in all respects natural things would exist more truly in the divine mind, by the ideas of them, than in themselves. For which reason, in fact, Plato held that the *separate* man was the true man,[19] and that man, as he exists in matter, is man only by participation. But since matter enters into

---

[19]Cf. St. Augustine, *Epist.* III (PL 33, 64); *Epist.* CXVIII, 3 (PL 33, 441).—Cf. also Aristotle, *Metaph.*, I, 6 (987b 7).

the being of natural things, we must say that natural things have a truer being absolutely in the divine mind than in themselves, because in that mind they have an uncreated being, but in themselves a created being. But to be this particular being, namely, a man or a horse, this they have more truly in their own nature than in the divine mind, because it belongs to human nature to be material, which, as existing in the divine mind, it is not. Even so a house has nobler being in the architect's mind than in matter; yet a material house is called a house more truly than the one which exists in the mind, since the former is actual, the latter only potential.

Reply Obj. 4. Although evils are in God's knowledge, as being comprehended by that knowledge, yet they are not in God as created by Him, or preserved by Him, or as having a likeness in Him. For they are known by God through the likenesses of good things. Hence it cannot be said that evils are life in God. Those things that at no time exist may be called life in God in so far as life means understanding only, and inasmuch as they are understood by God; but not in so far as life implies a source of operation.

Question 19
The Will of God
(*In Twelve Articles*)

After considering the things belonging to the divine knowledge, we consider what belongs to the divine will. The first consideration is about the divine will itself; the second, about what belongs to His will absolutely;[1] the third, about what belongs to the intellect in relation to His will.[2] About His will itself there are twelve points of inquiry: (1) Whether there is will in God? (2) Whether God wills things other than Himself? (3) Whether whatever God wills, He wills necessarily? (4) Whether the will of God is the cause of things? (5) Whether any cause can be assigned to the divine will? (6) Whether the divine will is always fulfilled? (7) Whether the will of God is mutable? (8) Whether the will of God imposes necessity on the things willed? (9) Whether God wills evil? (10) Whether God has free choice? (11) Whether the *will of sign is* distinguished in God? (12) Whether five signs of will are rightly held of the divine will?

---

[1] Q. 20.   [2] Q. 22.

First Article
Whether There Is Will in God?

We proceed thus to the First Article:

Objection 1. It seems that there is no will in God. For the object of will is the end and the good. But we cannot assign any end to God. Therefore there is no will in God.

Obj. 2. Further, will is a kind of appetite. But appetite, since it is directed to things not possessed, implies imperfection, which cannot be imputed to God. Therefore there is no will in God.

Obj. 3. Further, according to the Philosopher, the will is a moved mover.[3] But God is the first mover, Himself unmoved, as is proved in *Physics* viii.[4] Therefore there is no will in God.

On the contrary, The Apostle says (*Rom.* xii. 2): *That you may prove what is the will of God.*

I answer that, There is will in God, just as there is intellect: since will follows upon intellect. For as natural things have actual being by their form, so the intellect is actually knowing by its intelligible form. Now everything has this disposition towards its natural form, that when it does not have it, it tends towards it; and when it has it, it is at rest therein. It is the same with every natural perfection, which is a natural good. This disposition to good in things without knowledge is called *natural appetite.* Whence also intellectual natures have a like disposition to good as apprehended through an intelligible form, so as to rest therein when possessed, and when not possessed to seek to possess it; both of which pertain to the will. Hence in every intellectual being there is will, just as in every sensible being there is animal appetite. And so there must be will in God, since there is intellect in Him. And as His knowing is His own being, so is His willing.

Reply Obj. 1. Although nothing apart from God is His end, yet He Himself is the end with respect to all things made by Him. And He is the end by His essence, for by His essence He is good, as was shown above:[5] for the end has the aspect of good.

Reply Obj. 2. Will in us belongs to the appetitive part, which, although named from appetite, has not for its only act to seek what it does not possess, but also to love and delight in what it does possess. In this respect will is said to be in God, as always possessing the good which is its object; since, as we have already said, it is not in essence distinct from this good.

---

[3]*De An.*, III, 10 (433b 16).   [4]Aristotle, *Phys.*, VIII, 6 (258 10).   [5]Q. 6, a. 3. [Not in this volume]

Reply Obj. 3. A will, of which the principal object is a good outside itself, must be moved by another: but the object of the divine will is His goodness, which is His essence. Hence, since the will of God is His essence, it is not moved by another than itself, but by itself alone (in the same sense, of course, in which understanding and willing are said to be movements). This is what Plato meant when he said that the first mover moves himself.[6]

Second Article
Whether God Wills Things Other than Himself?

We proceed thus to the Second Article:—

Objection 1. It seems that God does not will things other than Himself. For the divine will is the divine being. But God is not other than Himself. Therefore He does not will things other than Himself.

Obj. 2. Further, the object willed moves the one who wills, as the appetible the appetite, as is stated in *De anima* iii.[7] If, therefore, God wills anything apart from Himself, His will must be moved by another; which is impossible.

Obj. 3. Further, if what is willed suffices the one who wills, he seeks nothing beyond it. But His own goodness suffices God, and completely His will. Therefore God does not will anything other than Himself.

Obj. 4. Further, acts of the will are multiplied according to their objects. If, therefore, God wills Himself and things other than Himself, it follows that the act of His will is manifold, and consequently His being, which is His will. But this is impossible. Therefore God does not will things other than Himself.

On the contrary, The Apostle says (*1 Thess.* iv. 3): *This is the will of God, your sanctification.*

I answer that, God wills not only Himself, but also things other than Himself. This is clear from the comparison made above. For natural things have a natural inclination not only towards their own proper good, to acquire it if not possessed, and, if possessed, to rest therein; but also to diffuse their own good among others so far as possible. Hence we see that every agent, in so far as it is perfect and in act, produces its like. It pertains, therefore, to the nature of the will to communicate as far as possible to others the good possessed; and especially does this pertain to the divine will, from which all perfection is derived in some kind of likeness. Hence,

---

[6]Cf. above, q. 9, a. 1, ad. 1. [Not in this volume]   [7]Aristotle, *De An.*, III, 10 (433b 17).

if natural things, in so far as they are perfect, communicate their good to others, much more does it pertain to the divine will to communicate by likeness its own good to others as much as is possible. Thus, then, He wills both Himself to be, and other things to be; but Himself as the end, and other things as ordained to that end, inasmuch as it befits the divine goodness that other things should be partakers therein.

Reply Obj. 1. Although in God to will is really the same as to be, yet they differ logically, according to the different ways of understanding them and signifying them, as is clear from what has been already said.[8] For when we say that God exists, no relation to any other thing is implied, as we do imply when we say that God wills. Therefore, although He is not anything other than Himself, yet He does will things other than Himself.

Reply Obj. 2. In things willed for the sake of the end, the whole reason for our being moved is the end; and this it is that moves the will, as most clearly appears in things willed only for the sake of the end. He who wills to take a bitter draught, in doing so wills nothing else than health; and this alone moves his will. It is different with one who takes a draught that is pleasant, which anyone may will to do, not only for the sake of health, but also for its own sake. Hence, although God wills things other than Himself only for the sake of the end, which is His own goodness, it does not follow that anything else moves His will, except His goodness. So, as He understands things other than Himself by understanding His own essence, so He wills things other than Himself by willing His own goodness.

Reply Obj. 3. From the fact that His own goodness suffices the divine will, it does not follow that it wills nothing other than itself, but rather that it wills nothing except by reason of its goodness. Thus, too, the divine intellect: although its perfection consists in its knowledge of the divine essence, yet in that essence it knows other things.

Reply Obj. 4. As the divine knowing is one, as seeing the many only in the one, in the same way the divine willing is one and simple, as willing the many only through the one, that is, through its own goodness.

Third Article
Whether Whatever God Wills He Wills Necessarily?

We proceed thus to the Third Article:—

Objection 1. It seems that whatever God wills He wills necessarily. For everything eternal is necessary. But whatever God wills, He wills from

---

[8]Q. 13, a. 4. [Not in this volume]

eternity, for otherwise His will would be mutable. Therefore whatever He wills, He wills necessarily.

Obj. 2. Further, God wills things other than Himself inasmuch as He wills His own goodness. Now God wills His own goodness necessarily. Therefore He wills things other than Himself necessarily.

Obj. 3. Further, whatever belongs to the nature of God is necessary, for God is of Himself necessary being, and the source of all necessity, as was above shown.[9] But it belongs to His nature to will whatever He wills; since in God there can be nothing over and above His nature, as is stated in *Metaph.* v.[10] Therefore whatever He wills, He wills necessarily.

Obj. 4. Further, being that is not necessary, and being that is possible not to be, are one and the same thing. If, therefore, God does not necessarily will a thing that He wills, it is also possible for Him not to will it, and therefore possible for Him to will what He does not will. And so the divine will is contingent, with respect to choosing determinately among these things; and also imperfect, since everything contingent is imperfect and mutable.

Obj. 5. Further, on the part of that which is indifferent to one or the other of two things, no action results unless it is inclined to one or the other by some other being, as the Commentator says on *Physics* ii.[11] If, then, the will of God is indifferent with regard to anything, it follows that His determination to a given effect comes from another; and thus He has some cause prior to Himself.

Obj. 6. Further, whatever God knows He knows necessarily. But as the divine knowledge is His essence, so is the divine will. Therefore whatever God wills He wills necessarily.

On the contrary, The Apostle says (*Ephes* i. 11): *Who worketh all things according to the counsel of His will.* Now, what we work according to the counsel of the will, we do not will necessarily. Therefore God does not will necessarily whatever He wills.

I answer that, There are two ways in which a thing is said to be necessary, namely, absolutely, and by supposition. We judge a thing to be absolutely necessary from the relation of the terms, as when the predicate forms part of the definition of the subject: thus it is necessary that man is an animal; or as when the subject forms part of the notion of the predicate: thus it is necessary that a number must be odd or even. In this way it is not necessary that Socrates sits: hence it is not necessary absolutely, but

---

[9]Q. 2, a. 3.   [10]Aristotle, *Metaph.*, IV, 5 (1015b 15).   [11]*Phys.*, II, comm. 48 (IV, 3iv).

it may be so by supposition; for, granted that he is sitting, he must necessarily sit, as long as he is sitting.

Accordingly, as to things willed by God, we must observe that He wills something of absolute necessity; but this is not true of all that He wills. For the divine will has a necessary relation to the divine goodness, since that is its proper object. Hence God wills the being of His own goodness necessarily, even as we will our own happiness necessarily, and as any other power has a necessary relation to its proper and principal object, for instance the sight to color, since it is of its nature to tend to it. But God wills things other than Himself in so far as they are ordered to His own goodness as their end. Now in willing an end we do not necessarily will things that conduce to it, unless they are such that the end cannot be attained without them; as, we will to take food to preserve life, or to take a ship in order to cross the sea. But we do not will necessarily those things without which the end is attainable, such as a horse for a stroll, since we can take a stroll without a horse. The same applies to other means. Hence, since the goodness of God is perfect and can exist without other things, inasmuch as no perfection can accrue to Him from them, it follows that for Him to will things other than Himself is not absolutely necessary. Yet it can be necessary by supposition, for supposing that He wills a thing, then He is unable not to will it, as His will cannot change.

Reply Obj. 1. From the fact that God wills from eternity whatever He wills, it does not follow that He wills it necessarily, except by supposition.

Reply Obj. 2. Although God wills necessarily His own goodness, He does not necessarily will things willed because of His goodness; for it can exist without other things.

Reply Obj. 3. It is not natural to God to will any of those other things that He does not will necessarily; and yet it is not unnatural or contrary to His nature, but voluntary.

Reply Obj. 4. Sometimes a necessary cause has a non-necessary relation to an effect, owing to a deficiency in the effect, and not in the cause. Thus, the sun's power has a non-necessary relation to some contingent events on this earth owing to a defect, not in the solar power, but in the effect that proceeds not necessarily from the cause. In the same way, that God does not necessarily will some of the things that He wills, does not result from defect in the divine will, but from a defect belonging to the nature of the thing willed, namely, that the perfect goodness of God can be without it; and such defect accompanies every created good.

Reply Obj. 5. A naturally contingent cause must be determined to act by some external being. The divine will, however, which by its nature is necessary, determines itself to will things to which it has no necessary relation.

Reply Obj. 6. Just as the divine being is necessary of itself, so is the divine willing and the divine knowing; but the divine knowing has a necessary relation to the thing known; not the divine willing, however, to the thing willed. The reason for this is that knowledge is of things as they exist in the knower; but the will is related to things as they exist in themselves. Since, then, all other things have a necessary being inasmuch as they exist in God, but no absolute necessity to be necessary in themselves, in so far as they exist in themselves, it follows that God knows necessarily whatever He knows, but does not will necessarily whatever He wills.

Fourth Article
Whether the Will of God Is the Cause of Things?

We proceed thus to the Fourth Article:—

Objection 1. It seems that the will of God is not the cause of things. For Dionysius says: As *our sun, not by reasoning nor by choice, but by its very being, enlightens all things that can participate in its light, so the divine good by its very essence pours the rays of its goodness upon everything that exists.*[12] But every voluntary agent acts by reasoning and choice. Therefore God does not act by will; and so His will is not the cause of things.

Obj. 2. Further, the first in any order is that which is essentially so; thus in the order of burning things, that comes first which is fire by its essence. But God is the first agent. Therefore He acts by His essence; and that is His nature. He acts then by nature, and not by will. Therefore the divine will is not the cause of things.

Obj. 3. Further, whatever is the cause of anything, because it itself is such a thing, is a cause by nature, and not by will. For fire is the cause of heat, as being itself hot; whereas an architect is the cause of a house, because he wills to build it. Now Augustine says, *Because God is good, we exist.*[13] Therefore God is the cause of things by His nature, and not by His will.

Obj. 4. Further, of one thing there is one cause. But the cause of created things is the knowledge of God, as was said before.[14] Therefore the will of God cannot be considered the cause of things.

On the contrary, It is said (*Wis.* xi. 26), *How could anything endure, if Thou wouldst not?*

---

[12]*De Div. Nom.*, IV, 1 (PG 3, 693). [13]*De Doc. Christ.*, I, 32 (PL 34, 32).
[14]Q. 14, a. 8.

I answer that, We must hold that the will of God is the cause of things, and that He acts by the will, and not, as some have supposed, by a necessity of His nature.

This can be shown in three ways: First, from the order itself of agent causes. Since both *intellect and nature* act for an end, as is proved in *Physics* ii.,[15] the natural agent must have the end and the necessary means predetermined for it by some higher intellect; as, the end and definite movement is predetermined for the arrow by the archer. Hence the intellectual and voluntary agent must precede the agent that acts by nature. Hence, since God is first in the order of agents, He must act by intellect and will.

This is shown, secondly, from the character of a natural agent, to which it belongs to produce one and the same effect; for nature operates in one and the same way, unless it be prevented. This is because the nature of the act is according to the nature of the agent, and hence as long as it has that nature, its acts will be in accordance with that nature; for every natural agent has a determinate being. Since, then, the divine being is undetermined, and contains in Himself the full perfection of being, it cannot be that He acts by a necessity of His nature, unless He were to cause something undetermined and indefinite in being; and that this is impossible has been already shown.[16] He does not, therefore, act by a necessity of His nature, but determined effects proceed from His own infinite perfection according to the determination of His will and intellect.

Thirdly, it is shown by the relation of effects to their cause. For effects proceed from the agent that causes them in so far as they pre-exist in the agent; since every agent produces its like. Now effects pre-exist in their cause after the mode of the cause. Therefore, since the divine being is His own intellect, effects pre-exist in Him after the mode of intellect, and therefore proceed from Him after the same mode. Consequently, they proceed from Him after the mode of will, for His inclination to put in act what His intellect has conceived pertains to the will. Therefore the will of God is the cause of things.

Reply Obj. 1. Dionysius in these words does not intend to exclude election from God absolutely, but only in a certain sense, in so far, that is, as He communicates His goodness not merely to certain beings, but to all; whereas election implies a certain distinction.

Reply Obj. 2. Because the essence of God is His intellect and will, from the fact of His acting by His essence it follows that He acts after the mode of intellect and will.

---

[15]Aristotle, *Phys.*, II, 5 (196b 21).   [16]Q. 7, a. 2. [Not in this volume]

Reply Obj. 3. Good is the object of the will. The words, therefore, *Because God is good, we exist*, are true inasmuch as His Goodness is the reason of His willing all other things, as was said before.

Reply Obj. 4. Even in us the cause of one and the same effect is knowledge as directing it, whereby the form of the thing to be done is conceived, and will as commanding it, since the form as it is only in the intellect is not determined to exist or not to exist actually, except by the will. Hence, the speculative intellect has nothing to say as to operation. But the power of the agent is cause, as executing the effect, since it denotes the immediate principle of operation. But in God all these things are one.

Fifth Article
Whether Any Cause Can Be Assigned to the Divine Will?

We proceed thus to the Fifth Article:—

Objection 1. It seems that some cause can be assigned to the divine will. For Augustine says: *Who would venture to say that God made all things irrationally?*[17] But to a voluntary agent, the reason for acting is also the cause of willing. Therefore the will of God has some cause.

Obj. 2. Further, in things made by one who wills to make them, and whose will is influenced by no cause, there can be no cause assigned except the will of him who wills. But the will of God is the cause of all things, as has been already shown. If, then, there is no cause of His will, in the whole realm of natural things we cannot seek any cause, except the divine will alone. Thus all the sciences would be in vain, since science seeks to assign causes to effects. This seems inadmissible, and therefore we must assign some cause to the divine will.

Obj. 3. Further, what is done by the one who wills, because of no cause, depends absolutely on his will. If, therefore, the will of God has no cause, it follows that all things made depend absolutely on His will, and have no other cause. But this also is not admissible.

On the contrary, Augustine says: *Every efficient cause is greater than the thing effected. But nothing is greater than the will of God. We must not then seek for a cause of it.*[18]

I answer that, In no wise has the will of God a cause. In proof of which we must consider that, since the will follows from the intellect, the cause explaining the willing of one who wills is the same as the cause explaining the knowing of one who knows. The case with the intellect is this: that if

---

[17]*Lib. 83 Quaest.*, q. 46 (PL 40, 30).   [18]*Op. cit.*, q. 28 (PL 40, 18).

the principle and its conclusion are understood separately from each other, the understanding of the principle is the cause that the conclusion is known. But if the intellect perceives the conclusion in the principle itself, apprehending both the one and the other at the same glance, in this case the knowledge of the conclusion would not be caused by understanding the principles, since a thing cannot be its own cause; and yet, it would be true that the intellect would understand the principles to be the cause of the conclusion. It is the same with the will, with respect to which the end stands in the same relation to the means as principles to the conclusions in the intellect.

Hence, if anyone in one act wills an end, and in another act the means to that end, his willing the end will be the cause of his willing the means. This cannot be the case if in one act he wills both end and means; for a thing cannot be its own cause. Yet it will be true to say that he wills to order to the end the means to the end. Now as God by one act understands all things in His essence, so by one act He wills all things in His goodness. Hence, as in God to understand the cause is not the cause of His understanding the effect (for He understands the effect in the cause), so, in Him, to will an end is not the cause of His willing the means; yet He wills the ordering of the means to the end. Therefore He wills this to be as means to that; but He does not will this because of that.

Reply Obj. 1. The will of God is reasonable, not because anything is to God a cause of willing, but in so far as He wills one thing to be because of another.

Reply Obj. 2. Since God wills effects to proceed from definite causes, for the preservation of order in the universe, it is not unreasonable to seek for causes secondary to the divine will. It would, however, be unreasonable to do so, if such were considered as primary, and not as dependent on the will of God. In this sense Augustine says: *Philosophers in their vanity have thought fit to attribute contingent effects to other causes, being utterly unable to perceive the cause that is above all others, the will of God.*[19]

Reply Obj. 3. Since God wills that effects be because of their causes, all effects that presuppose some other effect do not depend solely on the will of God, but on something else besides: but the first effect depends on the divine will alone. Thus, for example, we may say that God willed man to have hands to serve his intellect by their work, and an intellect, that he might be man; and willed him to be man that he might enjoy Him, or for the completion of the universe. But this cannot be reduced to further cre-

---

[19]*De Trin.*, III, 2 (PL 42, 871).

ated secondary ends. Hence such things depend on the simple will of God; but the others on the order of other causes.

Sixth Article
Whether the Will of God Is Always Fulfilled?

We proceed thus to the Sixth Article:—

Objection 1. It seems that the will of God is not always fulfilled. For the Apostle says (*1 Tim.* ii. 4): *God will have all men to be saved, and to come to the knowledge of the truth.* But this does not happen. Therefore the will of God is not always fulfilled.

Obj. 2. Further, as is the relation of knowledge to truth, so is that of the will to good. Now God knows all truth. Therefore He wills all good. But not all good actually exists; for much more good might exist. Therefore the will of God is not always fulfilled.

Obj. 3. Further, since the will of God is the first cause, it does not exclude intermediate causes. But the effect of a first cause may be hindered by a defect of a secondary cause; as the effect of the locomotive power of the body may be hindered by the incapacity of a leg. Therefore the effect of the divine will may be hindered by a defect of the secondary causes. The will of God, therefore, is not always fulfilled.

On the contrary, It is said (*Ps.* cxiii. 11): *God hath done all things, whatsoever He would.*

I answer that, The will of God must needs always be fulfilled. In proof of which we must consider that, since an effect is conformed to the agent according to its form, the rule is the same with agent causes as with formal causes. The rule in forms is this: that although a thing may fall short of any particular form, it cannot fall short of the universal form. For though a thing may fail to be a man or a living being, for example, yet it cannot fail to be a being. Hence the same must happen in agent causes. Something may escape the order of any particular agent cause, but not the order of the universal cause under which all particular causes are included; and if any particular cause fails of its effect, this is because of the hindrance of some other particular cause, which is included within the order of the universal cause. Therefore, an effect cannot possibly escape the order of the universal cause. This is clearly seen also in corporeal things. For it may happen that a star is hindered from producing its effects; yet whatever effect does result within the realm of corporeal things, as a consequence of this hindrance of a corporeal cause, must be referred through intermediate causes to the universal influence of the first heavens.

Since, then, the will of God is the universal cause of all things, it is impossible that the divine will should not produce its effect. Hence that which seems to depart from the divine will in one order, returns into it in another; as does the sinner, who by sin falls away from the divine will as much as lies in him, yet falls back into the order of that will, when by its justice he is punished.

Reply Obj. 1. The words of the Apostle, *God will have all men to be saved*, etc., can be understood in three ways. First, by a restricted application, in which case they would mean, as Augustine says, *God wills all men to be saved that are saved, not because there is no man whom He does not wish saved, but because there is no man saved whose salvation He does not will.*[20] Secondly, they can be understood as applying to every class of individuals, not to every individual of each class; in which case they mean that God wills some men of every class and condition to be saved, males and females, Jews and Gentiles, great and small, but not all of every condition. Thirdly, according to Damascene, they are understood of the antecedent will of God; not of the consequent will.[21] This distinction must not be taken as applying to the divine will itself, in which there is nothing antecedent or consequent, but to the things willed.

To understand this we must consider that everything, in so far as it is good, is willed by God. A thing taken in its primary sense, and absolutely considered, may be good or evil, and yet, when some additional circumstances are taken into account, by a consequent consideration may be changed into the contrary. Thus that a man should live is good; and that a man should be killed is evil, absolutely considered. But if in a particular case we add that a man is a murderer or dangerous to society, to kill him is a good; that he live is an evil. Hence it may be said of a just judge, that antecedently he wills all men to live; but consequently wills the murderer to be hanged. In the same way, God antecedently wills all men to be saved, but consequently wills some to be damned, as His justice exacts. Nor do we will absolutely what we will antecedently, but rather we will it in a qualified manner; for the will is directed to things as they are in themselves, and in themselves they exist under particular conditions. Hence we will a thing absolutely inasmuch as we will it when all particular circumstances are considered; and this is what is meant by willing consequently. Thus it may be said that a just judge wills absolutely the hanging of a murderer, but in a qualified manner he would will him to live, namely, inasmuch as he is a man. Such a qualified will may be called a velleity rather than an

---

[20]*Enchir.*, 103 (PL 40, 280).   [21]*De Fide Orth.*, II, 29 (PG 94, 968).

absolute will. Thus it is clear that whatever God wills absolutely takes place; although what He wills antecedently may not take place.

Reply Obj. 2. An act of the cognitive power takes place according as the thing known is in the knower; while an act of the appetitive power is directed to things as they exist in themselves. But all that can have the nature of being and truth is virtually in God, though it does not all exist in created things. Therefore God knows all truth, but does not will all good, except in so far as He wills Himself, in Whom all good exists virtually.

Reply Obj. 3. A first cause can be hindered in its effect by deficiency in the secondary cause, when it is not the universal first cause, including under itself all causes; for then the effect could in no way escape the order of this cause. And thus it is with the will of God, as was said above.

Seventh Article
Whether the Will of God Is Changeable?

We proceed thus to the Seventh Article:—

Objection 1. It seems that the will of God is changeable. For the Lord says (*Gen.* vi. 7): *It repenteth Me that I have made man.* But whoever repents of what he has done, has a changeable will. Therefore God has a changeable will.

Obj. 2. Further, it is said in the person of the Lord: *I will speak against a nation and against a kingdom, to root out, and to pull down, and to destroy it; but if that nation shall repent of its evil, I also will repent of the evil that I have thought to do to them* (*Jer.* xviii. 7, 8). Therefore God has a changeable will.

Obj. 3. Further, whatever God does, He does voluntarily. But God does not always do the same thing, for at one time He ordered the law to be observed and at another time forbade it. Therefore He has a changeable will.

Obj. 4. Further, God does not will of necessity what He wills, as was said before. Therefore He can both will and not will the same thing. But whatever can incline to either of two opposites is changeable; as that which can exist and not exist is changeable substantially, and that which can exist in a place or not in that place is changeable locally. Therefore God is changeable as regards His will.

On the contrary, It is said: *God is not as a man, that He should lie, nor as the son of man, that He should be changed* (*Num.* xxiii. 19).

I answer that, The will of God is entirely unchangeable. On this point we must consider that to change the will is one thing; to will that certain things should be changed is another. For it is possible to will a thing to be done now and its contrary afterwards, and yet for the will to remain permanently the same; whereas the will would be changed if one should begin to will what before he had not willed, or cease to will what he had willed before. This cannot happen, unless we presuppose change either in the knowledge or in the disposition of the substance of the one who wills. For since the will is concerned with the good, a man may in two ways begin to will a thing. In one way, when that thing begins to be good for him, and this does not take place without a change in him. Thus when the cold weather begins, it becomes good to sit by the fire; though it was not so before. In another way, when he knows for the first time that a thing is good for him, though he did not know it before. For, after all, we take counsel in order to know what is good for us. Now it has already been shown that both the substance of God and His knowledge are entirely unchangeable.[22] Therefore His will must be entirely unchangeable.

Reply Obj. 1. These words of the Lord are to be understood metaphorically, and according to the likeness of our nature. For when we repent, we destroy what we have made; although we may even do so without change of will, as, when a man wills to make a thing, at the same time intending to destroy it later. Therefore, God is said to have repented by way of comparison with our mode of acting, in so far as by the deluge He removed from the face of the earth man whom He had previously made.

Reply Obj. 2. The will of God, as it is the first and universal cause, does not exclude intermediate causes that have power to produce certain effects. Since, however, all intermediate causes are inferior in power to the first cause, there are many things in the divine power, knowledge and will that are not included in the order of inferior causes. Thus in the case of the raising of Lazarus, one who looked only at inferior causes could have said: *Lazarus will not rise again;* but looking at the divine first cause, he could have said: *Lazarus will rise again.* And God wills both: that is, that a thing shall happen in the order of the inferior cause, but that it shall not happen in the order of the higher cause; or He may will conversely. We may say, then, that God sometimes declares that a thing shall happen according as it falls under the order of inferior causes (for example, the dispositons of nature or the merits of men), which yet does not happen, as not being in the designs of the divine and higher cause. Thus He foretold to Ezechias: *Take order with thy house, for thou shalt die, and not live* (*Isa.* xxxviii. 1). Yet this did not take place, since from eternity it was otherwise disposed in the divine knowledge and will, which is unchangeable. Hence

---

[22]Q. 9, a. 1; q. 14, a. 15. [Not in this volume]

Gregory says: *The sentence of God changes, but not His counsel*[23]—that is to say, the counsel of His will. When therefore He says, *I also will repent,* His words must be understood metaphorically. For men seem to repent, when they do not fulfill what they have threatened.

Reply Obj. 3. It does not follow from this argument that God has a will that changes, but that He wills that things should change.

Reply Obj. 4. Although God's willing a thing is not by absolute necessity, yet it is necessary by supposition, because of the unchangeableness of the divine will, as has been said above.

Eighth Article
Whether the Will of God Imposes Necessity on the Things Willed?

We proceed thus to the Eighth Article:—

Objection 1. It seems that the will of God imposes necessity on the things willed. For Augustine says: *No one is saved, except whom God has willed to be saved. He must therefore be asked to will it; for if He wills it, it must necessarily be.*[24]

Obj. 2. Further, every cause that cannot be hindered produces its effect necessarily, because, as the Philosopher says, *nature always works in the same way, if there is nothing to hinder it.*[25] But the will of God cannot be hindered. For the Apostle says (*Rom.* ix. 19): *Who resisteth His will?* Therefore the will of God imposes necessity on the things willed.

Obj. 3. Further, whatever is necessary by its antecedent cause is necessary absolutely; it is thus necessary that animals should die, being compounded of contrary elements. Now things created by God are related to the divine will as to an antecedent cause, whereby they have necessity. For this conditional proposition is true: *if God wills a thing, it comes to pass:* and every true conditional proposition is necessary. It follows therefore that all that God wills is necessary absolutely.

On the contrary, All good things that exist God wills to be. If therefore His will imposes necessity on the things willed, it follows that all good happens of necessity; and thus there is an end of free choice, counsel, and all other such things.

I answer that, The divine will imposes necessity on some things willed, but not on all. The reason of this some have chosen to assign to intermediate causes, holding that what God produces by necessary causes is necessary, and what He produces by contingent causes contingent.

---

[23]*Moral.*, XVI, 10 (PL 75, 1127). [24]*Enchir.*, 103 (PL 40, 280).
[25]Aristotle, *Phys.* II, 8 (199b 18).

This does not seem to be a sufficient explanation, for two reasons. First, because the effect of a first cause is contingent because of the secondary cause, from the fact that the effect of the first cause is hindered by deficiency in the second cause, as the sun's power is hindered by a defect in the plant. But no defect of a secondary cause can hinder God's will from producing its effect. Secondly, because if the distinction between the contingent and the necessary is to be referred only to secondary causes, this must mean that the distinction itself escapes the divine intention and will; which is inadmissible.

It is better therefore to say that this happens because of the efficacy of the divine will. For when a cause is efficacious to act, the effect follows upon the cause, not only as to the thing done, but also as to its manner of being done or of being. Thus from defect of active power in the seed it may happen that a child is born unlike its father in accidental points, which belong to its manner of being. Since then the divine will is perfectly efficacious, it follows not only that things are done, which God wills to be done, but also that they are done in the way that He wills. Now God wills some things to be done necessarily, some contingently, so that there be a right order in things for the perfection of the universe. Therefore to some effects He has attached unfailing necessary causes, from which the effects follow necessarily; but to others defectible and contingent causes, from which effects arise contingently. Hence it is not because the proximate causes are contingent that the effects willed by God happen contingently; but God has prepared contingent causes for them because He has willed that they should happen contingently.

Reply Obj. 1. By the words of Augustine we must understand a necessity in things willed by God that is not absolute, but conditional. For the conditional proposition that *if God wills a thing, it must necessarily be*, is necessarily true.

Reply Obj. 2. From the very fact that nothing resists the divine will, it follows not only that those things happen that God wills to happen, but that they happen necessarily or contingently according to His will.

Reply Obj. 3. Consequents have necessity from their antecedents according to the mode of the antecedents. Hence things effected by the divine will have that kind of necessity that God wills them to have, either absolute or conditional. Not all things, therefore, are necessary absolutely.

Ninth Article
Whether God Wills Evils?

We proceed thus to the Ninth Article:—

Objection 1. It seems that God wills evils. For every good that exists, God wills. But it is a good that evil should exist. For Augustine says: *Although evil in so far as it is evil is not a good, yet it is good that not only good things should exist, but also evil things.*[26] Therefore God wills evil things.

Obj. 2. Further, Dionysius says: *Evil would conduce to the perfection of everything, i.e.,* the universe.[27] And Augustine says: *Out of all things is built up the admirable beauty of the universe, wherein even that which is called evil, properly ordered and disposed, commends the good the more evidently, so that the good be more pleasing and praiseworthy when contrasted with evil.*[28] But God wills all that pertains to the perfection and beauty of the universe, for this is what God desires above all things in His creatures. Therefore God wills evils.

Obj. 3. Further, that evil should exist, and should not exist, are contradictory opposites. But God does not will that evil should not exist; otherwise, since various evils do exist, God's will would not always be fulfilled. Therefore God wills that evils should exist.

On the contrary, Augustine says: *No wise man is the cause of another man becoming worse. Now God surpasses all men in wisdom. Much less therefore is God the cause of man becoming worse: and when He is said to be the cause of a thing, He is said to will it.*[29] Therefore it is not by God's will that man becomes worse. Now it is clear that every evil makes a thing worse. Therefore God does not will evils.

I answer that, Since the good and the appetible are the same in nature, as was said before,[30] and since evil is opposed to good, it is impossible that any evil, as such, should be sought for by the appetite, either natural, or animal, or by the intellectual appetite which is the will. Nevertheless evil may be sought accidentally, so far as it accompanies a good, as appears in each of the appetites. For a natural agent does not intend privation or corruption; he intends the form to which is yet annexed the privation of some other form, and the generation of one thing, which yet implies the corruption of another. For when a lion kills a stag, his object is food, which yet is accompanied by the killing of the animal. Similarly the fornicator has merely pleasure for his object, which is yet accompanied by the deformity of sin.

Now the evil that accompanies one good is the privation of another good. Never therefore would evil be sought after, not even accidentally, unless the good that accompanies the evil were more desired than the good

---

[26]*Enchir.*, XCVI (PL 40, 276).   [27]*De Div. Nom.*, IV, 19 (PG 3, 717).
[28]*Enchir.*, X (PL 40, 236).   [29]*Lib. 83 Quaest.*, q. 3 (PL 40, 11).   [30]Q. 5, a. 1. [Not in this volume]

of which the evil is the privation. Now God wills no good more than He wills His own goodness; yet He wills one good more than another. Hence He in no way wills the evil of sin, which is the privation of right order towards the divine good. The evil of natural defect, or of punishment, He does will, by willing the good to which such evils are attached. Thus, in willing justice He wills punishment; and in willing the preservation of the order of nature, He wills some things to be naturally corrupted.

Reply Obj. 1. Some have said that although God does not will evil, yet He wills that evil should be or be done, because, although evil is not a good yet it is good that evil should be or be done.[31] This they said because things evil in themselves are ordered to some good end; and this order they thought was expressed in the words *that evil should be* or *be done.* This, however, is not correct; since evil is not of itself ordered to good, but accidentally. For it is outside the intention of the sinner that any good should follow from his sin; as it was outside the intention of tyrants that the patience of the martyrs should shine forth from all their persecutions. It cannot therefore be said that such an ordering to good is implied in the statement that it is a good thing that evil should be or be done, since nothing is judged by that which pertains to it accidentally, but by that which belongs to it essentially.

Reply Obj. 2. Evil does not contribute towards the perfection and beauty of the universe, except accidentally, as was said above. Therefore, in saying that *evil would conduce to the perfection of the universe,* Dionysius draws this conclusion as the consequence of false premises.

Reply Obj. 3. The statements that evil comes to be and that it does not come to be are opposed as contradictories; yet the statements that anyone wills evil to be and that he wills it not to be, are not so opposed, since either is affirmative. God therefore neither wills evil to be done, nor wills it not to be done; but He wills to permit evil to be done, and this is a good.

Tenth Article
Whether God Has Free Choice?

We proceed thus to the Tenth Article:—

Objection 1. It seems that God has not free choice. For Jerome says, in a homily on the prodigal son: *God alone it is Who is not liable to sin, nor can be liable: all others, as having free choice, can be inclined to either side.*[32]

---

[31]Hugh of St. Victor, *De Sacram.,* I, iv, 13 (PL 176, 239); *Summa Sent.,* I, 13 (PL 176, 66).—Cf. Peter Lombard, *Sent.,* I, xlvi, 3 (I, 280).   [32]*Epist.* XXI (PL 22, 393).

Obj. 2. Further, free choice is a faculty of the reason and will, by which good and evil are chosen. But God does not will evil, as has been said. Therefore there is not free choice in God.

On the contrary, Ambrose says: *The Holy Spirit divideth unto each one as He will, namely, according to the free choice of the will, not in obedience to necessity.*[33]

I answer that, We have free choice with respect to what we do not will of necessity, or by natural instinct. That we will to be happy does not pertain to free choice but to natural instinct. Hence other animals, that are moved to act by natural instinct, are not said to be moved by free choice. Since then God wills His own goodness necessarily, but other things not necessarily, as was shown above, He has free choice with respect to what He does not will necessarily.

Reply Obj. 1. Jerome seems to deny free choice to God, not absolutely, but not as regards the turning to sin.

Reply Obj. 2. Since the evil of sin consists in turning away from the divine goodness, by which God wills all things, as was above shown, it is manifestly impossible for Him to will the evil of sin; yet He can choose one of two opposites, inasmuch as He can will a thing to be or not to be. In the same way we ourselves can, without sin, will to sit down and not will to sit down.

Eleventh Article
Whether the Will of Sign Is to Be Distinguished in God?

We proceed thus to the Eleventh Article:—

Objection 1. It seems that the will of sign is not to be distinguished in God. For as the will of God is the cause of things, so is His wisdom. But there are no signs of the divine wisdom. Therefore, neither ought there to be signs of the divine will.

Obj. 2. Further, every sign that is not in agreement with what it signifies is false. If therefore the signs of the divine will are not in agreement with that will, they are false. But if they do agree, they are superfluous. No signs therefore of the divine will are to be recognized.

On the contrary, The will of God is one, since it is the very essence of God. Yet sometimes it is spoken of as many, as in the words of *Ps.* cx. 2: *Great are the works of the Lord, sought out according to all His wills.* Therefore, sometimes the sign must be taken for the will.

---

[33]*De Fide*, 6 (PL 16, 592).

I answer that, Some things are said of God in their strict sense, others by metaphor, as appears from what has been said before.[34] When certain human passions are predicated of the Godhead metaphorically, this is done because of a likeness in the effect. Hence a thing that is in us a sign of some passion is signified metaphorically in God under the name of that passion. Thus with us it is usual for an angry man to punish, so that punishment becomes an expression of anger. Therefore punishment itself is signified by the name of anger, when anger is attributed to God. In the same way, what is usually with us an expression of will is sometimes metaphorically called will in God; just as when anyone lays down a precept, it is a sign that he wishes that precept obeyed. Hence a divine precept is sometimes called by metaphor the will of God, as in the words: *Thy will be done on earth, as it is in heaven* (*Matt.* vi. 10). There is, however, this difference between will and anger, that anger is never attributed to God properly, since in its primary meaning it includes passion; whereas will is attributed to Him properly. Therefore in God there are distinguished will in its proper sense and will as attributed to Him by metaphor. Will in its proper sense is called the *will of good pleasure*, and will metaphorically taken is the *will of sign*, inasmuch as the sign itself of will is called will.

Reply Obj. 1. Knowledge is not the cause of a thing being done, unless through the will. For we do not put into act what we know, unless we will to do so. Accordingly, signs are not attributed to knowledge, but to will.

Reply Obj. 2. Signs of will are called divine wills, not as being signs that God wills anything, but because what in us are the usual signs of our will, are called *divine wills* in God. Thus punishment is not a sign that there is anger in God; but it is called anger in Him, from the fact that it is a sign of anger in ourselves.

Twelfth Article
Whether Five Signs of Will Are Rightly Held of the Divine Will?

We proceed thus to the Twelfth Article:—

Objection 1. It seems that five signs of will—namely, *prohibition, precept, counsel, operation,* and *permission*—are not rightly held of the divine will. For the same things that God bids us do by His precept or counsel, these He sometimes operates in us; and the same things that He prohibits, these He sometimes permits. They ought not therefore to be enumerated as distinct.

Obj. 2. Further, God works nothing unless He will it, as the Scripture

---

[34]Q. 13, a. 3. [Not in this volume]

says (*Wis.* xi. 26). But the will of sign is distinct from the will of good pleasure. Therefore operation ought not to be comprehended in the will of sign.

Obj. 3. Further, operation and permission pertain to all creatures in common, since God works in them all, and permits some action in them all. But precept, counsel and prohibition pertain to rational creatures only. Therefore they do not come rightly under one division, not being of one order.

Obj. 4. Further, evil happens in more ways than does good, since *good happens in one way, but evil in all kinds of ways,* as is declared by the Philosopher,[35] and Dionysius.[36] It is not right therefore to propose one sign only in the case of evil—namely, prohibition—and two—namely, counsel and precept—in the case of good.

I answer that, These signs are so called because by them we are accustomed to show that we will something. A man may show that he wills something, either by himself or by means of another. He may show it by himself, by doing something either directly or indirectly and accidentally. He shows it directly when he works in his own person; in that way the sign of his will is said to be *operation.* He shows it indirectly, by not hindering the doing of a thing; for *what removes an impediment is called an accidental mover.*[37] In this the sign is called *permission.* He declares his will by means of another when he orders another to perform a work, either by insisting upon it as necessary by *precept,* and by *prohibiting* its contrary; or by persuasion, which is a part of *counsel.*

Since the will of man makes itself known in these ways, the same five are sometimes named divine wills, in the sense of being signs of that will. That *precept, counsel* and *prohibition* are called the will of God is clear from the words of *Matt.* vi. 10: *Thy will be done on earth as it is in heaven.* That *permission,* and *operation* are called the will of God is clear from Augustine, who says: *Nothing is done, unless the Almighty wills it to be done, either by permitting it, or by actually doing it.*[38]

Or it may be said that permission and operation refer to present time, permission being with respect to evil, operation with regard to good. While as to future time, prohibition is in respect to evil, precept to good that is necessary, and counsel to good that is of supererogation.

Reply Obj. 1. There is nothing to prevent anyone declaring his will about the same matter in different ways; thus we find many names that

---

[35]*Eth.*, II, 6, (1106b 35). [36]*De Div. Nom.*, IV, 30 (PG 3, 729).
[37]Aristotle, *Phys.*, VIII, 4 (255b 24). [38]*Enchir.*, XCV (PL 40, 276).

mean the same thing. Hence there is no reason why the same thing should not be the subject of precept, operation, counsel, prohibition or permission.

Reply Obj. 2. As God may by metaphor be said to will what by His will, properly understood, He wills not, so He may by metaphor be said to will what He does, properly speaking, will. Hence there is nothing to prevent the same thing from being the object of the will of good pleasure and of the will of sign. But operation is always the same as the will of good pleasure, while precept and counsel are not, both because the former regards the present, and the two latter the future, and because the former is of itself the effect of the will, while the latter is the effect as fulfilled by means of another.

Reply Obj. 3. Rational creatures are masters of their own acts; and for this reason certain special signs of the divine will are proposed for them, inasmuch as God ordains rational creatures to act voluntarily and of themselves. Other creatures act only as moved by the divine operation; therefore only operation and permission are concerned with these.

Reply Obj. 4. All evil of sin, though happening in many ways, agrees in being out of harmony with the divine will. Hence with regard to evil, only one sign is proposed, that of prohibition. On the other hand, good stands in various relations to the divine goodness, since there are good deeds without which we cannot attain to the fruition of that goodness, and these are the subject of precept; and there are other goods by which we attain to it more perfectly, and these are the subject of counsel. Or it may be said that counsel is concerned not only with the obtaining of greater good, but also with the avoiding of lesser evils.

Question 20

God's Love

(*In Four Articles*)

We next consider those things that pertain absolutely to the will of God. In the appetitive part of the human soul there are found both the passions of the soul, as joy, love, and the like; and the habits of the moral virtues, as justice, fortitude, and the like. Hence we shall first consider the love of God, and secondly his justice and mercy. About the first there are four points of inquiry: (1) Whether love exists in God? (2) Whether He loves all things? (3) Whether he loves one thing more than another? (4) Whether He loves better things more?

First Article
Whether Love Exists in God?

We proceed thus to the First Article:—

Objection 1. It seems that love does not exist in God. For in God there are no passions. Now love is a passion. Therefore love is not in God.

Obj. 2. Further, love, anger, sorrow, and the like, are mutually divided against one another. But sorrow and anger are not attributed to God, unless by metaphor. Therefore neither is love attributed to Him.

Obj. 3. Further, Dionysius says: *Love is a uniting and binding force.*[1] But this cannot take place in God, since He is simple. Therefore love does not exist in God.

On the contrary, It is written: *God is love* (*1 John* iv. 16).

I answer that, We must needs assert that in God there is love, because love is the first movement of the will and of every appetitive power. For since the acts of the will and of every appetitive power tend towards good and evil as to their proper objects, and since good is essentially and especially the object of the will and the appetite, whereas evil is only the object secondarily and indirectly (as opposed to good): it follows that the acts of the will and appetite that regard good must naturally be prior to those that regard evil; thus, for instance, joy is prior to sorrow, love to hate. For what exists of itself is always prior to that which exists through another.

Again, the more universal is naturally prior to what is less so. Hence the intellect is first directed to universal truth, and in the second place to particular and special truths. Now there are certain acts of will and appetite that regard good under some special condition, as joy and delight regard good present and possessed; whereas desire and hope regard good not as yet possessed. Love, however, regards good universally, whether possessed or not. Hence love is naturally the first act of will and appetite; for which reason all the other appetitive movements presuppose love as their root and origin. For nobody desires anything nor rejoices in anything, except as a good that is loved; nor is anything an object of hate except as opposed to the object of love. Similarly, it is clear that sorrow, and other things like to it, refer to love as to their first principle. Hence, in whomsoever there is will and appetite, there must also be love: since if the first is wanting, all that follows is also wanting. Now it has been shown that will is in God.[2] Hence we must attribute love to Him.

Reply Obj. 1. The cognitive power does not move except through the medium of the appetitive: and just as in ourselves the universal reason

---

[1]*De Div. Nom.*, IV, 15 (PG 3, 713).   [2]Q. 19, a. 1.

moves through the medium of the particular reason, as is stated in *De anima* iii.,[3] so in ourselves the intellectual appetite, which is called the will, moves through the medium of the sensitive appetite. Hence, in us the sensitive appetite is the proximate motive-power of our bodies. Some bodily change therefore always accompanies an act of the sensitive appetite, and this change affects especially the heart, which is the first source of movement in animals. Therefore acts of the sensitive appetite, inasmuch as they have annexed to them some bodily change, are called passions; whereas acts of the will are not so called. Love, therefore, and joy and delight are passions, in so far as they denote acts of the sensitive appetite; but in so far as they denote acts of the intellective appetite, they are not passions. It is in this latter sense that they are in God. Hence the Philosopher says: *God rejoices by an operation that is one and simple.*[4] And for the same reason He loves without passion.

Reply Obj. 2. In the passions of the sensitive appetite there may be distinguished a certain material element—namely, the bodily change—and a certain formal element, which is on the part of the appetite. Thus in anger, as the Philosopher says,[5] the material element is the surging of the blood about the heart; but the formal, the appetite for revenge. Again, as regards the formal element of some passions, a certain imperfection is implied, as in desire, which is of the good we have not, and in sorrow, which is about the evil we have. This applies also to anger, which supposes sorrow. Certain other passions, however, as love and joy, imply no imperfection. Since therefore none of these can be attributed to God on their material side, as has been said, neither can those that even on their formal side imply imperfection be attributed to Him; except metaphorically, and from likeness of effects, as has already been shown.[6] On the other hand, those that do not imply imperfection, such as love and joy, can be properly predicated of God, though without attributing passion to Him, as was said before.

Reply Obj. 3. An act of love always tends towards two things: to the good that one wills, and to the person for whom one wills it: since to love a person is to will good for that person. Hence, inasmuch as we love ourselves, we will good for ourselves; and, so far as possible, union with that good. In this sense, love is called a unitive force even in God, yet without implying composition; for the good that He wills for Himself is none other than Himself, Who is good by His essence, as was shown above.[7]

---

[3]*De An.*, III, 11 (434a 20).   [4]*Eth.*, VII, 14 (1154b 26).   [5]Aristotle, *De An.*, I, 1 (403a 30).   [6]Q. 3, a. 2, ad 2; q. 19, a. 11.   [7]Q. 6, a. 3. [Not in this volume]

And by the fact that anyone loves another, he wills good to that other. Thus he puts the other, as it were, in the place of himself, and regards the good done to him as done to himself. So far love is a binding force, since it joins another to ourselves, and refers his good to our own. And in this way too the divine love is a binding force, in as much as God wills good to others; yet without implying any composition in God.

Second Article
Whether God Loves All Things?

We proceed thus to the Second Article:—

Objection 1. It seems that God does not love all things. For according to Dionysius, love places the lover outside himself, and causes him to pass, as it were, into the object of his love.[8] But it is not admissible to say that God is placed outside of Himself, and passes into other things. Therefore it is inadmissible to say that God loves things other than himself.

Obj. 2. Further, the love of God is eternal. But things apart from God are not from eternity; except in God. Therefore God does not love anything, except as it exists in Himself. But as existing in Him, it is no other than Himself. Therefore God does not love things other than Himself.

Obj. 3. Further, love is twofold—the love, namely, of desire, and the love of friendship. Now God does not love irrational creatures with the love of desire, since He needs no creature outside Himself. Nor with the love of friendship, since there can be no friendship with irrational creatures, as the Philosopher shows.[9] Therefore God does not love all things.

Obj. 4. Further, it is written (*Ps.* v. 7): *Thou hatest all the workers of iniquity.* Now nothing is at the same time hated and loved. Therefore God does not love all things.

On the contrary, It is said (*Wis.* xi. 25): *Thou lovest all things that are, and hatest none of the things which Thou hast made.*

I answer that, God loves all existing things. For all existing things, in so far as they exist, are good, since the being of a thing is itself a good; as is likewise whatever perfection it possesses. Now it has been shown above that God's will is the cause of all things.[10] It must needs be, therefore, that a thing has some being, or any kind of good, only inasmuch as it is willed by God. To every existing thing, then, God wills some good. Hence, since to love anything is nothing else than to will good to that

---

[8]*De Div. Nom.*, IV, 13 (PG 3, 712).   [9]*Eth.*, VIII, 2 (1155b 27).   [10]Q. 19, a. 4.

thing, it is manifest that God loves everything that exists. Yet not as we love. Because, since our will is not the cause of the goodness of things, but is moved by it as by its object, our love, whereby we will good to anything, is not the cause of its goodness; but conversely its goodness, whether real or imaginary, calls forth our love, by which we will that it should preserve the good it has, and receive besides the good it has not, and to this end we direct our actions: whereas the love of God infuses and creates goodness in things.

Reply Obj. 1. A lover is placed outside himself, and made to pass into the object of his love, inasmuch as he wills good to the beloved, and works for that good by his providence even as he works for his own. Hence Dionysius says: *On behalf of the truth we must make bold to say even this, that He Himself, the cause of all things, by His abounding love and goodness, is placed outside Himself by His providence over all existing things.*[11]

Reply Obj. 2. Although creatures have not existed from eternity, except in God, yet because they have been in Him from eternity, God has known them eternally in their proper natures, and for that reason has loved them; even as we, by the likenesses of things within us, know things existing in themselves.

Reply Obj. 3. Friendship cannot exist except towards rational creatures, who are capable of returning love and of communicating with one another in the various works of life, and who may fare well or ill, according to the changes of fortune and happiness; even as towards them is benevolence, properly speaking, exercised. But irrational creatures cannot attain to loving God, nor to any share in the intellectual and beatific life that He lives. Strictly speaking, therefore, God does not love irrational creatures with the love of friendship, but as it were with the love of desire, in so far as He orders them to rational creatures, and even to Himself. Yet this is not because He stands in need of them, but only because of His goodness, and of the services they render to us. For we can desire a thing for others as well as for ourselves.

Reply Obj. 4. Nothing prevents one and the same thing from being loved under one aspect, while it is hated under another. God loves sinners in so far as they are existing natures; for thus they both are and are from Him. In so far as they are sinners, they are not, and they fail of being; and this is not in them from God. Hence under this aspect, they are hated by Him.

---

[11]*De Div. Nom.*, IV, 13 (PG 3, 712).

Third Article
Whether God Loves All Things Equally?

We proceed thus to the Third Article:—

Objection 1. It seems that God loves all things equally. For it is said: *He hath equally care of all* (*Wis.* vi. 8). But God's providence over things comes from the love wherewith He loves them. Therefore He loves all things equally.

Obj. 2. Further, the love of God is His essence. But God's essence does not admit of degree; neither therefore does His love. He does not therefore love some things more than others.

Obj. 3. Further, as God's love extends to created things, so do His knowledge and will extend. But God is not said to know some things more than others; nor to will one thing more than another. Neither therefore does He love some things more than others.

On the contrary, Augustine says: *God loves all things that He has made, and among them rational creatures more, and of these especially those who are members of His only-begotten Son; and much more than all, His only-begotten Son Himself.*[12]

I answer that, Since to love a thing is to will it good, anything may be loved more or less in a twofold way. In one way on the part of the act of the will itself, which is more or less intense. In this way, God does not love some things more than others, because He loves all things by an act of the will that is one, simple, and always the same. In another way, on the part of the good itself that a person wills for the one whom he loves. In this way we are said to love that being more than another, for whom we will a greater good, even though our will is not more intense. In this way we must needs say that God loves some things more than others. For since God's love is the cause of goodness in things, as has been said, no one thing would be better than another, if God did not will greater good for one than for another.

Reply Obj. 1. God is said to have equally care of all, not because by His care He deals out equal good to all, but because He administers all things with a like wisdom and goodness.

Reply Obj. 2. This argument is based on the intensity of love on the part of the act of the will, which is the divine essence. But the good that God wills for His creatures is not the divine essence. Therefore there is no reason why it may not vary in degree.

Reply Obj. 3. To understand and to will signify only acts, and do not

[12] *Tract.* CX, super *Ioann.*, XVII, 23 (PL 35, 1924).

include in their meaning objects from the diversity of which God may be said to know or will more or less; as has been said with respect to God's love.

Fourth Article
Whether God Always Loves Better Things More?

We proceed thus to the Fourth Article:—

Objection 1. It seems that God does not always love better things more. For it is manifest that Christ is better than the whole human race, being God and man. But God loved the human race more than He loved Christ; for it is said: *He spared not His own Son, but delivered Him up for us all* (*Rom.* viii. 32). Therefore God does not always love better things more.

Obj. 2. Further, an angel is better than a man. Hence it is said of man: *Thou hast made him a little less than the angels* (*Ps.* viii. 6). But God loved men more than He loved the angels, for it is said: *Nowhere doth He take hold of the angels, but of the seed of Abraham He taketh hold* (*Heb.* ii. 16). Therefore God does not always love the better things more.

Obj. 3. Further, Peter was better than John, since he loved Christ more. Hence the Lord, knowing this to be true, asked Peter, saying: *"Simon, son of John, lovest thou Me more than these?"* (*Jo.* xxi. 15). Yet Christ loved John more than He loved Peter. For as Augustine says, commenting on the words, "Simon, son of John, lovest thou Me?" *By this very mark is John distinguished from the other disciples, not that He loved him only, but that He loved him more than the rest.*[13] Therefore God does not always love better things more.

Obj. 4. Further, the innocent man is better than the repentant, since repentance is, as Jerome says, *a second plank after shipwreck.*[14] But God loves the penitent more than the innocent; since He rejoices over him the more. For it is said: *I say to you that there shall be joy in heaven upon one sinner that doth penance, more than upon ninety-nine just who need not penance* (*Luke* xv. 7). Therefore God does not always love better things more.

Obj. 5. Further, the just man who is merely foreknown is better than the predestined sinner. Now God loves the predestined sinner more, since He wills for him a greater good, namely, life eternal. Therefore God does not always love better things more.

On the contrary, Everything loves what is like it, as appears from what is written (*Ecclus.* xiii. 19): *Every beast loveth its like.* Now the more like God a thing is, the better it is. Therefore, better things are more loved by God.

---

[13] *Tract.* CXXIV (PL 35, 1971).　　[14] *In Isaiam*, II, super III, 8 (PL 24, 66).

I answer that, It must be said, according to what has gone before, that God loves better things more. For it has been shown that God's loving one thing more than another is nothing else than His willing for that thing a greater good: because God's will is the cause of goodness in things, and the reason why some things are better than others is that God wills for them a greater good. Hence it follows that He loves better things more.

Reply Obj. 1. God loves Christ not only more than He loves the whole human race, but more than He loves the entire created universe: because He willed for Him the greater good in giving Him *a name that is above all names (Phil.* ii. 9); so that by God's will Christ was true God. Nor did anything of His excellence diminish when God delivered Him up to death for the salvation of the human race; rather did He become thereby a glorious conqueror: *The government was placed upon His shoulder,* according to *Isa.* ix. 6.

Reply Obj. 2. God loves the human nature assumed by the Word of God in the person of Christ more than He loves all the angels; for that nature is better, especially on the ground of union with the Godhead. But speaking of human nature in general, and comparing it with the angelic, the two are found equal in the order of grace and of glory, since according to *Apoc.* xxi. 17, *the measure of a man and of an angel* is the same; yet so that, in this respect, some angels are found nobler than some men, and some men nobler than some angels. But as to the condition of their natures, an angel is better than a man. God therefore did not assume human nature because, absolutely speaking, He loved man more, but because the needs of man were greater; just as the master of a house may give some costly delicacy to a sick servant, that he does not give to his own son who is well.

Reply Obj. 3. This doubt concerning Peter and John has been solved in various ways. Augustine interprets it mystically, and says that the active life, signified by Peter, loves God more than the contemplative, signified by John, because the former is more conscious of the miseries of this present life, and therefore the more ardently desires to be freed from them, and reach God.[15] But God, he says, loves the contemplative life more, since He preserves it longer. For it does not end, as the active life does, with the ending of the life of the body.

Some, on the other hand, say that Peter loved Christ more in His members, and therefore was loved more by Christ also, for which reason

---

[15] *Tract.* CXXIV, super *Ioann.,* XXI, 20 (PL 35, 1974).

He gave him the care of the Church,[16] but that John loved Christ more in Himself, and so was loved more by Him; on which account Christ commended His mother to his care. Still others say that it is uncertain which of them loved Christ more with the love of charity, and uncertain also which of them God loved more and ordained to a greater degree of glory in eternal life.[17] Peter is said to have loved more, in regard to a certain promptness and fervor, whereas John was more loved, with respect to certain marks of familiarity which Christ showed to him rather than to others, because of his youth and purity. And there are others who say that Christ loved Peter more, from his more excellent gift of charity; but John more, from his gifts of intellect.[18] Hence, absolutely speaking, Peter was the better and the more beloved; but, in a certain sense, John was the better, and was loved the more.

However, it seems presumptuous to pass judgment on these matters, since *the Lord* and no other *is the weigher of spirits* (*Prov.* xvi. 2).

Reply Obj. 4. The penitent and the innocent are related as exceeding and exceeded. For whether innocent or penitent, those are the better and the better loved who have more grace. Now, other things being equal, innocence is the nobler thing and the more beloved. Yet God is said to rejoice more over the penitent than over the innocent, because often penitents rise from sin more cautious, humble, and fervent. Hence Gregory commenting on these words says that, *In battle, the general loves the soldier who after flight returns and bravely pursues the enemy, more than him who has never fled, but has never done a brave deed.*[19]

Or it may be answered that an equal gift of grace is greater in relation to a penitent sinner who merited punishment than to an innocent person who did not merit it; just as a hundred pieces of gold are a greater gift to a poor man than to a king.

Reply Obj. 5. Since God's will is the cause of goodness in things, the goodness of one who is loved by God is to be reckoned according to the time when some good is to be given to him by the divine goodness. According therefore to that time when a greater good is to be given by the divine will to the predestined sinner, the sinner is the better; although at another time he may be worse than the innocent man; for there is even a time when he is neither good nor bad.

---

[16]St. Albert, *In III Sent.*, d. xxxi, a. 12 (XXVIII, 593).   [17]Cf. St. Bernard, *Serm. de Diversis*, XXIX (PL 183, 622).   [18]Cf. St. Albert, *Enarr. in Ioann.* (XXIV, 13).   [19]*In Evang.*, II, hom. 34 (PL 76, 1248).

Question 21
The Justice and Mercy of God
(*In Four Articles*)

After considering the divine love, we must treat of God's justice and mercy. Under this head there are four points of inquiry: (1) Whether there is justice in God? (2) Whether His justice can be called truth? (3) Whether there is mercy in God? (4) Whether in every work of God there are justice and mercy?

First Article
Whether There Is Justice in God?

We proceed thus to the First Article:—

Objection 1. It seems that there is no justice in God. For justice and temperance are divided as members of the same class. But temperance does not exist in God: neither therefore does justice.

Obj. 2. Further, he who does whatsoever he wills and pleases does not work according to justice. But, as the Apostle says: *God worketh all things according to the counsel of his will* (*Ephes.* i. 11). Therefore justice cannot be attributed to Him.

Obj. 3. Further, the act of justice is to pay what is due. But God is no man's debtor. Therefore justice does not belong to God.

Obj. 4. Further, whatever is in God is His essence. But justice cannot belong to the divine essence. For Boethius says: *Good refers to the essence; justice to the act.*[1] Therefore justice does not belong to God.

On the contrary, It is said (*Ps.* x. 8): *The Lord is just, and hath loved justice.*

I answer that, There are two kinds of justice. The one consists in mutual giving and receiving, as in buying and selling, and other kinds of communication and exchange. This justice the Philosopher calls *commutative justice,* which directs exchange and the communication of business.[2] This does not belong to God, since, as the Apostle says: *Who hath first given to Him, and recompense shall be made him?* (*Rom.* xi. 35). The other kind of justice consists in distribution, and is called *distributive justice,* whereby a ruler or a steward gives to each what his rank deserves. As, then, the proper order displayed in ruling a family or any kind of multitude evinces justice of this kind in the ruler, so the order of the universe,

---

[1]*De Hebdom.* (PL 64, 1314).   [2]*Eth.*, V, 4 (1131b 25).

which is seen both in effects of nature and in effects of will, shows forth the justice of God. Hence Dionysius says: *We must needs see that God is truly just, in seeing how He gives to all existing things what is proper to the condition of each; and preserves the nature of each one in the order and with the powers that properly belong to it.*[3]

Reply Obj. 1. Certain of the moral virtues are concerned with the passions, as temperance with concupiscence, fortitude with fear and temerity, meekness with anger. Such virtues as these can be attributed to God only metaphorically, since, as was stated above, in God there are no passions,[4] nor a sensitive appetite, which is, as the Philosopher says, the subject of those virtues.[5] On the other hand, certain moral virtues are concerned with works of giving and expending: such are justice, liberality and magnificence; and these reside not in the sensitive power, but in the will. Hence, there is nothing to prevent our attributing these virtues to God; although not in reference to civil matters, but in such acts as befit Him. For, as the Philosopher says, it would be absurd to praise God for His political virtues.[6]

Reply Obj. 2. Since the apprehended good is the object of the will, it is impossible for God to will anything but what His wisdom approves. For wisdom is, as it were, His law of justice, in accordance with which His will is right and just. Hence, what He does according to His will He does justly; as we do justly what we do according to law. But whereas law comes to us from some higher power, God is a law unto Himself.

Reply Obj. 3. To each one is due what is his own. Now that which is ordered to a man is what is said to be his own. Thus, the master owns the servant, and not conversely, for that is free which is its own master. In the word *debt*, therefore, there is implied a certain exigency or necessity on the part of one being towards another being to which it is ordered. Now a two-fold order has to be considered in things: the one, whereby one created thing is ordained to another, as the parts to the whole, accident to substance, and all things whatsoever to their end; the other, whereby all created things are ordered to God. Thus in the divine operations, a debt may be regarded in two ways, as due either to God, or to creatures; and in either way God pays what is due. *God has a debt to Himself* that there should be fulfilled in creatures what His will and wisdom contain, and what manifests His goodness. In this respect God's justice regards what befits Him; inasmuch as He renders to Himself what is due to Himself.

---

[3]*De Div. Nom.*, VIII, 7 (PG 3, 896).   [4]Q. 20, a. 1., ad 1.   [5]*Eth.* III, 10 (11117b 24).   [6]*Op. cit.*, X, 8 (1178b 10).

There is also a debt to each creature that it should possess what is ordered to it; thus it is due to man to have hands, and that other animals should serve him. Thus also God carries out justice, when He gives to each thing what is due it according to its nature and condition. This debt, however, is derived from the first; since what is due each thing is due to it as ordered to it according to the divine wisdom. And although God in this way pays each thing its due, yet He Himself is not the debtor, since He is not ordered to other things, but rather other things to Him. Justice, therefore, in God is sometimes spoken of as the fitting accompaniment of His goodness; sometimes as the reward of merit. Anselm touches on both views where he says: *When Thou dost punish the wicked, it is just, since it agrees with their deserts; and when Thou dost spare the wicked, it is also just, since it befits Thy goodness.*[7]

Reply Obj. 4. Although justice refers to an act, this does not prevent its being the essence of God; since even that which is of the essence of a thing may be a principle of action. But good does not always refer to an act, since a thing is called good not merely with respect to its acts, but also with respect to the perfection in its essence. For this reason it is said that the good is related to the just as the general to the special.

Second Article
Whether the Justice of God Is Truth?

We proceed thus to the Second Article:—

Objection 1. It seems that the justice of God is not truth. For justice resides in the will, since, as Anselm says, it is *the rectitude of the will;*[8] whereas truth resides in the intellect, as the Philosopher says, *Metaph.* vi.[9] and *Ethics* vi.[10] Therefore justice does not pertain to truth.

Obj. 2. Further, according to the Philosopher, truth is a virtue distinct from justice.[11] Truth therefore does not pertain to the nature of justice.

On the contrary, It is said (*Ps.* lxxxiv. 11): *Mercy and truth have met each other:* where truth stands for justice.

I answer that, Truth consists in the equation of intellect and thing, as was said above.[12] Now the intellect that is the cause of the thing is related to it as its rule and measure: whereas the converse is the case with the intellect that receives its knowledge from things. When, therefore, things are the measure and rule of the intellect, truth consists in the equation of

---

[7]*Proslog.*, X (PL 158, 233).   [8]*De Ver.*, XII (PL 158, 482).   [9]*Metaph.*, V, 4 (1027b 27).   [10]*Eth.*, VI, 2 (1139a 27).   [11]*Op. cit.*, IV, 7 (1127a 34). [12]Q. 16, a. 1. [Not in this volume]

the intellect to the thing; as happens in ourselves. For according as a thing is, or is not, our thoughts or our words about it are true or false. But when the intellect is the rule or measure of things, truth consists in the equation of things to the intellect; just as the work of an artist is said to be true when it is in accordance with his art.

Now as works of art are related to the art, so are works of justice related to the law with which they accord. Therefore, God's justice, which has established in things the order conforming to the rule of His wisdom, which is the law of His justice, is fittingly called truth. Thus we too speak of the truth of justice in human affair.

Reply Obj. 1. Justice, as to the law that governs, resides in the reason or intellect; but as to the command whereby our actions are governed according to the law, it resides in the will.

Reply Obj. 2. The truth of which the Philosopher is speaking in this passage, is that virtue whereby a man shows himself in word and deed such as he really is. Thus it consists in the conformity of the sign with the thing signified; and not in that of the effect with its cause and rule: as has been said regarding the truth of justice.

Third Article
Whether Mercy Can Be Attributed to God?

We proceed thus to the Third Article:—

Objection 1. It seems that mercy cannot be attributed to God. For mercy is a kind of sorrow, as Damascene says.[13] But there is no sorrow in God; and therefore there is no mercy in Him.

Obj. 2. Further, mercy is a relaxation of justice. But God cannot remit what pertains to His justice. For it is said (*2 Tim.* ii 13): *If we believe not, He continueth faithful: He cannot deny Himself.* But he would deny Himself, as the *Gloss* says, if He should deny His words.[14] Therefore mercy is not becoming to God.

On the contrary, It is said (*Ps.* cx. 4): *He is a merciful and gracious Lord.*

I answer that, Mercy is especially to be attributed to God, provided it be considered in its effect, but not as an affection of passion. In proof of which it must be observed that a person is said to be merciful [*misericors*] as being, so to speak, sorrowful at heart [*miserium cor*]; in other words, as being affected with sorrow at the misery of another as though it were his own. Hence it follows that he endeavors to dispel the misery of this other, as if it

---

[13]*De Fide Orth.*, II, 14 (PG 94, 932).   [14]*Glossa interl.* (VI, 125r); Peter Lombard, *In II Tim.*, super II, 13 (PL 192, 370).

were his; and this is the effect of mercy. To sorrow, therefore, over the misery of others does not belong to God; but it does most properly belong to Him to dispel that misery, whatever be the defect we call misery. Now defects are not removed, except by the perfection of some kind of goodness; and the primary source of goodness is God, as was shown above.[15]

It must, however, be considered that to bestow perfections on things pertains not only to the divine goodness, but also to the divine justice, liberality and mercy; yet under different aspects. The communicating of perfection absolutely considered, pertains to goodness, as was shown above;[16] in so far as perfections are given to things according to what is due them, it is a work of justice, as has been already said; in so far as God does not bestow them for His own use, but only because of His goodness, it belongs to liberality in so far as perfections given to things by God expel defects, it belongs to mercy.

Reply Obj. 1. This argument is based on mercy regarded as an affection of passion.

Reply Obj. 2. God acts mercifully, not indeed by going against His justice, but by doing something more than justice. Thus a man who pays another two hundred pieces of money, though owing him only one hundred, does nothing against justice, but acts liberally or mercifully. The case is the same with one who pardons an offense committed against him; for in remitting it he may be said to bestow a gift. Hence the Apostle calls remission a forgiving: *Forgive one another, as Christ has forgiven you* (*Ephes.* iv. 32). Hence it is clear that mercy does not destroy justice, but in a sense is the fulness thereof. And thus it is said: *Mercy exalteth itself above judgment* (*Jas.* ii. 13).

Fourth Article
Whether in Every Work of God There Are Mercy and Justice?

We proceed thus to the Fourth Article:—

Objection 1. It seems that not in every work of God are mercy and justice. For some works of God are attributed to mercy, as the justification of the sinners; and others to justice, as the damnation of the wicked. Hence it is said: *Judgment without mercy to him that hath not done mercy* (*Jas.* ii. 13). Therefore not in every work of God do mercy and justice appear.

Obj. 2. Further, the Apostle attributes the conversion of the Jews to justice and truth, but that of the Gentiles to mercy (*Rom.* xv. 8). Therefore not in every work of God are there justice and mercy.

---

[15]Q. 6, a. 4. [Not in this volume]   [16]Q. 6, a. 1. [Not in this volume]

Obj. 3. Further, many just persons are afflicted in this world; which is unjust. Therefore not in every work of God are there justice and mercy.

Obj. 4. Further, it is the part of justice to pay what is due, but of mercy to relieve misery. Thus both justice and mercy presuppose something in their works whereas creation presupposes nothing. Therefore in creation neither mercy nor justice is found.

On the contrary, It is said (*Ps.* xxiv. 10): *All the ways of the Lord are mercy and truth.*

I answer that, Mercy and truth are necessarily found in all God's works, provided mercy be taken to mean the removal of any kind of defect. Not every defect, however, can properly be called a misery, but only defect in a rational nature whose lot is to be happy; for misery is opposed to happiness. For this necessity there is a reason, because since a debt paid according to the divine justice is one due either to God, or to some creature, neither the one nor the other can be lacking in any work of God: for God can do nothing that is not in accord with His wisdom and goodness. It is in this sense, as we have said, that anything is said to be a debt on the part of God. Likewise, whatever is done by Him in created things, is done according to proper order and proportion; wherein consists the nature of justice. Thus justice must exist in all God's works.

Now the work of divine justice always presupposes the work of mercy; and is founded thereupon. For nothing is due to creatures, except on the supposition of something already existing or already known in them. Again, if this is due to a creature, it must be due because of something that precedes. And since we cannot go on to infinity, we must come to something that depends only on the goodness of the divine will—which is the ultimate end. We may say, for instance, that to possess hands is due to man because of his rational soul; and his rational soul is due to him that he may be man; and his being man is for the sake of the divine goodness. So in every work of God, viewed at its primary source, there appears mercy. In all that follows, the power of mercy remains, and works indeed with even greater force; as the influence of the first cause is more intense than that of second causes. For this reason does God out of the abundance of His goodness bestow upon creatures what is due them more bountifully than is proportionate to their deserts: since less would suffice for preserving the order of justice than what the divine goodness confers; because between creatures and God's goodness there can be no proportion.

Reply Obj. 1. Certain works are attributed to justice, and certain others to mercy, because in some justice appears more forcibly and in others mercy. Yet even in the damnation of the reprobate mercy is seen, which, though it does not totally remit, yet somewhat alleviates, in punishing short of what is deserved.

In the justification of the sinner justice is seen, when God remits sins because of love, though He Himself has mercifully infused that love. So we read of Magdalen: *Many sins are forgiven her, because she hath loved much* (*Luke* vii. 47).

Reply Obj. 2. God's justice and mercy appear both in the conversion of the Jews and of the Gentiles. But an aspect of justice appears in the conversion of the Jews which is not seen in the conversion of the Gentiles, inasmuch as the Jews were saved because of the promises made to their fathers.

Reply Obj. 3. Justice and mercy appear in the punishment of the just in this world, since by afflictions lesser faults are cleansed in them, and they are the more raised up from earthly affections to God. As to this Gregory says: *The evils that press on us in this world force us to go to God.*[17]

Reply Obj. 4. Although creation presupposes nothing in the universe, yet it does presuppose something in the knowledge of God. In this way too the idea of justice is preserved in creation, inasmuch as things are brought into being in a manner that accords with the divine wisdom and goodness. And the idea of mercy is also preserved in the transition of creatures from non-being to being.

Question 22
The Providence of God
(*In Four Articles*)

Having considered all that relates to the will absolutely, we must now proceed to those things which have relation to both the intellect and the will, namely providence, in relation to all created things; predestination and reprobation, and all that is connected with them, in relation especially to man as ordered to his eternal salvation.[1] For in the science of morals, after the moral virtues themselves, comes the consideration of prudence, to which providence would seem to belong. Concerning God's providence there are four points of inquiry: (1) Whether providence is suitably

---

[17]*Moral.*, XXVI, 13 (PL 76, 360).
[1]Q. 23. [Not in this volume]

assigned to God? (2) Whether everything comes under divine providence? (3) Whether divine providence is immediately concerned with all things? (4) Whether divine providence imposes any necessity upon what it foresees?

First Article
Whether Providence Can Suitably Be Attributed to God?

We proceed thus to the First Article:—

Objection 1. It seems that providence is not becoming to God. For providence, according to Tully, is a part of prudence.[2] But since, according to the Philosopher, prudence gives good counsel,[3] it cannot belong to God, Who never has any doubt for which He should take counsel. Therefore providence cannot belong to God.

Obj. 2. Further, whatever is in God is eternal. But providence is not anything eternal, *for it is concerned with existing things* that are not eternal, according to Damascene.[4] Therefore there is no providence in God.

Obj. 3. Further, there is nothing composite in God. But providence seems to be something composite, because it includes both the intellect and the will. Therefore providence is not in God.

On the contrary, It is said (*Wis.* xiv. 3): *But Thou, Father, governeth all things by providence.*

I answer that, It is necessary to attribute providence to God. For all the good that is in things has been created by God, as was shown above.[5] Good is found in things not only as regards their substance, but also as regards their order towards an end and especially their last end, which, as was said above, is the divine goodness.[6] This good of order existing in created things is itself created by God. Now God is the cause of things by His intellect, and therefore it is necessary that the exemplar of every effect should pre-exist in Him, as is clear from what has gone before.[7] Hence, the exemplar of the order of things towards their end must necessarily pre-exist in the divine mind; and the exemplar of things ordered towards an end, is properly speaking, providence. For providence is the chief part of prudence, to which two other parts are directed—namely, remembrance of the past, and understanding of the present; inasmuch as from the remembrance of what is past and the understanding of what is present, we gather how to provide for the future. Now it belongs to pru-

---

[2]*De Invent.*, II, 53 (p. 147[b]).   [3]*Eth.*, VI, 5 (1140a 26).   [4]*De Fide Orth.*, II, 29 (PG 94, 964).   [5]Q. 6, a. 4. [Not in this volume]   [6]Q. 21, a. 4. [7]Q. 19, a. 4.

dence, according to the Philosopher, *to direct other things towards an end,*[8] whether in regard to oneself—as for instance, a man is said to be prudent, who orders well his acts towards the end of life—or in regard to others subject to him, in a family, city, or kingdom; in which sense it is said (*Matt.* xxiv. 45): a *faithful and wise servant, whom his lord hath appointed over his family.* In this second way prudence or providence may suitably be attributed to God. For in God Himself there can be nothing ordinable towards an end, since He is the last end. Hence, the very exemplar of the order of things towards an end is in God called providence. Whence Boethius says that *Providence is the divine reason itself which, seated in the Supreme Ruler, disposes all things;*[9] which disposition may refer either to the exemplar of the order of things towards an end, or to the exemplar of the order of parts in the whole.

Reply Obj. 1. According to the Philosopher, *Prudence, strictly speaking, commands all that "eubulia" has rightly counselled and "synesis" rightly judged.*[10] Whence, though to take counsel may not be fitting to God, insofar as counsel is an inquiry into matters that are doubtful, nevertheless to give a command as to the ordering of things towards an end, the right reason of which He possesses, does belong to God, according to *Ps.* cxlviii. 6: *He hath made a decree, and it shall not pass away.* In this manner both prudence and providence belong to God. At the same time, it may also be said that the very exemplar of things to be done is called counsel in God; not because of any inquiry necessitated, but from the certitude of the knowledge, to which those who take counsel come by inquiry. Whence it is said: *Who worketh all things according to the counsel of His will* (*Ephes.* i. 11).

Reply Obj. 2. Two things pertain to the care of providence—namely, the *exemplar of order,* which is called providence and disposition; and the *execution of order,* which is termed government. Of these, the first is eternal, and the second is temporal.

Reply Obj. 3. Providence resides in the intellect; but it presupposes the act of willing the end. For no one gives a precept about things done for an end, unless he wills that end. Hence likewise prudence presupposes the moral virtues, by means of which the appetitive power is directed towards good, as the Philosopher says.[11] But even supposing that providence were equally related to the divine will and intellect, this would not affect the divine simplicity, since in God both the will and intellect are one and the same thing, as we have said above.[12]

---

[8]*Eth.,* VI, 12 (1144a 8).   [9]*De Consol.,* IV, prose 6 (PL 63, 814).   [10]*Eth.,* VI, 9 (1142b 31); 10 (1143b 8).   [11]Aristotle, *Eth.,* VI, 13 (1144b 32). [12]Q. 19, a. 1; a. 4, ad 2.

Second Article
Whether Everything Is Subject to the Providence of God?

We proceed thus to the Second Article:—

Objection 1. It seems that not everything is subject to divine providence. For nothing foreseen can happen by chance. If then everything has been foreseen by God, nothing will happen by chance. And thus chance and fortune disappear; which is against common opinion.

Obj. 2. Further, a wise provider excludes any defect or evil, as far as he can, from those over whom he has a care. But we see many evils existing in things. Either, then, God cannot hinder these, and thus is not omnipotent; or else He does not have care for everything.

Obj. 3. Further, whatever happens of necessity does not require providence or prudence. Hence, according to the Philosopher: *Prudence is the right reason of contingent things concerning which there is counsel and choice.*[13] Since, then, many things happen from necessity, everything cannot be subject to providence.

Obj. 4. Further, whatsoever is left to itself cannot be subject to the providence of a governor. But men are left to themselves by God, in accordance with the words: *God made man from the beginning, and left him in the hand of his own counsel (Ecclus.* xv. 14). And particularly in reference to the wicked: *I let them go according to the desires of their heart (Ps.* lxxx. 13). Everything, therefore, cannot be subject to divine providence.

Obj. 5. Further, the Apostle says (*1 Cor.* ix. 9): *God doth not care for men*; and we may say the same of other irrational creatures. Thus everything cannot be under the care of divine providence.

On the contrary, It is said of divine wisdom: *She reacheth from end to end mightily, and ordereth all things sweetly (Wis.* viii. 1).

I answer that, Certain persons totally denied the existence of providence, as Democritus and the Epicureans,[14] maintaining that the world was made by chance. Others taught that incorruptible substances only were subject to providence, while corruptible substances were not in their individual being, but only according to their species; for in this respect they are incorruptible.[15] They are represented as saying (*Job* xxii. 14): *The clouds are His covert; and He doth not consider our things; and He walketh about the poles of heaven.* Rabbi Moses, however, excluded men from the

---

[13]*Eth.,* VI, 5 (1140a 35); 7 (1141b 9); 13 (1144b 27).   [14]Cf. Nemesius, *De Nat. Hom.,* XLIV (PG 40, 795).   [15]According to St. Thomas himself (*In I Sent.,* d. xxxix, q. 2, a. 2), this opinion is attributed to Aristotle and expressly held by Averroes.—Cf. Maimonides, *Guide,* III, 17 (p. 282); Averroes, *In Metaph.,* XII, comm. 52 (VIII, 158v).

generality of corruptible things, because of the excellence of the intellect which they possess, but in reference to all else that suffers corruption he adhered to the opinion of the others.[16]

We must say, however, that all things are subject to divine providence, not only in general, but even in their own individual being. This is made evident thus. For since every agent acts for an end, the ordering of effects towards that end extends as far as the causality of the first agent extends. Whence it happens that in the effects of an agent something takes place which has no reference towards the end, because the effect comes from some other cause outside the intention of the agent. But the causality of God, Who is the first agent, extends to all beings not only as to the constituent principles of species, but also as to the individualizing principles; not only of things incorruptible, but also of things corruptible. Hence all things that exist in whatsoever manner are necessarily directed by God towards the end; as the Apostle says: *Those things that are of God are well ordered* (*Rom.* xiii. 1). Since, therefore, the providence of God is nothing other than the notion of the order of things towards an end, as we have said, it necessarily follows that all things, inasmuch as they participate being, must to that extent be subject to divine providence. It has also been shown that God knows all things, both universal and particular.[17] And since His knowledge may be compared to the things themselves as the knowledge of art to the objects of art, as was said above,[18] all things must of necessity come under His ordering; as all things wrought by an art are subject to the ordering of that art.

Reply Obj. 1. There is a difference between universal and particular causes. A thing can escape the order of a particular cause, but not the order of a universal cause. For nothing escapes the order of a particular cause, except through the intervention and hindrance of some other particular cause; as, for instance, wood may be prevented from burning by the action of water. Since, then, all particular causes are included under the universal cause, it is impossible that any effect should escape the range of the universal cause. So far then as an effect escapes the order of a particular cause, it is said to be by chance or fortuitous in respect to that cause; but if we regard the universal cause, outside whose range no effect can happen, it is said to be foreseen. Thus, for instance, the meeting of two servants, although to them it appears a chance circumstance, has been fully foreseen by their master, who has purposely sent them to meet at the one place, in such a way that the one has no knowledge of the other.

---

[16]*Guide*, III, 17 (p. 286).   [17]Q. 14, a. 11. [Not in this volume]   [18]Q. 14, a. 8. [Not in this volume]

Reply Obj. 2. It is otherwise with one who is in charge of a particular thing, and one whose providence is universal, because a particular provider excludes all defects from what is subject to his care as far as he can; whereas one who provides universally allows some little defect to remain, lest the good of the whole should be hindered. Hence, corruption and defects in natural things are said to be contrary to some particular nature, yet they are in keeping with the plan of universal nature, inasmuch as the defect in one thing yields to the good of another, or even to the universal good: for the corruption of one is the generation of another, and through this it is that a species is kept in existence. Since God, then, provides universally for all being, it belongs to His providence to permit certain defects in particular effects, that the perfect good of the universe may not be hindered; for if all evil were prevented, much good would be absent from the universe. A lion would cease to live, if there were no slaying of animals; and there would be no patience of martyrs if there were no tyrannical persecution. Thus Augustine says: *Almighty God would in no wise permit evil to exist in His works, unless He were so almighty and so good as to produce good even from evil.*[19] It would appear that it was because of these two arguments to which we have just replied, that some were persuaded to consider corruptible things—*i.e.*, things in which chance and evil are found—as removed from the care of divine providence.

Reply Obj. 3. Man is not the author of nature; but he uses natural things for his own purposes in his works of art and virtue. Hence human providence does not reach to that which takes place in nature from necessity; but divine providence extends thus far, since God is the author of nature. Apparently it was this argument that moved those who withdrew the course of nature from the care of divine providence, attributing it rather to the necessity of matter, as did Democritus, and others of the ancients.[20]

Reply Obj. 4. When it is said that God left man to himself, this does not mean that man is exempt from divine providence, but merely that he has not a prefixed operating power determined to only the one effect; as in the case of natural things, which are only acted upon as though directed by another towards an end: for they do not act of themselves, as if they directed themselves towards an end, like rational creatures, through the possession of free choice, by which these are able to take counsel and make choices. Hence it is significantly said: *In the hand of his own counsel.* But since the very act of free choice is traced to God as to a cause, it necessar-

---

[19]*Enchir.*, XI (PL 40, 236).   [20]Cf. Aristotle, *Metaph.*, I, 3 (983b 7); 4 (985b 5).

ily follows that everything happening from the exercise of free choice must be subject to divine providence. For human providence is included under the providence of God as a particular cause under a universal cause. God, however, extends His providence over the just in a certain more excellent way than over the wicked, inasmuch as He prevents anything happening which would impede their final salvation. For *to them that love God, all things work together unto good* (*Rom.* viii. 28). But from the fact that He does not restrain the wicked from the evil of sin, He is said to abandon them. This does not mean that He altogether withdraws His providence from them; otherwise they would return to nothing, if they were not preserved in existence by His providence. This was the reason that had weight with Tully, who withdrew human affairs, concerning which we take counsel, from the care of divine providence.[21]

Reply Obj. 5. Since a rational creature has, through its free choice, control over its actions, as was said above,[22] it is subject to divine providence in an especial manner: something is imputed to it as a fault, or as a merit, and accordingly there is given to it something by way of punishment or reward. In this way the Apostle withdraws oxen from the care of God: not, however, that individual irrational creatures escape the care of divine providence, as was the opinion of the Rabbi Moses.[23]

Third Article
Whether God Has Immediate Providence Over Everything?

We proceed thus to the Third Article:—

Objection 1. It seems that God has not immediate providence over all things. For whatever pertains to dignity must be attributed to God. But it belongs to the dignity of a king that he should have ministers, through whose mediation he provides for his subjects. Therefore much less has God Himself immediate providence over all things.

Obj. 2. Further, it belongs to providence to order all things to an end. Now the end of everything is its perfection and its good. But it pertains to every cause to bring its effect to good; and therefore every agent cause is a cause of the effect over which it has providence. If therefore God were to have immediate providence over all things, all secondary causes would be withdrawn.

Obj. 3. Further, Augustine says that, *It is better to be ignorant of some things than to know them, for example, ignoble things,*[24] and the Philosopher

---

[21]*De Divinat.*, II, 5 (p. 69).   [22]Ad 4, and q. 19, a. 10.   [23]*Guide*, III, 17 (p. 286).   [24]*Enchir.*, XVII (PL 40, 239).

says the same.[25] But whatever is better must be attributed to God. Therefore He has not immediate providence over ignoble and wicked things.

On the contrary, It is said (*Job* xxxiv. 13): *What other hath He appointed over the earth? or whom hath He set over the world which He made?* On which passage Gregory says: *Himself He ruleth the world which He Himself hath made.*[26]

I answer that, Two things belong to providence—namely, the exemplar of the order of things foreordained towards an end, and the execution of this order, which is called government. As regards the first of these, God has immediate providence over everything, because he has in His intellect the exemplars of everything, even the smallest; and whatsoever causes He assigns to certain effects, He gives them the power to produce those effects. Whence it must be that He has pre-comprehended the order of those effects in His mind. As to the second, there are certain intermediaries of God's providence, for He governs things inferior by superior, not because of any defect in His power, but by reason of the abundance of His goodness; so that the dignity of causality is imparted even to creatures. Thus Plato's opinion, as narrated by Gregory of Nyssa, is removed.[27] He taught a threefold providence. First, one which belongs to the supreme Deity, Who first and foremost has provision over spiritual things, and thus over the whole world as regards genus, species, and universal causes. The second providence, which is over the individuals of all that can be generated and corrupted, he attributed to the divinities who circulate in the heavens; that is, certain separate substances, which move corporeal things in a circular motion. The third providence, which is over human affairs, he assigned to demons, whom the Platonic philosophers placed between us and the gods, as Augustine tells us.[28]

Reply Obj. 1. It pertains to a king's dignity to have ministers who execute his providence. But the fact that he does not know the plans of what is done by them arises from a deficiency in himself. For every operative science is the more perfect, the more it considers the particular things where action takes place.

Reply Obj. 2. God's immediate provision over everything does not exclude the action of secondary causes, which are the executors of His order, as was said above.[29]

Reply Obj. 3. It is better for us not to know evil and ignoble things,

---

[25]*Metaph.*, XI, 10 (1074b 32).   [26]*Moral.*, XXIV, 20 (PL 76, 314).   [27]Cf. Nemesius, *De Nat. Hom.*, XLIV (PG 40, 794).   [28]*De Civit. Dei*, IX, 1 (PL 41, 257); VIII, 14 (PL 41, 238).   [29]Q. 19, a. 5 and 8.

insofar as by them we are impeded in our knowledge of what is better and higher (for we cannot understand many things simultaneously), and insofar as the thought of evil sometimes perverts the will towards evil. This does not hold true of God, Who sees everything simultaneously at one glance, and Whose will cannot turn in the direction of evil.

Fourth Article
Whether Providence Imposes Any Necessity on What It Foresees?

We proceed thus to the Fourth Article:—

Objection 1. It seems that divine providence imposes necessity upon what it foresees. For every effect that has an essential cause (present or past) which it necessarily follows, comes to be of necessity; as the Philosopher proves.[30] But the providence of God, since it is eternal, precedes its effect, and the effect flows from it of necessity; for divine providence cannot be frustrated. Therefore divine providence imposes a necessity upon what it foresees.

Obj. 2. Further, every provider makes his work as stable as he can, lest it should fail. But God is most powerful. Therefore He assigns the stability of necessity to things whose providence He is.

Obj. 3. Further, Boethius says: *Fate from the immutable source of providence binds together human acts and fortunes by the indissoluble connexion of causes.*[31] It seems therefore that providence imposes necessity upon what it foresees.

On the contrary, Dionysius says that *to corrupt nature is not the work of providence.*[32] But it is in the nature of some things to be contingent. Divine providence does not therefore impose any necessity upon things so as to destroy their contingency.

I answer that, Divine providence imposes necessity upon some things; not upon all, as some believed.[33] For to providence it belongs to order things towards an end. Now after the divine goodness, which is an extrinsic end to all things, the principal good in things themselves is the perfection of the universe; which would not be, were not all grades of being found in things. Whence it pertains to divine providence to produce every grade of being. And thus for some things it has prepared necessary causes, so that they happen of necessity; for others contingent causes, that they

---

[30]*Metaph.*, V, 3 (1027a 30).   [31]*De Consol.*, IV, prose 6 (PL 63, 817).   [32]*De Div. Nom.*, IV, 33 (PG 3, 733).   [33]The Stoics: cf. Nemesius, *De Nat. Hom.*, XXXVII (PG 40, 752).

may happen by contingency, according to the disposition of their proximate causes.

Reply Obj. 1. The effect of divine providence is not only that things should happen *somehow*; but that they should happen either by necessity or by contingency. Therefore whatsoever divine providence ordains to happen infallibly and of necessity, happens infallibly and of necessity; and what the divine providence plans to happen contingently, happens contingently.

Reply Obj. 2. The order of divine providence is unchangeable and certain, so far as all things foreseen happen as they have been foreseen, whether from necessity or from contingency.

Reply Obj. 3. The indissolubility and unchangeableness, of which Boethius speaks, pertain to the certainty of providence, which does not fail to produce its effect, and that in the way foreseen; but they do not pertain to the necessity of the effects. We must remember that, properly speaking, *necessary* and *contingent* are consequent upon being as such. Hence the mode both of necessity and of contingency falls under the foresight of God, Who provides universally for all being; not under the foresight of causes that provide only for some particular order of things.

III

THE GOD OF CHRISTIAN FAITH

When we enter the world of Christian Theology proper, we enter the world of the Trinity and the Incarnation. Here both the scientific nature of theological argumentation that leads us to new sure conclusions or brings us back to more fundamental principles or premises underlying what the Christian Church holds as true and the declarative approaches to the articles of the Creed considered in themselves point to further extensions and adjustments of philosophers' metaphysical principles, whether they be those of Aristotle and the Platonists or those of the Arab and Jewish thinkers. The revelation of the Trinity did not just present Aquinas with a belief to be defended. It stretched his mind: It presented him with a belief that helped him better understand the attributes of God, as well as the meaning of the Scriptures, the affirmations of the Fathers, and the declarations of the Creeds. Defensive theology, overcoming heretical positions, is not just a matter of building a protective turret. It is a form of declarative theology: It is Aquinas's way of helping himself and other Christians understand the basic truths of the faith by examining the contentions and grounds supporting heretical positions and coming to a better understanding of why they are false.

Anyone reading Boethius's *On The Trinity* would realize how much he had to adapt Aristotle's theory of relations to treat the more subtle view of relations a Christian must bring to an understanding of the Trinity. Aristotle's *Categories* never could plumb the depths of the nature of relation as manifested by a Trinity of persons in one God. Aristotle never had a clue whereby he could understand subsistent relations. The Philosopher had only a theory of accidental relations. In dealing with God's simplicity in Part II, we stressed that simplicity meant lack of composition. A theory of subsistent relations must be able to ground a plurality of relations without admitting composition. In some of the five ways of proving the existence of God, we saw explicitly (in the others implicitly) that God is one God. These philosophical views still remain: God is simple and there is only one God. The Christian doctrine of the Trinity cannot and does not involve composition in God, nor does it mean that there are three gods. If the understanding of God's goodness leads us to an understanding of goodness beyond the goodness we experience in any creature, then, how much more does the teaching of a trinity of persons in one God lead us to an understanding of the kind of plurality that does not involve composition? We can notice the subtle adjustments Boethius had to make. These adjustments were not made for only Aristotle's theory of relation. They entailed a whole new view of relations.

Many questions of the First Part of the *Summa Theologica* that deal with the technical aspect of Trinitarian Theology center on declarative theology's role of clarifying terms. Aquinas notes:

> Since, as Jerome remarks, a heresy arises from words wrongly used, when we speak of the Trinity we must proceed with care and with befitting modesty; because, as Augustine says, *nowhere is error more harmful, the quest more toilsome, the finding more fruitful.* Now, in treating of the Trinity, we must beware of two opposite errors, and proceed cautiously between them—namely, the error of Arius, who posited a Trinity of substances with the Trinity of persons, and the error of Sabellius, who posited a unity of person with the unity of essence.
>
> Thus, to avoid the error of Arius we must shun the use of the terms *diversity* and *difference* in God, lest we take away the unity of essence; we may, however, use the term *distinction* because of the relative opposition. . . .
>
> To avoid the heresy of Sabellius, on the other hand, we must shun the term *singularity* lest we take away the communicability of the divine essence.[1]

Before we turn to the teachings of Arius and Sabellius and the need for linguistic precision to avoid their errors, it is important to consider a few general points about theological language. Theological language, like philosophical language, is a technical language aimed at as much precision as the object we speak about allows.[2] Furthermore, Theology's magnified use of philosophical vocabulary, giving it new meaning, follows a long Christian tradition of extending the meaning of words. *Sacramentum* (sacrament) in the pagan world meant the soldier's oath of allegiance. *Catechumenus* (catechumen), originally a Greek word for "learner," was simply transliterated by the Roman military to indicate "an army recruit"; Christians used it to indicate a person preparing for baptism in the Christian faith. *Paganus* (pagan), the soldier's word for a "civilian," became the Christian term for those who did not belong to the army of Christ. All these words, as well as many others, took on new Christian meanings.[3]

---

[1]*Summa Theologica*, I, q. 31, a. 2.   [2]Aristotle, *Nicomachean Ethics*, I, c.3 (1094b 23–28)   [3]Stephen F. Brown, "Theology and Philosophy," in *Medieval Latin: an Introduction and Bibliographical Guide*, ed. F. A. C. Mantello and A. G. Rigg (Washington, DC: The Catholic University of America Press, 1996) 267–287, esp. 268.

Theological terms of a more technical nature likewise had to be newly coined by Christians. The pagan Romans themselves had difficulties translating the Greek word *soter*. Cicero used the word *servator*, a term applied to Jupiter, and explained its meaning by saying "*soter*, one who gives protection." Of course, the translators of the Old Latin Bible did not want to use the term *servator* associated with Jupiter, so they coined the term *salvator* (savior) that was based on their new verb *salvare*. Tertullian (died c. 220) suggested the alternative *salutificator* and Arnobious (died c. 327) spoke of Christ as *sospitator*. By the time of Augustine (died 430), however, *salvator* was welcomed without much apology to the Latin grammarians who often mocked Christian coinage. Augustine bodly used *salvator*. He simply noted that the pagan grammarians might ask, "What kind of Latin is a word like *salvator*?" but Christians are more interested in truth than in the human limits of Latin grammar. *Salvare* and *salvator* did not exist earlier in the pagan Latin language, Augustine explained, because before the coming of Christ, there simply was no Savior. When Christ the Savior came to the Latins, Augustine argued, then the word *salvator* also came.[4]

The two most characteristic or proper doctrines of the Christian faith are the Trinity of Persons in God and the Incarnation of Christ. With respect to the first, the Christian faith holds that there is one God who is Father, Son, and Holy Spirit. Aquinas presents one of its scriptural warrants from the *First Epistle of John* (5:7): "*There are three who bear witness in heaven, the Father, the Word, and the Holy Ghost. (1 John v. 7) To those who ask, Three what? we answer, with Augustine, Three persons. Therefore, there are but three persons in God.*"[5] Yet how could this be explained without falling into *modalism* (the belief that there is only one divine essence and that the Father, Son, and Holy Spirit are not distinct persons or substances but only different manifestations of this one divine essence) or *tritheism* (the belief that the Father, Son, and Holy Spirit each have a distinct divine essence and thus are three distinct gods)? Christian belief concerning the incarnate Christ is affirmed by Aquinas in his *Commentary on the Gospel of Saint John*: " . . . We should know that we can consider two things in Christ: his nature and person. In Christ there is a distinc-

---

[4]Augustine, *Sermon 299*, n. 6: "Christus, inquit, 'Jesus,' id est Christus Salvator. Hoc est enim latine Jesus. Nec quaerant grammatici quam sit latinum, sed Christiani quam verum. Salus enim latinum nomen est. Salvare et salvator non fuerunt haec latina antequam veniret Salvator: quando ad latinos venit, et haec latina fecit."

[5]*Summa Theologica*, I, q. 30, a. 2, *On the contrary*.

tion in nature, but not in person, which is one and the same in the two natures, since the human nature in Christ was assumed into a oneness of person."[6]

Attempts to explain and defend these teachings required greater and greater clarity in rethinking not only the *Categories* of Aristotle but also the categories of natural things and their appropriate application to God. Some thirty years before Thomas Aquinas, William of Auxerre, in his *Summa aurea*, declared:

> In desiring, however, to demonstrate divine realities by means of reasons, we will start out from suitable reasons, not from reasons that are characteristic of the world of natural realities. For that is how heretics were led astray: they wanted to apply to the divine world qualities that are proper to natural created things. It is as if they wanted to make creatures and the Creator into equals. Arius was deceived in this way. It is indeed generally true in the world of nature that when there are many individuals there are also many natures—for example, when there are many men there are also many humanities, and when there are many donkeys there are also many donkey natures. Arius wanted to apply this general rule to the divine world in the following way: The Father, the Son, and the Holy Spirit are many persons, therefore they have many natures. Now, the Father has a divine nature, and there is only one divine nature; so the Son does not have a divine nature but some other nature that is distinct from the divine. It follows that the Son of God is not God but a pure creature. And this is what Arius admitted, being led astray by his deceptive analogy from the world of creatures. In a similar way Sabellius also was deceived. Since it is generally true in the case of created things that one nature belongs to one individual, it follows that because the divine nature is unique, it can belong to only one person. Now the divine nature belongs to the Father, the Son, and the Holy Spirit. So just as the Father, the Son, and the Holy Spirit are one being, they are also one person. Thus Sabellius claimed that when the Father wants to be the Father he is the Father; and when he wants to be the Son he is the Son; and when he wants to be the Holy Spirit he is the Holy Spirit. Therefore Sabellius confused the persons, making, as it were, the three into one; while Arius, on the other hand, separated off a nature or substance for each person.[7]

---

[6]*Commentary on the Gospel of Saint John*, lect. 7, n. 175.   [7]William of Auxerre, *Summa aurea*, I, ed. J. Ribaillier, 18–19: "Volentes autem ostendere rationibus res divinas, ex convenientibus rationibus procedemus, non ex eis que sunt [proprie] rerum naturalium. Ideo enim decepti fuerunt heretici, quia rationes proprias rerum naturalium volebant applicare rebus divinis, quasi volentes adequare naturam suo Creatori. Sic deceptus fuit Arius. Cum enim in rebus naturalibus

Arius and his followers also realized the importance of vocabulary. When the councils of Nicea and Constantinople adopted St. Basil's (died 379) formula *mia ousia, treis hypostaseis* (one substance, three persons) to combat Arius's Trinitarian modalism, the Arians argued that *ousia* is both untranslatable and nonscriptural.[8] In brief, for them vocabulary does not count, and scriptural terms have no meaning or intelligibility behind them that other terms might present more clearly. Saint Basil and the council Fathers at Nicea and Constantinople found it necessary to contradict this view, declaring that vocabulary does have importance and that nonscriptural language can help us better understand the meanings of scriptural language.

To avoid the errors of Arius and Sabellius, and others, and thereby to bring out the truth of Christian faith, Catholic theologians patiently attempted to make their language precise. This continuing effort is manifest not only in Aquinas's main theological texts but also in his commentaries on Scripture and his sermons. Theologians, including Aquinas, also have searched for better analogies to bring further light to the truths of the faith, especially the truths of the Trinity and Incarnation. In doing so, they have attempted to stress the difference and limits of their examples in comparison to the marvelous realities they were trying to describe.

They do this even when they try to illuminate one scriptural passage by a more evident one or to directly qualify the natural language of a vivid scriptural expression. We can see this when Aquinas corrects Arius:

> Again, we cannot say that the Father pre-established a beginning of duration for his Son by his own will, because God the Father does not generate

---

generaliter verum sit quod plurium plures sint naturae, ut plurium hominum plures humanitates et plurium asinorum plures asinitates, voluit Arius applicare hanc regulam rebus divinis sic: Pater et Filius et Spiritus Sanctus sunt plures; ergo plures sunt eorum naturae; sed Pater habet deitatem et una sola est deitas; ergo Filius non habet deitatem sed aliam naturam quam sit deitas. Ex hoc sequitur quod Filius Dei non sit Deus, sed creatura pura, quod ipse concessit deceptus fantastica similitudine rerum naturalium. Eodem modo Sabellius deceptus fuit. Cum enim verum generaliter in rebus sit quia una natura [unius] solius est; sed deitas est unica natura; ergo unius solius est; sed ipsa est Patris et Filii et Spiritus Sancti; ergo sicut Pater et Filius et Spiritus Sanctus sunt unum, ita sunt unus. Et ideo dixit Sabellius quod Pater quando vult est Pater, quando vult est Filius, quando vult est Spiritus Sanctus. Ipse ergo Sabellius personas confundit quasi de tribus faciens unam; Arius vero separavit naturam sive substantiam personarum." [8]Cf. Marius Victorinus, *Against Arius*, 2.6.

the Son by his will, as the Arians held, but naturally: for God the Father, understanding himself, conceives the Word, and so God the Father did not exist prior to the Son. An example of this, *to a limited degree*, appears in fire and in the brightness issuing from it: for this brightness issues *naturally and without succession* from the fire. Again, *if the fire were eternal, its brightness would be coeternal with it.* This is why the Son is called the brightness of the Father: "the brightness of his glory" (Heb. 1:3). *But this example lacks an illustration of the identity of nature.* And so we call him Son, *although in human sonship we do not find coeternity:* for *we must attain our knowledge of divine things from many likenesses in material things, for one likeness is not enough.*[9]

We also can see it in the way Aquinas deals with councils. This is most evident when he is dealing with the Incarnation and thus with conciliar declarations in regard to Christ's nature and person, especially in his *Sermon on the Apostles' Creed.* Photinus held a number of heretical beliefs: that Christ, for example, was a very good man who, like other good men, became God's son by adoption. Thus, Christ did not exist before Mary and began to exist when he was conceived of her. Scripture refutes this position. Christian faith, based on Scripture, holds that Christ is the Son of God by nature and that He is from eternity. The Nicene Creed records this in the words "The only Son of God" and "eternally begotten of the Father."

Sabellius admitted that Christ existed before Mary yet denied the distinction between the Person of the Father and the Person of the Son. He believed the Father himself became incarnate and the person of the Father is the same as the person of Christ. Yet, as we all realize, no one is sent by himself, so the Creed announced "God from God and Light from Light."

Arius admitted that Christ existed before Mary and that the Person of the Father was distinct from that of the Son. Yet he made Christ purely a creature, albeit the highest of all temporal creatures, and claimed that Christ did not share the divine nature. This explains the Nicene statement that Christ is "one in being with the Father."

Each of these heresies is contradicted in Saint John's speaking of the Word:

> We must observe then that various things have various ways of generating. In God, generation is different from the generation of other things, so we cannot obtain a notion of divine generation except though the generation of that creature which approaches nearest to a likeness to God.

---

[9]*Commentary on the Gospel of Saint John,* Lecture 1, n. 41.

Now, as we have stated, nothing is so like God as the human soul. And the manner of generation in the soul is that a man by his soul conceives something which is called the concept of the mind. This concept proceeds from the soul as from its father, and is called the word of the mind or of man. Accordingly the soul by thought generates its word.

Thus the Son of God is nothing else but the Word of God, not like the word that is uttered externally (for this is transitory) but as the word conceived inwardly. Therefore this same Word of God is of one nature with God and equal to God.[10]

The words of Saint John thus destroy the heresy of Photinus when Saint John says, "In the beginning was the Word"; that of Sabellius when he says, "and the Word was with God"; and that of Arius when he says, "and the Word was God."[11]

It is evident that when attempting to illuminate our limited understanding of the Trinity, Aquinas depends not only on the Scriptures and on the Councils but also on the authority of the Fathers of the Church. In regard to the Trinity, he appeals to Basil, Alcuin, Bede, Chrysostom, and Hilary.[12] Most of all, he appeals to Augustine. Moreover, none of these authorities is followed without serious consideration and, when necessary, criticism.

In his commentary on the first verse of Saint John's Gospel, where the evangelist speaks of the Word who was in the beginning with God and who was God, Aquinas explains the text with the help of Augustine: "And so Augustine (*On the Trinity* IX, 5) sees a likeness of the Trinity in the soul insofar as the mind understands itself. . . ."[13] For, the Word, the likeness of the Father, is well exemplified by the mind's self-understanding in which it sees a likeness of itself. Yet Aquinas pulls us back and explains how the analogy limps by discussing how the Word differs from our own mental word.[14] He follows the warnings of Augustine[15] and William of Auxerre[16] concerning the proper assistance that natural things, in this case even natural spiritual things, can provide for the understanding of the mysteries of God.

In his third way of explaining these limits of human analogies, Aquinas indicates that our word is not of the same nature as we are, whereas the divine Word is the same nature as God. For, in God, to understand and to be are the same, as Aquinas indicated when he spoke of the divine

---

[10]*Sermon II on the Apostles' Creed*, B. 1. [11]*Ibid.* [12]*Commentary on the Gospel of Saint John*, Lecture 1, n. 51. [13]*Ibid.*, n. 25. [14]*Ibid.*, nn. 26–28. [15]Augustine, *On the Trinity*, I, c. 1. [16]Cf. above, n. 7.

attributes and their identity with God's being. " . . . The Word of the divine intellect is not an accident but belongs to its nature. Thus it must be subsistent, because whatever is in the nature of God is God."[17] Aquinas continually looks for stronger and more suitable analogies to illustrate Theological truths, yet he always indicates their limits.

As we can see by studying the texts of Part III, Aquinas's presentation of Scripture, the Councils, and the Fathers, as well as his use of analogies, clearly demonstrate that in all his Theological efforts he aims at discovering and revealing deep insights from his various sources. He continues in the tradition of Augustine and Anslem as his faith strives to seek understanding.

---

[17] *Ibid.*, n. 28.

THE TRIUNE GOD

Summa Theologica

Part One

Question 30

The Plurality of Persons in God

(*In Four Articles*)

We are now led to consider the plurality of the persons; about which there are four points of inquiry: (1) Whether there are many persons in God? (2) How many are they? (3) What numeral terms signify in God? (4) The community of the term *person*.

First Article
Whether There Are Many Persons in God?

We proceed thus to the First Article:—

Objection 1. It would seem that there are not many persons in God. For person is *the individual substance of a rational nature.* If then there are many persons in God, there must be many substances; which appears to be heretical.

Obj. 2. Further, plurality of absolute properties does not make a distinction of persons, either in God, or in ourselves. Much less therefore is this effected by a plurality of relations. But in God there is no plurality but of relations.[1] Therefore there cannot be many persons in God.

Obj. 3. Further, Boethius says of God that *this is truly one which has no number.*[2] But plurality implies number. Therefore there are not many persons in God.

Obj. 4. Further, where number is, there is whole and part. Thus, if in God a number of persons exists, there must be whole and part in God; which is inconsistent with the divine simplicity.

On the contrary, Athanasius says*: One is the person of the Father, another of the Son, another of the Holy Ghost.*[3] Therefore the Father, and the Son, and the Holy Ghost are many persons.

---

[1]Q. 28, a. 3. [Not in this volume]   [2]*De Trin.*, III (PL 64, 1251).   [3]Cf. *Symb. "Quicumque"* (Denzinger, no. 39).

I answer that, It follows from what precedes that there are many persons in God. For it was shown above that this term *person* signifies in God a relation as subsisting in the divine nature.[4] It was also established that there are many real relations in God.[5] Hence it follows that there are many realities subsistent in the divine nature; which means that there are many persons in God.

Reply Obj. 1. The definition of *person* includes *substance*, not as meaning the essence, but the *suppositum*, which is made clear by the addition of the term *individual*. To signify substance thus understood, the Greeks use the name *hypostasis*. So, as we say *three persons*, they say *three hypostases*. We are not, however, accustomed to say three substances, lest we be understood to mean three essences or natures, by reason of the equivocal signification of the term.

Reply Obj. 2. The absolute properties in God, such as goodness and wisdom, are not mutually opposed; and hence, neither are they really distinguished from each other. Therefore, although they subsist, nevertheless they are not many subsistent realities—that is, many persons. But the absolute properties in creatures do not subsist, although they are really distinguished from each other, as whiteness and sweetness; on the other hand, the relative properties in God both subsist, and are really distinguished from each other.[6] Hence the plurality of such properties suffices for the plurality of persons in God.

Reply Obj. 3. The supreme unity and simplicity of God exclude every kind of plurality taken absolutely, but not plurality of relations; for relations are predicated relatively, and thus they do not imply composition in that of which they are predicated, as Boethius teaches in the same book.[7]

Reply Obj. 4. Number is twofold, simple or absolute, as two, three and four; and number as existing in things numbered, as two men and two horses. So, if number in God is taken absolutely or abstractedly, there is nothing to prevent whole and part from being in Him; and thus number in Him is only in our way of understanding, for number regarded apart from things numbered exists only in the intellect. But if number be taken as it is in the things numbered, in that sense, as existing in creatures, one is part of two, and two of three, as one man is part of two men, and two of three. This however does not apply to God, because the Father is of the same magnitude as the whole Trinity, as we shall show further on.[8]

---

[4]Q. 29, a. 4. [Not in this volume]   [5]Q. 28, a. 1, 3 and 4. [Not in this volume]
[6]Q. 28, a. 3 [Not in this volume]; q. 29, a. 4. [Not in this volume]   [7]*De Trin.*, VI (PL 64, 1354).   [8]Q. 42, a. 4, ad 3. [Not in this volume]

Second Article
Whether There Are More than Three Persons in God?

We proceed thus to the Second Article:—

Objection 1. It would seem that there are more than three persons in God. For the plurality of persons in God arises from the plurality of the relative properties, as was stated above. But there are four relations in God, as was stated above,[9] namely paternity, filiation, common spiration and procession. Therefore there are four persons in God.

Obj. 2. The nature of God does not differ from His will more than from His intellect. But in God, one person proceeds from the will, as Love; and another proceeds from His nature, as Son. Therefore another proceeds from His intellect, as Word, besides the one Who proceeds from His nature, as Son. Thus again it follows that there are not only three persons in God.

Obj. 3. Further, the more perfect a creature is, the more intrinsic are its operations; as a man has understanding and will beyond other animals. But God infinitely excels every creature. Therefore in God not only is there a person proceeding from the will, and another from the intellect, but also in an infinite number of ways. Therefore there is an infinite number of persons in God.

Obj. 4. Further, it is from the infinite goodness of the Father that He communicates Himself infinitely in the production of a divine person. But also in the Holy Ghost there is infinite goodness. Therefore the Holy Ghost produces a divine person; and that person another; and so to infinity.

Obj. 5. Further, everything within a determinate number is measured, for number is a measure. But the divine persons are immense, as we say in the Creed of Athanasius: *The Father is immense, the Son is immense, the Holy Ghost is immense.*[10] Therefore the persons are not contained within the number three.

On the contrary, It is said: *There are three who bear witness in heaven, the Father, the Word, and the Holy Ghost (1 John* v. 7). To those who ask, *Three what?* we answer, with Augustine, *Three persons.*[11] Therefore there are but three persons in God.

I answer that, As was explained above, there can be only three persons in God. For it was shown above that the many persons are the many subsisting relations really distinct from each other. But a real distinction between the divine relations can come only from relative opposition.

---

[9]Q. 28, a. 4. [Not in this volume]   [10]Cf. *Symb. "Quicumque"* (Denzinger, no. 39).   [11]*De Trin.*, VII, 4; 6; V, 9 (PL 42, 940; 943; 913).

Therefore two opposite relations must needs refer to two persons: and if any relations are not opposite, they must needs belong to the same person. Since then paternity and filiation are opposite relations, they belong necessarily to two persons. Therefore the subsisting paternity is the person of the Father and the subsisting filiation is the person of the Son. The other two relations are not opposed to either of these, but they are opposed to each other; therefore these two cannot belong to one person. Hence either one of them must belong to both of the aforesaid persons, or one must belong to one person, and the other to the other. Now, procession cannot belong to the Father and the Son, or to either of them; for thus it would follow that the procession of the intellect, which in God is generation (wherefrom paternity and filiation are derived), would issue from the procession of love (whence spiration and procession are derived); and thus the person generating and the person generated would proceed from the person spirating. This is against what was laid down above.[12] We must consequently admit that spiration belongs to the person of the Father and to the person of the Son, inasmuch as it has no relative opposition either to paternity or to filiation; and consequently that procession belongs to the other person who is called the person of the Holy Ghost, who proceeds by way of love, as was above explained.[13] Therefore only three persons exist in God, the Father, the Son, and the Holy Ghost.

Reply Obj. 1. Although there are four relations in God, one of them, spiration, is not separated from the person of the Father and of the Son, but belongs to both; and thus, although it is a relation, it is not called a property, because it does not belong to only one person, nor is it a personal relation—*i.e.*, constituting a person. The three relations—paternity, filiation, and procession—are called personal properties, constituting as it were the persons; for paternity is the person of the Father, filiation is the person of the Son, procession is the person of the Holy Ghost proceeding.

Reply Obj. 2. That which proceeds by way of intellect, as a word, proceeds according to likeness, as does also that which proceeds by way of nature. Hence, as was explained above, the procession of the divine Word is the very same as generation by way of nature.[14] But love, as such, does not proceed as the likeness of that whence it proceeds, even though in God love is co-essential as being divine; and therefore the procession of love is not called generation in God.

Reply Obj. 3. As man is more perfect than other animals, he has a

---

[12]Q. 27, a. 3, ad 3. [Not in this volume]   [13]Q. 27, a. 4. [Not in this volume]
[14]Q. 27, a. 2 [Not in this volume]; q. 28, a. 4. [Not in this volume]

greater number of intrinsic operations than other animals, because his perfection is something composite. Hence the angels, who are more perfect and more simple, have fewer intrinsic operations than man, for they have no imagination, sensation, or the like. In God, however, there exists only one real operation—that is, His essence. How there are in Him two processions was above explained.[15]

Reply Obj. 4. This argument would hold if the Holy Ghost possessed another goodness apart from the goodness of the Father; for then if the Father produced a divine person by His goodness, the Holy Ghost also would do so. But the Father and the Holy Ghost have one and the same goodness. Nor is there any distinction between them except by the personal relations. So goodness belongs to the Holy Ghost, as derived from another; and it belongs to the Father, as the principle of its communication to another. The opposition of relation does not allow the relation of the Holy Ghost to be joined with the relation which is the principle of another divine person; because He Himself proceeds from the other persons who are in God.

Reply Obj. 5. A determinate number, if taken as a simple number, existing in the intellect only, is measured by *one*. But when we speak of a number of things as applied to the persons in God, the notion of measure has no place, because the magnitude of the three persons is the same,[16] and the same is not measured by the same.

Third Article
Whether Numeral Terms Denote Anything Real in God?

We proceed thus to the Third Article:—

Objection 1. It would seem that numeral terms denote something real in God. For the divine unity is the divine essence. But every number is unity repeated. Therefore every numeral term in God signifies the essence; and therefore it denotes something real in God.

Obj. 2. Further, whatever is said of God and of creatures belongs to God in a more eminent manner than to creatures. But numeral terms denote something real in creatures; therefore much more so in God.

Obj. 3. Further if numeral terms do not denote anything real in God, and are introduced simply in a negative and removing sense, as plurality is employed to remove unity, and unity to remove plurality, it follows that a vicious circle results, confusing the intellect and obscuring the truth; and

---

[15]Q. 27, a. 3 and 5. [Not in this volume]   [16]Q. 42, a. 1 and 4. [Not in this volume]

this ought not to be. Therefore it must be said that numeral terms denote something real in God.

On the contrary, Hilary says: *If we admit companionship*—that is, plurality—*we exclude the idea of oneness and of solitude;*[17] and Ambrose says: *When we say one God, unity excludes a plurality of gods; it does not imply quantity in God.*[18] Hence we see that these terms are applied to God in order to remove something, and not to denote anything positive.

I answer that, The Master of the *Sentences* considers that numeral terms do not denote anything positive in God, but have only a negative meaning.[19] Others, however, assert the contrary.[20]

In order to resolve this point, we may observe that all plurality is a consequence of some division. Now division is twofold. One is material, and is division of the continuous; from this results number, which is a species of quantity. Number in this sense is found only in material things, which have quantity. The other kind of division is called formal, and is effected by opposite or diverse forms; and this kind of division results in a multitude, which does not belong to a genus, but is transcendental in the sense in which being is divided by one and by many. Only this kind of multitude is found in immaterial things.

Some,[21] considering only that multitude which is a species of discrete quantity, and seeing that such quantity has no place in God, asserted that numeral terms do not denote anything real in God, but remove something from Him. Others, considering the same kind of multitude, said that as knowledge exists in God according to the strict sense of the word, but not according to the genus to which it belongs (as in God there is no such thing as a quality), so number exists in God in the proper sense of number, but not according to the genus to which it belongs, which is quantity.

But our view of the problem is that numeral terms predicated of God are not derived from number which is a species of quantity, for in that sense they could bear only a metaphorical sense in God, like other corporeal properties, such as length, breadth, and the like; but that they are taken from multitude in a transcendental sense. Now multitude so understood has relation to the many of which it is predicated, as *one* convertible with *being* is related to being; which kind of oneness does not add anything to being, except only a negation of division, as we saw when treating

---

[17]*De Trin.*, IV (PL 10, 111).   [18]*De Fide*, I, 2 (PL 16, 555).   [19]Peter Lombard, *Sent.*, I, xxiv, 1 (I, 153).   [20]A common opinion at Paris, according to St. Bonaventure, *In I Sent.* d. xxiv, a. 2, q. 1, concl. (I, 426).   [21]Peter Lombard, *Sent.*, I, xxiv, 1 (I, 154).

of the divine unity.[22] For *one* signifies undivided being. So, of whatever we say *one*, we signify its undivided reality: thus, for instance, *one* applied to man signifies the undivided nature or substance of a man. In the same way, when we speak of many things, multitude in this latter sense points to those things as being each undivided in itself. But number, if taken as a species of quantity, denotes an accident added to being; as also does *one* which is the principle of that number.

Therefore numeral terms in God signify the things of which they are said, and beyond this they add only negation, as was stated. In this respect the Master of the *Sentences* was right. So when we say, the essence is one, the term *one* signifies the essence undivided; and when we say the person is *one*, it signifies the person undivided; and when we say the persons are *many*, we signify the persons and their individual undividedness; for it is of the very nature of multitude that it should be composed of units.

Reply Obj. 1. One, as it is a transcendental, is wider and more general than substance and relation; so likewise is multitude. Hence in God, *one* may mean both substance and relation, according to the context. Still the very signification of such names adds a negation of division, beyond substance and relation; as was explained above.

Reply Obj. 2. Multitude, which denotes something real in creatures, is a species of quantity, and cannot be used when speaking of God: unlike transcendental multitude, which adds only indivision to those of which it is predicated. Such a kind of multitude is applicable to God.

Reply Obj. 3. *One* does not exclude multitude, but division, which logically precedes one or multitude. Multitude does not remove unity, but division from each of the individuals which compose the multitude. This was explained when we treated of the divine unity.[23]

It must be observed, nevertheless, that the arguments to the contrary do not sufficiently prove the point advanced. For although the idea of solitude is excluded by plurality, and the plurality of gods by unity, it does not follow that these terms express this signification alone. For blackness is excluded by whiteness; nevertheless, the term whiteness does not signify the mere exclusion of blackness.

Fourth Article
Whether This Term *Person* Can
Be Common to the Three Persons?

We proceed thus to the Fourth Article:—

---

[22]Q. 11, a. 1. [Not in this volume]   [23]Q. 11, a. 2, ad 4. [Not in this volume]

Objection 1. It would seem that this term *person* cannot be common to the three persons. For nothing is common to the three persons but the essence. But this term *person* does not signify the essence directly. Therefore, it is not common to all three.

Obj. 2. Further, the common is the opposite to the incommunicable. But the very meaning of person is that it is incommunicable; as appears from the definition given by Richard of St. Victor.[24] Therefore, this term *person* is not common to all the three persons.

Obj. 3. Further, if the name *person* is common to the three, it is common either really, or logically. But it is not so really, otherwise the three persons would be one person; nor again is it so logically, otherwise *person* would be a universal. But in God there is neither universal nor particular, neither genus nor species, as we proved above.[25] Therefore this term *person* is not common to the three.

On the contrary, Augustine says that when we ask, *Three what?* we say, *Three persons,* because what a person is, is common to them.[26]

I answer that, The very mode of expression itself shows that this term *person* is common to the three when we say *three persons*; just as when we say *three men* we show that *man* is common to the three. Now it is clear that this is not community of a real thing, as if one essence were common to the three; otherwise there would be only one person among the three, just as there is one essence.

What is meant by such a community has been variously determined by those who have examined the subject. Some[27] have called it a community of exclusion, because the definition of *person* contains the word *incommunicable*. Others[28] thought it to be a community of intention, as the definition of person contains the word *individual*; as we say that to be a *species* is common to horse and ox. Both of these explanations, however, are excluded by the fact that *person* is not a name of exclusion nor of intention, but the name of a reality.

We must therefore affirm that even in human affairs this name *person* is common by a community of idea, not as genus or species, but as a vague individual thing. The names of genera and species, as man or animal, are given to signify the common natures themselves, but not the intentions of those common natures, signified by the terms *genus* or *species*. The vague individual thing, as *some man*, signifies the common nature with the

---

[24]Q. 29, a. 3, ad 4. [Not in this volume]   [25]Q. 3, a. 5.   [26]*De Trin.*, VII, 4; 6; V, 9 (PL 42, 940; 943; 913).   [27]William of Auxerre, *Summa Aurea*, I, tr. 6, ch. 2 (fol. 10c).   [28]Cf. Alex. of Hales, *Summa Theol.*, II, no. 389 (I, 573).

determinate mode of existence of singular things—that is, something self-subsisting, as distinct from others. But the name of a designated singular thing signifies that which distinguishes the determinate thing; as the name Socrates signifies this flesh and this bone. But there is this difference—that the term *some man* signifies the nature, or the individual on the part of its nature, with the mode of existence of singular things; while this name *person* is not given to signify the individual on the part of the nature, but the subsistent reality in that nature. Now this is common in idea to the divine persons, that each of them subsists distinctly from the others in the divine nature. Thus this name *person* is common in idea to the three divine persons.

Reply Obj. 1. This argument is founded on a real community.

Reply Obj. 2. Although person is incommunicable, yet the mode itself of incommunicable existence can be common to many.

Reply Obj. 3. Although this community is logical and not real, yet it does not follow that in God there is universal or particular, or genus, or species; both because neither in human affairs is the community of person the same as community of genus or species, and because the divine persons have one being, whereas genus and species and every other universal are predicated of many which differ in being.

Question 31

What Belongs to the Unity or Plurality in God

(*In Four Articles*)

We now consider what belongs to the unity or plurality in God; which gives rise to four points of inquiry: (1) Concerning the term *Trinity.* (2) Whether we can say that the Son is other than the Father? (3) Whether an exclusive term, which seems to exclude otherness, can be joined to an essential name in God? (4) Whether it can be joined to a personal term?

First Article
Whether There Is a Trinity in God?

We proceed thus to the First Article:—

Objection 1. It would seem there is not a trinity in God. For every name in God signifies substance or relation. But this name *trinity* does not signify the substance; otherwise it would be predicated of each one of the persons: nor does it signify relation; for it is not said as a relative name. Therefore the name *Trinity* is not to be applied to God.

Obj. 2. Further, this name *trinity* is a collective term, since it signifies multitude. But such a name does not apply to God; as the unity of a collective name is the least of unities, whereas in God there exists the greatest possible unity. Therefore this name *trinity* does not apply to God.

Obj. 3. Further, every triple is threefold. But in God there is not triplicity, since triplicity is a kind of inequality. Therefore neither is there a trinity in God.

Obj. 4. Further, all that exists in God exists in the unity of the divine essence, because God is His own essence. Therefore, if a Trinity exists in God, it exists in the unity of the divine essence; and thus in God there would be three essential unities; which is heresy.

Obj. 5. Further, in all that is said of God, the concrete is predicated of the abstract; for Deity is God and paternity is the Father. But the Trinity cannot be called triple; otherwise there would be nine realities in God; which, of course, is erroneous. Therefore the name trinity is not to be applied to God.

On the contrary, Athanasius says: *Unity in Trinity, and Trinity in Unity is to be revered.*[1]

I answer that, The name *Trinity* in God signifies the determinate number of persons. And so the plurality of persons in God requires that we should use the name trinity; because what is indeterminately signified by plurality, is signified by trinity in a determinate manner.

Reply Obj. 1. In its etymological sense, this name *Trinity* seems to signify the one essence of the three persons, according as trinity may mean three-in-one. But in the strict meaning of the term, it rather signifies the number of persons of one essence; and on this account we cannot say that the Father is the Trinity, as He is not three persons. Yet it does not mean the relations themselves of the Persons, but rather the number of persons related to each other; and hence it is that the name in itself is not used as a relative name.

Reply Obj. 2. Two things are implied in a collective term, plurality of the *supposita*, and a unity of some kind of order. For *people* is a multitude of men comprehended under a certain order. As to the first point, this name *trinity* is like collective names; but as to the second, it differs from them, because in the divine Trinity not only is there unity of order, but with this there also is unity of essence.

Reply Obj. 3. *Trinity* is taken in an absolute sense, for it signifies the threefold number of persons. *Triplicity* signifies a proportion of inequal-

---

[1] Cf. *Symb.* *"Quicumque"* (Denzinger, no. 39).

ity; for it is a species of unequal proportion, according to Boethius.[2] Therefore in God there is not triplicity, but Trinity.

Reply Obj. 4. In the divine Trinity is to be understood both number and the persons numbered. So when we say, *Trinity in Unity,* we do not place number in the unity of the essence, as if we meant three times one; but we place the Persons numbered in the unity of nature, just as the *supposita* of a nature are said to exist in that nature. On the other hand, we say *Unity in Trinity,* meaning that the nature is in its supposita.

Reply Obj. 5. When we say, the *Trinity is threefold,* by reason of the number implied, we signify the multiplication of that number by itself; since the word threefold implies a distinction in the *supposita* of which it is spoken. Therefore it cannot be said that the Trinity is threefold, otherwise it follows that, if the Trinity be threefold, there would be three *supposita* of the Trinity; as when we say, *God is triune,* it follows that there are three *supposita* of the Godhead.

Second Article
Whether the Son Is Other than the Father?

We proceed thus to the Second Article:—

Objection 1. It seems that the Son is not other than the Father. For *other* is a relative term implying diversity of substance. If, then, the Son is other than the Father, He must be different from the Father; which is contrary to what Augustine says, namely, that when we speak of three persons, *we do not mean to imply diversity.*[3]

Obj. 2. Further, whosoever are other from one another, differ in some way from one another. Therefore, if the Son is other than the Father, it follows that He differs from the Father; which is against what Ambrose says, that *the Father and the Son are one in Godhead; nor is there any difference in substance between them, nor any diversity.*[4]

Obj. 3. Further, the term alien is taken from *alius* [other]. But the Father is not alien from the Son, for Hilary says that *in the divine persons there is nothing diverse, nothing alien, nothing separable.*[5] Therefore the Son is not other than the Father.

Obj. 4. Further, the terms *other person* and *other thing* [*alius et aliud*] have the same meaning, differing only in gender. So if the Son is another person from the Father, it follows that the Son is a thing apart from the Father.

---

[2]*Arithm.,* I, 23 (PL 63, 1101).   [3]*De Trin.,* VII, 4 (PL 42, 940).   [4]*De Fide,* I, 2 (PL 16, 555).   [5]*De Trin.,* VII (PL 10, 233).

On the contrary, Augustine says: *There is one essence of the Father and Son and Holy Ghost, in which the Father is not one thing, the Son another, and the Holy Ghost another; although the Father is one person, the Son another, and the Holy Ghost another.*[6]

I answer that, Since, as Jerome remarks, a heresy arises from words wrongly used,[7] when we speak of the Trinity we must proceed with care and with befitting modesty; because, as Augustine says, *nowhere is error more harmful, the quest more toilsome, the finding more fruitful.*[8] Now, in treating of the Trinity, we must beware of two opposite errors, and proceed cautiously between them—namely, the error of Arius, who posited a Trinity of substances with the Trinity of persons,[9] and the error of Sabellius, who posited a unity of person with the unity of essence.[10]

Thus, to avoid the error of Arius we must shun the use of the terms *diversity* and *difference* in God, lest we take away the unity of essence; we may, however, use the term *distinction* because of the relative opposition. Hence, whenever we find the terms *diversity* or *difference* of Persons used in an authentic work, these terms *diversity* or *difference* are taken to mean *distinction.* But lest the simplicity and singleness of the divine essence be taken away, the terms *separation* and *division,* which belong to the parts of a whole, are to be avoided. Lest equality be taken away, we avoid the use of the term *disparity.* And lest we remove *likeness,* we avoid the terms *alien* and *discrepant.* For Ambrose says that *in the Father and the Son there is no discrepancy, but one Godhead;*[11] and according to Hilary, as quoted above, *in God there is nothing alien, nothing separable.*[12]

To avoid the heresy of Sabellius, on the other hand, we must shun the term *singularity,* lest we take away the communicability of the divine essence. Hence Hilary says: *It is sacrilege to assert that the Father and the Son are separate in Godhead.*[13] We must avoid the term *only* [*unici*] lest we take away the number of persons. Hence Hilary says in the same book: *We exclude from God the idea of singularity or uniqueness.*[14] Nevertheless, we can say *the only Son,* for in God there is no plurality of Sons. Yet, we do not say *the only God,* for Deity is common to many. We avoid the term *confused,* lest we take away from the Persons the order of their nature. Hence Ambrose says: *What is one is not confused, and there is no multiplicity*

---

[6]Cf. Fulgentius, *De Fide ad Petrum,* I (PL 65, 674).   [7]Cf. Peter Lombard, *Sent.,* IV, xiii, 2 (II, 818).   [8]*De Trin.,* I, 3 (PL 42, 822).   [9]Cf. St. Augustine, *De Haeres.,* 49 (PL 42, 39).   [10]Cf. *op. cit.,* 41 (PL 42, 32).   [11]*De Fide,* 1, 2 (PL 16, 555).   [12]*De Trin.,* VII (PL 10, 233).   [13]*Ibid.*   [14]*Ibid.* (PL 10, 231).

where there is no difference.[15] The term *solitary* is also to be avoided, lest we take away the society of the three persons; for, as Hilary says, *We confess neither a solitary God nor a God with diversity.*[16]

This term *other* [*alius*], however, in the masculine gender, means only a distinction of *suppositum*; and hence we can properly say that the *Son is other than the Father*, because He is another *suppositum* of the divine nature, just as He is another person and another hypostasis.

Reply Obj. 1. *Other*, being like the name of a particular thing, refers to the *suppositum*; and so, there is sufficient reason for using it, where there is a distinct substance in the sense of hypostasis or person. But diversity requires a distinct substance in the sense of essence. Thus we cannot say that the Son is diverse from the Father, although He is *other*.

Reply Obj. 2. *Difference* implies distinction of form. There is one form only in God, as appears from the text, *Who, when He was in the form of God* (*Phil.* ii. 6). Therefore, the term *difference* does not properly apply to God, as appears from the authority quoted. Yet Damascene employs the term *difference* in the divine persons, as meaning that the relative property is signified by way of form. Hence he says that the hypostases do not differ from each other in substance, but according to determinate properties.[17] But *difference* is taken for distinction, as was above stated.

Reply Obj. 3 The term *alien* [*alienum*] means what is extraneous and dissimilar; which is not expressed by the term *other* [*alius*]; and therefore we say that the Son is *other* than the Father, but not that He is anything *alien*.

Reply Obj. 4. The neuter gender is formless, whereas the masculine is formed and distinct; and so is the feminine. So the common essence is properly and aptly expressed by the neuter gender; but by the masculine and feminine is expressed the determined subject in the common nature. Hence also in human affairs, if we ask, *Who* is this man? we answer, *Socrates*, which is the name of the *suppositum*; whereas, if we ask, *What* is he? we reply, *A rational and mortal animal*. So, because in God distinction is by the persons, and not by the essence, we say that the Father is other than the Son, but not something else; while conversely we say that they are one thing, but not one person.

---

[15]*De Fide*, I, 2 (PL 16, 555).   [16]*De Trin.*, IV (PL 10, 111).   [17]*De Fide Orth.*, III, 5 (PG 94, 1000).

Third Article
Whether the Exclusive Word *Alone* Should Be Added to an Essential Term in God?

We proceed thus to the Third Article:—

Objection 1. It would seem that the exclusive word *alone* [*solus*] is not to be added to an essential term in God. For, according to the Philosopher, *He is alone who is not with another.*[18] But God is with the angels and the souls of the saints. Therefore we cannot say that God is alone.

Obj. 2. Further, whatever is joined to an essential term in God can be predicated of every person *per se*, and of all the persons together; for, as we can properly say that God is wise, we can say the Father is a wise God, and the Trinity is a wise God. But Augustine says: *We must consider the opinion that the Father is not true God alone.*[19] Therefore God cannot be said to be alone.

Obj. 3. Further, if this expression *alone* is joined to an essential term, it would be so joined as regards either the personal predicate or the essential predicate. But it cannot be the former, as it is false to say, *God alone is Father*, since man also is a father; nor, again, can it be applied as regards the latter, for, if this saying were true, *God alone creates*, it would follow that the *Father alone creates*, as whatever is said of God can be said of the Father; and it would be false, as the Son also creates. Therefore this expression *alone* cannot be joined to an essential term in God.

On the contrary, It is said, *To the King of ages, immortal, invisible, the only God* (*1 Tim.* I. 17).

I answer that, This term *alone* can be taken as a categorematical term, or as a syncategorematical term. A categorematical term is one which ascribes absolutely its meaning to a given *suppositum*; as, for instance, *white* to man, as when we say a *white man*. If the term *alone* is taken in this sense, it cannot in any way be joined to any term in God; for it would mean solitude in the term to which it is joined; and it would follow that God was solitary, against what is above stated. A syncategorematical term signifies the order of the predicate to the subject, as this expression, *every one* or *no one*; and likewise the term *alone*, as excluding every other *suppositum* from the predicate. Thus, when we say, *Socrates alone writes*, we do not mean that Socrates is solitary, but that he has no companion in writing, though many others may be with him. In this way, nothing prevents

---

[18]*Soph. Elench.*, XXII (178a 39).　　[19]*De Trin.*, VI, 9 (PL 42, 930).

the term *alone* being joined to any essential term in God, as excluding the predicate from all things but God; as if we said, *God alone is eternal,* because nothing but God is eternal.

Reply Obj. 1. Although the angels and the souls of the saints are always with God, nevertheless, if a plurality of persons did not exist in God, He would be alone or solitary. For solitude is not removed by association with anything that is extraneous in nature; and thus one is said to be alone in a garden, though many plants and animals are with him in the garden. Likewise, God would be alone or solitary, though angels and men were with Him, supposing that several persons were not within Him. Therefore the society of angels and of souls does not take away absolute solitude from God; much less does it remove respective solitude, in reference to a predicate.

Reply Obj. 2. This expression *alone,* properly speaking, does not affect the predicate, which is taken formally, for it refers to the suppositum, as excluding any other *suppositum* from the one which it qualifies. But the adverb *only,* being exclusive, can be applied either to subject or to predicate. For we can say, *Only Socrates*—that is, no one else—*runs*; and, *Socrates only runs*—that is, he does nothing else. Hence it is not properly said that the Father is God alone, or the Trinity is God alone, unless some implied meaning be assumed in the predicate, as, for instance, *The Trinity is God, Who alone is God.* In that sense it can be true to say that the Father is that God who alone is God, if the relative be referred to the predicate, and not to the *suppositum.* So, when Augustine says that the Father is not God alone, but that the Trinity is God alone, he speaks expositively, as he might explain the words, *"To the King of ages, invisible, the only God,"* as applying not to the Father, but to the Trinity alone.

Reply Obj. 3. The term *alone* can be joined to an essential term in both ways. For this proposition, *God alone is Father,* can mean two things, because the *Father* can signify the person of the Father, and then it is true, for no man is that person; or it can signify only the relation, and thus it is false, because the relation of paternity is found also in others, though not in a univocal sense. Likewise it is true to say God alone creates; nor does it follow, *therefore the Father alone creates,* because, as logicians say, an exclusive expression so fixes the term to which it is joined that what is said exclusively of that term cannot be said exclusively of an individual contained in that term: for instance, from the proposition, *Man alone is a mortal rational animal,* we cannot conclude, *therefore Socrates alone is such.*

Fourth Article
Whether an Exclusive Expression Can Be Joined to the Personal Term?

We proceed thus to the Fourth Article:—

Objection 1. It would seem that an exclusive expression can be joined to a personal term, even though the predicate is common. For our Lord, speaking to the Father, said: *That they may know Thee, the only true God* (*Jo* xvii. 3). Therefore the Father alone is true God.

Obj. 2. Further, He said: *No one knows the Son but the Father* (*Matt.* xi 27); which means that the Father alone knows the Son. But to know the Son is common. Therefore the same conclusion follows.

Obj. 3. Further, an exclusive expression does not exclude what enters into the concept of the term to which it is joined. Hence it does not exclude the part, nor the universal; for it does not follow that if we say *Socrates alone is white,* therefore *his hand is not white,* or that *man is not white.* But one person is in the concept of another; as the Father is in the concept of the Son; and conversely. Therefore, when we say, The Father alone is God, we do not exclude the Son, nor the Holy Ghost; so that such a mode of speaking is true.

Obj. 4. Further, the Church sings: *Thou alone art Most High, O Jesus Christ.*[20]

On the contrary, This proposition *The Father alone is God* includes two assertions—namely, that the Father is God, and that no other besides the Father is God. But this second proposition is false, for the Son who is God, is other than the Father. Therefore this is false, The Father alone is God; and the same can be said of similar expressions.

I answer that, When we say, *The Father alone is God,* such a proposition can be taken in several senses. If *alone* means solitude in the Father, it is false in a categorematical sense; but if taken in a syncategorematical sense, it can again be understood in several ways. For if it excludes [all others] from the form of the subject, it is true; so that the sense is, *the Father alone is God*—that is, *He who, with no other is the Father, is God.* In this way Augustine explains the point when he says: *We say the Father alone, not because He is separate from the Son, or from the Holy Ghost, but because they are not the Father together with Him.*[21] This, however, is not the usual way of speaking, unless we understand another implication, as though we said *He who alone is called the Father is God.* But in the strict sense, the exclusion affects the predicate. And thus the proposition is false if it excludes

---

[20]In the *Gloria* of the Mass.   [21]*De Trin.*, VI, 7 (PL 42, 929).

another in the masculine gender, but it is true if it excludes it in the neuter; because the Son is another person than the Father, but not another thing; and the same applies to the Holy Ghost. But because this expression *alone* refers, properly speaking, to the subject, it tends to exclude another Person rather than other things. Hence such a way of speaking is not to be taken too literally, but it should be respectfully expounded, whenever we find it in an authentic work.

Reply Obj. 1. When we say, *Thee the only true God*, we do not understand it as referring to the person of the Father, but to the whole Trinity, as Augustine expounds.[22] Or, if understood of the person of the Father, the other persons are not excluded by reason of the unity of essence; for *only* excludes *another* thing, as was above explained.

The same Reply can be given to *Obj. 2.* For an essential term applied to the Father does not exclude the Son or the Holy Ghost, by reason of the unity of essence. Hence we must understand that in the text quoted the term *no one* [*nemo*] is not the same as *no man* [*nullus homo*] which the word itself would seem to signify (for the person of the Father could not be excepted), but is taken according to the usual way of speaking, in a distributive sense, to mean any rational nature.

Reply Obj. 3. The exclusive expression does not exclude what enters into the concept of the term to which it is adjoined, if they do not differ in *suppositum*, as part and universal. But the Son differs in *suppositum* from the Father; and so there is no parity.

Reply Obj. 4. We do not say absolutely that the Son alone is Most High; but that He alone is Most High *with the Holy Ghost, in the glory of God the Father*.

Question 32
The Knowledge of the Divine Persons
(*In Four Articles*)

We proceed to inquire concerning the knowledge of the divine persons; and this involves four points of inquiry: (1) Whether the divine persons can be known by natural reason? (2) Whether notions are to be attributed to the divine persons? (3) The number of the notions. (4) Whether we may have various contrary opinions concerning these notions?

---

[22]*Op. cit.*, VI, 9 (PL 42, 930).

First Article
Whether the Trinity of the Divine Persons
Can Be Known by Natural Reason?

We proceed thus to the First Article:—

Objection 1. It would seem that the trinity of the divine persons can be known by natural reason. For philosophers came to the knowledge of God not otherwise than by natural reason.[1] Now we find that they have said many things about the trinity of persons. For Aristotle says: *Through this number*—namely, three—*we bring ourselves to acknowledge the greatness of one God, surpassing all things created.*[2] And Augustine says: *I have read in their works,* that is, in the books of the Platonists, *not in so many words, but enforced by many and various reasons, that in the beginning was the Word, and the Word was with God, and the Word was God,*[3] and so on; in which passage the distinction of persons is laid down. We read, moreover, in the *Gloss* on *Rom.* i. and *Exod.* viii. that the magicians of Pharoah failed in the third sign[4]—that is, as regards knowledge of a third person—*i.e.,* of the Holy Ghost, and thus it is clear that they knew at least two persons. Likewise Trismegistus says*: The monad begot a monad, and reflected upon itself its own desire.*[5] By which words the generation of the Son and the procession of the Holy Ghost seem to be indicated. Therefore knowledge of the divine persons can be obtained by natural reason.

Obj. 2. Further, Richard of St. Victor says: *I believe without doubt that not only probable but even necessary arguments can be found for any explanation of the truth.*[6] So even to prove the Trinity some have brought forward an argument based on the infinite goodness of God, which communicates itself infinitely in the procession of the divine persons;[7] while some are moved by the consideration that *no good thing can be joyfully possessed without partnership.*[8] Augustine, on the other hand, proceeds to prove the trinity of persons by the procession of the word and of love in our own mind;[9] and we have followed him in this.[10] Therefore the trinity of persons can be known by natural reason.

---

[1]Cf. R. Arnou, "Platonisme des Pères" (*Dict. de théol. cath.*, XII, 2, 1935, coll. 2322–2327). [2]*De Caelo*, I, i (268a 13). [3]*Confess.*, VII, 9 (PL 32, 740). [4]*Glossa ordin.*, super *Exod.* VIII, 19 (I, 140E).—Cf. St. Isidore, *Quaest. in Vet. Test.*, *In Exod.*, XIV, super VIII, 19 (PL 83, 293).—Cf. also St. Augustine, *Epist.* LV., ch. 16 (PL 33, 119). [5]Pseudo-Hermes Trismegistus, *Lib. 24 Philosoph.*, prop. 1 (p. 31). [6]*De Trin.* (PL 196, 892). [7]Alexander of Hales, *Summa Theol.*, I, no. 295 (I, 414); St. Bonaventure, *Itin. Mentis in Deum*, VI (V, 310). [8]Richard of St. Victor, *De Trin.*, III, 3 (PL 196, 917). [9]*De Trin.*, IX, 4 (PL 42, 963). [10]Q. 27, a. 1 and 3. [Not in this volume]

Obj. 3. Further, it seems to be superfluous to teach what cannot be known by natural reason. But it may not be said that the divine teaching on the Trinity is superfluous. Therefore the trinity of persons can be known by natural reason.

On the contrary, Hilary says, *Let man not think to reach the sacred mystery of generation by his own mind.*[11] And Ambrose says, *It is impossible to know the secret of generation. The mind fails, the voice is silent.*[12] But the trinity of the divine persons is distinguished by origin of generation and procession.[13] Since, therefore, man cannot know, and with his understanding attain to, that for which no necessary argument can be given, it follows that the trinity of persons cannot be known by reason.

I answer that, It is impossible to attain to the knowledge of the Trinity by natural reason. For, as was above explained,[14] man cannot obtain a knowledge of God by natural reason except from creatures. Now creatures lead us to the knowledge of God, as effects do to their cause. Accordingly, by natural reason we can know of God only that which of necessity belongs to Him as the cause [*principium*] of all things, and we have used this as a fundamental principle in treating of God.[15] Now, the creative power of God is common to the whole Trinity; and hence it belongs to the unity of the essence, and not to the distinction of the persons. Therefore, by natural reason we can know what belongs to the unity of the essence, but not what belongs to the distinction of the persons.

Whoever, then, tries to prove the trinity of persons by natural reason, detracts from faith in two ways. First, as regards the dignity of faith itself, which consists in its being concerned with invisible things that exceed human reason; wherefore the Apostle says that *faith is of things that appear not* (*Heb.* xi. 1), and the same Apostle says also, *We speak wisdom among the perfect, but not the wisdom of this world, nor of the princes of this world; but we speak the wisdom of God in a mystery which is hidden* (*1 Cor.* ii. 6, 7). Secondly, as regards the utility of drawing others to the faith. For when anyone in the endeavor to prove what belongs to faith brings forward arguments which are not cogent, he falls under the ridicule of the unbelievers: since they suppose that we base ourselves upon such arguments, and that we believe on their account.

Therefore, we must not attempt to prove what is of faith, except by authority alone, to those who receive the authority; while as regards oth-

---

[11]*De Trin.,* II (PL 10, 58).   [12]*De Fide,* I, 10 (PL 16, 566).   [13]Q. 30, a. 2.
[14]Q. 12, a. 4, 11 and 12. [Not in this volume]   [15]Q. 12, a. 12. [Not in this volume]

ers, it suffices to prove that what faith teaches is not impossible. Hence it is said by Dionysius: *Whoever wholly resists Scripture, is far off from our philosophy; whereas if he regards the truth of the sacred writings we are agreed in following the same rule.*[16]

Reply Obj. 1. The philosophers did not know the mystery of the trinity of the divine persons by its proper attributes, namely, paternity, filiation, and procession; according to the Apostle's words, *We speak the wisdom of God which none of the princes of the world*—i.e., "the philosophers," according to the *Gloss*[17]—*knew* (*1 Cor.* ii. 6). Nevertheless, they knew some of the essential attributes appropriated to the persons, as power to the Father, wisdom to the Son, goodness to the Holy Ghost; as will later on appear.[18] So, when Aristotle said, *By this number, etc.,*[19] we must not take it as if he affirmed a threefold number in God, but that he wished to say that the ancients used the threefold number in their sacrifices and prayers because of some perfection residing in the number three. In the Platonic books also we find, *In the beginning was the word,*[20] not as meaning the Person begotten in God, but as meaning the ideal model whereby God made all things, and which is appropriated to the Son. And even though it be said that they knew these were appropriated to the three persons, yet they are said to have failed in the third sign—that is, in the knowledge of the third person, because they deviated from the goodness appropriated to the Holy Ghost, in that, knowing God, *they did not glorify Him as God* (*Rom.* i. 21); or because the Platonists, asserting the existence of one Primal Being whom they also declared to be the father of the universe,[21] then maintained the existence of another substance beneath him, which they called *mind*[22] or the *paternal intellect,*[23] containing the models of all things, as Macrobius relates.[24] They did not, however, assert the existence of a third separate substance which might correspond to the Holy Ghost. Now we do not thus assert that the Father and the Son differ in substance, which was the error of Origen and Arius, who in this followed the Platonists.[25] When Trismegistus says, *Monad begot monad, etc.,*[26] this does not refer to the generation of the Son, or to the procession

---

[16]*De Div. Nom.*, II, 2 (PG 3, 640).   [17]*Glossa interl.* (VI, 36r); Peter Lombard, *In I Cor.* (PL 191, 1548).   [18]Q. 39, a. 7. [Not in this volume]   [19]*De Caelo*, I, 1 (268a 13).   [20]Cf. St. Augustine, *Confess.*, VII, 9 (PL 32, 740).   [21]Macrobius, *In Somn. Scipion.*, I, 14 (p. 539).   [22]*Op. cit.*, I, 2 (p. 482); 14 (p. 540).   [23]St. Albert, *Metaph.*, I, tr. 4, ch. 12 (VI, 82); *De 15 Problem.*, problem. I (p. 34).   [24]*In Somn. Scipion.*, I, 2 (p. 482).   [25]Cf. St. Jerome, *Epist.* LXXXIV, 1 (PL 22, 746).   [26]Pseudo-Hermes Trismegistus, *Lib. 24 Philosoph.*, prop. 1 (p. 31).

of the Holy Ghost, but to the production of the world. For one God produced one world by reason of His love for Himself.

Reply Obj. 2. Reasoning may be brought forward for anything in a twofold way: firstly, for the purpose of furnishing sufficient proof of some principle, as in natural science, where sufficient proof can be brought to show that the movement of the heavens is always of a uniform velocity. Reasoning is employed in another way, not as furnishing a sufficient proof of a principle, but as showing how the remaining effects are in harmony with an already posited principle; as in astronomy the theory of eccentrics and epicycles is considered as established, because thereby the sensible appearances of the heavenly movements can be explained; not, however, as if this proof were sufficient, since some other theory might explain them. In the first way we can prove that *God is one*, and the like. In the second way, arguments may be said to manifest the Trinity; that is to say, given the doctrine of the Trinity, we find arguments in harmony with it. We must not, however, think that the trinity of persons is adequately proved by such reasons. This becomes evident when we consider each point; for the infinite goodness of God is manifested also in creation, because to produce from nothing is an act of infinite power. For if God communicates Himself by His infinite goodness, it is not necessary that an infinite effect should proceed from God: but that, according to its own mode and capacity, the effect should receive the divine goodness. Likewise, when it is said that the joyous possession of good requires partnership, this holds in the case of a person not having perfect goodness: hence he needs to share in the good of someone of his fellows, in order to have the goodness of complete happiness. Nor is the divine image in the intellect an adequate proof about anything in God, since intellect is not in God and ourselves univocally. Hence, Augustine says that by faith we arrive at knowledge, and not conversely.[27]

Reply Obj. 3. There are two reasons why the knowledge of the divine persons was necessary for us. It was necessary for the right idea of creation. The fact of saying that God made all things by His Word excludes the error of those who say that God produced things by necessity. When we say that in Him there is a procession of love, we show that God produced creatures not because He needed them, nor because of any other extrinsic reason, but because of the love of His own goodness. So Moses, when he had said, *In the beginning God created heaven and earth*, subjoined, *God said, Let there be light*, to manifest the divine Word; and then

---

[27] *Tract.* XXVI, super *Ioann.*, VI, 64 (PL 35, 1618).

said, *God saw the light that it was good* (*Gen.* i. 1, 3, 4), to show the proof of the divine love. The same is also found in the other works of creation.

In another way, and chiefly, that we may think rightly concerning the salvation of the human race, accomplished by the Incarnate Son, and by the gift of the Holy Ghost.

Second Article
Whether There Are Notions in God?

We proceed thus to the Second Article:—

Objection 1. It would seem that in God there are no notions. For Dionysius says: *We must not dare to say anything of God but what is taught to us by the Holy Scripture.*[28] But Holy Scripture does not say anything concerning notions. Therefore there are none in God.

Obj. 2. Further, all that exists in God belongs to the unity of the essence or the trinity of the persons. But the notions do not belong to the unity of the essence, nor to the trinity of the persons; for neither can what belongs to the essence be predicated of the notions: for instance, we do not say that paternity is wise or creates; nor can what belongs to the persons be so predicated: for example, we do not say that paternity begets, nor that filiation is begotten. Therefore notions are not found in God.

Obj. 3. Further, we do not require to presuppose any abstract notions as principles of knowing things which are devoid of composition: for they are known of themselves. But the divine persons are supremely simple. Therefore we are not to suppose any notions in God.

On the contrary, Damascene says: *We recognize the difference of the hypostases* (*i.e., persons*), *in the three properties; i.e., in the paternal, the filial, and the processional.*[29] Therefore we must admit properties and notions in God.

I answer that, Prepositinus, considering the simplicity of the persons, said that in God there were no properties or notions; and so wherever they occur, he explains them as being abstract terms standing for the concrete.[30] For as we are accustomed to say, *I beseech your kindness—i.e., you who are kind*—so, when we speak of paternity in God, we mean God the Father.

But, as was shown above, the use of concrete and abstract names in God is not in any way repugnant to the divine simplicity,[31] for we always

---

[28]*De Div. Nom.*, I, 1; 2 (PG 3, 588).   [29]*De Fide Orth.*, III, 5 (PG 94, 1000).
[30]Cf. the reference in the Ottawa edition of *Sum. Theol.*, I, q. 32, a. 2 (col. 211a 8).
[31]Q. 3, a. 3, ad 1.

name a thing as we understand it. Now, our intellect cannot attain to the very simplicity of the divine essence, considered in itself, and therefore our intellect apprehends and names divine things in its own way, that is, according to what is found in sensible things whence its knowledge is derived. What happens in the case of sensible things is this: we use abstract terms to signify simple forms; and to signify subsistent beings we use concrete terms. In the same way, likewise, we signify divine things, as was above stated, by abstract names in order to express their simplicity;[32] whereas, to express their subsistence and completeness, we use concrete names.

But essential names must not be the only ones used in the abstract and in the concrete, as when we say *Deity* and *God*, or *wisdom* and *wise;* but the same must apply to the personal names, so that we may say *paternity* and *Father.*

Two chief motives for this can be cited. The first arises from the issue posed by heretics. For since we confess the Father, the Son and the Holy Ghost to be one God and three persons, to those who ask: *Whereby are They one God? and whereby are they three persons?* as we answer that they are one in essence or deity, so there must also be some abstract terms whereby we may answer that the persons are distinguished; and these are the properties or notions signified by an abstract term, as paternity and filiation. Therefore the divine essence is signified as *What;* and the person as *Who;* and the property as *Whereby.*

The second motive: one Person in God is related to two Persons— namely, the person of the Father to the person of the Son and to the person of the Holy Ghost. This is not, however, by one relation; otherwise it would follow that the Son also and the Holy Ghost would be related to the Father by one and the same relation. Hence, since relation alone multiplies the Trinity, it would follow that the Son and the Holy Ghost would not be two persons. Nor can it be said with Prepositinus[33] that, just as God is related in one way to creatures, although creatures are related to Him in diverse ways, so the Father is related by one relation to the Son and to the Holy Ghost, although these two persons are related to the Father by two relations. For, since the specific nature of the relative is that it refers to another, it must be said that two relations are not specifically different if but one opposite relation corresponds to them. For the relations of lord and father must differ specifically according to the difference of filiation and servitude. Now, all creatures are related to God as His creatures by one

---

[32] *Ibid.*   [33] Cf. above, note 30 of the present article.

specific relation. But the Son and the Holy Ghost are not related to the Father by one and the same kind of relation. Hence there is no parity.

Further, in God there is no need to admit any real relation to the creature;[34] but there is no reason against multiplying logical relations in God. But in the Father there must be a real relation to the Son and to the Holy Ghost. Hence, corresponding to the two relations of the Son and of the Holy Ghost, whereby they are related to the Father, we must understand two relations in the Father, whereby He is related to the Son and to the Holy Ghost. Hence, since there is only one Person of the Father, it is necessary that the relations should be separately signified in the abstract; and these are what we mean by properties and notions.

Reply Obj. 1. Although the notions are not mentioned in Holy Scripture, yet the persons are mentioned, comprising the idea of notions, as the abstract is contained in the concrete.

Reply Obj. 2. In God the notions have their significance not after the manner of realities, but by way of certain ideas whereby the persons are known; although in God these notions or relations are real, as was stated above.[35] Therefore, whatever has order to any essential or personal act, cannot be applied to the notions; for this is against their mode of signification. Hence we cannot say that paternity begets, or creates, or is wise, or is intelligent. Essential names, however, which are not ordered to any act, but simply remove creaturely conditions from God, can be predicated of the notions; for we can say that paternity is eternal, or immense, or the like. So, too, because of the identity in God, substantive terms, whether personal or essential, can be predicated of the notions; for we can say that paternity is God, and that paternity is the Father.

Reply Obj. 3. Although the persons are simple, still, without prejudice to their simplicity, the proper natures of the persons can be abstractly signified, as was above explained.

Third Article
Whether There Are Five Notions?

We proceed thus to the Third Article:—

Objection 1. It would seem that there are not five notions. For the notions proper to the persons are the relations whereby they are distinguished from each other. But the relations in God are only four.[36] Therefore the notions are only four in number.

---

[34]Q. 28, a. 1, ad 3. [Not in this volume]   [35]Q. 28, a. 1. [Not in this volume]
[36]Q. 28, a. 4. [Not in this volume]

Obj. 2. Further, because there is only one essence in God, He is called one God; and because in Him there are three persons, He is called the Triune God. Therefore, if in God there are five notions, He may be called quinary; which cannot be allowed.

Obj. 3. Further, if there are five notions for the three persons in God, there must be in some one person two or more notions, as in the person of the Father there is innascibility, paternity and common spiration. Either these three notions differ really, or not. If they differ really, it follows that the person of the Father is composed of several realities. But if they differ only logically, it follows that one of them can be predicated of another, so that we can say that, just as the divine goodness is the same as the divine wisdom by reason of their identity in reality, so common spiration is paternity; which is not to be admitted. Therefore there are not five notions.

Obj. 4. *On the contrary*, It seems that there are more than five. For the Father is *from no one*, and hence the notion of *innascibility;* so from the Holy Ghost *no other person proceeds*. It would thus seem that the notions total six.

Obj. 5. Further, as the Father and the Son are the common origin of the Holy Ghost, so it is common to the Son and the Holy Ghost to proceed from the Father. Therefore, as one notion is common to the Father and the Son, so there ought to be one notion common to the Son and to the Holy Ghost.

I answer that, A notion is the proper idea whereby we know a divine Person. Now the divine persons are multiplied by reason of their origin: and origin includes the idea of *someone from whom another comes*, and of *someone that comes from another;* and in these two ways a person can be known. Therefore the Person of the Father cannot be known by the fact that He is from another, but by the fact that He is from no one; and thus the notion that belongs to Him is called *innascibility*. As the source of another, He can be known in two ways, because as the Son is from Him, the Father is known by the notion of *paternity;* and as the Holy Ghost is from Him, He is known by the notion of *common spiration*. The Son can be known as begotten by another, and thus He is known by *filiation;* and also by another person proceeding from Him, the Holy Ghost, and thus He is known in the same way as the Father is known, by *common spiration*. The Holy Ghost can be known by the fact that He is from another, or from others, and thus He is known by *procession;* but not by the fact that another is from Him, as no divine person proceeds from Him.

Therefore there are five notions in God: *innascibility, paternity, filia-tion, common spiration,* and *procession.* Of these only four are relations, for *innascibility* is not a relation, except by reduction, as will appear later.[37] Four only are properties. For *common spiration* is not a property, because it belongs to two persons. Three are personal notions—*i.e.,* constituting persons, namely, *paternity, filiation,* and *procession. Common spiration* and *innascibility* are called notions of Persons, but not personal notions, as we shall explain further on.[38]

Reply Obj. 1. Besides the four relations, another notion must be admitted, as was above explained.

Reply Obj. 2. The divine essence is signified as a reality, and likewise the persons are signified as realities; whereas the notions are signified as ideas which make known the persons. Therefore, although God is one by unity of essence, and triune by trinity of persons, nevertheless, He is not quinary by the five notions.

Reply Obj. 3. Since the real plurality in God is founded only on relative opposition, the several properties of one Person, as they are not relatively opposed to each other, do not differ really. Nor again are they predicated of each other, because they are different ideas of the persons. In the same way, we do not say that the attribute of power is the attribute of knowledge, although we do say that His knowledge is His power.

Reply Obj. 4. Since Person implies dignity, as was stated above,[39] we cannot derive a notion of the Holy Ghost from the fact that no person is from Him. For this does not belong to His dignity, as it belongs to the authority of the Father that He is from no one.

Reply Obj. 5. The Son and the Holy Ghost do not agree in one special mode of existence derived from the Father; as the Father and the Son agree in one special mode of producing the Holy Ghost. But the principle on which a notion is based must be something special. Thus no parity of reasoning exists.

Fourth Article
Whether We May Have Various
Contrary Opinions about the Notions?

We proceed thus to the Fourth Article:—

Objection 1. It would seem that we may not have various contrary opinions of the notions: For Augustine says: *No error is more dangerous than*

---

[37]Q. 33, a. 4, ad 3. [Not in this volume]   [38]Q. 40, a. 1, ad 1. [Not in this volume]   [39]Q. 29, a. 3, ad 2. [Not in this volume]

any as regards the Trinity;[40] to which mystery the notions assuredly belong. But contrary opinions must be in some way erroneous. Therefore it is not right to have contrary opinions of the notions.

Obj. 2. Further, the persons are known by the notions. But contrary opinions concerning the persons are not permissible. Therefore neither can there be any such about the notions.

On the contrary, The notions are not articles of faith. Therefore different opinions of the notions are permissible.

I answer that, Anything is of faith in two ways. *Directly*, and such are truths that come to us principally as divinely taught, as the trinity and unity of God, the Incarnation of the Son, and the like; and concerning these truths a false opinion of itself involves heresy, especially if it be held obstinately. A thing is of faith *indirectly*, if the denial of it involves as a consequence something against faith, as, for instance, if anyone said that Samuel was not the son of Elcana; for it follows that the divine Scripture would be false. Concerning such things anyone may have a false opinion without danger of heresy, before the matter has been considered or settled as involving consequences against faith, and particularly if no obstinacy be shown; whereas when it is manifest, and especially if the Church has decided that consequences follow against faith, then the error cannot be free from heresy. For this reason, many things are now considered as heretical which were formerly not so considered, as their consequences are now more manifest.

So we must conclude that we may, without danger of heresy, entertain contrary opinions about the notions, if we do not mean to uphold anything at variance with faith. If, however, anyone should entertain a false opinion of the notions, knowing or thinking that consequences against the faith would follow, he would lapse into heresy.

By what has been said all the objections may be solved.

---

[40]*De Trin.*, I, 3 (PL 42, 822).

GOD INCARNATE

I. *Commentary on the Gospel of Saint John*
Lecture 1

> 1 In the beginning was the Word;
> and the Word was with God;
> and the Word was God.
> 2 He was in the beginning with God.

23 John the Evangelist, as already indicated, makes it his principal object to show the divinity of the Incarnate Word. Accordingly, his Gospel is divided into two parts. In the first he states the divinity of Christ; in the second he shows it by the things Christ did in the flesh (2:1). In regard to the first, he does two things. First he shows the divinity of Christ; secondly he sets forth the manner in which Christ's divinity is made known to us (1:14). Concerning the first he does two things. First he treats of the divinity of Christ; secondly of the incarnation of the Word of God (1:6).

Because there are two items to be considered in each thing, namely, its existence and its operation or power, first he treats the existence of the Word as to his divine nature; secondly of his power or operation (1:3). In regard to the first he does four things. First he shows when the Word was: **In the beginning was the Word**; secondly where he was: **and the Word was with God**; thirdly what he was: **and the Word was God**; fourthly, in what way he was: **He was in the beginning with God.** The first two pertain to the inquiry "whether something exists"; the second two pertain to the inquiry "what something is."

24 With respect to the first of these four we must examine the meaning of the statement, **In the beginning was the Word.** And here three things present themselves for careful study according to the three parts of this statement. First it is necessary to investigate the name **Word**; secondly the phrase **in the beginning**; thirdly the meaning of the Word **was in the beginning.**

Source: Saint Thomas Aquinas, *Commentary on the Gospel of Saint John*, Part I, translated by J. A. Weisheipl and F. R. Archer (Albany: Magi Books, 1980). Reprinted by permission of the publisher. Numbers follow the original Latin divisions.

25 To understand the name **Word** we should note that according to the Philosopher [*On Interpretation* 16a3] vocal sounds are signs of the affections that exist in our soul. It is customary in Scripture for the things signified to be themselves called by the names of their signs, as in the statement, "And the rock was Christ" (1 Cor 10:4). It is fitting that what is within our soul, and which is signified by our external word, be called a "word." But whether the name "word" belongs first to the exterior vocal sound or to the conception in our mind, is not our concern at present. However, it is obvious that what is signified by the vocal sound, as existing interiorly in the soul, exists prior to the vocal expression inasmuch as it is its actual cause. Therefore if we wish to grasp the meaning of the interior word, we must first look at the meaning of that which is exteriorly expressed in words.

Now there are three things in our intellect: the intellectual power itself, the species of the thing understood (and this species is its form, being to the intellect what the species of a color is to the eye), and thirdly the very activity of the intellect, which is to understand. But none of these is what is signified by the exterior vocal word: for the name "stone" does not signify the substance of the intellect because this is not what the one naming intends; nor does it signify the species, which is that by which the intellect understands, since this also is not the intention of the one naming; nor does it signify the act itself of understanding since to understand is not an action proceeding to the exterior from the one understanding, but an action remaining within. Therefore, that is properly called an interior word which the one understanding forms when understanding.

Now the intellect forms two things, according to its two operations. According to its operation which is called "the understanding of indivisibles," it forms a definition; while according to its operation by which it unites and separates, it forms an enunciation or something of that sort. Hence, what is thus formed and expressed by the operation of the intellect, whether by defining or enunciating, is what the exterior vocal sound signifies. So the Philosopher says that the notion (*ratio*) which a name signifies is a definition. Hence, what is thus expressed, i.e., formed in the soul, is called an interior word. Consequently it is compared to the intellect, not as that by which the intellect understands, but as that in which it understands, because it is in what is thus expressed and formed that it sees the nature of the thing understood. Thus we have the meaning of the name "word."

Secondly, from what has been said we are able to understand that a word is always something that proceeds from an intellect existing in act;

and furthermore, that a word is always a notion (*ratio*) and likeness of the thing understood. So if the one understanding and the thing understood are the same, then the word is a notion and likeness of the intellect from which it proceeds. On the other hand, if the one understanding is other than the thing understood, then the word is not a likeness and notion of the one understanding but of the thing understood, as the conception which one has of a stone is a likeness of only the stone. But when the intellect understands itself, its word is a likeness and notion of the intellect. And so Augustine (*On the Trinity* IX, 5) sees a likeness of the Trinity in the soul insofar as the mind understands itself, but not insofar as it understands other things.

It is clear then that it is necessary to have a word in any intellectual nature, for it is of the very nature of understanding that the intellect in understanding should form something. Now what is formed is called a word, and so it follows that in every being which understands there must be a word.

However, intellectual natures are of three kinds: human, angelic and divine; and so there are three kinds of words. The human word, about which it is said in the Psalm (13:1): "The fool said in his heart, 'There is no God.'" The angelic word, about which it is said in Zechariah (1:9), and in many places in Sacred Scripture, "And the angel said to me." The third is the divine word, of which Genesis (1:3) says, "And God said, 'Let there be light.'" So when the Evangelist says, **In the beginning was the Word,** we cannot understand this as a human or angelic word, because both these words have been made since man and angel have a cause and principle of their existence and operation, and the word of a man or an angel cannot exist before they do. The word the Evangelist had in mind he shows by saying that this word was not made, since all things were made by it. Therefore, the word about which John speaks here is the Word of God.

26 We should note that this Word differs from our own word in three ways. The first difference, according to Augustine, is that our word is formable before being formed, for when I wish to conceive the notion of a stone, I must arrive at it by reasoning. And so it is in all other things that are understood by us, with the sole possible exception of the first principles which, since they are known in a simple manner, are known at once without any discourse of reason. So as long as the intellect, in so reasoning, casts about this way and that, the formation is not yet complete. It is only when it has conceived the notion of the thing perfectly that for the first time it has the notion of the complete thing and a word. Thus in our

mind there is both a "cogitation," meaning the discourse involved in an investigation, and a word, which is formed according to a perfect contemplation of the truth. So our word is first in potency before it is in act. But the Word of God is always in act. In consequence, the term "cogitation" does not properly speaking apply to the Word of God. For Augustine says (*On the Trinity* XV): "The Word of God is spoken of in such a way that cogitation is not included, lest anything changeable be supposed in God." Anselm was speaking improperly when he said: "For the supreme Spirit to speak is for him to look at something while cogitating."

27 The second difference is that our word is imperfect, but the divine Word is most perfect. For since we cannot express all our conceptions in one word, we must form many imperfect words through which we separately express all that is in our knowledge. But it is not that way with God. For since he understands both himself and everything else through his essence, by one act, the single divine Word is expressive of all that is in God, not only of the Persons but also of creatures; otherwise it would be imperfect. So Augustine says: "If there were less in the Word than is contained in the knowledge of the One speaking it, the Word would be imperfect; but it is obvious that it is most perfect; therefore, it is only one." "God speaks once" (Jb 33:14).

28 The third difference is that our word is not of the same nature as we; but the divine Word is of the same nature as God. And therefore it is something that subsists in the divine nature. For the understood notion which the intellect is seen to form about some thing has only an intelligible existence in our soul. Now in our soul, to understand is not the same as the nature of the soul, because our soul is not its own operation. Consequently, the word which our intellect forms is not of the essence of our soul, but is an accident of it. But in God, to understand and to be are the same; and so the Word of the divine intellect is not an accident but belongs to its nature. Thus it must be subsistent, because whatever is in the nature of God is God. Thus Damascene says that God is a substantial Word, and a hypostasis, but our words are concepts in our mind.

29 From the above it is clear that the Word, properly speaking, is always understood as a Person in the Divinity, since it implies only something expressed by the one understanding; also, that in the Divinity the Word is the likeness of that from which it issues; and that it is co-eternal with that from which it issues, since it was not first formable before being formed, but was always in act; and that it is equal to the Father, since it is perfect and expressive of the whole being of the Father; and that it is coessential and consubstantial with the Father, since it is his substance.

It is also clear that since in every nature that which issues forth and has a likeness to the nature from which it issues is called a son, and since this Word issues forth in a likeness and identity to the nature from which it issues, it is suitable and appropriately called a "Son," and its production is called a generation.

So now the first point is clear, the meaning of the term **Word**.

30 There are four questions on this point, two of them from Chrysostom. The first is: Why did John the Evangelist omit the Father and begin at once with the Son, saying, **In the beginning was the Word?**

There are two answers to this. One is that the Father was known to everyone in the Old Testament, although not under the aspect of Father, but as God; but the Son was not known. And so in the New Testament, which is concerned with our knowledge of the Word, he begins with the Word or Son.

The other answer is that we are brought to know the Father through the Son: "Father, I have manifested your name to the men whom you have given to me" (below 17:6). And so wishing to lead the faithful to a knowledge of the Father, the Evangelist fittingly began with the Son, at once adding something about the Father when he says, **and the Word was with God.**

31 The second question is also from Chrysostom. Why did he say **Word** and not "Son," since, as we have said, the Word proceeds as Son?

There are also two answers to this. First, because "son" means something begotten, and when we hear of the generation of the Son, someone might suppose that this generation is the kind he can comprehend, that is, a material and changeable generation. Thus he did not say "Son," but **Word**, which signifies an intelligible proceeding, so that it would not be understood as a material and changeable generation. And so in showing that the Son is born of the Father in an unchangeable way, he eliminates a faulty conjecture by using the name **Word**.

The second answer is this. The Evangelist was about to consider the Word as having come to manifest the Father. But since the idea of manifesting is implied better in the name "Word" than in the name "Son," he preferred to use the name **Word**.

32 The third question is raised by Augustine in his book *Eighty-three Questions;* and it is this. In Greek, where we have "Word," they have "Logos"; now since "Logos" signifies in Latin both "notion" and "word" [i.e., *ratio et verbum*], why did the translators render it as "word" and not "notion," since a notion is something interior just as a word is?

I answer that "notion" [*ratio*], properly speaking, names a conception of the mind precisely as in the mind, even if through it nothing exterior comes to be; but "word" signifies a reference to something exterior. And so because the Evangelist, when he said "Logos," intended to signify not only a reference to the Son's existence in the Father, but also the operative power of the Son, by which, through him, all things were made, our predecessors preferred to translate it "Word," which implies a reference to something exterior, rather than "notion," which implies merely a concept of the mind.

33 The fourth question is from Origen, and is this. In many passages, Scripture, when speaking of the Word of God, does not simply call him the Word, but adds "of God," saying, "the Word of God," or "of the Lord": "The Word of God on high is the foundation of wisdom" (Sir 1:5); "His name is the Word of God" (Rv 19:13). Why then did the Evangelist, when speaking here of the Word of God, not say, "In the beginning was the Word of God," but said **In the beginning was the Word?**

I answer that although there are many participated truths, there is just one absolute Truth, which is Truth by its very essence, that is, the divine act of being (*esse*); and by this Truth all words are words. Similarly, there is one absolute Wisdom elevated above all things, that is, the divine Wisdom, by participating in which all wise persons are wise. Further, there is one absolute Word, by participating in which all persons having a word are called speakers. Now this is the divine Word which of itself is the Word elevated above all words. So in order that the Evangelist might signify this supereminence of the divine Word, he pointed out this Word to us absolutely without any addition.

And because the Greeks, when they wished to signify something separate and elevated above everything else, did this by affixing the article to the name (as the Platonists, wishing to signify the separated substances, such as the separated good or the separated man, called them the good *per se*, or man *per se*), so the Evangelist, wishing to signify the separation and elevation of that Word above all things, affixed an article to the name "Logos," so that if it were stated in Latin we would have "*the* Word."

34 Secondly, we must consider the meaning of the phrase, **In the beginning**. We must note that according to Origen, the word *principium* has many meanings [such as "principle," "source," or "beginning"]. Since the word *principium* implies a certain order of one thing to another, one can find a *principium* in all those things which have an order. First of all, order is found in quantified things; and so there is a principle of number

and lengths, as for example, a line. Second, order is found in time; and so we speak of a "beginning" of time, or of duration. Third, order is found in learning; and this in two ways: as to nature, and as to ourselves, and in both cases we can speak of a "beginning": "By this time you ought to be teachers" (Heb 5:12). As to nature, in Christian doctrine the beginning and principle of our wisdom in Christ, inasmuch as he is the Wisdom and Word of God, i.e., in his divinity. But as to ourselves, the beginning is Christ himself inasmuch as the Word has become flesh, i.e., by his incarnation. Fourth, an order is found in the production of a thing. In this perspective there can be a *principium* on the part of the thing generated, that is, the first part of the thing generated or made; as we say that the foundation is the beginning of a house. Another *principium* is on the part of the generator, and in this perspective there are three "principles": of intention, which is the purpose, which motivates the agent; of reason, which is the idea in the mind of the maker; and of execution, which is the operative faculty. Considering these various ways of using the term, we now ask how *principium* is used here when it says, **In the beginning was the Word**.

35 We should note that this word can be taken in three ways. In one way so that *principium* is understood as the Person of the Son, who is the principle of creatures by reason of his active power acting with wisdom, which is the conception of the things that are brought into existence. Hence we read: "Christ the power of God and the wisdom of God" (1 Cor 1:24). And so the Lord said about himself: "I am the *principium* who also speaks to you" (below 8:25). Taking *principium* in this way, we should understand the statement, **In the beginning was the Word**, as though he were saying, "The Word was in the Son," so that the sense would be: The Word himself is the *principium*, principle, in the sense in which life is said to be "in" God, when this life is not something other than God. And this is the explanation of Origen. And so the Evangelist says In the beginning here in order, as Chrysostom says, to show at the very outset the divinity of the Word by asserting that he is a principle because, as determining all, a principle is most honored.

36 In a second way *principium* can be understood as the Person of the Father, who is the principle not only of creatures, but of every divine process. It is taken this way in "Yours is princely power (*principium*) in the day of your birth" (Ps 110:3). In this second way one reads **In the beginning was the Word** as though it means, "The Son was in the Father." This is Augustine's understanding of it, as well as Origen's. The Son, however, is said to be in the Father because both have the same essence. Since the Son is his own essence, then the Son is in whomsoever the Son's

essence is. Since, therefore, the essence of the Son is in the Father by con-substantiality, it is fitting that the Son be in the Father. Hence it says below (14:10): "I am in the Father and the Father is in me."

37 In a third way, *principium* can be taken for the beginning of dura-tion, so that the sense of **In the beginning was the Word** is that the Word was before all things, as Augustine explains it. According to Basil and Hilary, this phrase shows the eternity of the Word.

The phrase **In the beginning was the Word** shows that no matter which beginning of duration is taken, whether of temporal things which is time, or of aeviternal things which is the aeon, or of the whole world or any imagined span of time reaching back for many ages, at that beginning the Word already was. Hence Hilary says (*On the Trinity* VII): "Go back season by season, skip over the centuries, take away ages. Set down what-ever you want as the beginning in your opinion: the Word already was." And this is what Proverbs (8:23) says: "The Lord possessed me in the beginning of his ways, before he made anything." But what is prior to the beginning of duration is eternal.

38 And thus the first explanation asserts the causality of the Word; the second explanation affirms the consubstantiality of the Word with the Father, who utters the Word; and the third explanation affirms the co-eternity of the Word.

39 Now we should consider that it says that the Word was (*erat*), which is stated in the past imperfect tense. This tense is most appropriate for designating eternal things if we consider the nature of time and of the things that exist in time. For what is future is not yet in act; but what is at present is in act, and by the fact that it is in act what is present is not described as having been. Now the past perfect tense indicates that some-thing has existed, has already come to an end, and has now ceased to be. The past imperfect tense, on the other hand, indicates that something has been, has not yet come to an end, nor has ceased to be, but still endures. Thus, whenever John mentions eternal things he expressly says "was" (*erat*, past imperfect tense), but when he refers to anything temporal he says "has been" (*fuit*, past perfect tense), as will be clear later.

But so far as concerns the notion of the present, the best way to desig-nate eternity is the present tense, which indicates that something is in act, and this is always the characteristic of eternal things. And so it says in Exodus (3:14): "I am who am." And Augustine says: "He alone truly is whose being does not know a past and a future."

40 We should also note that this verb **was**, according to the Gloss, is not understood here as indicating temporal changes, as other verbs do, but as signifying the existence of a thing. Thus it is also called a substantive verb.

41 Someone may ask how the Word can be co-eternal with the Father since he is begotten by the Father: for a human son, born from a human father, is subsequent to his father.

I answer that there are three reasons why an originative principle is prior in duration to that which derives from that principle. First of all, if the originative principle of anything precedes in time the action by which it produces the thing of which it is the principle; thus a man does not begin to write as soon as he exists, and so he precedes his writing in time. Secondly, if an action is successive; consequently, even if the action should happen to begin at the same time as the agent, the termination of the action is nevertheless subsequent to the agent. Thus, as soon as fire has been generated in a lower region, it begins to ascend; but the fire exists before it has ascended, because the motion by which it tends upward requires some time. Thirdly, by the fact that sometimes the beginning of a thing depends on the will of its principle, just as the beginning of a creature's coming-to-be depends on the will of God, such that God existed before any creature.

Yet none of these three is found in the generation of the divine Word. God did not first exist and then begin to generate the Word: for since the generation of the Word is nothing other than an intelligible conception, it would follow that God would be understanding in potency before understanding in act, which is impossible. Again, it is impossible that the generation of the Word involve succession: for then the divine Word would be unformed before it was formed (as happens in us who form words by "cogitating"), which is false, as was said. Again, we cannot say that the Father pre-established a beginning of duration for his Son by his own will, because God the Father does not generate the Son by his will, as the Arians held, but naturally: for God the Father, understanding himself, conceives the Word; and so God the Father did not exist prior to the Son.

An example of this, to a limited degree, appears in fire and in the brightness issuing from it: for this brightness issues naturally and without succession from the fire. Again, if the fire were eternal, its brightness would be coeternal with it. This is why the Son is called the brightness of the Father: "the brightness of his glory" (Heb 1:3). But this example lacks an illustration of the identity of nature. And so we call him Son, although in human sonship we do not find coeternity: for we must attain our knowledge of divine things from many likenesses in material things, for one likeness is not enough. The Council of Ephesus says that the Son always coexists with the Father: for "brightness" indicates his unchangeability, "birth" points to the Word himself, but the name "Son" suggests his consubstantiality.

42 And so we give the Son various names to express his perfection, which cannot be expressed by one name. We call him "Son" to show that he is of the same nature as the Father; we call him "image" to show that he is not unlike the Father in any way; we call him "brightness" to show that he is coeternal; and he is called the "Word" to show that he is begotten in an immaterial manner.

43 Then the Evangelist says, and **the Word was with God**, which is the second clause in his account. The first thing to consider is the meaning of the two words which did not appear in the first clause, that is, **God**, and **with**; for we have already explained the meanings of "Word," and "beginning." Let us continue carefully by examining these two new words, and to better understand the explanation of this second clause, we must say something about the meaning of each so far as it is relevant to our purpose.

44 At the outset, we should note that the name "God" signifies the divinity concretely and as inherent in a subject, while the name "deity" signifies the divinity in the abstract and absolutely. Thus the name "deity" cannot naturally and by its mode of signifying stand for a [divine] person, but only for the [divine] nature. But the name "God" can, by its natural mode of signifying, stand for any one of the [divine] persons, just as the name "man" stands for any individual (*suppositum*) possessing humanity. Therefore, whenever the truth of a statement or its predicate require that the name "God" stand for the person, then it stands for the person, as when we say, "God begets God." Thus, when it says here that **the Word was with God**, it is necessary that **God** stand for the person of the Father, because the preposition **with** signifies the distinction of the Word, which is said to be **with God**. And although this preposition signifies a distinction in person, it does not signify a distinction in nature, since the nature of the Father and of the Son is the same. Consequently, the Evangelist wished to signify the person of the Father when he said **God**.

45 Here we should note that the preposition **with** signifies a certain union of the thing signified by its grammatical antecedent to the thing signified by its grammatical object, just as the preposition "in" does.

However, there is a difference, because the preposition "in" signifies a certain intrinsic union, whereas the preposition **with** implies in a certain way an extrinsic union. And we state both in divine matters, namely, that the Son is *in* the Father and *with* the Father. Here the intrinsic union pertains to consubstantiality, but the extrinsic union (if we may use such an expression, since "extrinsic" is improperly employed in divine matters) refers only to a personal distinction, because the Son is distinguished from the Father by origin alone. And so these two words designate both a consubstantiality in nature and distinction in person: consubstantiality inasmuch as a certain union is implied; but distinction, inasmuch as a certain otherness is signified as was said above.

The preposition "in," as was said, principally signifies consubstantiality, as implying an intrinsic union and, by way of consequence, a distinction of persons, inasmuch as every preposition is transitive. The proposition "with" principally signifies a personal distinction, but also a consubstantiality inasmuch as it signifies a certain extrinsic, so to speak, union. For these reasons the Evangelist specifically used here the preposition "with" in order to express the distinction of the person of the Son from the Father, saying, **and the Word was with God**, that is, the Son was with the Father as one person with another.

46 We should note further that this preposition **with** has four meanings, and these eliminate four objections. First, the preposition **with** signifies the subsistence of its antecedent, because things that do not subsist of themselves are not properly said to be "with" another; thus we do not say that a color is with a body, and the same applies to other things that do not subsist of themselves. But things that do subsist of themselves are properly said to be "with" another; thus we say that a man is with a man, and a stone with a stone.

Secondly, it signifies authority in its grammatical object. For we do not, properly speaking, say that a king is with a soldier, but that the soldier is with the king. Thirdly, it asserts a distinction. For it is not proper to say that a person is with himself, but rather that one man is with another. Fourthly, it signifies a certain union and fellowship. For when some person is said to be with another, it suggests to us that there is some social union between them.

Considering these four conditions implied in the meaning of this preposition **with**, the Evangelist quite appropriately joins to the first clause, **In the beginning was the Word**, this second clause, **and the Word was with God**. For if we omit one of the three explanations of, **In** the beginning was the Word (namely, the one in which *principium* was understood as the Son), certain heretics make a twofold objection against each of the other explanations (namely, the one in which *principium* means the same as "before all things," and the one in which it is understood as the Father). Thus there are four objections, and we can answer these by the four conditions indicated by this preposition with.

47 The first of these objections is this. You say that the Word was in the beginning, i.e., before all things. But before all things there was nothing. So if before all things there was nothing, where then was the Word? This objection arises due to the imaginings of those who think that whatever exists is somewhere and in some place. But this is rejected by John when he says, with God, which indicates the union mentioned in the last of the four conditions. So, according to Basil, the meaning is this: Where was the Word? The answer is: with God; not in some place, since he is unsurroundable, but he is with the Father, who is not enclosed by any place.

48 The second objection against the same explanation is this. You say that the Word was in the beginning, i.e., before all things. But whatever exists before all things appears to proceed from no one, since that from which something proceeds seems to be prior to that which proceeds from it. Therefore, the Word does not proceed from another. This objection is rejected when he says, the Word was with God, taking "with" according to its second condition, as implying authority in what is causing. So the meaning, according to Hilary, is this: From whom is the Word if he exists before all things? The Evangelist answers: the Word was with God, i.e., although the Word has no beginning of duration, still he does not lack a *principium* or author, for he was with God as his author.

49 The third objection, directed to the explanation in which *principium* is understood as the Father, is this. You say that In the beginning was the Word, i.e., the Son was in the Father. But that which is in something does not seem to be subsistent, as a hypostasis; just as the whiteness in a body does not subsist. This objection is solved by the statement, the Word was with God, taking "with" in its first condition, as implying the subsistence of its grammatical antecedent. So according to Chrysostom, the meaning is this: In the beginning was the Word, not as an accident, but he was with God, as subsisting, and a divine hypostasis.

50 The fourth objection, against the same explanation, is this. You say that the Word was in the beginning, i.e., in the Father. But whatever is in something is not distinct from it. So the Son is not distinct from the Father. This objection is answered by the statement, and the Word was with God, taking "with" in its third condition, as indicating distinction.

Thus the meaning, according to Alcuin and Bede, is this: **The Word was with God**, and he was "in" the Father by a consubstantiality of nature, while still being "with" him through a distinction in person.

51 And so, **and the Word was with God**, indicates: the union of the Word with the Father in nature, according to Basil; their distinction in person, according to Alcuin and Bede; the subsistence of the Word in the divine nature, according to Chrysostom; and the authorship of the Father in relation to the Word, according to Hilary.

52 We should also note, according to Origen, that **the Word was with God** shows that the Son has always been with the Father. For in the Old Testament it says that the word of the Lord "came" to Jeremiah or to someone else, as is plain in many passages of sacred Scripture. But it does not say that the word of the Lord was "with" Jeremiah or anyone else, because the word "comes" to those who begin to have the word after not having it. Thus the Evangelist did not say that the Word "came" to the Father, but was "with" the Father, because, given the Father, the Word was with him.

53 Then he says, **and the Word was God**. This is the third clause in John's account, and it follows most appropriately considering the order of teaching. For since John had said both *when* and *where* the Word was, it remained to inquire *what* the Word was, that is, **the Word was God**, taking "Word" as the subject, and "God" as the predicate.

54 But since one should first inquire what a thing is before investigating where and when it is, it seems that John violated this order by discussing these latter first.

Origen answers this by saying that the Word of God is with man and with God in different ways. The Word is with man as perfecting him, because it is through him that man becomes wise and good: "She makes friends of God and prophets" (Wis 7:27). But the Word is not with God as though the Father were perfected and enlightened by him. Rather, the Word is with God as receiving natural divinity from him, who utters the Word, and from whom he has it that he is the same God with him. And so, since the Word was with God by origin, it was necessary to show first that the Word was in the Father and with the Father before showing that the Word was God.

55 This clause also enables us to answer two objections which arise from the foregoing. The first is based on the name "Word," and is this. You say that **In the beginning was the Word**, and that the Word was **with God**. Now it is obvious that "word" is generally understood to sig-

nify a vocal sound and the statement of something necessary, a manifest-ing of thoughts. But these words pass away and do not subsist. Accordingly, someone could think that the Evangelist was speaking of a word like these.

According to Hilary and Augustine, this question is sufficiently answered by the above account. Augustine says (Homily 1 *On John*) that it is obvious that in this passage "Word" cannot be understood as a state-ment because, since a statement is in motion and passes away, it could not be said that **In the beginning was the Word**, if this Word were some-thing passing away and in motion. The same thing is clear from **and the Word was with God**: for to be "in" another is not the same as to be "with" another. Our word, since it does not subsist, is not "with" us, but "in" us; but the Word of God is subsistent, and therefore "with" God. And so the Evangelist expressly says, and the **Word was with God**. To entirely remove the ground of the objection, he adds the nature and being of the Word, saying, **and the Word was God**.

56 The other question comes from his saying, **with God**. For since "with" indicates a distinction, it could be thought that **the Word was with God**, i.e., the Father, as distinct from him in nature. So to exclude this he adds at once the consubstantiality of the Word with the Father, saying, **and the Word was God**. As if to say: the Word is not separated from the Father by a diversity of nature, because the Word itself is God.

57 Note also the special way of signifying, since he says, **the Word was God**, using "God" absolutely to show that he is not God in the same way in which the name of the deity is given to a creature in Sacred Scripture. For a creature sometimes shares this name with some added qualification, as when it says, "I have appointed you the God of Pharoah" (Ex 7:1), in order to indicate that he was not God absolutely or by nature, because he was appointed the god of someone in a qualified sense. Again, it says in the Psalm (81:6): "I said, 'You are gods.'"—as if to say: in my opinion, but not in reality. Thus the Word is called God absolutely because he is God by his own essence, and not by participation, as men and angels are.

58 We should note that Origen disgracefully misunderstood this clause, led astray by the Greek manner of speaking. It is the custom among the Greeks to put the article before every name in order to indicate a distinction. In the Greek version of John's Gospel the name "Word" in the statement, **In the beginning was the Word**, and also the name "God" in the statement, **and the Word was with God**, are prefixed by the article, so as to read "the Word" and "the God," in order to indicate the eminence and distinction of the Word from other words, and the prin-

cipality of the Father in the divinity. But in the statement, **the Word was God**, the article is not prefixed to the noun "God," which stands for the person of the Son. Because of this Origen blasphemed that the Word, although he was Word by essence, was not God by essence, but is called God by participation; while the Father alone is God by essence. And so he held that the Son is inferior to the Father.

59 Chrysostom proves that this is not true, because if the article used with the name "God" implied the superiority of the Father in respect to the Son, it would never be used with the name "God" when it is used as a predicate of another, but only when it is predicated of the Father. Further, whenever said of the Father, it would be accompanied by the article. However, we find the opposite to be the case in two statements of the Apostle, who calls Christ "God," using the article. For in Titus (2:13) he says, "the coming of the glory of the great God and our Savior Jesus Christ," where "God" stands for the Son, and in the Greek the article is used. Therefore, Christ is the great God. Again he says (Rom 9:5): "Christ, who is God over all things, blessed forever," and again the article is used with "God" in the Greek. Further, in 1 John (5:20) it says: "That we may be in his true Son, Jesus Christ; he is the true God and eternal life." Thus, Christ is not God by participation, but truly God. And so the theory of Origen is clearly false.

Chrysostom gives us the reason why the Evangelist did not use the article with the name "God," namely, because he had already mentioned God twice using the article, and so it was not necessary to repeat it a third time, but it was implied. Or, a better reason would be that "God" is used here as the predicate and is taken formally. And it is not the custom for the article to accompany names used as predicates, since the article indicates separation. But if "God" were used here as the subject, it could stand for any of the persons, as the Son or the Holy Spirit; then, no doubt, the article would be used in the Greek.

60 Then he says, **He was in the beginning with God**. This is the fourth clause and is introduced because of the preceding clause. For from the Evangelist's statement that **the Word was God**, two false interpretations could be held by those who misunderstand. One of these is by the pagans, who acknowledge many and different gods, and say that their wills are in opposition. For example, those who put out the fable of Jupiter fighting with Saturn; or as the Manicheans, who have two contrary principles of nature. The Lord said against this error (Dt 6:4): "Hear O Israel: The Lord our God is one Lord."

Since the Evangelist had said, **the Word was with God; and the Word was God,** they could adduce this in support of their error by understanding the God with whom the Word is to be one [God], and the Word to be another, having another, or contrary, will to the former; and this is against the law of the Gospel. And so to exclude this he says, **He was in the beginning with God,** as if to say, according to Hilary: I say that the Word is God, not as if he has a distinct divinity, but he is with God, that is, in the one same nature in which he is. Further, lest his statement, **and the Word was God,** be taken to mean that the Word has an opposed will, he added that the Word **was in the beginning with God,** namely, the Father; not as divided from him or opposed, but having an identity of nature with him and a harmony of will. This union comes about by the sharing of the divine nature in the three persons, and by the bond of the natural love of the Father and the Son.

61 The Arians were able to draw out another error from the above. They think that the Son is less than the Father because it says below (14:28): "The Father is greater than I." And they say the Father is greater than the Son both as to eternity and as to divinity of nature. And so to exclude this the Evangelist added: **He was in the beginning with God.** For Arius admits the first clause, **In the beginning was the Word,** but he will not admit that *principium* should be taken for the Father, but rather for the beginning of creatures. So he says that the Word was in the beginning of creatures, and consequently is in no sense coeternal with the Father. But this is excluded, according to Chrysostom, by this clause, **He was in the beginning,** not of creatures, but **in the beginning with God,** i.e., whenever God existed. For the Father was never alone without the Son or Word, but **He,** that is, the Word, was always **with God.**

62 Again, Arius admits that the Word was God, but nevertheless inferior to the Father. This is excluded by what follows. For there are two attributes proper to the great God which Arius attributed solely to God the Father, that is, eternity and omnipotence. So in whomever these two attributes are found, he is the great God, than whom none is greater. But the Evangelist attributes these two to the Word. Therefore, the Word is the great God, and not inferior. He says the Word is eternal when he states, **He was in the beginning with God,** i.e., the Word was with God from eternity, and not only in the beginning of creatures (as Arius held), but with God, receiving being and divinity from him. Further, he attributes omnipotence to the Word when he adds, **Through him all things came into being.**

63 Origen gives a rather beautiful explanation of this clause, **He was in the beginning with God**, when he says that it is not separate from the first three, but is in a certain sense their epilogue. For the Evangelist, after he had indicated that truth was the Son's and was about to describe his power, in a way gathers together in a summary form, in this fourth clause, what he had said in the first three. For in saying **He**, he understands the third clause; by adding **was in the beginning**, he recalls the first clause; and by adding **with was in the beginning**, he recalls the first clause; and by adding **with God**, he recalls the second, so that we do not think that the Word which was in the beginning is different than the Word which was God; but this Word which was God **was in the beginning with God**.

64 If one considers these four propositions well, he will find that they clearly destroy all the errors of the heretics and of the philosophers. For some heretics, as Ebion and Cerinthus, said that Christ did not exist before the Blessed Virgin, but took from her the beginning of his being and duration; for they held that he was a mere man, who had merited divinity by his good works. Photinus and Paul of Samosata, following them, said the same thing. But the Evangelist excludes their errors saying, **In the beginning was the Word**, i.e., before all things, and in the Father from eternity. Thus he did not derive his beginning from the Virgin.

Sabellius, on the other hand, although he admitted that the God who took flesh did not receive his beginning from the Virgin, but existed from eternity, still said that the person of the Father, who existed from eternity, was not distinct from the person of the Son, who took flesh from the Virgin. He maintained that the Father and Son were the same person; and so he failed to distinguish the trinity of persons in the deity. The Evangelist says against this error, **and the Word was with God**, i.e., the Son was with the Father, as one person with another.

Eunomius declared that the Son is entirely unlike the Father. The Evangelist rejects this when he says, **and the Word was God**. Finally, Arius said that the Son was less than the Father. The Evangelist excludes this by saying, **He was in the beginning with God**, as was explained above.

65 These words also exclude the errors of the philosophers. For some of the ancient philosophers, namely, the natural philosophers, maintained that the world did not come from any intellect or through some purpose, but by chance. Consequently, they did not place at the beginning as the cause of things a reason or intellect, but only matter in flux; for example,

atoms, as Democritus thought, or other material principles of this kind as different philosophers maintained. Against these the Evangelist says, **In the beginning was the Word,** from whom, and not from chance, things derive their beginning.

Plato, however, thought that the Ideas of all the things that were made were subsistent, i.e., existing separately in their own natures; and material things exist by participating in these. For example, he thought men existed through the separated Idea of man, which he called Man *per se.* So lest you suppose, as did Plato, that this Idea through which all things were made be Ideas separated from God, the Evangelist adds, **and the Word was with God.**

Other Platonists, as Chrysostom relates, maintained that God the Father was most eminent and first, but under him they placed a certain mind in which there were the likenesses and ideas of all things. So lest you think that the Word was with the Father in such a way as to be under him and less than he, the Evangelist adds, **and the Word was God.**

Aristotle, however, thought that the ideas of all things are in God, and that in God, the intellect, the one understanding, and what is understood, are the same. Nevertheless, he thought that the world is coeternal with him. Against this the Evangelist says, **He,** the Word alone, **was in the beginning with God,** in such a way that **He** does not exclude another person, but only another coeternal nature.

66 Note the difference in what has been said between John and the other Evangelists: how he began his Gospel on a loftier plane than they. They announced Christ the Son of God born in time: "When Jesus was born in Bethlehem" (Mt 2:1): but John presents him existing from eternity: **In the beginning was the Word.** They show him suddenly appearing among men: "Now you dismiss your servant, O Lord, in peace, according to your word; because my eyes have seen your salvation" (Lk 2:29); but John says that he always existed with the Father: **and the Word was with God.** The others show him as a man: "They gave glory to God who had given such authority to men" (Mt 9:8); but John says that he is God: **and the Word was God.** The others say he lives with men: "While living in Galilee, Jesus said to them" (Mt 17:21); but John says that he has always been with the Father: **He was in the beginning with God.**

67 Note also how the Evangelist designedly uses the word was (*erat*) to show that the Word of God transcends all times: present, past and future. It is as though he were saying: He was beyond time: present, past and future, as the Gloss says.

Lecture 7

14a And the Word was made flesh, and made his dwelling among us.

165 Having explained the necessity for the Word's coming in the flesh as well as the benefits this conferred, the Evangelist now shows the way he came (v 14a). He thus resumes the thread with his earlier statement, he **came unto his own.** As if to say: The Word of God came unto his own. But lest anyone suppose that he came by changing his location, he shows the manner in which he came, that is, by an incarnation. For he came in the manner in which he was sent by the Father, by whom he was sent, i.e., he was made flesh. "God sent his Son made from a woman" (Gal 4:4). And Augustine says about this that "He was sent in the manner in which he was made."

According to Chrysostom, however, he is here continuing the earlier statement, **he gave them power to become the sons of God.** As if to say: If you wonder how he was able to give this power to men, i.e., that they become sons of God, the Evangelist answers: because **the Word was made flesh,** he made it possible for us to be made sons of God. "God sent his Son . . . so that we might receive our adoption as sons" (Gal 4:5).

But according to Augustine, he is continuing the earlier statement, **who are born from God.** For since it seemed a hard saying that men be born from God, then, as though arguing in support of this and to produce belief in the existence of the Word, the Evangelist adds something which seems less seemly, namely, that **the Word was made flesh.** As if to say: Do not wonder if men are born from God, because **the Word was made flesh,** i.e., God became man.

166 It should be noted that this statement, **the Word was made flesh,** has been misinterpreted by some and made the occasion of error. For certain ones have presumed that the Word became flesh in the sense that he or something of him was turned into flesh, as when flour is made into bread, and air becomes fire. One of these was Eutyches, who postulated a mixture of natures in Christ, saying that in him the nature of God and of man was the same. We can clearly see that this is false because, as was said above, "the Word was God." Now God is immutable, as is said, "I am the Lord, and I do not change" (Mal 3:6). Hence in no way can it be said that he was turned into another nature. Therefore, one must say in opposition to Eutyches, **the Word was made flesh,** i.e., the Word assumed flesh, but not in the sense that the Word himself is that flesh. It is

as if we were to say: "The man became white," not that he is that white-ness, but that he assumed whiteness.

167 There were others who, although they believed that the Word was not changed into flesh but assumed it, nevertheless said that he assumed flesh without a soul; for it he had assumed flesh with a soul, the Evangelist would have said, "the Word was made flesh with a soul." This was the error of Arius, who said that there was no soul in Christ, but that the Word of God was there in place of a soul.

The falsity of this opinion is obvious, both because it is in conflict with Sacred Scripture, which often mentions the soul of Christ, as: "My soul is sad, even to the point of death" (Mt 26:38), and because certain affections of the soul are observed in Christ which can not possibly exist in the Word of God or in flesh alone: "He began to be sorrowful and troubled" (Mt 26:37). Also, God cannot be the form of a body. Nor can an angel be united to a body as its form, since an angel, according to its very nature, is separated from body, whereas a soul is united to a body as its form. Consequently, the Word of God cannot be the form of a body.

Furthermore, it is plain that flesh does not acquire the specific nature of flesh except through its soul. This is shown by the fact that when the soul has withdrawn from the body of a man or a cow, the flesh of the man or the cow is called flesh only in an equivocal sense. So if the Word did not assume flesh with a soul, it is obvious that he did not assume flesh. But **the Word was made flesh**; therefore, he assumed flesh with a soul.

168 And there were others who, influenced by this, said that the Word did indeed assume flesh with a soul, but this soul was only a sensitive soul, not an intellectual one; the Word took the place of the intellectual soul in Christ's body. This was the error of Apollinaris. He followed Arius for a time, but later in the face of the [scriptural] authorities cited above, was forced to admit a soul in Christ which could be the subject of these emotions. But he said this soul lacked reason and intellect, and that in the man Christ their place was taken by the Word.

This too is obviously false, because it conflicts with the authority of Sacred Scripture in which certain things are said of Christ that cannot be found in his divinity, nor in a sensitive soul, nor in flesh alone; for example, that Christ marvelled, as in Matthew (8:10). For to marvel or wonder is a state which arises in a rational and intellectual soul when a desire arises to know the hidden cause of an observed effect. Therefore, just as sadness compels one to place a sensitive element in the soul of Christ, against Arius, so marvelling or amazement forces one to admit, against Apollinaris, an intellectual element in Christ.

The same conclusion can be reached by reason. For as there is no flesh without a soul, so there is no human flesh without a human soul, which is an intellectual soul. So if the Word assumed flesh which as animated with a merely sensitive soul to the exclusion of a rational soul, he did not assume human flesh; consequently, one could not say: "God became man."

Besides, the Word assumed human nature in order to repair it. Therefore, he repaired what he assumed. But if he did not assume a rational soul, he would not have repaired it. Consequently, no fruit would have accrued to us from the incarnation of the Word; and this is false. Therefore, **the Word was made flesh**, i.e., assumed flesh which was animated by a rational soul.

169 But you may say: If the Word did assume flesh with such a soul, why did the Evangelist not mention "rational soul," instead of only "flesh," saying, **the Word was made flesh**? I answer that the Evangelist had four reasons for doing this.

First, to show the truth of the incarnation against the Manichaeans, who said that the Word did not assume true flesh, but only imaginary flesh, since it would not have been becoming for the Word of the good God to assume flesh, which they regarded as a creature of the devil. And so to exclude this the Evangelist made special mention of the flesh, just as Christ showed the truth of the resurrection to the disciples when they took him for a spirit, saying: "A spirit does not have flesh and bones, as you see that I have" (Lk 24:39).

Secondly, to show the greatness of God's kindness to us. For it is evident that the rational soul has a greater conformity to God than does flesh, and that it would have been a great sign of compassion if the Word had assumed a human soul, as being conformed to himself. But to assume flesh too, which is something far removed from the simplicity of his nature, was a sign of a much greater, indeed, of an incomprehensible compassion. As the Apostle says (1 Tim 3:16): "Obviously great is the mystery of godliness which appeared in the flesh." And so to indicate this, the Evangelist mentioned only flesh.

Thirdly, to demonstrate the truth and uniqueness of the union in Christ. For God is indeed united to other holy men, but only with respect to their soul; so it is said: "She [wisdom] passes into holy souls, making them friends of God and prophets" (Wis 7:27). But that the Word of God is united to flesh is unique to Christ, according to the Psalmist: "I am alone until I pass" (Ps 140:10). "Gold cannot equal it" (Jb 28: 17). So the evangelist, wishing to show the uniqueness of the union in Christ, mentioned only the flesh, saying, **the Word was made flesh**.

Fourthly, to suggest its relevance to man's restoration. For man was weak because of the flesh. And thus the Evangelist, wishing to suggest that the coming of the Word was suited to the task of our restoration, made special mention of the flesh in order to show that the weak flesh was repaired by the flesh of the Word. And this is what the Apostle says: "The law was powerless because it was weakened by the flesh. God, sending his Son in the lifeness of sinful flesh and in reparation for sin, condemned sin in his flesh" (Rom 8.3).

170 A question arises as to why the Evangelist did not say that the Word assumed flesh, but rather that **the Word was made flesh**. I answer that he did this to exclude the error of Nestorius. He said that in Christ there were two persons and two sons, [one being the Son of God] the other being the son of the Virgin. Thus he did not admit that the Blessed Virgin was the mother of God.

But if this were so, it would mean that God did not become man, for one particular *suppositum* cannot be predicated of another. Accordingly, if the person or *suppositum* of the Word is different than the person or *suppositum* of the man, in Christ, then what the Evangelist says is not true, namely, **the Word was made flesh**. For a thing is made or becomes something in order to be it; if, then, the Word is not man, it could not be said that the Word became man. And so the Evangelist expressly said **was made**, and not "assumed," to show that the union of the Word to flesh is not such as was the "lifting up" of the prophets, who were not "taken up" into a unity of person, but for the prophetic act. This union is such as would truly make God man and man God, i.e., that God would be man.

171 There were some, too, who, misunderstanding the manner of the incarnation, did indeed admit that the aforesaid assumption was terminated at a oneness of person, acknowledging in God one person of God and man. But they said that in him there were two hypostases, i.e., two *supposita*; one of the human nature, created and non-eternal, and the other of the divine nature, non-created and eternal. This is the first opinion presented in the *Sentences* (III, d6).

According to this opinion the proposition, "God was made man and man was made God," is not true. Consequently, this opinion was condemned as heretical by the Fifth Council, where it is said: "If anyone shall assert one person and two hypostases in the Lord Jesus Christ, let him be anathema." And so the Evangelist, to exclude any assumption not terminated at a oneness of person, says, **was made**.

172 If you ask how the Word is man, it must be said that he is man in the way that anyone is man, namely, as having human nature. Not that the Word is human nature itself, but he is a divine *suppositum* united to a human nature. The statement, **the Word was made flesh**, does not indicate any change in the Word, but only in the nature newly assumed into the oneness of a divine person. **And the Word was made flesh** through a union to flesh. Now a union is a relation. And relations newly said of God with respect to creatures do not imply a change on the side of God, but on the side of the creature relating in a new way to God.

173 Now follows, **and made his dwelling among us**. This is distinguished in two ways from what went before. The first consists in stating that above the Evangelist dealt with the incarnation of the Word when he said, **the Word was made flesh**; but now he touches on the manner of the incarnation, saying, **and made his dwelling among** us. For according to Chrysostom and Hilary, by the Evangelist saying **the Word was made flesh**, someone might think that he was converted into flesh and that there are not two distinct natures in Christ, but only one nature compounded from the human and divine natures. And so the Evangelist, excluding this, added, **and made his dwelling among us**, i.e., in our nature, yet so as to remain distinct in his own. For what is converted into something does not remain distinct in its nature from that into which it is converted.

Furthermore, something which is not distinct from another does not dwell in it, because to dwell implies a distinction between the dweller and that in which it dwells. But the Word dwelt in our nature; therefore, he is distinct in nature from it. And so, inasmuch as human nature was distinct from the nature of the Word in Christ, the former is called the dwelling place and temple of the divinity, according to John (2:21): "But he spoke of the temple of his body."

174 Now although what is said here by these holy men is orthodox, care must be taken to avoid the reproach which some receive for this. For the early doctors and saints were so intent upon refuting the emerging errors concerning the faith that they seemed meanwhile to fall into the opposite ones. For example, Augustine, speaking against the Manichaeans, who destroyed the freedom of the will, disputed in such terms that he seemed to have fallen into the heresy of Pelagius. Along these lines, John the Evangelist added, **and made his dwelling among us**, so that we would not think there was a mingling or transformation of natures in Christ because he had said, **the Word was made flesh**.

Nestorius misunderstood this phrase, **and made his dwelling among us,** and said that the Son of God was united to man in such a way that there was not one person of God and of man. For he held that the Word was united to human nature only by an indwelling through grace. From this, however, it follows that the Son of God is not man.

175 To clarify this we should know that we can consider two things in Christ: his nature and person. In Christ there is a distinction in nature, but not in person, which is one and the same in the two natures, since the human nature in Christ was assumed into a oneness of person. Therefore, the indwelling which the saints speak of must be referred to the nature, so as to say, he **made his dwelling among** us, i.e., the nature of the Word inhabited our nature; not according to the hypostasis or person, which is the same for both natures in Christ.

176 The blasphemy of Nestorius is further refuted by the authority of Sacred Scripture. For the Apostle calls the union of God and man an emptying, saying of the Son of God: "He, being in the form of God . . . emptied himself, taking the form of a servant" (Phil 2:6). Clearly, God is not said to empty himself insofar as he dwells in the rational creature by grace, because then the Father and the Holy Spirit would be emptying themselves, since they too are said to dwell in man through grace: for Christ, speaking of himself and of the Father says, "We will come to him and make our home with him" (below 14:23); and of the Holy Spirit the Apostle says: "The Spirit of God dwells in us" (1 Cor 3:16).

Furthermore, if Christ was not God as to his person, he would have been most presumptuous to say: "I and the Father are one" (below 10:30), and "Before Abraham came to be, I am," as is said below (8:58). Now "I" refers to the person of the speaker. And the one who was speaking was a man, who, as one with the Father, existed before Abraham.

177 However, another connection [besides that given in 173] with what went before is possible, by saying that above he dealt with the incarnation of the Word, but that now he is treating the manner of life of the incarnate Word, saying, he **made his dwelling among** us, i.e., he lived on familiar terms with us apostles. Peter alludes to this when he says, "During all the time that the Lord Jesus came and went among us" (Acts 1:21). "Afterwards, he was seen on earth" (Bar 3:38).

178 The Evangelist added this for two reasons. First, to show the marvelous likeness of the Word to men, among whom he lived in such a way as to seem one of them. For he not only willed to be like men in nature, but also in living with them on close terms without sin, in order to draw to himself men won over by the charm of his way of life.

Secondly, to show the truthfulness of his [the Evangelist's] statements. For the Evangelist had already said many great things about the Word, and was yet to mention more wonderful things about him; and so that his testimony would be more credible he took as a proof of his truthfulness the fact that he had lived with Christ, saying, he **made his dwelling among us**. As if to say: I can well bear witness to him, because I lived on close terms with him. "We tell you . . . what we have heard, what we have seen with our eyes" (1 Jn 1:1); "God raised him up on the third day, and granted that he be seen, not by all the people, but by witnesses preordained by God," that is, "to us who ate and drank with him" (Acts 10:40).

Sermon II
And in Jesus Christ His Only Son, Our Lord

A. Christ is the Son of God

Not only must Christians believe in one God, and that He is the Creator of heaven and earth and of all things, but they must also believe that God is the Father, of Whom Christ is the True Son.

1. The Scriptural evidence. As St. Peter says in his second canonical Epistle, this is no fable, but an ascertained fact proved by the voice on the mountain: "For we have not by following artificial fables made known to you the power and the presence of our Lord Jesus Christ, but we were eyewitnesses of His greatness. For He received from God the Father honor and glory, the voice coming down to Him from the excellent glory: 'This is my beloved Son, in Whom I am well pleased. Hear ye Him.' And we heard this voice brought from heaven when we were with Him in the holy mount."[1]

Moreover, on several occasions Jesus Christ called God His Father, and Himself the Son of God. The apostles and holy fathers reckoned this among the articles of faith, saying, *And (I believe) in Jesus Christ, His* (i.e., God's) *only Son.*

2. Heresies regarding this doctrine. However, there were heretics who believed this in a distorted sense:

a. Photinus asserted that Christ is the Son of God in the same way as any other good men, who by leading a good life, merit to be called God's sons by adoption through doing God's will. Thus Christ Who led a good life and did the will of God merited to be called a Son of God. Photinus held, in fact, that Christ did not exist before the Blessed Virgin, and that He began to exist when He was con-

---

Source: The Three Greatest Prayers, translated by L. Shapcote (Manchester, NH: Sophia Institute Press, 1990). Reprinted by permission of the publisher. The divisions of the original are followed.

[1] 2 Pet. 1:16–18

ceived of her. Thus he erred in two ways: first, by denying that Christ was the Son of God by nature; and second by asserting that with regard to His whole being, Christ began to exist in time. Our faith, however, holds that Christ is the Son of God by nature, and that He is from eternity.

Now Holy Scripture explicitly contradicts Photinus on both counts. Against the first it states not only that Christ is the Son, but also that He is the only begotten Son: "The only begotten Son Who is in the bosom of the Father, He hath declared Him."[2] Against the second it states: "Before Abraham was, I am"[3] (and it is undeniable that Abraham existed before the Blessed Virgin). For this reason, against the first error the holy Fathers added in another Creed,[4] *the only Son of God;* and against the second, *eternally begotten of the Father.*

b. Sabellius, although he said that Christ was before the Blessed Virgin, denied the distinction between the Person of the Father and the Person of the Son. He said that the Father Himself became incarnate, so that the Person of the Father is the same as that of Christ. But this is erroneous, since it removes the Trinity of Persons, contrary to the words of John 8:16: "I am not alone, but I and the Father Who sent me." It is plain that no one is sent by himself. Accordingly Sabellius lied, and therefore in the [Nicene] Creed of the Fathers, was added *God from God, Light from Light.* In other words, we must believe in God Who is the Son of God the Father, and in God the Son, Who is the Light of the Father Who is Light.

c. Arius, while admitting that Christ was before the Blessed Virgin and that the Person of the Father was distinct from that of the Son, nevertheless attributed to Christ three things: first, that the Son of God is a creature; second, that He is the highest of all creatures made by God, not from eternity but in the course of time; and third, that God the Son was not of the same nature as God the Father, and that therefore He was not truly God.

But this again is erroneous and contrary to the authority of Holy Scripture. For it is said: "I and the Father are one"[5] (i.e., one in nature). Consequently, as the Father always was, so also was the Son; and as the Father is true God, so also is the Son. Accordingly,

---

[2]John 1:18   [3]John 8:58   [4]The Nicene Creed   [5]John 10:30

whereas Arius asserted that Christ was a creature, it is said by the Fathers in the [Nicene] Creed, *true God from true God.* And whereas he said that Christ was not from eternity but from time, on the contrary it is said in the [Nicene] Creed, *begotten not made.* And against his assertion that Christ was not of the same nature as the Father, it was added in the [Nicene] Creed, *one in being with the Father.*

It is clear then that we must believe that Christ is the only-begotten of God and the true Son of God; that He has always existed together with the Father; that the Person of the Son is distinct from the Person of the Father; and that He is one of nature with the Father. This, however, in the present life we believe by faith, but we shall know it by perfect vision in eternal life. Accordingly for our own consolation we shall make a few observations on this point.

B. Christ is the Word of God

1. How this may be understood. We must observe then that various things have various ways of generating. In God, generation is different from the generation of other things, so we cannot obtain a notion of divine generation except through the generation of that creature which approaches nearest to a likeness to God.

Now, as we have stated, nothing is so like God as the human soul. And the manner of generation in the soul is that a man by his soul conceives something which is called the concept of the mind. This concept proceeds from the soul as from its father, and is called the word of the mind or of man. Accordingly the soul by thought generates its word.

Thus the Son of God is nothing else but the Word of God, not like the word that is uttered externally (for this is transitory) but as the word conceived inwardly. Therefore this same Word of God is one nature with God and equal to God.

Thus in speaking of the Word of God, St. John destroys three heresies: first, the heresy of Photinus, when John says, "In the beginning was the Word"; second, that of Sabellius, when he says, "and the Word was with God"; and third, that of Arius, when he says, "and the Word was God."[6]

---

[6]John 1:1

Now a word is not in us in the same way as it is in God. In us our own word is accidental;[7] but in Him, the Word of God is the same as God Himself, since there is nothing in God that is not the divine essence. Yet no one can say that God has not a Word, for it would follow that God is most foolish. Therefore, just as God always was, so also His Word always was. Even as a craftsman makes all things by means of the form or word which he has preconceived in his mind, so, too, God makes all things by His Word as by His art: "All things were made by Him."[8]

2. How we ought to respond to God's words. If, then, God's Word is His Son, and all His words bear a certain likeness to that Word:

a. **We ought to be willing to hear God's words,** for it is a sign that we love God if we willingly hear His words.

b. **We ought also to believe God's words,** since thereby the Word of God (i.e., Christ Who is God's Word) dwells in us, or to quote the Apostle: "That Christ may dwell in your hearts by faith."[9] And, "You have not His word abiding in you."[10]

c. **The Word of God abiding in us should be continually in our thoughts,** since not only should we believe in Him, but also meditate upon Him; otherwise we would derive no profit from His presence. In fact, meditation of this kind is of great assistance against sin: "In my heart I have hidden Thy words that I may not sin against Thee."[11] Again, it is said of the just man, "Day and night he shall meditate on His law."[12] And it is said of the Blessed Virgin that she "kept all these words, pondering on them in her heart."[13]

d. **We ought to communicate God's Word to others** by admonishing them, preaching to them, and inflaming their hearts. Thus the Apostle wrote to the Ephesians, "Let no evil speech proceed from your mouth, but that which is good unto edification."[14] And to the Colossians, "Let the word of Christ dwell in you abundantly: in all wisdom teaching and admonishing one another."[15] And to Tim-

---

[7]*Accidental* in this context means "not of the essence."   [8]John 1:3
[9]Eph. 3:17   [10]John 5:38   [11]Ps. 118:11   [12]Ps. 1:2   [13]Luke 2:19   [14]Eph. 4:29   [15]Col. 3:16

othy, "Preach the word, be insistent in season and out of season, reprove, entreat, rebuke in all patience and doctrine."[16]

e. We ought to put God's words into practice: "Be ye doers of the word and not hearers only, deceiving yourselves."[17]

3. The Virgin Mary responded to God in all of these ways. These five precepts were observed by the Blessed Virgin in their order when she begot the Word of God. First she *heard:* "The Holy Spirit shall come upon thee."[18] Then she *consented* by faith: "Behold the handmaid of the Lord."[19] Third, she *held and bore Him* in her womb. Fourth, she *brought Him forth* and gave birth to Him. Fifth, she *nourished and fed* Him. Hence the Church sings, "The Virgin alone gave her heaven-filled breast to the king of angels."[20]

Sermon III
He Was Conceived by the Holy Spirit and Born of the Virgin Mary

As we have shown, a Christian must believe not only that Christ is the Son of God, but also that He became man. Thus, St. John, having said many subtle things about the Word of God that are hard to understand,[21] goes on to tell us of the Incarnation, saying, "And the Word was made flesh."[22]

A. Analogies by which to understand the Incarnation

In order to throw some light on this subject, I shall illustrate it by means of two examples.

1. The spoken word. In the first place, without doubt, nothing is more like the Word of God than the unvoiced word that is conceived in man's heart. Now the word conceived in the heart is unknown to all except the one who conceives it; it is first known to others when the voice gives utterance to it. Thus the Word of God while yet in the bosom of the Father was known to the Father alone; but when He was

---

[16]2 Tim. 4:2   [17]Jas. 1:22   [18]Luke 1:35   [19]Luke 1:38
[20]Fourth Responsory, Office of the Circumcision, *Dominican Breviary*
[21]John 1:1–13   [22]John 1:14

clothed with flesh as a word is clothed with the voice, then He was first made manifest and known: "Afterwards He was seen on earth and conversed with men."[23]

2. The written word. Another example lies in the fact that although the voiced word is known through hearing, it is not seen or touched; but when it is written, it is both seen and touched. In like manner, the Word of God became both visible and tangible when He was, as it were, written on our flesh.

Just as the parchment on which the king's word is written is called the king's word, so the man united to God's Word in unity of person is called the Word of God: "Take thee a great book and write in it with a man's pen."[24] And therefore the holy Apostles said, *Who was conceived by the Holy Spirit and born of the Virgin Mary.*

B. Errors regarding the Incarnation

On this point there arose many errors, which is why the holy Fathers at the Council of Nicea made several additions in another Creed[25] whereby all these errors stand condemned.

1. Origen said that Christ was born and came into the world in order to save the demons also, and so he asserted that all the demons would be saved at the end of the world. But this is contrary to Holy Scripture, for it said: "Depart from me, ye cursed, into everlasting fire, that was prepared for the devil and his angels."[26] Therefore, in order to exclude this, the following clause was added: *For us men* (not for the demons) *and for our salvation*, thus stressing God's love for us.

2. Photinus admitted that Christ was born of the Virgin Mary, but asserted that He was a mere man, Who by leading a good life and doing God's will, merited to become a son of God, even as other holy men. And against this it is said: "I came down from heaven, not to do my will, but the will of Him Who sent me."[27] Now it goes without saying that He would not have come down from there unless He had been there, and if He were a mere man He would not have been in heaven. Therefore, in order to exclude this, the following words were added: *He came down from heaven.*

---

[23]Bar. 3:38   [24]Isa. 8:1   [25]The Nicene Creed   [26]Matt. 25:41
[27]John 6:38

3. The Manicheans said that although the Son of God always existed, and came down from heaven, yet He had flesh not really but only apparently. But this is false, since it was unbecoming for the Teacher of truth to have anything false about Him. Therefore since He had flesh ostensibly, He really had it. Thus it is said: "Handle and see; for a spirit hath not flesh and bones, as you see me to have."[28] Therefore, in order to exclude this, they added, [29] *And He took flesh.*

4. Ebion,[30] who was of Jewish nationality, said that Christ was born of the Blessed Virgin from sexual intercourse and fecundation by the male seed. But this is false, since the Angel said, "For that which is conceived in her is of the Holy Spirit."[31] Therefore the holy Fathers excluded this by adding, *By the power of the Holy Spirit.*

5. Valentine, while confessing that Christ was conceived by the Holy Spirit, taught that the Holy Spirit fashioned a heavenly body which He placed in the Virgin's womb; this was Christ's body. Thus the Blessed Virgin's cooperation was reduced to her serving as a place for Christ's body. Hence Valentine said that Christ's body passed through the Blessed Virgin as through a channel. But this is false, because the Angel said, "The Holy One that shall be born of thee shall be called the Son of God."[32] And the Apostle says, "When the fullness of time came, God sent His Son made of a woman."[33] For this reason they added, *Born of the Virgin Mary.*

6. Arius and Apollinarius said that though Christ was the Word of God born of the Virgin Mary, He had no soul but the Godhead in lieu thereof. But this is contrary to Scripture, for Christ said, "Now is my soul troubled"[34] and "My soul is sorrowful even unto death."[35] The holy Fathers excluded this by adding, *And became man*, because a man is composed of a soul and a body. So Christ had whatever a man can have, except sin.

7. Eutyches. In that He is said to have become man, all the aforesaid errors stand condemned, as well as all possible errors, especially that of

---

[28]Luke 24:39   [29]Currently this is translated: *And became man.*   [30]The Ebionites were a sect whose doctrines were a mixture of Gnosticism and Judaism. [31]Matt. 1:20   [32]Luke 1:35   [33]Gal. 4:4   [34]John 12:27   [35]Matt. 26:38

Eutyches, who maintained that the divine and human natures were mixed together so as to form one nature in Christ that is neither purely divine nor purely human. This is false, since in that case He would not be a man, and this would be contrary to the words, "And became man."

8. Nestorius. The error of Nestorius also stands condemned, for he said that the Son of God was united to man solely by indwelling. But this is false, because then He would not *be* a man, but *in* a man. That He became man is declared by the Apostle: "He was in habit found as a man."[36] "Ye seek to kill me, a man who have spoken the truth to you, which I have heard of God."[37]

C. Benefits of belief in the Incarnation

From what has been said we may gather a few points for our instruction:

1. Our faith is strengthened. For instance, if anyone were to tell us about a distant country which he had never visited, we would not believe him to the same extent as if he had been there. Accordingly, before Christ came into the world, the patriarchs, prophets, and John the Baptist said certain things about God, but men did not believe them as they believe Christ Who was with God, Who indeed was one with God. For this reason our faith is very strong, seeing that we have received it from Christ: "No man has ever seen God; the only begotten Son, Who is in the bosom of the Father, He hath declared Him."[38] So it is that many mysteries of faith have been made known to us after the coming of Christ, which until then were hidden.

2. Our hope is raised, because it is evident that God's Son took our flesh and came to us not for a trifling reason, but for our exceedingly great good. He bound Himself to us, as it were, by deigning to take a human soul and body and to be born of a Virgin, in order to bestow His Godhead on us. Thus He became man that man might become God: "By Whom we have access through faith into this grace wherein we stand; and glory in the hope of the glory of the sons of God."[39]

3. Our charity is inflamed, because there is no greater proof of God's love than that God the Creator became a creature, that our Lord

---

[36]Phil. 2:7   [37]John 8:40   [38]John 1:18   [39]Rom. 5:2

became our brother, and that the Son of God became the Son of man: "God so loved the world that He gave His only begotten son."[40] The very thought of this should kindle and inflame our hearts with the love of God.

4. We are encouraged to keep our souls pure, because our nature was ennobled and raised through being united to God, to the extent of being assumed into union with a divine Person. Thus after the Incarnation the Angel would not allow St. John to worship him,[41] whereas an angel had suffered this from even the greatest patriarchs.[42] Consequently, man ought to bear this exaltation in mind, and in consideration of it should disdain to debase himself and his nature by falling into sin. For this reason St. Peter says, "By Whom He hast given us most great and precious promises; that by these you may be made partakers of the divine nature, flying the corruption of that concupiscence which is in the world."[43]

5. Our desire to go to Christ is inflamed. For a man whose brother is king in a far distant country will have a great longing to go to him, to be with and stay with him. Thus, seeing that Christ is our brother, we should long to be with Him and to be united to Him: "Wheresoever the body is, there will the eagles be gathered together."[44] The Apostle also desired "to be dissolved and to be with Christ."[45] This same desire increases in us when we meditate on Christ's Incarnation.

Sermon IV

He Suffered under Pontius Pilate,
Was Crucified, Died and Was Buried

A. Christ's death is difficult to conceive

Just as a Christian is required to believe in the Incarnation of the Son of God, so is it necessary that he believe in His Passion and Death, because as Augustine says, "His birth would have profited us nothing had we not profited by His Redemption."

---

[40]John 3:16   [41]Rev. 22:8,9   [42]Cf. Gen. 18:2; 19:1–2   [43]2 Pet. 1:4
[44]Matt. 24:28   [45]Phil. 1:23

That Christ did indeed die for us is so hard to conceive that scarcely is our mind able to grasp it; in fact it is utterly beyond our understanding. The Apostle insinuates this when he says, "I work a work in your days, a work which you will not believe if any man shall tell it to you."[46] In fact, so great is God's favor and love in our regard that He has done more for us than we are able to understand. However, we are not to believe that Christ suffered death in such a way that His Godhead died, but that His human nature died; for He died not as God, but as man. This may be illustrated by examples.

1. The analogy in ourselves. It is clear that when a man dies, it is not the soul, but the body or the flesh that dies when body and soul are separated. Accordingly when Christ died, it was not His Godhead that died, but His human nature. But surely if the Jews did not kill His Godhead, they sinned no more than if they had killed any other man.

I reply that a man who bespatters a king's robe is as guilty as though he had bespattered the king himself. Hence the Jews, though they could not slay God, yet for slaying the human nature wherewith Christ was clothed, were punished as though they had slain the Godhead.

2. The analogy of a king's parchment. As we have said above, the Son of God is the Word of God, and the Word of God was made flesh even as the king's word is inscribed on parchment. If, then, one were to tear the king's parchment, he would be held as guilty as if he had torn the king's word. Hence the Jews are held to be as guilty as if they had slain the Word of God.

B. Why Christ suffered for us

But what need was there for the Word of God to suffer for us? That the need was great may be assigned to two reasons. One was the need for a remedy for sin; the other was the need for an example of what we ought to do.

1. Christ's passion remedies the evils incurred through sin. We find a remedy inasmuch as Christ's Passion proves a remedy for all the evils that we incur through sin. These evils are of five kinds:

a. The stain of sin. For when a man sins, he defiles his soul. Just as virtue is the soul's beauty, so is sin its stain: "How happeneth it,

---

[46]Acts 13:41 (quoting Hab. 1:5)

O Israel, that thou are in thy enemies' land? . . . Thou art defiled with the dead."[47] This is removed by Christ's Passion, for Christ by His Passion poured out His blood as a laver in which sinners are cleansed. "He hath washed us from our sins in His own blood."[48] Now the soul is cleansed by Christ's blood in Baptism, which from Christ's blood derives the power of regeneration. Consequently, when a man defiles himself with sin, he does an injury to Christ, and sins more grievously than before he was baptized: "A man making void the law of Moses dieth without any mercy under two or three witnesses; how much more, think you, he deserveth worse punishments who hath trodden underfoot the Son of God and hath esteemed the blood of the testament unclean?"[49]

b. The anger of God. For just as a carnal man loves carnal beauty, so does God love spiritual beauty, which is that of the soul. When, therefore, the soul is defiled by sin, God is offended and the sinner becomes an object of His hatred: "To God the wicked and his wickedness are hateful."[50] But Christ's Passion removes this, because He atoned to God the Father for sin, for which man himself was unable to atone. Christ's charity and obedience were greater than the sin and disobedience of the first man: "When we were enemies we were reconciled to God by the death of His Son."[51]

c. Weakness, which we incur because a man thinks that if he sins once he will be able afterwards to refrain from sinning, whereas it is quite the reverse that happens. For by the first sin he is weakened and is more inclined to sin again; also sin has a greater power over him. Moreover, so far as he is concerned, he puts himself in a state from which there is no escape—like a man who jumps into a well— except by the power of God. So after man had sinned, our nature was weakened and corrupted, and thus man was more prone to sin.

But Christ diminished this weakness and infirmity, although He did not remove it altogether. And yet man is so strengthened and sin is so weakened by Christ's Passion, that sin has no longer such power over him. Man, by the help of God's grace bestowed in the Sacraments, which derive their efficacy from Christ's Passion, is able to endeavor to arise from his sins. Thus says the Apostle, "Our

---

[47]Bar. 3:10,11   [48]Rev. 1:5   [49]Heb. 10:28, 29   [50]Wisd. 14:9
[51]Rom. 5:10

old man is crucified with Him, that the body of sin may be destroyed."[52] For before Christ's Passion there were few who lived without falling into mortal sin, whereas afterwards many have lived and are living without mortal sin.

d. The debt of punishment, which we incur because God's justice demands that whoever sins should be punished. Now punishment is awarded according to guilt. Thus, since the guilt of mortal sin is infinite, being against the infinite good (namely, God) Whose commandments the sinner holds in contempt, it follows that the punishment due to mortal sin is infinite.

But Christ by His Passion delivered us from this punishment which He bore Himself: "He bore our sins in His body"[53] (i.e., the punishment due to our sins). For His Passion was so efficacious that it suffices to atone for all the sins of the whole world, even of a hundred thousand worlds.

For this reason when a man is baptized he is released from all his sins; so also it is that a priest forgives sins; and again that the more a man conforms to the Passion of Christ, the more is he pardoned and the more grace he merits.

e. Banishment from the kingdom. Those who offend their king are compelled to leave the kingdom, and thus on account of sin man is banished from paradise. For this reason, immediately after he had sinned Adam was banished from paradise and the gates of Eden were closed.

But Christ by His Passion opened the gates and recalled the exiles to the kingdom. For when Christ's side was pierced, the gates of paradise were opened, and by the shedding of His blood the stain of sin was wiped away, God was appeased, man's weakness was removed, his punishment was expiated, and the exiles were called back to the kingdom. Hence the thief received the immediate response, "This day shalt thou be with me in Paradise."[54] This had not been said of old—not to Adam, not to Abraham, not to David. But "this day" (i.e., as soon as the gates were opened) the thief having sought pardon, found it: "Having . . . confidence in the entering into the holies by the blood of Christ."[55]

---

[52]Rom. 6:6   [53]1 Pet. 2:24   [54]Luke 23:43   [55]Heb. 10:19

2. Christ's passion as a model of virtues

Accordingly it is clear how profitable was Christ's Passion as a remedy, but it is not less profitable as an example. For as St. Augustine says, Christ's Passion affords us a model in all the circumstances of life, since whoever wishes to lead a perfect life needs only to despise what Christ despised on the Cross and to desire what He desired. There is no virtue an example of which we do not find on the Cross.

a. Charity. If you seek an example of charity, "greater love hath no man than that he lays down his life for his friends,"[56] and this Christ did on the Cross. If He laid down His life for us, we should not deem it a hardship to suffer any evils whatever for His sake: "What shall I render unto the Lord for all the things which He hath rendered to me?"[57]

b. Patience. If you seek an example of patience, you will find a most perfect example on the Cross. For a man's patience is proved to be great on two counts: either when he suffers great evils patiently or when he suffers that which he is able to avoid yet does not avoid.

Now Christ suffered greatly on the Cross: 'O all ye that pass by the way, attend and see if there be any sorrow like unto my sorrow."[58] And He suffered patiently inasmuch as "when He suffered He threatened not."[59] "He shall be led as a sheep to the slaughter, and shall be dumb as a lamb before His shearer."[60]

Moreover He could have escaped but did not escape: "Thinkist thou that I cannot ask my Father and He will give me presently more than twelve legions of angels?"[61] Great therefore was Christ's patience on the Cross: "Let us run by patience to the fight proposed to us; looking on Jesus the author and finisher of faith Who, having joy set before Him, endured the Cross, despising the shame."[62]

c. Humility. If you seek an example of humility, look on the Crucified. Although He was God, He chose to be judged by Pontius Pilate and to suffer death: "Thy cause hath been judged as that of the wicked"[63] Truly *as that of the wicked* because: "Let us condemn

---

[56]John 15:13   [57]Ps. 115:12   [58]Lam. 1:12   [59]1 Pet. 2:23
[60]Isa. 53:7   [61]Matt. 26:53   [62]Heb. 12:1,2   [63]Job 36:17

Him to a most shameful death."[64] The Master chose to die for His servant; the Life of the Angels suffered death for man: "Made obedient unto death."[65]

d. Obedience. If you seek an example of obedience, follow Him Who was made obedient to the Father even unto death: "As by the disobedience of one man, many were made sinners, so also by the obedience of one, many shall be made just."[66]

e. Contempt for earthly things. If you seek an example of contempt for earthly things, follow Him, the King of kings and Lord of lords, in Whom are the treasures of wisdom; and see Him on the Cross, despoiled, derided, spat upon, scourged, crowned with thorns, served with gall and hyssop, dead. Therefore, take no account of your apparel or possessions, since "they parted my garments amongst them";[67] nor of honors, since I suffered Myself to be jeered at and scourged; nor of rank, since they plaited a crown of thorns and placed it on my head; nor of pleasures, since "in my thirst they gave me vinegar to drink."[68] Thus Augustine in commenting on Heb. 12:2 ("Who, having joy set before Him, endured the Cross, despising the shame") says, "Christ the man despised all earthly things in order to teach us to despise them."

---

[64]Wisd. 2:20   [65]Phil. 2:8   [66]Rom. 5:19   [67]Ps. 21:19   [68]Ps. 68:22

KEY TO AQUINAS'S SOURCES

The sources given in Aquinas's texts and listed below should be quite easy to find in most cases, simply by looking up the author. For example, St. Bonaventure's works will be found in the standard Latin editions of this author edited at Quaracchi, Italy, in the ten-volume collection of his *Opera omnia* (or collected works). Others, however, are found in particular collections or editions that are noted in the footnotes to Aquinas's texts. The following short introduction to such collections and editions will make it easier to find the location of the reference.

Aristotle	*Aristotelis Opera*, ed. I. Bekker (Berlin: G. Reimerum, 1831–70).
CCL	*Corpus Christianorum Series Latina* (Turnhout, Belgium: Brepols, 1954—).
Conc.	*Enchiridion symbolorum, definitionum et declarationum de rebus fidei et morum*, ed. H Denzinger and C. Bannwart (Freiburg, Germany: B. Herder, 1913).
CSEL	*Corpus Scriptorum Ecclesiasticorum Latinorum* (Vienna: C. Geroldi and Hoelder, Pichler and Tempsky, 1866—).
Glossa interlinearis	*Biblia sacra cum glossa . . . et postilla Nicolai Lyrani* (Paris, 1590 and Lyons, 1545).
Glossa ordinaria	In *Biblia sacra* above.

Albert

De 15 Problem.	*De quindecim problematibus* (On fifteen Problems)
Enarr. in Ioann.	*Enarrationes in Ioannis Evangelium* (Comments on the Gospel of John)
In IV Sent.	*Commentarium in Sententias* (Commentary on the Sentences of Peter Lombard)
Metaph.	*Commentarium in Metaphysicam Aristotelis* (Commentary on the Metaphysics of Aristotle)

Alexander of Hales

Summa Theol.	*Summa Theologica* (Theological Summa)

Ambrose

De Fide	Exposition on the Christian Faith
In Luc.	*Homiliae in Lucam* (Homilies on Luke's Gospel)

Anonymous   *De causis* (On Causes)

Anselm

De Ver.	*De veritate* (On Truth)
Proslog.	*Proslogium* (Proslogion)

Aristotle

De An.	*De anima* (On the Soul)
De Caelo	On the Heavens
De Interpretatione	On Interpretation
De Part. Anim.	*De partibus animalium* (On the Parts of Animals)
De Plantis	On Plants
Metaph.	*Metaphysica* (Metaphysics)
Nic. Ethics or *Eth.*	*Ethica Nicomachea* (Nicomachean Ethics)
Phys.	*Physica* (Physics)
Post. Anal.	*Analytica Posteriora* (Posterior Analytics)
Soph. Elench.	*De sophisticis elenchis* (On Sophistical Refutations)

Augustine

Confess.	*Confessiones* (Confessions)
Contra Faust.	*Contra Faustum* (Against Faustus)
Contra Julian.	*Contra Julianum* (Against Julian)
De Civit. Dei	*De civitate Dei* (The City of God)
De Doc. Christ.	*De doctrina Christiana* (On Christian Teaching)
De Fide et Oper.	*De fide et operibus* (On Faith and Works)
De Genesi ad Litt.	*De Genesi ad litteram* (Literal Meaning of Genesis)
De Haeres.	*De haeresibus* (On Heresies)
De Praedest. Sanct.	*De praedestinatone Sanctorum* (On the Predestination of the Saints)
De Serm. Dom.	*De Sermone Domini* (On the Lord's Prayer)
De Trin.	*De Trinitate* (On the Trinity)
De Util. Cred.	*De utilitate credendi* (On the Necessity of Believing)
De Vera Relig.	*De vera religione* (On True Religion)
Enchir.	*Enchiridion* (Handbook)
Epist.	*Epistolae* (Letters)
Lib. 83 Quaest.	*Liber 83 quaestionum* (83 Different Questions)
Quaest. Evang.	*Quaestiones super Evangelia* (Questions on the Gospels)
Serm.	*Sermones* (Sermons)
Tract. super Ioann.	*Tractatus super Ioannis Evangelium* (Treatises on the Gospel of John)

Averroes
In Metaph.   *Commentarium in Metaphysicam Aristotelis* (Commentary on Aristotle's *Metaphysics*)

Bernard
Serm. de Diversis   *Sermones de diversis* (Sermons on Different Subjects)

Boethius
Arithm.   *De musica* (Fundamentals of Music)
De Consol.   *De consolatione philosophiae* (The Consolation of Philosophy)
De Differ. Top.   *De differentiis topicis* (On Topical Differences)
De Hebdom.   *De hebdomadibus* (On the Hebdomads)
De Trin.   *De Trinitate* (On the Trinity)
In Cat. Arist.   *In Categorias Aristotelis* (On Aristotle's Categories)
In Top. Cicer.   *In Ciceronis Topica* (On the Topics of Cicero)

Bonaventure
In Hexaëm.   *Collationes in Hexaëmeron* (Sermons on the Six Days of Creation)
Itin. Mentis in Deum   *Itinerarium Mentis in Deum* (Journey of the Mind to God)
Sent., In I Sent., In II Sent., etc.   *Commentarium in Sententias* (Commentary on the *Sentences* of Peter Lombard)

Chyrsostom
In Matt.   *Homiliae in Matthaeum* (Homilies on the Gospel of St. Matthew)

Cicero
De Divinat.   *De divinatione* (On Divination)
De Invent.   *De inventione* (On Discovery)
De Officiis   *De officiis* (On Duties)

Cicero (Pseudo-)
Rhetor. ad Herenn.   *Rhetorica ad Herennum* (Rhetoric for Herennus)

Commentator   Cf. Averroes

Conc. Arausic., II   *Acta Concilii Secundi Arausicani* (Acts of the Second Council of Orange)

Conc. Chalced.	*Acta Concilii Chalcedonensis* (Acts of the Council of Chalcedon)
Conc. Ephes.	*Acta Concilii Ephesini* (Acts of the Council of Ephesus)
Damascene	See John Damascene.

Dionysius Areopagita (Pseudo-)

De Cael. Hier.	*De caelesti hierarchia* (On the Celestial Hierarchy)
De Div. Nom.	*De divinis nominibus* (On the Divine Names)
De Eccles. Hier.	*De ecclesiastica hierarchia* (On the Ecclesiastical Hierarchy)

Fulgentius

De Fide ad Petrum	To Peter concerning the Faith
Glossa Interl. or *Glossa interlinearis*	Interlineary Gloss on the Scriptures
Glossa ordino. or *Glossa ordinaria*	Ordinary Gloss on the Scriptures

Gratian

Decretum	Decretum

Gregory the Great

In Evang. or *Hom.*	*Homiliae in Evangelia* (Homilies on the Gospels)
In Ezech.	*Homiliae in Ezechielem* (Homilies on Ezechiel)
Moral.	*Moralia in Job* (On the Book of Job)

Hermes Trismegistus (Pseudo-)

Lib. 24 Philosoph.	*Liber viginti quattuor Philosophorum* (Book of the 24 Philosophers)

Hilary

De Trinitate	On the Trinity

Hugh of St. Victor

De Sacram.	*De Sacramentis fidei Christianae* (On the Sacraments of the Christian Faith)
De Scriptur. et Scriptor. Sacris	*De scripturis et scriptoribibus sacris* (On the Scriptures and Sacred Writers)

Summa Sent.   *Summa Sententiarum* (Summa of Sentences)

Isidore
Quaest. in Vet. Test.   *Quaestiones in Vetus Testamentum* (Questions
                                      on the Old Testament)

Jerome
Comm. in Esaiam or   *Commentarium in Isaiam prophetam*
  Isaiam   (Commentary on Isaiah the Prophet)
Ep. 21 ad Damasum
Ep. 22
Ep. 56 ad Pammachium
Ep. 70 ad Magnum
Epist. or *Ep.*   (Letters)
In Osee   *Commentarium in Osee prophetam*
                                      (Commentary on Hosea the Prophet)
Liber psalmorum   Commentary on the Book of Psalms

John Damascence
De Fide Orth.   *De fide orthodoxa* (On the Orthodox Faith)

Macrobius
In Somn. Scipion.   *In somnium Scipionis* (The Dream of Scipio)

Maimonides, Moses
Guide   *Dux neutrorum* (Guide for the Perplexed)

Nemesius Emesenus
De Nat. Hom.   *De natura hominis* (On the Nature of Man)

Origen
De principiis   *Periarchon* (On First Principles)

Peter Lombard
Glossa   Glosses on Scripture
In I Cor.   *Commentarium in Epistolam I ad Corinthios*
                                      (Commentary on the First Letter to the
                                      Corinthians)
In Gal.   *Commentarium in Epistolam ad Galatas*
                                      (Commentary on the Letter to the
                                      Galatians)
In Rom.   *Commentarium in Epistolam ad Romanos*
                                      (Commentary on the Letter to the
                                      Romans)

In II Tim.	*Commentarium in Epistolam II ad Timotheum* (Commentary on the Second Letter to Timothy)
Sent.	*Sententiae* (Sentences)

Richard of St. Victor
De Trin. — *De Trinitate* (On the Trinity)

Robert Grosseteste
Hexaëm. — *Hexaëmeron* (On the Six Days of Creation)

Robert Kilwardby
De Nat. Theol. — *De natura theologiae* (On the Nature of Theology)

Rufinus
In Symb. Apost. — *In Symbolum Apostolorum* (Commentary on the Apostles' Creed)

Symb. Nicaeno-Constantinopolitanum — *Symbolum Nicaeno-Constantinopolitanum* (The Nicene Creed)

Symb. "Quicumque" — *Symbolum "Quicumque"* (The Creed beginning with "Whoever")

Theophanes
Chronographia — Chronography

Thomas Aquinas — See the Bibliography.

Tully — See Cicero.

Vigilius Thapsensis
De unitate Trinitatis — On the Unity of the Trinity

William of Auxerre
Summa Aurea — The Golden Summa

BIBLIOGRAPHY

Works of St. Thomas Aquinas

For a detailed bibliography of Thomas Aquinas's works, see the adaptation of Giles Emery's French bibliography that was made for the English edition of Jean-Pierre Torrell, *Saint Thomas Aquinas: The Person and His Work*, 330–61.

General Theological Works

Scriptum super libros Sententiarum. (no English trans.)

Summa contra Gentiles. (*Saint Thomas Aquinas, On the Truth of the Catholic Faith*, 5 vols. Ed. A. C. Pegis, J. F. Anderson, V. J. Bourke, C. J. O'Neill. Garden City: Image Books, 1955–57. Reprinted by the University of Notre Dame Press, IN, 1975.)

Summa Theologiae or *Summa Theologica.* (*Summa Theologiae*. 60 vols. Ed. T. Gilby and T. C. O'Brien. London and New York: Blackfriars, 1964–73.)

Disputed Questions

De anima. (*Saint Thomas Aquinas, Questions on the Soul*. Trans. J. H. Robb. Milwaukee: Marquette University Press, 1984.)

De malo. (*Saint Thomas Aquinas, Disputed Questions on Evil*. Trans. J. and J. Oesterle. Notre Dame, IN: University of Notre Dame Press, 1983.)

De potentia. (*Saint Thomas Aquinas, On the Power of God*. 3 vols. Ed. L. Shapcote. London: Blackfriars, 1932–34.)

De quolibet I–XII. (*Saint Thomas Aquinas. Quodlibetal Questions 1 and 2*. Trans. S. Edwards [Mediaeval Sources in Translation, 27]. Toronto: Pontifical Institute of Medieval Studies, 1983.)

De spiritualibus creaturis. (*Saint Thomas Aquinas. On Spiritual Creatures*. Trans. M. C. Fitzpatrick and J. J. Wellmuth. Milwaukee: Marquette University Press, 1949.)

De unione Verbi incarnati. (no English trans.).

De veritate. (*Saint Thomas, On Truth*. 3 vols. Trans. R. W. Mulligan, J. V. McGlynn, R. W. Schmidt. Chicago: H. Regnery, 1952–54.)

De virtutibus. (*On the Virtues* [in general]. Trans. J. P. Reid. Providence: Providence College Press, 1951. *On Charity*. Trans. L. H. Kenzierski. Milwaukee: Marquette University Press, 1960.)

Commentaries on the Bible

Catena aurea. (*Saint Thomas Aquinas. Catena aurea: Commentary on the Four Gospels*. 4 vols. Trans. M. Pattison, J. D. Dalgairns, and T. D. Ryder. Oxford: J. Parker, 1874.)

Inaugural sermons on Scripture: "Rigans montes de superioribus" and "Hic est liber mandatorum Dei." (The first was translated into English by S. Tugwell, *Albert and Thomas. Selected Writings*. Mahwah, NY: Panlist Press, 1988.)

Postilla super Psalmos. (no English trans.).

Super epistolas Pauli Apostoli. (*Saint Thomas Aquinas. Commentary on Saint Paul's Epistle to the Galatians*. Trans. F. R. Larcher. Albany: Magi Books, 1966. *Commentary on Saint Paul's Epistle to the Ephesians*. Trans. M. L. Lamb. Albany: Magi Books, 1966. *Commentary on Saint Paul's First Letter to the Thessalonians*. Trans. F. R. Archer and M. Duffy. Albany: Magi Books, 1969. *Commentary on Saint Paul's Letter to the Philippians*. Trans. F. R. Larcher. Albany: Magi Books, 1969.)

Super Ieremiam et Threnos. (no English trans.).

Super Ioannem. (*Saint Thomas Aquinas. Commentary on the Gospel of Saint John*, part I. Trans. J. A. Weisheipl and F. R. Larcher. Albany: Magi Books, 1980.)

Super Iob ad litteram. (*The Literal Exposition on Job: A Scriptural Commentary concerning Providence*. Trans. A. Damico [Classics of Religious Studies, 7]. Atlanta: Scholars Press, 1989.)

Super Isaiam ad litteram. (no English trans.).

Super Matthaeum. (no English trans.).

Commentaries on Aristotle's Works

De anima. (*Aristotle's De anima with the Commentary of St. Thomas Aquinas*. Trans. K. Foster and S. Humphries. New Haven: Yale University Press, 1951. Reprinted by Dumb Ox Books, Notre Dame, IN, 1994.)

De sensu et sensato. (English trans. in preparation).

Super Analytica Posteriora. (*Saint Thomas Aquinas. Exposition of the Posterior Analytics of Aristotle*. Trans. F. R. Archer. Albany: Magi Books, 1970.)

Super De caelo et mundo. (*Exposition of Aristotle's Treatise on the Heavens*. Trans. P. Conway and F. R. Larcher. Columbus: College of St. Mary of the Springs, photocopy, 1963–64.)

Super De generatione et corruptione. (*On Generation and Corruption*. Trans. P. Conway and W. H. Kane. Columbus: College of St. Mary of the Springs, photocopy, n. d.)

Super libros Ethicorum. (*Saint Thomas Aquinas. Commentary on the Nicomachean Ethics*. 2 vols. Trans. C. I. Litzinger. Chicago: Regnery, 1964. Reprinted by Dumb Ox Books, Notre Dame, IN, 1993.)

Super libros Politicorum. (English trans. in preparation).

Super Metaphysicam. (*Saint Thomas Aquinas. Commentary on the Metaphysics of Aristotle.* 2 vols. Trans. J. P. Rowan. Chicago: Regnery, 1964. Reprinted by Dumb Ox Books, Notre Dame, IN, 1995.)

Super Meteora. (*On Meterology.* Trans. P. Conway and F. R. Larcher. Columbus: College of St. Mary of the Springs, photocopy, 1964.)

Super Perihermenias. (*Aristotle on Interpretation: Commentary by St. Thomas and Cajetan.* Trans. J. T. Oesterle. Milwaukee: Marquette University Press, 1962.)

Super Physicam. (*Thomas de Aquino: Commentary on Aristotle's "Physics."* Trans. R. J. Blackwell et ali. New Haven: Yale University Press, 1963.)

Commentaries on Boethius, Pseudo-Dionysius, and the *Liber De causis*

Super Boethium De hebdomadibus. (no English trans.).

Super Boethium De Trinitate. (*Saint Thomas Aquinas. Faith, Reason, and Theology: Questions I–IV of His Commentary on the De Trinitate of Boethius. Saint Thomas Aquinas. The Division and Methods of the Sciences: Questions V and VI of his Commentary on the De Trinitate of Boethius* [Mediaeval Sources in Translation, 3 and 32]. Trans. A. A. Maurer. Toronto: Pontifical Institute of Mediaeval Studies, 1986 and 1987.)

Super librum De causis. (*St. Thomas Aquinas, Commentary on the Book of Causes.* Trans. V. A. Guagliaro, C. R. Hess, and R. C. Taylor. Washington, DC: The Catholic University of America Press, 1996.)

Super librum Dionysii De divinis nominibus. (no English trans.).

Special Treatises

Compendium theologiae. (*Compendium of Theology.* Trans. C. Vollert. St. Louis: Herder, 1952.)

De ente et essentia. (*Aquinas on Being and Essence.* Trans. A. A. Maurer. Toronto: Pontifical Institute of Mediaeval Studies, 1968.)

De principiis naturae. (Complete trans. found in *The Pocket Aquinas.* Trans. V. J. Bourke. New York: Pocket Books, 1973.)

De regno. (*On Kingship, to the King of Cyprus.* Trans. G. B. Phelan and I. T. Eschmann. Toronto: Pontifical Institute of Mediaeval Studies, 1949.)

De substantiis separatis. (*Treatise on Separate Substances.* Trans. F. J. Lescoe. West Hartford: St. Joseph's College, 1959.)

Minor Works

Collationes in decem praecepta. (*The Commandments of God.* Trans. L. Shapcote. London: Blackfriars, 1937.)

Collationes in orationem dominicam, in Symbolum Apostorum, in salutationem angeli-
   cam. (*The Three Greatest Prayers.* Trans. L. Shapcote. Manchester, NH: Sophia
   Institute Press, 1990.)

Contra errores Graecorum. (no English trans.).

De articulis fidei. (Partial trans. J. B. Collins, part 2. "On the Sacraments," *Cate-
   chetical Instructions of St. Thomas.* New York: Wagner, 1953.)

De emptione et venditione ad tempus. ("On Buying and Selling on Credit." *Irish
   Ecclesiastical Record* 31 [1928]: 159–65.)

De forma absolutionis. (no English trans.).

De iudiciis astrorum. (no English trans.).

De mixtione elementorum. ("On the Combining of the Elements." Trans. V. R. Larkin. *Isis* 51 [1960]: 67–72.)

De motu cordis. ("On the movement of the Heart." Trans. V. R. Larkin. *Journal of
   the History of Medicine* 15 [1960]: 22–30.)

De operationibus occultis naturae. (*The Letter of St. Thomas Aquinas De occultis operi-
   bus naturae* [Philosophical Studies, 42]. Trans. J. B. McAllister. Washington,
   DC: The Catholic University of America Press, 1939.)

De rationibus fidei ad Cantorem Antiochenum. (Partial trans. H. Nash. "Why Did
   God the Son Become Man?" Chapter 5 of *Life of the Spirit.* London: Blackfriars, 1952.)

De secreto. (English summary in V. J. Bourke, *Aquinas' Search for Wisdom.* Milwaukee: Bruce Publishing Company, 1965, 143–46.)

De sortibus. (no English trans.).

Epistola ad Bernardum. (Partial trans. V. J. Bourke. *Aquinas's Search for Wisdom.*
   Milwaukee: Bruce Publishing Company, 1965, 114–15.)

Epistola ad ducissam Brabantiae. ("On the Government of Jews in Aquinas,"
   Aquinas: Selected Political Writings. Ed. A. P. d'Entrèves. Trans. J. G. Dawson.
   Oxford: B. Blackwell, 1948, 84–95.)

Officium de festo Corporis Christi. (no English trans.).

Responsio ad lectorem Bisuntinum. (no English trans.).

Responsiones ad lectorem Venetum. (no English trans.).

Responsio ad magistrum Ioannem de Vercellis. (no English trans.).

Bibliographical Sources

Bourke, V. J. *Thomistic Bibliography, 1920–1940.* St. Louis: The Modern School-
   man, 1945.

———, and T. L. Miethe. *Thomistic Bibliography, 1940–1978.* Westport, CT:
   Greenwood Press, 1980.

Ingardia, R. *Thomas Aquinas: International Bibliography, 1977–1990*. Bowling Green, KY: The Philosophy Documentation Center, 1992.

Secondary Sources

Adams, R. M. *The Virtue of Faith and Other Essays in Philosophical Theology.* New York: Oxford University Press, 1987.

Aertsen, J. A. *Nature and Creature. Thomas Aquinas's Way of Thought.* (Studien und Texte zur Geistesgeschichte des Mittelalters, 21). Leiden, Netherlands: Brill, 1988.

Alfaro, J. "Fides in terminologia biblica." in *Gregorianum* 42 (1961): 463–505.

———. "Supernaturalitas fidei iuxta S. Thomam." *Gregorianum* 44 (1963): 501–42; 731–57.

Ashley, B. *Thomas Aquinas: The Gifts of the Holy Spirit.* Hyde Park, NY: New City Press, 1995.

Balthasar, H. Urs von. "Theology and Holiness." In *Explorations in Theology I, The Word Made Flesh*. San Francisco: Ignatius Press, 1989.

Bazán, B. C., G. Franzen, J. F. Wippel, and D. Jacquart. *Les questions disputées et es questions quodlibétiques dans les facultés de théologie, de droit et de médecine* (Typologie des sources du moyen âge occidental, 44–45). Turnhout, Belgium: Brepols, 1985.

Bellemare, R. "Credere: Note sur la définition thomiste." *Revue de l'Université d'Ottawa* 30 (1960): 37–47.

Biffi, I. *I misteri di Cristo in Tommaso d'Aquino.* Preface by M.-D. Chenu. Milan: Jaca Book, 1994.

Blanchette, O. *The Perfection of the Universe According to Aquinas: A Teleological Cosmology.* University Park: Pennsylvania State University, 1992.

Bouillard, Henri. *Conversion et grâce chez Thomas d'Aquin.* Paris: Aubier, 1944.

Bourassa, F., S. J. *De missionibus et inhabitatione personarum divinarum.* Rome: Pontificia Universitas Gregorianum, 1970.

———. "Rôle personnel de Personnes et relations distinctes aux personnes." *Sciences ecclésiastiques* 7 (1955): 151–72.

Bourgeois, D. "'Inchoatio vitae eternae.' La dimension eschatologique de la vertu théologale de foi chez saint Thomas d'Aquin." *Sapienza* 27 (1974): 272–314.

Boyer, C. "L'image de la Trinité. Synthèse de la pensée Augustinienne." *Gregorianum* 5 (1946): 173–99, 333–52.

Boyle, L., O.P. "Alia lectura fratris Thome." *Mediaeval Studies* 45 (1983): 418–29.

———. *The Setting of the Summa theologiae of Saint Thomas* (The Gilson Lecture Series, 5). Toronto: Pontifical Institute of Medieval Studies, 1982.

Burrell, D. D., C.S.C. *Aquinas: God and Action*. Notre Dame, IN: University of Notre Dame Press, 1979.

———. *Exercises in Religious Understanding*. Notre Dame, IN: University of Notre Dame Press, 1974.

———. *Knowing the Unknowable God: Ibn-Sina, Maimonides, and Aquinas*. Notre Dame, IN: University of Notre Dame Press, 1986.

Casciaro Ramirez, J. M. "Contributión al studio de las fuentes arabes y rabinicas en la doctrina de Sto. Tomás sobre la Profecia." *Estudios Biblicos* 18/2 (1959): 117–48.

Cessario, R. *Christian Faith and the Theological Life*. Washington, DC: The Catholic University of America Press, 1996.

———. "Is Aquinas's *Summa* only about Grace." In *Ordo sapientiae et amoris. Image et message de saint Thomas d'Aquin à travers les récentes études historiques, herméneutiques et doctrinales (Hommage au Professeur Jean-Pierre Torrell O.P. à l'occasion de son 65e anniversaire)*, ed. C.-J. Pinto de Oliveira. Fribourg, Switzerland: Éditions universitaires, 1993.

Chenu, M.-D. *La Théologie comme science au XIIIe siècle (Bibliothèque Thomiste, vol. 33)*, 2nd ed. Paris: J. Vrin, 1943.

———. "Le plan de la *Somme théologique* de saint Thomas." *Revue Thomiste* 47 (1939): 93–107.

———. "Psychologie de la foi dans la théologie du 13ème siècle." In *Études d'histoire littéraire et doctrinale du 13ème siècle*. Paris: J. Vrin, 1932.

———. *St. Thomas d'Aquin et la théologie (Maîtres spirituels, vol. 17)*. Paris: Éditions du Seuil, 1959.

———. *Toward Understanding Saint Thomas*. Trans. A.-M. Landry and D. Hughes. Chicago: Regnery, 1964.

Corbin, M. *Le chemin de la théologie chez Thomas d'Aquin* (Bibliothèque des Archives de Philosophie, n.s., vol. 16). Paris: Beauchesne, 1964.

Cottier, G. "Les motifs de crédibilité de la Révélation selon saint Thomas" in *Nova et Vetera* 65 (1990): 161–79.

Crosson, F., and B. Marshall. "Postliberal Thomism Again." *The Thomist* 56 (1992): 481–524.

Cunningham, F. L. B., O.P. *The Indwelling of the Trinity. A Historico-Doctrinal Study of the Theory of St. Thomas Aquinas*. Dubuque: Priory Press, 1955.

Davies, B., O.P. *The Thought of Thomas Aquinas*. Oxford: Oxford University Press, 1992.

De Beaurecueil, M.-J Serge de Laugier, O.P. "L'homme, image de Dieu selon saint Thomas d'Aquin." *Études et recherches: Cahiers de théologie et de philosophie* 8 (1952): 45–82; 9 (1955): 151–72.

Dedek, J. F. *Experimental Knowledge of the Indwelling Trinity. An Historical Study of the Doctrine of St. Thomas.* Mundelein, IL: St. Mary of the Lake Seminary, 1958.

Dewan, Lawrence, O.P. "St. Thomas, Aristotle, and Creationism." *Dionysius* 15 (1991): 81–90.

Dulles, A. *The Assurance of Things Hoped For: A Theology of Christian Faith.* New York: Oxford University Press, 1994.

———. *The Craft of Theology. From Symbol to System.* New York: Crossroad, 1971.

Dumont, C. "La réflexion sur la méthode théologique. Un moment capital: le dilemme posé au XIIIe siècle." *Nouvelle revue théologique* 83 (1961): 1034–50; 84 (1962): 17–35.

Dupré, L. "L'acte de foi chez Kierkegaard." *Revue philosophique de Louvain* 54 (1958): 418–55.

Duroux, B. *La psychologie de la foi chez S. Thomas d'Aquin.* Tournai, Belgium: Descleé de Brouwer, 1963.

Elders, L. *Faith and Science. An Introduction to St. Thomas' "Expositio in Boethii De Trinitate."* Rome: Herder, 1974.

———. "La méthode suivie par saint Thomas d'Aquin dans la composition de la *Somme de théologie.*" *Nova et Vetera* 66 (1991): 178–192.

———. "Les citations de saint Augustin dans la Somme Théologique de saint Thomas d'Aquin." *Doctor communis* 40 (1987): 115–167.

———. *The Philosophical Theology of St. Thomas Aquinas* (Studien und Texte zur Geistesgeschichte des Mittelalters). Leiden, Netherlands: E. J. Brill, 1990.

Emery, G., *La Trinité créatrice. Trinité et création dans les commentarires aux Sentences de Thomas d'Aquin et de ses précurseurs Albert le Grand et Bonaventure* (*Bibliothèque Thomiste*, vol. 47). Paris: J. Vrin, 1995.

———. "Le Père et l'oeuvre de la création selon le Commentarire des Sentences de S. Thomas d'Aquin." *Ordo sapientiae et amoris* (Fribourg, Switzerland: Editions universitaries, 1993), 85–117.

Flint, T. "Two Accounts of Providence." In *Divine and Human Action*, ed. Thomas Morris. Ithaca: Cornell University Press, 1988, 147–81.

Fogelin, R. J. "A Reading of Aquinas's Five Ways." *American Catholic Philosophical Quarterly* 27 (1990): 305–13.

Gardeil, A. "Dons du Saint Esprit II. Partie documentaire et historique." *Dictionnaire de théologie catholique* 4/2; 1728–1781.

———. "Le plan de la *Somme théologique.*" In *S. Thomas d'Aquin, Somme Théologique: La théologie* (Ia Prologue et Q. 1). Paris; Tournai, Belgium; and Rome: Desclée de Brouwer, 1968, 66–105.

Garrigou-Lagrange, R., *The Theological Virtues.* Vol. 1, *On Faith.* St. Louis: B. Herder, 1965.

Gauthier, R.-A. *Introduction historique au tome I de l'édition bilingue de la "Summa contra Gentiles."* Trans. R. Bernier et M. Corvez. Paris: Lethielleux, 1961, 7–123.

———. Introduction to *Somme contre les gentiles.* Ed. H. Hude. Paris: Éditions universitaires, 1993.

Geach, P. T. *The Virtues.* Cambridge: Cambridge University Press, 1977.

Geenen, C. G. "Saint Thomas et les Pères." *Thomas d'Aquin, Dictionnaire de Théologie Catholique* 15/1: 738–61.

Gilson, E. *The Christian Philosophy of St. Thomas Aquinas.* Trans. L. Shook, C.S.B. New York: Random House, 1956.

———. *History of Christian Philosophy in the Middle Ages.* London: Sheed and Ward, 1955.

Glorieux, P. "La Christologie du *Compendium theologiae*." *Sciences ecclésiastiques* 13 (1961): 7–34.

———. "L'enseignement au Moyen Âge. Techniques et méthodes en usage à la Faculté de Théologie de Paris au XIIIe siècle." *Archives d'histoire doctrinale et littéraire du moyen âge* 35 (1968): 65–186.

Grabmann, M. *Die theologische Erkenntnis- und Einleitungslehre des hl. Thomas von Aquin auf Grund seiner Schrift "In Boethium de Trinitate."* Freiburg, Switzerland: Paulusverlag, 1948.

Greenstock, D. L. "Exemplar Causality and the Supernatural Order." *The Thomist* 16 (1953): 1–31.

Guzie, Tad W. "The Act of Faith according to St. Thomas: A Study in Theological Methodology." *The Thomist* 19 (1965): 239–80.

Hall, D. C. *The Trinity. An Analysis of St. Thomas Aquinas' "Exposition of the De Trinitate of Boethius"* (Studien und Texte zur Geistesgeschichte des Mittelalters, 33). Leiden, Netherlands: Brill, 1992.

Hankey, W. "The Place of the Psychological Image of the Trinity in the Arguments of Augustine's *De Trinitate*, Anselm's *Monologion*, and Aquinas' *Summa theologiae*." in *Dionysius* 3 (1979): 99–110.

Hayden, D. "Notes on Aristotelian Dialectic in Theological Method." *The Thomist* 20 (1957): 383–418.

Hayen, A. "La structure de la *Somme théologique* et Jésus." *Sciences ecclésiastiques* 12 (1960): 59–82.

Hibbs, T. S. *Dialectic and Narrative in Aquinas: An Interpretation of the "Summa contra Gentiles."* Notre Dame, IN: University of Notre Dame Press, 1995.

Hill, William J. *The Three-Personed God. The Trinity as a Mystery of Salvation.* Washington, DC: The Catholic University of America Press, 1982.

Hislop, I., O.P. "Man, the Image of the Trinity, according to St. Thomas." *Dominican Studies* 3 (1950): 1–9.

Hoenen, M. J. F. M., and A. de Libera, *Albertus Magnus und der Albertismus. Deutsche philosophische Kultur des Mittelalters* (Studien und Texte zur Geistesgeschichte des Mittelalters, 48). Leiden, Netherlands; New York; and Cologne: Brill, 1995.

Jenkins, J. I., C.S.C. "Aquinas on the Veracity of the Intellect." *The Journal of Philosophy*, 88 (1991): 623–32.

———. "Expositions of the Text: Aquinas's Aristotelian Commentaries." *Medieval Philosophy and Theology* 5 (1996): 39–62.

———. *Knowledge and Faith in Thomas Aquinas*. Cambridge: Cambridge University Press, 1997.

Jordan, M. D. *The Alleged Aristotelianism of Thomas Aquinas* (Gilson Lecture, 15). Toronto: Pontifical Institute of Mediaeval Studies, 1992.

———. "The Names of God and the Being of Names." *The Existence and Nature of God*, ed. A. Freddoso. Notre Dame, IN: University of Notre Dame Press, 1983, 161–90.

———. *On Faith. "Summa theologiae," Part 2–2, Questions 1–16 of St. Thomas Aquinas*. Notre Dame, IN: University of Notre Dame Press, 1990.

Kenny, A. *The Five Ways*. London: Routledge and Kegan Paul, 1969.

———. *What is Faith?* Oxford: Oxford University Press, 1992.

Klubertanz, G. *Habits and Virtues*. New York: Appleton-Century-Croft, 1965.

Kretzmann, N. *The Metaphysics of Theism: Aquinas's Natural Theology in the "Summa contra Gentiles" I*. Oxford: Clarendon, 1997.

———, and E. Stump (ed.). *The Cambridge Companion to Aquinas*. Cambridge: Cambridge University Press, 1993.

Labourdette, M.-M. "La théologie, intelligence de la foi." *Revue thomiste* 46 (1946): 5–44.

———. "La vie théologale selon saint Thomas: L'affection dans la foi." *Revue thomiste* 60 (1960): 364–80.

———. "La vie théologale selon saint Thomas: L'objet de la foi." *Revue thomiste* 58 (1958): 597–622.

Lafont, G., O.S.B. "Simbolo degli Apostoli et methodo teologico: Il *Compendium Theologiae* di San Tommaso." *La Scuola Cattolica* 102 (1974): 557–68.

———. *Structures et Méthode dans la Somme théologique de saint Thomas d'Aquin*. Paris: Desclée de Brouwer, 1961.

Leclercq, J. "L'idéal du théologien au moyen âge. Textes inédits." *Revue des sciences religieuses* 21 (1947): 121–48.

Libera, A. de. *Penser au Moyen Âge*. Paris: Éditions du Seuil, 1991.

Lindbeck, G. A. *The Nature of Doctrine: Religion and Theology in a Postliberal Age*. Philadelphia: Westminster Press, 1984.

Lonergan, B. *Verbum. Word and Idea in Aquinas*. Notre Dame, IN: University of Notre Dame Press, 1970.

MacDonald, S. "Theory of Knowledge." In *The Cambridge Companion to Aquinas*, ed. N. Kretzmann and E. Stump. New York: Cambridge University Press, 1993, 160–96.

Mackey, L. "Entreatments of God: Reflections on Aquinas' Five Ways." *Franciscan Studies* 37 (1977): 105–19.

Mascall, E. L. "Faith and Reason: Anselm and Aquinas," *Journal of Theological Studies* 14 (1963): 67–90.

Matthys, M. "Quid ratio naturalis doceat de possibilitate visionis beatae secundum S. Thomam in *Summa contra Gentiles*." *Divus Thomas* (Piacenza) 39 (1936): 201–28.

Maurer, A. A. "St. Thomas on the Sacred Name 'Tetragrammaton.'" *Mediaeval Studies* 34 (1972): 275–86.

McInerny, R. *The Logic of Analogy: An Interpretation of St. Thomas*. The Hague: M. Nijhoff, 1961.

Ménard, E. *La tradition: Révélation, Écriture, Église selon saint Thomas d'Aquin* [Studia, 18]. Paris: Desclée de Brouwer, 1964.

Mitterer, A. "Die sieben Gaben des Hl. Giestes nach der Väterlehre." *Zeitschrift für katholische Theologie* 49 (1925): 529–66.

Moreau, J. "Le platonisme dans la 'Somme théologique.'" *Tommaso d'Aquino nel suo settimo centenario* (*Atti del congresso internazionale*, Rome/Naples, 17–24 April 1974), vol. I, 238–47.

Mulard, R. "Desir naturel de connaître et vision béatifique." *Revue des sciences philosophiques et théologiques* 14 (1925): 5–19.

O'Meara, T. F. "Grace as a Theological Structure in the *Summa Theologiae* of Thomas Aquinas." *Revue de Théologie ancienne et médiévale* 55 (1988): 130–53.

Parente, P. "De munere rationis naturalis in actu fidei eliciendo." *Doctor Communis* 3 (1950): 10–21.

Patfoort, A. "L'unité de la Ia Pars et le mouvement interne de la Somme théologique de S. Thomas d'Aquin" in *Revue des sciences philosophiques et théologiques* 47 (1963): 513–44.

———. *L'unité d'être dans le Christ d'après S. Thomas. À la croisée de l'ontologie et de la christologie*. Paris: Desclée de Brouwer, 1964.

———. *Saint Thomas d'Aquin. Les clés d'une théologie*. Paris: Desclée de Brouwer, 1983.

Pelikan, J. *The Christian Tradition. A History of the Development of Doctrine. The Growth of Medieval Theology* (*600–1300*). Chicago and London: University of Chicago, 1978.

Penelhum, T. "The Analysis of Faith in St. Thomas Aquinas." *Religious Studies* 3 (1977): 133–54.

Persson, P. E. "Le plan de la *Somme théologique* et le rapport *ratio-revelatio*." *Revue philosophique de Louvain* 56 (1958): 545–75.

Philippe, P. "Le plan des Sentences de Pierre Lombard d'après S. Thomas." *Bulletin Thomiste* 3 (1930–33): Notes et communications, 131–54.

Pieper, J. *Guide to Thomas Aquinas*. Trans. R. Winston and C. Winston. Notre Dame, IN: University of Notre Dame Press, 1962.

———. *The Silence of St. Thomas: Three Essays*. Trans. J. Murray and D. O'Connor, New York: Pantheon Books, 1957.

Pinckaers, S. "Le désir naturel de voir Dieu." *Nova Et Vetera* 51 (1976): 255–73.

———. "Recherche de la signification véritable du terme 'speculatif.'" *Nouvelle Revue Théologique* 81 (1959): 673–95.

Plantinga, A. *Does God Have a Nature?* Milwaukee: Marquette University Press, 1980.

Potts, T. "Aquinas on Belief and Faith." In *Inquiries into Medieval Philosophy*, ed. J. F. Ross. Westport: Greenwood Publishing, 1971.

Pritzl, L. "Aristotle: Ways of Truth and Ways of Opinion." *Proceedings of the American Catholic Philosophical Association* 67 (1993): 241–52.

Riga, P. "The Act of Faith in Augustine and Aquinas." *The Thomist* 35 (1971): 143–74.

Ross, J. "Aquinas on Belief and Knowledge." In *Essays Honoring Allan B. Wolter*, ed. W. A. Frank and G. J. Etzkorn. St. Bonaventure, NY: The Franciscan Institute Press, 1985, 245–69.

Rousselot, P. *The Eyes of Faith*. Trans. J. Donceel and A. Dulles. New York: Fordham University Press, 1990.

Ruello, F. *La christologie de Thomas d'Aquin*. (*Théologie historique*, vol. 76). Paris: Beauchesne, 1987.

———. "Saint Thomas et Pierre Lombard. Les relations trinitaires et la structure du commentarire des *Sentences* de saint Thomas d'Aquin." In *San Tommaso, Fonti e riflessi del suo pensiero* (*Studi Tomistici*, vol. 1). Rome: Pontificia Accademia Romana di S. Tommaso d'Aquino, 1974, 176–209.

Schillebeeckx, E. *Revelation and Theology*. Vol. I, *What Is Theology?* Trans. N. D. Smith. New York: Sheed and Ward, 1967–68.

Schmitz, K. "St. Thomas and the Appeal to Experience." *Catholic Theological Society of America Proceedings* 47 (1992): 1–20.

Sertillanges, A.-D. *L'idée de création et ses retentissments en philosophie*. Paris: Aubier, 1945.

Somme, L. "La rôle du Saint-Esprit dans la vie chrétienne, selon saint Thomas d'Aquin." *Sedes Sapientiae* 26 (1988): 11–29.

Stumpf, E. "Aquinas on the Foundations of Knowledge." In *Aristotle and His Medieval Interpreters*, ed. R. Bosley and M. Tweedale. *Canadian Journal of Philosophy*, supplementary volume 17 (1991): 125–58.

————. and N. Kretzmann. "Absolute Simplicity." *Faith and Philosophy* 2 (1985): 353–82.

————. "Aquinas on Faith and Goodness." In *Being and Goodness: The Concept of the Good in Metaphysics and Philosophical Theology*, ed. S. MacDonald. Ithaca: Cornell University Press, 1991, 179–207.

Szabo, T., O.F.M. *De SS. Trinitate in creaturis refulgente: Doctrina S. Bonaventurae.* Rome: Orbis Catholicus-Herder, 1963.

Torrell, J.-P. *Saint Thomas Aquinas: The Person and His Work.* Trans. by Robert Royal. Vol. 1, *Saint Thomas Aquinas.* Washington, DC: The Catholic University of America Press, 1996.

Walz, A. *Saint Thomas Aquinas: A Biographical Study.* Trans. L. Bullough, O.P. Westminster, MD: Newman Press, 1951.

Weisheipl, J. A., O.P. *Friar Thomas d'Aquino. His Life, Thought, and Work.* Garden City: Doubleday, 1974.

————. "The Meaning of 'Sacra Docrina' in *Summa theologiae*, I, q. 1." *The Thomist* 38 (1974): 49–80.

White, V. *Holy Teaching, The Idea of Theology according to St. Thomas Aquinas, Aquinas Papers*, vol. 33. London: Blackfriars Publications, 1958.

Wippel, J. F. *Metaphysical Themes in Thomas Aquinas.* Washington, DC: The Catholic University of America Press, 1984.

Wolterstorff, N. "The Migration of the Theistic Arguments: From Natural Theology to Evidentialist Apologetics." In *Rationality, Religious Belief, and Moral Commitment*, ed. R. Augi and W. Wainwright. Ithaca: Cornell University Press, 1986, 38–81.